DATE			

Hopi Stories of Witchcraft, Shamanism, and Magic

Hopi Stories of Witchcraft, Shamanism, and Magic

Ekkehart Malotki and Ken Gary

Illustrations by Karen Knorowski

University of Nebraska Press
Lincoln and London

Library of Congress Cataloging-in-Publication Data
Malotki, Ekkehart.
Hopi stories of witchcraft, shamanism, and magic /
Ekkehart Malotki and Ken Gary; illustrations by
Karen Knorowski.
p. cm.
Includes bibliographical references.
ISBN 0-8032-3217-9 (cl: alk. paper)
1. Hopi Indians—Folklore.   2. Tales—Arizona.
3. Hopi magic.   I. Gary, Ken.   II. Title.
E99.H7M338   2001
398.2'089'9745—dc21
00-050316

Contents

Preface   vii

Introduction   xiii

The Stories

1   The Boy Who Encountered the Jimsonweed and
Four O'Clock Girls   1

2   The Man Who Was Buried Alive   8

3   How Old Spider Woman Came to the Rescue of the Yaya't   11

4   The Boy Who Wanted to Be a Medicine Man   15

5   The Tsa'kwayna Death Spirits   21

6   The Fate of Pongoktsina and His Wife   30

7   The Man Who Traveled to Maski, Home of the Dead,
to Bring Back His Wife   55

8   The Yaya't and Their Feats   65

9   An Oraibi Boy's Visit to Maski, Home of the Dead   69

10   The Snake Clan Boy and the Sorcerers   93

11   The Man Who Was Married to a Witch   104

12   How Coyote Came to Visit Maski, Home of the Dead   115

13   The So'yoko Ogre and His Wife   124

14   How Somaykoli Came to Shungopavi   136

15   The Boy Who Was Born from a Dead Mother   141

16   Kotsoylaptiyo and the Sorcerers   147

17   How the Snake Ceremony Came to Oraibi   161

18   A Flood at Oraibi   173

19   The Boy Who Became a Deer   185

20   The Woman Who Gave Birth to the Seeds   202

21 The Creation of the Morning and Evening Star   208
22 How the Pöqangw Brothers Stole the Lightning   212
23 The Poor Boy Who Wanted a Horse   219
24 How the Pöqangw Brothers Found Their Father   225
25 The Water Vessel Boy   236
26 A Famine at Oraibi   240
27 How the Zunis Killed the Hehey'a Kachinas   247
28 Yaapontsa, the Wind God   252
29 So'yoko and the Shungopavis   258
30 The Witch Owl   267
31 The Gambling Boy Who Married a Bear Girl   270
Glossary   284

Preface

The specific focus of *Hopi Stories of Witchcraft, Shamanism, and Magic* was inspired by two separate strands of my research life that have become ever more interwoven during the last ten years: Hopi ethnography and the study of paleoart in the form of rock engravings and rock paintings. In the late 1980s, the number of days I spent annually on the Hopi reservation tape-recording Hopi oral traditions—tales, legends, myths, songs, recipes, games, and any other cultural information that was volunteered to me—took a steep decline. Soon my visits to Hopiland ceased altogether, not only because several of my most knowledgeable consultant friends, such as Sidney Namingha Jr. and Michael Lomatuway'ma, had died, but also because the political conditions for field work underwent drastic changes. Nevertheless, I continued my Hopi research off the reservation, primarily aided by Michael's wife, Lorena Lomatuway'ma, who resides in Flagstaff. She provided cultural and linguistic insights not only for several of my oral literature publications but also for the comprehensive Hopi dictionary, which finally became available to the general public in 1998.

Addicted to the open spaces and canyonscapes of northern Arizona, I began to fill the personal and professional void created by my absence from the Hopi mesas by turning my attention to the phenomenon of rock art, that is, to the thousands of petroglyphic and pictographic sites that are scattered throughout the Four Corners states of Arizona, Utah, Colorado, and New Mexico. In the course of recording and photographing these sites, my efforts initially centered almost exclusively in the area of Petrified Forest National Park. I later extended my search for sites to the entire Colorado Plateau, eventually uncovering massive evidence for a predominantly Archaic rock art style which, at the time, was practically unknown to Southwestern archaeologists. I termed this newly emerging complex the Palavayu Anthropomorphic Style, since the art was confined to a geographic area of several thousand square miles I had previously named Palavayu, after the traditional Hopi appellation for the Little Colorado River.

Before long, in connection with my rupestrian work, I also became acquainted with the so-called shamanistic hypothesis. Spearheaded by David Lewis Williams in conjunction with his work on San rock paintings in southern Africa, this explanatory theory suggests that a large portion of rock paintings and engravings, especially of Archaic hunter-gatherer provenance, has its origins in visions, hallucinations, and altered states of consciousness experienced by religious specialists or shamans. As scientific model, the shamanistic hypothesis is heavily indebted to two relatively novel academic disciplines. The first of these is cognitive archaeology, which considers art no longer as simply epiphenomenal, that is, analytically irrelevant, but as a significant window into the human mind. The second is neuropsychology, which posits that the human nervous system is a biopsychological universal, implying that all *Homo sapiens sapiens* are "hard-wired" in the same way. For these reasons, the shamanistic hypothesis is testable and has great heuristic potential concerning our endeavors to unlock some of the meanings of rock art.

Palavayu Anthropomorphic Style rupestrian art has all the hallmarks of shamanistically created visionary imagery: a plethora of geometric designs, generally referred to as entoptic or endogenous phenomena; patterned-body anthropomorphs with associated animal spirit helpers and an array of power objects; chimerical monsters and other fantastic figures; metaphorical depictions of shamanic flight and transformation; skeletonization of humans and animals; anthropomorphs of distorted or attenuated proportions; and the recurrent portrayal of liminal animals such as serpents, dragonflies and owls. Perfectly matching the paradigm of trance imagery, these motifs consistently fit the visionary, somatic, and tactile hallucinations that typically originate from altered states of consciousness. In my eyes, they clearly demonstrate that much of Palavayu Anthropomorphic iconography is of shamanistic origin.

Unfortunately, the shaman-artists responsible for much of Palavayu Anthropomorphic Style art have been gone for several thousand years. Nothing is known about their beliefs, myths, rituals, and world view. Nor is it possible to debrief the rock art creators and look for answers to such burning questions as what motivated them to produce the images, whether they used hallucinogens to achieve trance, and whether the rock art sites functioned as vision quest locales. To bridge this knowledge gap, the shamanistic hypothesis frequently resorts to ethnographic analogy. The cardinal question, therefore, is to what extent present-day ethnographic information from Pueblo Indians, presumably descendants of the earlier Basketmaker and Archaic peoples, can be used to interpret much older shamanistically oriented rock art.

The Hopi Indians are no longer hunters and foragers, though they live today on their mesas only some seventy miles north of the northernmost boundary of the Palavayu area, home to the Archaic and Basketmaker people responsible for the Palavayu Anthropomorphic Style engravings. However, in the course of my Hopi field work, it quickly became apparent that shamanism did not die out with the emergence of maize cultivation in the Southwest. There was just too much evidence in Hopi culture, sometimes outright and sometimes in disguise, that vestigial shamanistic practices lasted into modern Pueblo times.

In a roundabout way, then, it was my longstanding enthusiasm for rock art, and especially the shamanistic explanatory theory, that led me to select these Hopi stories. All of them, even though dealing with witchcraft, shamanism, and magic, relate either directly or indirectly to the ideology of shamanism. Elements of shamanism have of course long been suspected in Hopi culture and have occasionally been pointed out, but they have never been analyzed systematically. The present compilation of narratives provided an incentive to do so. To my knowledge, this is the first time that such a detailed investigation of shamanistic influences has been undertaken for any Puebloan society in the American Southwest. Still, it is far from exhaustive, and the shamanistic background information presented in the introduction is heavily biased toward material embedded in Hopi oral literature. Moreover, aspects of Hopi religion were dealt with only marginally. A complete study of Hopi rituals and ceremonies would undoubtedly yield a great deal more shamanistic evidence, warranting book-length treatment of its own.

To carry out this challenging and time-consuming analysis, I solicited Ken Gary's assistance. He readily agreed not only to stylistically polish my translations of the Hopi story originals but also to search the corpus of published Hopi narratives for shamanistic motifs and merge his findings with mine in the introduction. In return for his substantial aid, I offered him co-authorship of this volume, which he gladly accepted. Well aware that without Ken's generous help this book would probably not have been completed, I can only assure him how deeply indebted and obliged I am.

With the exception of two overtly shamanistic stories, "The Boy Who Wanted to Be a Medicine Man" and "The Gambling Boy Who Married a Bear Girl," which were included in my *Hopi Animal Tales,* all other narratives compiled in this anthology have not been published previously in this form. They were freely shared with me by several of my principal Hopi consultants, all of whom became close friends in the course of the years that they collaborated with me. Five of them, Michael Lomatuway'ma, Sidney Namingha Jr., Rebecca Namingha, Silas Hoyungowa (all deceased), and Lorena Lomatuway'ma, were from the Third Mesa village of Hotevilla. Two, Leslie Koyawena from Shipaulovi and a Shungopavi man who preferred to remain anonymous (both also deceased), were from Second Mesa. Without the splendid memories of these storytellers and story rememberers this book would not exist. They must therefore be the principal recipients of my unqualified gratitude. All of them were sincerely concerned about the ever-accelerating loss of their oral traditions and not only readily consented to having their tales tape-recorded, but also actively encouraged me to preserve their priceless patrimony in print.

Specifically, the thirty-one narratives preserved here were collected as follows: "The Man Who Was Married to a Witch" and "How the Pöqangw Brothers Found Their Father" were obtained from Leslie Koyawena. Silas Hoyungowa volunteered "The Poor Boy Who Wanted a Horse." The anonymous man from Shungopavi contributed "How Old Spider Woman Came to the Rescue of the Yaya't," "The Man Who Traveled to Maski, Home of the Dead, to bring Back His Wife," "The Yaya't and Their Feats," "The Snake Clan Boy and the Sorcerers," "How Somaykoli Came to Shungopavi," "The Boy Who Became a Deer," "The Woman Who Gave Birth to the Seeds," "The Creation of the Morning and Evening Stars," "The Water Vessel Boy," "Yaapontsa, the Wind God," and "So'yoko and the Shungopavis." Sidney Namingha Jr. provided "The Boy Who Encountered the Jimsonweed and Four O'Clock Girls," "How the Snake Clan Came to Oraibi," "A Famine at Oraibi," "How the Zunis Killed the Hehey'a Kachinas," and "The Boy Who Wanted to Be a Medicine Mman." Michael Lomatuway'ma told "The Man Who Was Buried Alive," "How Coyote Came to Visit Maski, Home of the Dead," "The So'yoko Ogre and His Wife," "How the Pöqangw Brothers Stole the Lightning," and "The Witch Owl." Rebecca Namingha remembered "The Fate of Pongoktsina and His Wife."

Lorena Lomatuway'ma, finally, narrated "The Tsa'kwayna Death Spirits," "An Oraibi Boy's Visit to Maski, Home of the Dead," "The Boy Who Was Born from a Dead Mother," "Kotsoylaptiyo and the Sorcerers," "A Flood at Oraibi," and "The Gambling Boy Who Married a Bear Girl."

While I have always striven to present my translations jointly with the Hopi originals, not only for reasons of cultural sensitivity and authenticity but also to preserve the actual Hopi vernacular for posterity, the Hopi originals are omitted this time because the transcribed texts are still in raw, unedited shape. Just as spontaneously recorded English prose typically requires substantial editorial work before it can go to press, so of course do taped field recordings of Hopi oral literature.

My longtime Hopi research assistant, Michael Lomatuway'ma, who learned from me to read and write his language and who, for many years, edited all of my field materials contained in previous publications, died in 1987. He never got to work on the current narratives, most of which I only transcribed and translated during the last couple of years. His wife Lorena, with whom I continued my ethnographic and linguistic work for another decade, is blind, and hence incapable of continuing where Michael left off. I can thus only hope that those familiar with my earlier work will know me well enough not to suspect any inaccuracies or ethnocentric distortions in the present story collection.

The lino-cuts that accompany the individual stories were created, with great enthusiasm and dedication, by Karen Knorowski. Karen just graduated from Northern Arizona University with a bachelor of fine arts degree in printmaking. Her many-sided interests, including a great love for Native American folklore, as well as her artistic talents immediately qualified her for this task. For the many hours that she spent on the illustrations she too deserves my sincere gratitude.

Most of the stories presented here were collected, together with many others, during countless field sessions on the Hopi reservation from the late 1970s through the mid-1980s. This work was supported by Organized Research funds from Northern Arizona University. I would therefore like to thank all my colleagues who, during those years, sat on the various Organized Research committees and endorsed my research efforts. In particular I am grateful to Henry Hooper, associate provost at Northern Arizona University, who not only found my work worthwhile in those days, when he served as chair of the Organized Research Committee, but has remained a steadfast supporter of my scholarly endeavors until the present day. He also signed off on the camera-ready production of the manuscript, which was carried out with professional competence, as always, by Louella Holter, editor at the Ralph M. Bilby Research Center.

To Dan Boone, finally, imaging specialist at NAU's Bilby Research Center, I owe a special thank-you for formatting the artwork for camera-ready production. Some observations on the introduction were thankfully accepted from Donald Weaver. Last, but not least, I'm indebted to my copyeditor, Stephen Barnett, who very professionally and circumspectly added the final touches to the manuscript.

Introduction: Observations on Witchcraft, Shamanism, and Magic in Hopi Oral Traditions and Culture

The Hopi, like all other human beings, have an abiding fascination with magic and supernaturalism, and with everything that transcends rational explanation—as is amply demonstrated by the present collection of stories. In fact, the ideological underpinnings of Hopi culture are "magical" to a large degree and, as Courlander (1970: 159) states, "theology-centered" rather than technology-centered. Thus, in the Hopi worldview, tradition, myth, legend, and historical accounts can be equally valid records of experience and are often woven together in mythology and in rituals, where the spoken or sung word is held sufficient to "magically" cause the desired result. Although magic, in the broadest sense, permeates this collection of authentic Hopi narratives, two subsidiary themes predominate. The more explicit of these is witchcraft, a common and easily recognized motif in Hopi oral literature. Less apparent at first glance is the strong thread of shamanism that also runs through many of the stories.

Though witchcraft and shamanism are sometimes referred to as "black magic" and "white magic," respectively, distinguishing between them is not so easy. That the boundary separating witchcraft and shamanism is a narrow one, easily transgressed, is emphasized by Hodge's ([1910] 1969: 965) remarks: "Witchcraft may be defined as the art of controlling the will and well-being of another person by supernatural or occult means, usually to his detriment. If shamans possessed supernatural powers that could be exerted beneficially, it was naturally supposed that they might also be exerted with injurious results, and therefore, where shamanism was most highly developed, the majority of supposed witches, or rather wizards, were shamans." This general observation by Hodge also holds true for the Hopi, as can be gathered from the following statement by Titiev (1956: 54): "On the widespread belief that the same kind of power which causes an ailment can also cure it, the Hopi tend to equate their shamans with witches." For this reason, "all medicine men are regarded with a mixture of respect and fear."

Nevertheless, we have attempted to discuss witchcraft, shamanism, and magic separately as an introduction to the stories, which frequently weave together elements of all three. Regardless of which of these elements may predominate in a given story, magical devices, magical medicines, magical creatures, and magical landscapes make up the milieu in which the practitioners of black or white magic, or simply greater-than-human protagonists, operate.

Though the Hopis of today are increasingly foregoing their native language for English and abandoning traditional beliefs—among them the pervasive belief in black magic or witchcraft—the fact remains that this belief persisted well into modern times, perhaps as late as the early part of the twentieth century. Not unexpectedly, this belief is well attested in Hopi ethnography and in oral literature such as the stories here presented. Hopi shamanistic beliefs and practices, however, are another matter. Practically no ethnographic information is available on Hopi shamanism, and Levy—in the only published treatment of the topic—contends that shamanic societies among the Hopi were "weak and short-lived" (1994: 322) after their relatively late introduction, which, according to him, occurred after "the arrival of the Spaniards" (1994: 324).

We believe, however, that a careful review of Hopi folklore, religion, and mythology supports another perspective: that a shamanic worldview was once firmly institutionalized among the Hopi. Although shamanism is almost universally associated with hunter-gatherers, the emergence of horticulturists and farmers such as the Hopi does not imply that shamanism became extinct among them and had to be reinvented after the Spanish arrival as Levy (1994: 324) claims. The development of priestly societies engaged in elaborate fertility and rainmaking ceremonials may well have deprived shamans of much of the influence they had enjoyed in hunter-gatherer times. This marginalization, however, did not lead to a change in the most basic elements of shamanism and the hallmark techniques of individual practitioners: shamanic initiation, ecstatic transformation, and ritual flight; the use of animal familiars; and shamanic descent or ascent into tiered otherworlds. While no longer a religious cornerstone among Puebloan culture groups, shamanism's survival from an earlier time was assured because agriculturists continued to have the same metaphysical, psychic, healing, and fertility needs as their Archaic predecessors.

We believe the stories presented here contain elements that recall Hopi shamanistic practices, though perhaps in a more subtle way than they may present the world of witchcraft. Through the presentation of ethnographic insights volunteered to Ekkehart Malotki by Hopi consultants and a review of Hopi oral literature by Ken Gary for evidence of classic shamanistic motifs—motifs synthesized primarily from Eliade's *Shamanism* (1964) and Halifax's *Shamanic Voices* (1979)—we hope to show that shamanism was once firmly institutionalized among the Hopi, agriculturalists though they were and now remain. Although similarities between witchcraft, shamanism, and magic make it difficult to draw clear distinctions, fourteen motifs typical of shamanism are applicable to the stories:

magical flight
drumming, singing, and dance
healing and the power to restore life
human-animal metamorphosis
trips from one cosmic region to another
sacred tree/world tree/axis mundi
androgyny
dismemberment/skeletonization
rainbow or sunlight ascent
underworld as inverted image
cosmic mountain
bridge or dangerous passage/ordeals
psychopomp (guide or conductor of departed souls)
sacred politician

We conclude our observations with a discussion of Hopi magic and its part in these stories, especially as practiced by the Yaya't, a now-extinct society whose magic acts are tinged with shamanistic overtones.

Witchcraft

Witchcraft, once a powerful controlling agent in Hopi society, is rapidly losing its grip: Simmons's (1942: 76) view that "the Pueblos are obsessively preoccupied with the threat posed by adherents to the black craft and that this fear is endemic" no longer holds for the present. Modern Hopis do not suffer from witch phobia and are not averse to sharing their knowledge of the subject with cultural outsiders. Yet if the frequency with which the destructive motif of witchcraft is encountered in Hopi oral traditions is any indicator, it must have been extremely pervasive and deeply ingrained in Hopi culture at one time.

As not much ethnographic information has been previously published on Hopi sorcery, a series of folk statements volunteered to Malotki (1993: 150–87) by Hopi consultants forms the basis for most of the following discussion. These statements are supplemented by observations from Hopi oral literature. Of 123 published stories analyzed for the presence of witchcraft, shamanism, and magic elements, we noted thirty stories involving witchcraft. Only some of the major aspects of Hopi witchcraft from these sources can be discussed in this introduction; a more thorough treatment of this topic would easily fill a book of its own.

The general Hopi term for a sorcerer or witch, male or female, is *powaqa*. While this animate noun pluralizes as *popwaqt*, the same word, when distinguished by inanimate gender, conceptualizes the abstract notion of "witchcraft" or "sorcery." In this meaning the word is limited to singular usage only. Morphologically, the word *powaqa* is composed of the root *powa-* and the element *qa*, "one who/that which." Although this analysis ultimately may not be verifiable, the core semantics of *powa-* imply something like "change." Elsewhere Malotki (1983a: 461) has suggested the gloss "transform" for this morpheme. This can be deduced from such words as *powata*, "to make right, cure, or exorcise," *powalti*, "become purified or healed (as from insanity)," *powa'iwta*, "be purified or be back to normal," and others. The element is likewise manifested in the lunar appellation Powamuya, literally "transform-moon/month" (approximately February), during which the great purification ceremony popularly known as the Bean dance takes place. While the stem *powa-*, which is not attested by itself, embraces positive denotations in these words, predominantly negative ones adhere to it in *powaqa*, "sorcerer" or "witchcraft"; *powaqqatsi*, "way of life based on sorcery"; and the affiliated verb *povowaqa*, "to practice witchcraft or exercise black magic." In the light of its etymology, the term *powaqa*, "witch," can therefore be understood as "negative transformer," and *powaqa*, "witchcraft," as "practice of negative transformation." As will become evident, the sorcerer attempts to transform the world around him for his own personal gain and advantage, usually with negative consequences, including death, for his fellow humans.

Hopi definitions of the *powaqa*, "sorcerer," typically employ the label *nukpana*, which denotes "bad, wicked, evil person, evildoer, or villain." The special knowledge of black magic that he commands is characterized as *tuhisa*. It is exploited for selfish purposes only.

In the context of a narrative, sorcerers, when operating individually, are often specified according to gender and age. One encounters *powaqtiyo*, "witch boy," *powaqmana*, "witch girl," *powaqwuuti*, "witch woman," and *powaqtaqa*, "witch man," as well as their respective plural forms. When acting as a whole conclave, however, they are frequently referred to in Hopi oral literature under the derogatory appellation of *kwitavit*, "excrement or feces people, turds," after their mythical home base, Kwitavi, "Excrement Kiva." (The term *kwitavit* is limited in its linguistic usage to the dialect of the Third Mesa villages. Second Mesa speakers prefer the form *kwitam* for the same meaning). The Hopi rationalization for this supposedly self-imposed cover term on the part of the sorcerers is that by calling themselves by this odious name, they feigned humility, hoping to deflect attention from themselves and camouflage their true activities.

According to Hopi mythology, witchcraft previously reigned in Maski, the underworld. It and the general chaos and corruption of *koyaanisqatsi* were the primary motivation for all remaining good Hopis to seek a new beginning in the upper surface world. However, evil succeeded in emerging with them from their ancestral home. Interestingly, First Witch is sometimes a woman and sometimes a man. She justifies showing up at the emergence place of Sipaapuni with the excuse that she felt obliged to introduce the Hopi to the idea of life after death. Indirectly, she also hints at her responsibility for maintaining the institution of death in the new world, indicating rather mysteriously that death has its uses.

According to Titiev (1942: 549), "the Hopi believe that all witches are the descendants of a mythological character known as Spider Woman, who plays a prominent part in their stories of the beginning of human life on earth." Hopi consultants did not concur with this assessment of Spider Woman as the primordial witch. In their eyes, she is considered a powerful yet benevolent earth goddess who, like a dea ex machina, always helps those in distress. Considering La Barre's (1972: 268) theory that "gods are only charismatic power-wielding shamans, hypostatized after death," it seems much more plausible to see Old Spider Woman's origin as a female shaman.

In some emergence stories, such as in Stephen (1929: 8–9), the existence of a witch (this time a man) among the newly emerged Hopi is evidenced by the death of the chief's daughter soon after the people emerge from the Sipaapuni. Distraught, the chief threatens to take the witch by the throat and kill him, until the witch convinces him to look down the Sipaapuni. There he sees his little daughter seated against the door of a house near the base of the reed they had all used to climb out. She is brushing her hair and smiling up at her father, who is now mollified. In Voth's (1905: 11–12) version, it is the Kikmongwi's young son who dies, and the witch, rather than an anonymous witch figure, is someone close to and known by the chief. Using a form of divination (throwing a ball of meal into the air and watching whom it falls on), he finds that the witch is his nephew (his younger sister's son). The reason that witches so often travel in coyote form is apparent from Stephen, as Coyote is responsible for his own primordial act of malevolence. As Coyote was standing near the Sipaapuni, he threw a large flat stone down into the underworld. Before Coyote did this, the witch had told those present that in four days the chief's daughter would return to the upper world. Now extremely vexed, the witch exclaimed, "Now she can never come back." Coyote had succeeded in making death permanent.

According to Hopi belief, Palangw is the universal headquarters of all practitioners of black magic. It is located somewhere northeast of Hopi territory. Occasionally, a Hopi will identify it geographically with Canyon de Chelly. The *powaqki*, "Home of the Sorcerers," at Palangw is modeled exactly after the typical Hopi subterranean kiva: It is divided into upper and lower floors, with hierarchical implications for the double caste system of witches. Those who meet on the lower floor are called *atkyapopwaqt*, "lower floor sorcerers." They are the ruthlessly cruel and merciless ones. The *tuuwingaqwpopwaqt*, "upper floor sorcerers," are less cruel and can even be somewhat merciful.

Travel to Palangw is effected by the witches in many different disguises. According to Hopi belief, one frequent mode of travel is as a crow. In Hopi oral narratives, witches also use the nighthawk, the dove, the owl, the wolf, the fox, and of course, the coyote, the animal most frequently chosen. One important reason for sorcerers to congregate at Palangw is to induct *powaqwiwimkyam*, "witch neophytes," into the *powaqwimi*, their own demoniacal order. A person can become a sorcerer of his own free will, or a practitioner of witchcraft may attempt to persuade a child to join the ranks of evildoers. To protect them from this danger, parents discourage their children from sleeping over at other people's homes. Another method of recruiting novices is by kidnapping infants. To enter the parents' home, the sorcerer is often disguised as a fly, which buzzes in, picks up the child, and carries it off to Palangw. It is said that this is frequently accomplished at a very early age, such as the very night preceding the naming ceremony, which traditionally takes place twenty days after birth. The infant is immediately taken to a secret underground meeting place where initiation occurs (Beaglehole and Beaglehole 1935: 5).

As Titiev (1942: 550) has pointed out, the initiatory proceedings of sorcerers "are modeled on those of the highly regarded secret societies which conduct Hopi ceremonies. Thus, the novice must be introduced by a ceremonial father chosen from the ranks of the sorcerers, his head is washed in yucca suds, and he is given a new name." Most important, through this initiation the candidate acquires the faculty of transforming himself into the animal familiar or tutelary spirit of his godfather, such as the crow, bear, or cougar. By drawing on the supernatural powers inherent or attributed to the animal, he can now exercise his evil craft.

By assuming the shape of his godfather beast, a sorcerer is believed to acquire a second heart in addition to his human one. For this reason, the locution *lööq unangwa'ytaqa*, "two-hearted one," is commonly applied to him. The sorcerer's metamorphosis into the helping spirit is accomplished by somersaulting over a rolling hoop, or in one narrative, by putting his head into the hoop and "turning over" (Wallis 1936: 60–68). In this same story, the hoop is described as "covered with feathers into which the down of birds and the hair of animals were woven." It is not clear whether each sorcerer owns his own hoop or whether the hoop exists only at Palangw. In some cases, the sorcerer somersaults over a hoop and then travels to Palangw; in others he does so only after waiting in line in the kiva there. In some cases, the sorcerer is said to consume part of his familiar's heart before leaping over the hoop.

Sorcerers, in addition to the creatures already mentioned, are believed to operate in the guise of bats and big shiny flies, also known as skeleton flies. Of the domestic animals, cats and dogs qualify, but only if they are black. The appropriate Hopi terms for the latter are *tu'alangwmosa*, "witching cat," and *tu'alangwvooko*, "witching dog." Witching dogs are said to attract attention through their odd behavior. Either they bark and whine for no apparent reason or they dig up the ground around the house, which is usually interpreted as a bad omen. Hopis are very suspicious of these creatures and either avoid or destroy them.

One of the prime objectives of the Hopi *powaqa* is to lengthen his own existence on this earth. This he achieves by causing the death of one of his relatives. To kill his relative, the sorcerer must extract his victim's heart. This is accomplished, symbolically, with an instrument described as a spindle. After the heart has been extracted by twirling the spindle on the victim's chest, it is taken to Palangw and deposited in a special receptacle. Sorcerers who are reluctant to bring a relative's heart and try to cheat by substituting the heart of a domestic animal are found out and fail to extend their lives. The special receptacle has the power to announce to all present what kind of heart is being deposited by producing the characteristic call of the creature it belonged to.

In "The Man Who Was Married to a Witch" from the present collection, a man follows his wife when she sneaks away at night, only to find that she is a witch. As he spies from the hatch of the witch kiva, the witches discover that they cannot transform themselves by leaping over a hoop, a sure sign that a non-witch is watching. They find him there, and under the law of trespass, he is required to become one of them and bring back the heart of his beloved sister. He breaks down in sobs, unable to do this. In a deft combination of comedy and pathos by the storyteller, the man substitutes the heart of a turkey instead. However, instead of the substitute heart being revealed by the special receptacle, the man himself is changed into a turkey. The next morning, he is scolded for his weakness by his witch wife as she herds him along.

By killing a relative, the sorcerer adds four years to his life expectancy. Titiev's (1942: 550) claim that heart extraction must be performed annually was not confirmed by Hopi consultants. Since many things in Hopi culture occur or exist in sets of four, the statements of these consultants should hold credence.

While death-dealing witchcraft in the form of heart extraction is restricted to the sorcerer's own relatives, disease-causing black magic is not. One method involves lodging a pathogenic object in the body of the human target. The Hopi term for this foreign object charged with malignant power is *tuukyayni*. According to Titiev (1942: 551), "stiff deer hairs, red or black ants, centipedes, bits of bone or glass, and shreds of graveyard clothes are favorites." Beaglehole and Beaglehole (1935: 6) add porcupine quills, bones of a dead person, and excrement to this list of injurious objects. A large variety of objects is used, but sharpness and essential malevolence seem to be common characteristics. As Eliade (1964: 301) has pointed out, these injurious objects are not introduced *in concreto* but are inserted by the mental power of the sorcerer. That this is so, and has been so for a long time for the Hopi, is exemplified by the lament of the Kikmo-ngwi in the underworld regarding the prevalence of wickedness: "They use dead men's bones and bones [quills?] of the porcupine. They take the bone of a dead man, put power of some kind into it, then make you sick throughout your entire body so that you die" (Wallis 1936: 2). According to Beaglehole and Beaglehole (1935: 6), the Hopi *tuukyayni* are symbolically projected from the sorcerer's "left hand by flicking the fingers at the intended victim." Stephen (1894: 212) reports that the missile, which was also referred to as *powaqat ho'at*, "sorcerer's arrow," was launched by a "magic bow." An interesting twist on this theme is related in a narrative collected by Voth (1905: 126–31), wherein a beautiful young maiden is poisoned by an actual arrow smeared with rattlesnake venom in an "accident" arranged by witches. Hopis consulted additionally mentioned cowry shells and teeth of the dead as potential disease inflictors. The offending object was usually sucked out by a shaman, who thereby becomes "the antidemonic champion" (Eliade 1964: 508).

A second technique of inflicting misfortune or disease on a victim makes use of a bait object. Also known as "contagious magic," the use of a bait object is based on the principle of "contact," which implies that "things once conjoined must remain in the same sympathetic relation forever after, even if subsequently separated" (Jorgensen 1980: 297). Generally, it is a person's hair that the sorcerer will try to acquire as the bait, which is then treated in such a way that the unwitting donor meets with bad fortune or falls ill. Nor is the use of malevolent objects restricted to insertion into the body to cause disease; it is also a favored noninvasive and defensive technique of witches. In a narrative collected by Malotki (1997: 261), witches put a centipede into *pik'ami* batter, hoping to sting a young girl, and they put scorpions into her wedding boots for the same purpose (Malotki 1997: 267). In a story related by Curtis ([1922] 1970: 208), witches defend themselves against the Walpi *qaleetaqmongwi*, "warrior chief," in a contest of magic by flinging many *sotsava* (Olivella) shells, porcupine quills, and cactus thorns at him. One of the weapons the warrior chief uses in retaliation is hordes of bees, an anti-witch device reminiscent of one of the stories in the present collection, "Kotsoylaptiyo and the Sorcerers," wherein a boy uses a swarm of wasps to free his arm from the clamping jaws of a witch rabbit.

One favorite pastime of sorcerers is the pursuit of illicit sex. Stories sometimes portray this desire for illicit sex as simply another manifestation of the naturally mean spirit of witches, but frequently envy or jealousy plays a part, just as it might with normal human beings, especially when the male (and sometimes female) *kwitavit* feel that someone else they consider undeserving wins the beautiful but reluctant maiden or handsome, haughty boy. For instance, when the misshapen Kookopölö wins an extremely beautiful girl as his bride, the Turds do everything they can to get even and claim her for their own (Malotki 1997: 189). In another story, witches poison a beautiful maiden expressly so they can change themselves into coyotes, foxes, and wolves, steal her body from the graveyard, and take it back to the witch kiva. There they plan to change themselves back into men, revive her, and have sex with her. She is told explicitly that since she had persistently refused to marry any of the young men of the village, this is her fate (Voth 1905: 126–31). Finally, a young man is tricked into changing into a coyote so that his alleged friend (actually a witch) can steal his new wife. The boy finds to his chagrin that he can't change back, and it is only with the help of Old Spider Woman that he becomes human again, discovering that his wife has now married the witch. In retribution, he turns his former wife into an owl using medicine given him by Old Spider Woman.

Both male and female converts to witchcraft are believed to enter clandestinely the homes of people they are lusting after in order to satisfy their sexual desires. Within the complex of sexual witchcraft one special form produces what is generally referred to as *tuskyavu,* "love craziness," in its victim. To bring about this state of love madness, the love magician renders an individual helpless against his sexual desires by means of a *tuskyaptawi,* "charming song."

Beaglehole and Beaglehole (1935: 8) discuss the use of a special medicine bundle in love magic performed by sorcerers, a small package containing pieces of the woman's clothing, hair, turquoise, shells, and a crystal. The sorcerer holds the bundle in front of him and sings songs to it, joining the name of the man to the name of the woman.

This causes the woman to come to the man's bed. The sorcerer who is hired is paid by the gift of the man's sister or other female relative as his mistress.

Charming songs of a different nature also serve to assure the sorcerer's hunting success. Casting a spell on the game animals with the song causes the animals to offer themselves freely as prey.

Of course, the antisocial practices a sorcerer engages in are not directed only toward individuals. Epidemics and famines are typically blamed on witches. Thus, cloud control, which within the realm of agriculturists and horticulturists ultimately implies control over life-sustaining moisture, is frequently attempted by the sorcerer because it will impact a large group of people. To this extent, witches either channel clouds exclusively to their own fields and garden plots or cause rain-laden clouds to withdraw. Offensive odor is often used to make the clouds recede. Consultants relate stories of witches blowing their breath at the clouds through the malodorous bone of a diseased human corpse, or bending over, sticking their naked buttocks directly toward the clouds, and blowing through their spread legs.

In addition, practitioners of witchcraft are believed to unleash a host of crop-destroying pests, such as grasshoppers, kangaroo rats, prairie dogs, mice, and cutworms. These agents of destruction, combined with the sorcerer's own powers of averting imminent rain, constitute the classic formula for bringing about famine.

Realizing the ever-present danger of witchcraft, Hopi society prescribes a whole array of safeguards and taboos to separate a person from its malevolent influence. Geertz (1987: 115–17), in discussing conflict and controversy in Hopi society, points out that it is "steeped in an ideology that ultimately associates blatant individualism with witchcraft." He also notes that witchcraft is so abhorrent, in part, because the individual's usual main source of security, the family, is also the group from which the witch's life-extending murders must come. However, as disintegrative as witchcraft is, it also encourages behaving prophylactically, in an ethically correct manner, as a shield against supernatural attack. This array of prophylactic measures pertains to both the ceremonial and the secular context of Hopi life. The scope of this discussion does not permit a complete listing of these, but Beaglehole and Beaglehole (1935: 9) list a few common ones: Hair and combings should be burnt and not left on the floor or ground; clothes should be kept inside the house and not left lying around; a person should endeavor to maintain a good spirit; and in the old days, at least, it was thought that keeping the skin cold and tough by bathing in a spring each morning would repel the "bullets" of the witch.

Regardless of their skill, sorcerers are not immune to discovery. As a rule, when found out they will do their utmost to bribe their way out of a potentially fatal predicament. Note that the correct Hopi term for a witch that is seen or heard is *tu'alangw*, not *powaqa*. In the words of a Hopi consultant (Malotki 1993: 187), "A *tu'alangw* is visible when practicing. For example, when he is scaring someone. The *powaqa*, however, one cannot see when he is practicing his witchcraft against a person. He is clearly not a *tu'alangw*."

As soon as the recognized sorcerer realizes that his discoverer cannot be bribed, he resorts to pleading for his life. As one might expect, however, this plea is loaded with trickery. He may plead for just a few more days, typically four, actually meaning four years. If the discoverer relents and grants him his wish, the witch would live for four more years, during which time he would have the opportunity to extend his life once again through another relative's death. If the discoverer doesn't fall for the ruse, the witch dies in four days.

Regardless of whether they are discovered or not, in the end witches get their just deserts. As Titiev (1942: 556) rightly points out, "one of the most telling features of the Hopi attitude toward sorcerers is found in their religious notions. On the whole, Hopi religion is decidedly nonethical, but *poakam* [correctly, *popwaqt*] are severely punished in the other world." After manifold ordeals along his journey in the underworld, on the last leg of this journey the witch reaches the flaming fire pit, his final destination. Here a Kwaani'ytaqa (One Horn society member), in his role as psychopomp, makes sure that evildoers receive their deserved punishment, while the souls of the pure are permitted to proceed to paradise.

Shamanism

Prominent among the many human universals that are thought to hold for modern as well as ancient man is the phenomenon of religion. Thus, Brown (1991: 130–41), who in his *Human Universals* devotes an entire chapter to the notion of a "Universal People," believes that the "UP," as he refers to them, share a whole catalog of ritual and religious traits that, in his view, are best explained in terms of evolutionary psychology or psychobiology:

The UP have religious or supernatural beliefs in that they believe in something beyond the visible and palpable. They anthropomorphize and (some if not all of them) believe things that are demonstrably false. They also practice magic, and their magic is designed to do such things as to sustain and increase life and to win the attention of the opposite sex. They have theories of fortune and misfortune. They have ideas about how to explain disease and death. They see a connection between sickness and death. They try to heal the sick and have medicines for this purpose. The UP practice divination. And they try to control the weather. (Brown 1991: 139)

The Universal People "also dream and attempt to interpret their dreams" (Brown 1991: 139), and to "alter their moods or feelings" they will resort to psychotropic substances such as stimulants, narcotics, or intoxicants (Brown 1991: 136).

Probably the oldest religious paradigm that fits these parameters is shamanism. Nearly globally attested among extant hunter-gatherers (Bahn in Smith 1992: ix), there exists today a near-consensus of opinion among scholars—particularly those devoted to the understanding of Archaic ontology—that, the world over, hunter-gatherers of prehistoric antiquity also practiced a shamanistically oriented religion. This is equally true for the earliest immigrants into the Americas. According to La Barre (1972: 273), all evidence, be it archaeological, linguistic, cultural, or folkloristic, is in concord with the physical-anthropological view today that "the American Indians were unspecialized Mongoloids bearing a late-Paleolithic and Mesolithic paleo-Siberian hunting culture and religion." As they reached the New World, they brought with them shamanism, the ur-religion of hunting peoples.

The shaman, in his pivotal role as "broker" or "boundary player" (Bean and Vane 1978: 127) between the domains of the sacred and the profane, was essentially responsible for balancing the physical and psychic needs of his hunter-gatherer group. In addition, he was expected to carry out such variegated tasks as curing diseases, invoking hunting success, and divining the future. Most important perhaps, because it was crucial for the survival of his group, was the challenge of weather control (Eliade 1964: 304).

As a religious mediator between the natural and supernatural realms, the shaman meets these duties through communication with the spirit world by way of ecstatic trance or altered states of consciousness. To achieve a convincing trance experience, he resorts to a wide range of techniques: exposure to the elements, sensory deprivation brought on by physical exhaustion, sleep deprivation, prolonged solitude, thirsting and fasting, rhythmic and sonic driving such as drumming and dancing, hyperventilation, intense concentration, sexual abstinence, endurance of pain, and self-mutilation and self-torture. In addition to these nonchemical means of achieving an altered state of consciousness, the shaman, equipped with an extensive psychopharmacological knowledge, can induce powerful hallucinations through the use of psychoactive plants. Unlike Eliade (1964: 401), who deems the use of narcotics "a vulgar substitution for pure trance," La Barre (1980: 82) argues that the early Native Americans were essentially "culturally programmed" for a conscious exploitation of hallucinogenic plants.

Altered states of consciousness are a universal psychobiological phenomenon. David Lewis-Williams (1996: 126), in a decalogue of elements that he considers central to a generic characterization of hunter-gatherer shamanism, lists, as the defining criterion, the fact that shamanism is based on "a range of institutionalized" altered states of consciousness. According to Bourguignon (1974: 231–32), a cross-cultural survey of nearly five hundred societies from around the world determined that 90 percent of them had institutionalized forms of altered states of consciousness. More to the point in this context, it is significant that the incidence of institutionalization of these states for North American societies (Indian and Eskimo) was 97 percent.

Taxonomically, it has been suggested that the term "shaman" should be reserved strictly for "those practitioners of ecstasy in hunting and gathering societies of the world who utilize trance states and engage in healing and divination" (Dobkin de Rios and Winkelman 1989: 2). A second category, "shaman/healer" or "shamanistic healer," would be applied to practitioners in sedentary communities that are distinguished, socioeconomically, by horticulture, agriculture, or pastoralism. Such communities would be distinguished by hierarchial organization and political integration "beyond the level of local community" (Dobkin de Rios and Winkelman 1989: 2)

The demise of Archaic hunter-gatherer bands and the emergence of horticulturists and farmers does not imply that shamanism became extinct, at least not where the American Southwest is concerned. The development of priestly societies engaged in fertility and rainmaking ceremonies may have decreased the power that shamans enjoyed in hunter-gatherer times, but shamanism's survival was assured because agriculturists continued to have the same metaphysical, psychic, healing, and fertility needs as their ancestors.

In the large corpus of ethnographic data and traditional narratives Malotki collected in the course of his research among the Hopis, intimations of shamanic practices are tantalizingly few. Still, there is sufficient evidence that shamanism was once firmly institutionalized among these agriculturalists, and that Hopi culture has what might be regarded as a general shamanic view of the world "in which everything—not only animals but also plants and rocks, wind and rain—may be imbued with spirit" (Vitebsky 1995: 15). This view may be expressed in the wide variety of aspects of the natural world that have been given kachina form.

A few lexemes in the Hopi language provide some insight in this connection. The shaman was known as *povosqa* (plural *povosyaqam*) at Second Mesa and as *poosi'ytaqa* (plural *poosi'yyungqam*) in the Third Mesa dialect area. Etymologically connected to *poosi*, "eye," *povosqa* literally translates "one who does seeing," whereas *poosi'ytaqa* means "one who has an eye." "Seer" perhaps best captures the notion of the Hopi shaman, with "seeing" relating to the diagnosing and curing of illness and disease.

As a rule, this "seeing" was enhanced by the use of a *ruupi*, "crystal," the shaman's "third eye." For this reason, shamans were sometimes called *ruupi'yyungqam*, "crystal owners." Stephen (1936: 723), in referring to one specific shaman, says of him that he "can make powerful medicine" and "can see with his eyes the very spot affected when anyone is ill." While it is not clear whether the "eyes" in this quotation relate to the man's real eyes or, metaphorically, to his gazing stone, he does describe the utilization of such quartz crystals in a curing session arranged for his personal benefit:

> Taking the crystal between finger and thumb, sometimes in one hand, sometimes in the other, he placed it close to his eye and looked intently at me. Then he would hold the crystal at arm's length toward me. Then he would bend over so as to bring the crystal close up to me, and thus he swayed back and forth, in silence, occasionally making passes with his arms to and fro and toward me, for about four or five minutes. Suddenly he reached over me and pressed the crystal against my right breast, and just upon the region of a quite severe pain, which I had probably described to him, but, whether or no, he located the seat of the pain exactly. (Stephen 1936: 860)

Hopi oral literature contains a number of references to the use of crystals. Old Spider Woman, in a story about the destruction of Awat'ovi (Courlander 1982: 56), is described as using "some kind of glass thing. . . . Not ordinary glass, some special kind of glass" in a divining fashion to determine where a kidnapped woman had been taken. In a story of the destruction of Hisatsongoopavi (Old Shungo-pavi), the people of the village call a shaman from Walpi when a plan hatched by some village leaders to enlist the help of the Water Serpents backfires. "When the shaman arrived, he went in to the men and found them still huddled around their altar. Immediately he took out his crystal and peered through it at the chiefs. He saw that every one of them was evil" (Malotki 1993: 35). In still another story, this one concerning the destruction of the village of Pivanhonkyapi, Old Spider Woman uses her crystal once again to determine the whereabouts of a young wife who disappears while out getting water. The young wife had been abducted by a young man dressed as a kachina but who is actually a witch (Courlander 1971: 135). In Curtis ([1922] 1970: 209), the sorcerers feel that there are too many children and they create the cannibal monster Chaveyu [correctly, Tseeveyo], from juniper bark to eat them. Into the monster they insert a crystal for the heart and shells for the liver and lungs, singing over it to bring it to life.

Interestingly, this idea of a crystal for a heart is also at the center of Hopi ritual practice, both literally and figuratively, in the case of ritual puppets such as the Paalölöqangw, Kooyemsi, and Sa'lakw-manawyat. Termed *tunöshayni'at*, "his food bag," this puppet heart is usually a little bag containing cornmeal, a prayer stick, seeds, and a *ruupi*, or quartz crystal. Additionally, "crystals are used during altar ceremonies, either as a symbol in itself or to increase the efficacy of the ritual activity. For instance, it is often used to deflect the rays of the sun towards the medicine bowl in order to strike the contents with the energy of the sun" (Geertz 1987: 32 n. 25). Crystals are also used for various purposes in the Wuwtsim and Niman ceremonies (Parsons [1939] 1996: 607, 768).

At one time, all Hopi shamans had to be members of the so-called *poswimi*. Literally denoting "eye society" (Curtis [1922] 1970: 53), the word corresponds to our notion of "shaman society." Its individual members, termed *poovost* or *poswiwimkyam*, were basically men with "X-ray" vision. According to Stephen (1936: 281), who recorded much of the Hopi culture at the First Mesa community of Walpi in the 1890s, the *poswimi* was already wholly extinct at that time, although some of its members were still alive. Describing it as "a society of occult medciners," he refers to the actual *poovost* as "eye-seekers"

(Stephen 1894: 212). Titiev (1972: 69), in characterizing it as "the *real* curing society," reports that the last great medicine men at Oraibi passed away before 1906.

Few details are available on the selection criteria for a potential Hopi shaman or on how he acquired his knowledge. One can assume that membership into the shamanistic *poswimi* sodality was primarily obtained through an established initiation process, as is or was the case for other religious societies such as the Al, Kwan, Wuwtsim, and Taw. As a rule, this route required a ceremonial sponsor. That initiation was the standard way to gain access to the society is borne out linguistically by the lexeme *wimkya*, "initiated member," whose plural form occurs in the above-mentioned compound *poswiwimkyam*, "initiated members of the 'eye' society." The following single sentence corroborates this fact: *I' hapi poosi'ytaqa poswimit aw wimkya'iwta*, "It is indeed true that the shaman is an initiated member of the shaman society." Unfortunately, except for the following, no details of the actual initiation process have survived in the literature.

In Curtis ([1922] 1970: 53–55), Lomasi, the only surviving member of the *poswimi* at Walpi at that time, describes the process of his incomplete initiation, especially the part using crystals:

> I was placed before the three medicine-men, and after the singers had been dismissed, three smooth crystals, each somewhat larger than a bean, were laid in a row beside the fire. They told me to remove my clothing and sit beside the fireplace, and Káni, the leader, took one of the crystals, and while singing he slapped it against my breast over the heart. This was to give me a heart as hard and strong as the crystal. He rubbed it about over this spot, and then asked if I felt something, and although I answered no, he nevertheless said aloud, "It is well done!" Then the next man did the same thing, and thus I received the heart of a pósi-taka [correctly, *poosi'ytaqa*]. This ceremony they called ŭnán-vana [correctly, *unangwvana*, "to put in, insert heart"].

Absent from the Hopi ethnographic record are references to initiation by means of an intentional vision quest, one of the hallmarks of shamanism among many other Native American tribal groups. Biological inheritance is equally unattested. Evidence that involuntary dreams may occasionally have induced an individual to take up the office of the shaman is contained in a brief reference by Levy (1994: 319). In this case, a man who survived a lightning strike "later dreamed that he had been chosen by the cloud deities, who imbued him with their healing power."

One way in which a Hopi shaman apparently received his call was by virtue of his clan membership (Levy 1994: 319). Thus, Badger clansmen were prospective candidates because they were thought to be endowed with an innate ability to heal due to their totemic linkage with the badger. The significance of the animal in regard to the business of curing is preserved in a narrative collected by Stephen (1936: 860–61). Here, at the occasion of a kachina performance, Badger magically surfaces in the center of the dance court from the underworld "carrying a bundle on his back which contained all medicines. He said, 'I know all medicinal charms, and I have the feather to navo'chiwa [correctly, *naavootsiwa*], to drive away (expel) all bodily ills." Interestingly, the story concludes by mentioning that "the Badger who came up from Below was the first of the Po'boshtü" [correctly, Poovost].

Another standard method for a person to become a shamanic practitioner is through suffering an illness or by being saved in a life-threatening medical situation. Titiev (1942: 552), for example, alludes to such a scenario when he relates that a Hotevilla man from Third Mesa "made a vow in the course of a serious sickness that he would become a shaman if he survived."

Finally, qualification for the office of shaman was automatically assured in Hopi society when a person survived a lightning strike. The following folk statement collected by Malotki explains this cultural belief. Linguistically noteworthy in this connection is the fact that lightning strikes, in the eyes of the Hopi, are seen as happenings caused by *yooyangw*, "the rain," or *yooyoyangwt*, "the rains." Note that the pluralized form of this meteorological event is marked by the suffix -*t*, which, according to Hopi grammatical rules, can only be attached to nouns conceived of as animate.

> When the rain strikes you, you are either alone or in the company of somebody. If you are alone, the rain will revive you by itself; but only if you're a Hopi, because Hopis have fasting practices. If someone is with the person who got struck, one must not attempt to help the victim, but leave the place. The rains then restore the person by themselves. If the other person would stay, he would merely delay the rains. There are many who have clearly been struck by lightning that talk about this. For this reason also, one is not supposed to walk past a thing struck by lightning, nor does one approach it, until it has been properly purified.
>
> People also say that whenever a person survives a lightning strike, he gets initiated into the business of curing. By being struck, he gets to see things in a clear way and, as a result, learns the things that pertain to medicine and healing.

Titiev (1942: 522), too, mentions the causal link between the experience of a lightning strike and the cultural privilege of attaining the status of a curer. He adds, however, that in this particular case the person in question "later dreamed that the cloud deities had thus imbued him with some of their power, which he had to use on pain of death, for helping others."

In addition to being organized in a shamanic sodality, the Hopi shaman derived his supernatural potency from animal familiars. Also known as spirit helpers, companion animals, tutelary spirits, or spirit guides, they were the shaman's supernatural aides or alter egos that empowered him to perform his extraordinary manipulations and shamanic healing tasks. The Hopi term for an animal familiar seems to have been *na'at*, not, however, in its sense of "his biological father," but here with the implication of "his ceremonial father, his godfather." This is evident from the following text:

> Medicine men typically have animal familiars such as game animals or other creatures that roam the land. As a rule, the animal called upon as a godfather is that which one desires to equal in power. With the help of this animal the medicine man then practices the art of healing.
> The seer or shaman will sometimes call on a wolf as a godfather and even dress like one when he shamanizes. Others come to have the bear or eagle as a helping spirit. Even the little mouse will qualify, for it is very skillful. However, while medicine men will call on the powers of these animals, they never change into them. Still, they possess their hearts and may dress like them as they treat a patient. They have incorporated the magic skill of these animals. (Malotki 1993: 164–65)

The total identification of the shaman with his animal familiar is most obvious perhaps in his attempt to impersonate it in the course of the curing session. This impersonation is tantamount to shamanic transformation, as may be gathered from the following text:

> When I was still a child, a man by the name of Yoto used to shamanize. No sooner had he swallowed his medicine than something happened to him. This Yoto had a hawk for an animal father, and so he behaved and screamed like one. Like a hawk he had his wings spread out and flew up, even climbed on top of things. Shamans will typically have one of the game animals, bears, pronghorn, all sorts of beasts, even mountain lions, for helpers. Thus, with a bear for an animal familiar, he will act like one too. Growling like a bear he feels around his patients and removes from them the foreign objects that are causing the disease.

Levy's (1994: 315) claim that the bear was not among the animals used by the Hopi as tutelary spirits is not verified by this statement. Also, there is strong evidence for bear shamanism in at least three or four Hopi narratives. In "The Boy Who Wanted to Be a Medicine Man" from the present collection, a man changes into a bear and takes a boy to a kiva in the high forest (presumably on Nuvatukya-'ovi, the San Francisco Peaks), where he is whipped by kachinas with yucca strips until he is nothing but a pile of bones and meat. He is then covered with a robe and danced back to life, whereupon he returns to his village and becomes an excellent medicine man. In "The Gambling Boy Who Married a Bear Girl," also from the present collection, a boy marries a bear girl at the kiva of the bears on the San Francisco Peaks. He returns to his village and forgets her, however, and in a rage she kills him. In remorse, she brings him back to life, and he subsequently becomes a great healer. In Courlander (1982: 56–57), in a story regarding the destruction of Awat'ovi, Coyote Grandma turns herself into a bear to rescue a woman who has been abducted by witches. In a contest of power between animal familiars, Coyote Grandma's bear bests the witches' unspecified animal. Finally, in the present collection, in the story "The Man Who Traveled to Maski, Home of the Dead, to Bring Back His Wife," a huge bear, in the role of psychopomp, guards the path to Maski.

Because of a taboo that generally restricted the shaman from eating meat from the species of his helper (Whitley 1996: 8), only nonfood animals served in the role of shamanic familiars. Thus, in addition to the game animals, mountain lion, bear, wolf, and hawk referred to above, the stories mention the badger, mice, and the snake as potential "godfathers."

Strong corroboration for the employment of spirit animals comes from the realm of Hopi witchcraft. Described as *lööq unangwa'ytaqa,* "one who has two hearts," the Hopi sorcerer is believed to possess the heart of his godfather animal in addition to his own and can assume its guise while pursuing his evil intents (Malotki 1993: 63). While some of the animals serving him overlap with those aiding the shaman, others would never be called upon by the shaman, especially the coyote.

Human-animal metamorphosis recurs frequently in the Hopi stories analyzed, including the stories in the present collection. In the stories dealing with witchcraft, humans most frequently turn into coyotes, but they also turn into nighthawks, doves, crows, ravens, owls, wolves, and foxes. In other stories, which sometimes have themes reminiscent of shamanism, humans become a wide variety of animals, but never the coyote: deer, antelope, snipes, snakes (including rattlesnakes), bears, mountain lions, badgers, gophers, swallows, eagles, hawks, and in one case each, the mule, the stinkbug, and the owl. It is worth noting that the humans who turned into the stinkbug and the mule were on the way to Maski, and they were not pillars of virtue in their lifetimes. The final case, in the story "The Owl That Made Off With a Little Child" (Malotki 1998: 248), concerns a misbehaving child who is carried off by an owl with no overt tones of witchcraft.

The fact that witches also use owls may reflect an ambiguity in Hopi culture regarding the bird. Though frequently used by witches, three species of the owl are also deified in kachina form: *hootsoko,* "screech owl," *mongwu,* "great horned owl," and *salapmongwu,* "spruce owl." Fluffy clusters of owl feathers, called *mongtsitoma* or *mongtsakwa,* are worn on the masks of various kachina deities, for example, by the Badger kachina. In other positive uses, Hopi arrows are typically fletched with owl feathers, guaranteeing a near-silent flight, and owl feathers are used in *nakwakwusi,* "prayer feathers," to protect peach trees from killing frosts. The negative aspect of owls in Hopi culture is clearly borne out in oral literature, where due to its nocturnal ways and silent flight, the owl becomes one of the witch's preferred means of prowling in the night (Malotki 1993: 163). Occasionally branded *powaqmongwu,* "witch owl," the bird is also contemptuously called *tu'alangwmongwu,* "ghost owl" (Malotki 1985: 61). In the present collection, in the supposedly true story "The Witch Owl," a jealous woman uses the guise of an owl to make a rival woman's baby sick. She is shot by the irate husband while she is roosting outside the couple's home. The witch woman later dies of the gunshot wound she received as an owl.

There is convincing evidence that the Hopi shaman used the trance state to effect his cure. Levy (1994: 310), in recounting a personal experience when a healer from Second Mesa performed a sucking cure on him, points out that the trance state was induced by hyperventilation and lasted approximately one minute. While this relatively mild form of inducement was employed by a *tuuhikya,* that is, a regular medicine man, the bona fide shaman of old appears to have resorted to more powerful methods. This is strongly intimated in the following folk statement. In its reference to an unspecified *ngahu,* "medicine," it alleges that the Hopi shaman consumed a particular medicine that may have heightened his visionary command and the diagnostic faculties of his all-seeing eye:

> Long ago, when a person became sick, he went to a shaman. The shaman was of course an initiated member of the Shaman society. If he was not very sick, the shaman treated him at any time of the day. If the patient was gravely ill, though, he did his shamanic diagnosing only at night.
>
> Whenever the shaman was going to practice at night, he used a special medicine. Upon eating this medicine, it got like daylight for him. Or he smeared something across his eyes, and then it got as clear as day for him. This is what people say, so I know about it.
>
> After first swallowing some sort of medicine the shaman can see the foreign object planted by someone through black magic [*tuu-kyayni*] that is causing the ailment. He then removes this foreign object. Nowadays, no one practices this skill anymore. The medicine men certainly don't do it. Only those who had learned this technique and were properly initiated were like that.

As may be gathered from this testimonial, Jorgensen's (1980: 564) contention that Hopi shamans differed from the quintessential pattern of the North American shaman in that they lacked the use of the trance state is not borne out. Unfortunately, nothing concrete was remembered by Malotki's consultants about the substance of the ingested *ngahu* or its possible ingredients. Circumstantial evidence suggests, however, that it may have involved a vegetal hallucinogen.

Although the Hopi subsistence economy emphasized horticulture and agriculture over hunting and gathering, it is safe to assume that Hopi shamanic healers were thoroughly familiar with the flora of the various phytogeographical zones that made up their land. Their botanical expertise, acquired through a method of trial and error over centuries, must have included detailed information not only about every plant's growth cycle and seasonal availability but also about its edibility and usefulness.

Hopi shamans, moreover, must have been versed in all aspects of a plant's medicinal properties and capable of separating those that were beneficial from those that were harmful or even fatal. Their pharmacopoeia would also have contained an assortment of botanical hallucinogens. Among these would have been jimsonweed (*Datura* spp.), Indian tobacco (*Nicotiana trigonophylla*), four o'clock (*Mirabilis multiflora*), the hallucinogenic mushroom psilocybe (*Psilocybe coprophilia*), and fly agaric (*Amanita muscaria*). Of these, *Datura* appears to be the most qualified to have served the shamans as a hallucinogen and a consciousness-altering agent. It is also the one hallucinogenic substance most frequently referred to in the Puebloan ethnographic literature.

Tsimona, the Hopi term for *Datura*, is today vehemently shunned by the Hopi and decried as a *nukustusaqa*, "evil grass" (Malotki 1983b: 207). As Beaglehole and Beaglehole (1935: 42) report, in the eyes of some Hopis, the plant is believed to make anyone crazy who touches it; the antidote, in the case of a child, was for a mother to quickly bathe the child in her own urine. Malotki's consultants, on the other hand, insisted that only actual ingestion of the plant would have triggered this consequence: *Tsimonat hak sowe' tuskyaptingwu*, "Whoever eats jimsonweed goes mad."

Nonetheless, a list of specific *Datura* applications among the Hopi is found in Whiting (1966: 89). According to him, its use in medical diagnosis and treatment was primary. Thus, the root was allegedly chewed to induce visions by the medicine man while examining the patient. The plant was also employed to cure mean-spirited individuals of their meanness by holding them in a blanket over the smoldering leaves of the plant (Whiting 1966: 37). Furthermore, it was customary to replace absent ears on kachina masks with *Datura* flowers (Colton 1959: 14). Quite appropriately, one kachina who is always adorned with such ears is the Maswikkatsinmana. Also known as Tsimonmana, "Jimsonweed Girl" (Wright 1973: 253), it was her task to fetch Maasaw, the god of death, in the course of the Nevenwehekiw ceremony (Malotki and Lomatuway'ma 1987: 133–38).

A more indirect reference to the Hopis' use of *Datura* is contained in an ethnographic episode collected by Beaglehole and Beaglehole (1935: 9) where *poswiwimkyam*, "initiated members of the 'seer' or shamanic curing sodality," made use of a "medicine which made them stagger in their walk as if they were intoxicated." This happened while they were treating their patients by removing from them, with the aid of quartz crystals, pathogenic objects shot into the victims by sorcerers and witches. During a similar extraction of injurious objects, a Hopi medicine man gave the patient "something to chew that would cause him to dream and thus learn the identity of the witches who were after him" (Titiev 1972: 54).

In addition to exploiting the psychotropic properties of *Datura* as a chemical inducement of altered states of consciousness, the Hopi shamans also appear to have intentionally used it as a sight- and vision-altering drug. Unfortunately, the simple statement above that the shaman "smeared something across his eyes, whereupon it got as clear as day for him" does not specify the plant that was involved in the procedure. A similar practice is reported for the Zuni Indians, Hopi Pueblo neighbors to the southeast. Apparently the plant extracts, bits of the powdered root, were directly inserted into the eye (Stevenson [1904] 1985: 386).

On the basis of ethnographic analogy one can therefore posit that the Hopis too were familiar with the powerful belladonna alkaloids and employed them for mydriatic effect. These alkaloids derive their epithet from the Renaissance custom of Italian women who hoped to make themselves sexually irresistible *belle donnae*, "beautiful ladies," by enlarging their pupils (La Barre 1980: 63). According to Mills-paugh (1974: 502), mydriasis, or pupil dilation, one of the physiological symptoms in patients suffering from *Datura* intoxication, will, in extreme cases, cause photophobia to the point that a patient will gain the ability to see clearly at night but be abnormally intolerant of daylight.

One final piece of evidence that the Hopi were intimately familiar with the properties of *Datura* comes from an aspect of the plant that is rarely mentioned in the symptomatology of the hallucinogens. Apparently, one of the physiological side effects of belladonna alkaloids is sexual arousal and a heightening of sexual functions (Stone 1932: 55). Women in particular experience nymphomania, a condition that is vividly illustrated in "The Story of the 'Tsimonmamant' or Jimson Weed Girls" (Malotki 1983b: 204–20) and in the narrative "The Boy Who Encountered the Jimsonweed and Four O'clock Girls" in the present collection.

In addition to *Datura*, Whiting (1966: 30–31) mentions two other plants with psychotomimetic properties that the Hopi shamans exploited for pharmacodynamic assistance. Of these, the herb *palena*, as Whiting (1966: 100) readily admits, was never satisfactorily identified by him. Nothing is known besides the fact that its root was chewed by the medicine man "in order to induce visions and thus help him in locating the source of the trouble" (Whiting 1966: 30).

The same application procedure was true for four o'clock. Known as *soksi* in the Hopi dialect of Third Mesa, its root too was masticated "to induce vision while making diagnosis" (Whiting 1966: 75). Confirmation for the hallucinatory power of this plant was obtained in a statement collected by Malotki: *Hak soksit sowe' hiituy tuwa'ynumngwu,*

"Whenever someone eats four o'clock, he will see [have visions of] all sorts of beings."

Whether the plant also had the effect of an aphrodisiac like *Datura* is not known. Suffice it to say that in the story titled "The Boy Who Encountered the Jimsonweed and Four O'clock Girls," the plant appears personified in the form of the Sokmamant, or Four O'clock Girls, together with the Tsimonmamant, or Jimsonweed Girls. Perceived as socially offensive due to their aggressive nymphomaniac behavior, both are destroyed by the story's protagonist.

Nothing is known about the consumption of consciousness-altering mushrooms by Hopi shamanic practitioners, although both psilocybe (*Psilocybe coprophilia*) and fly agaric (*Amanita muscaria*), both strongly psychedelic, are native to the Colorado Plateau. The red-capped version of the latter is found, for example, in the ponderosa pine forests, and the former in deer and wapiti dung in the open park lands south of the Hopi territory. Generically termed *maskiisi*, which etymologically translates as "corpse-shade," mushrooms have traditionally been shunned as part of the Hopi diet. While it is tempting to link the morpheme *mas-*, "corpse, death" to trance, which, symbolically and metaphorically, is frequently described in terms of death or dying, its inherent meaning may simply relate to the poisonous nature of many mushrooms. In the total absence of Hopi ethnographic information, this question will have to remain unanswered.

Finally, there is tobacco, "supernatural plant *par excellence* of the American Indian" (La Barre 1972: 276), which was widely used for magico-religious and medicinal purposes in both Americas. Ingested in a multitude of ways, ranging from chewing, licking, drinking, snuffing, and smoking to administration through the skin and rectal injection by means of enemas (Wilbert 1994; Furst 1976), it is potent in nicotine, an alkaloid that produces a noticeable psychotropic effect. Belonging to the genus *Nicotiana*, a branch of the nightshade family, or Solanaceae (Wilbert 1994: 48), it was the primary hallucinogen of the shaman in far western North America, according to Whitley (1998: 146).

The Hopi use of the plant was not for reasons of hedonistic indulgence but rather was limited to a ritual context. A common element of Hopi stories, therefore, is the ritualistic use of tobacco when something important is to be discussed, or when *pahos*, or prayer feathers or sticks, have been made and the makers wish to "blow their desires" into them. To be more effective ceremonially, both *Nicotiana attenuata* and *Nicotiana trigonophylla*, the two native tobacco species occurring in the Hopi environment, were mixed with other plants. The resulting mixtures were known as *yoyviva*, "rain tobacco" (Whiting 1966: 89) or *omawviva*, "cloud tobacco" (Stephen 1936: 599). The billowing smoke, which was never inhaled but primarily dispensed from pipes, was thought to be associated with clouds and hence capable of bringing rain. Smoking is used in such a direct manner in a story of the demise of Sikyatki (Malotki 1993: 137). The protagonist is in a life or death race with a witch boy, and the smoke clouds produced by his uncles leave the kiva and drift over the racers, where the clouds are transformed into actual thunderheads. The witch boy, traveling in the form of a hawk for an advantage over the protagonist, becomes drenched and cannot fly. In addition, in its ascending form, smoke was believed to transmit the prayers of the people to the gods (Whiting 1966: 90). The importance of the plant in Hopi society is also evident from the fact that it served as totemic eponym to the Pipngyam, "Tobacco clan members."

No ethnographic evidence exists that the mind-altering plant was employed as a vehicle of ecstacy or altered states of consciousness by Hopi shamans. Its psychedelic effect may be alluded to in the term *pipsuwi*, "to get dizzy from smoking," but there is no evidence that this dizziness was exploited for supernatural visions, acquisition of power, or other shamanic quests.

Nevertheless, a possible clue that tobacco smoke may once have been ingested by Hopi shamans to induce altered states of consciousness is contained in the smoking-test motif encountered in Hopi oral literature. As a rule, the protagonist, to establish his legitimacy to a certain claim, is challenged to a test that consists of consuming or "smoking up" (*sowa*) a large pipe of tobacco—that is, inhaling rather than exhaling the smoke. In one such instance in the present collection of stories, "How the Pöqangw Brothers Found Their Father," the protagonists are miraculously aided in such an endeavor by a gopher who, by means of a reed that he secretly inserts in the smokers' rectums, channels the smoke harmlessly out of their bodies to his subterranean burrow. In a similar story (Curtis [1922] 1970: 196), a village crier chief, hunting for his missing son, is tested by the Winged-Snake Girl, who passes to him a clay pipe as large as a cooking pot filled with tobacco that she has tamped down with her foot. She admonishes him that he must inhale the smoke and not blow it out. In the meantime, however, Mole has been digging an opening under the chief so that the smoke passes through him and down into Mole's burrow. Winged-Snake Girl is amazed that he does not become sick. Elsewhere in Curtis ([1922] 1970: 212), Mole allows a man who has gone to the kiva of the bird monster Kwaatoko to pass a smoking trial, one of a number necessary before he can recover his stolen wife. Once again, the man is admonished by the monster to inhale, but Mole makes an opening under him and vents the smoke harmlessly out into the valley below.

One very common sensation reported during trance or an altered state is that of spatial displacement. It is this kinesthetic effect of weightlessness that suggests to the shaman that his soul is departing from his body and embarking on an extracorporeal journey to the spirit world. Commonly referred to as shamanic flight, modern nomenclature employs such terms as ecsomatic experience, translocation, aerial voyaging, astral projection, and exteriorization (Turpin 1994: 77–78).

Clinically known as depersonalization, this out-of-body phenomenon can be triggered by a host of inducing agents. Among those listed by Turpin (1994: 78), tobacco, fasting, and rhythmic driving in the form of dancing, drumming, and chanting are very much part of the Hopi cultural fabric. However, there is no ethnographic evidence that they were actively exploited for this purpose. Further, a review of Hopi oral literature turned up only one instance of drumming, in which Old Spider Woman plays the drum for her grandsons Pöqangwhoya and Palöngawhoya, who are practicing so they can go to Kiisiw, where kachinas live, and bring back a new dance (Courlander 1982: 221). A number of cases of dance and song are present in the oral literature, but they are not overtly related to out-of-body experiences. For example, the cicadas sing and play the flute to counter a blizzard (Malotki 1998: 179), and in the present collection, in the story "The So'yoko Ogre and His Wife," Billy Goat rattles and chants over So'yoko Woman's body, creating goats and sheep for the Hopi.

A much more probable candidate as a cause for the phenomenon of extracorporeal flight is *Datura*. Clinical studies show that the drug causes this sensation as one of the central somatic hallucinations experienced by a person under its influence. Of the two powerful alkaloids contained in the plant, scopolamine and hyoscyamine, it is especially the latter that conveys the peculiar feeling of flying (La Barre 1980: 63).

Mystical flight, a classic shamanistic motif, is probably the most widely attested metaphor for an altered state of consciousness in human culture. "The rapture induced by trance, when the soul of the ecstatic leaves the body and flies into the realm of spirits and gods, is indeed an act of transcendence" (Halifax 1979: 18). According to Eliade (1964: 478–79), at one time all men could reach heaven and could achieve this act of transcendence, whereas it is now given to the shaman, here on earth and as often as desired, to accomplish this "coming out of the body." Magical flight is clearly represented in the *paatuwvota*, "magic flying shield," of Hopi oral literature, and, as Vitebsky (1995: 70) asserts, such vehicles "express the shaman's extra-ordinary power of locomotion, which is not available to the unaided human body." Literally denoting "water-shield," the term *paatuwvota* also alludes to the rings in the water that ripple out in every direction when an object is cast into a pool. Serving supernaturals as their premier mode of transportation, the device is described as consisting of "two parts, with the lower one spinning and the upper one remaining still" (Malotki 1993: 307). Manufactured from lightweight cotton, the shield is said to be "woven in the manner of a Hopi wedding robe. The owner of such a vehicle needs only to climb aboard, tug on something and utter a command, whereupon the shield rises in the air" (Malotki 1993: 429), taking its occupant wherever he wishes to go.

Identical in function, but of a different construction and design, is the *tawiya*, "gourd." This flying machine is said to consist of two halves. Its rider, after climbing aboard and closing the upper half over himself, allegedly installs a tightly stretched sinew between the bottom of the gourd and its stem button. By twisting the sinew between his palms, the rider causes the flying machine to miraculously lift off and zoom along, emitting a humming noise (Malotki 1993: 135, 139).

In a manner similar to the motif of the flying carpet in Middle Eastern mythology, Hopi culture provides for the descent of a deceased person's soul to Maski. For example, in "An Oraibi Boy's Visit to Maski, Home of the Dead" from the present collection, a boy is transported for a portion of his journey on a ceremonial kilt, ac-companied by the sun. Unlike the conveyance symbols mentioned above, which are only used in a fictional, nonreligious context, the devices serving this purpose are part of the Hopi beliefs surrounding death and afterlife. Termed *hahawpi*, "climbing-down instrument," they are actual Hopi material culture items that are bestowed on their recipients according to gender, age, and marital status. Little boys and girls, for example, are expected to use their little *kwikwilhoya* and *tsirooya* blankets, respectively, both as shrouds and means to reach the other world. A married man employs the *hahawpiyungyapu*, a specially designed wicker plaque that is traditionally given to him as a bridegroom by his bride. A married woman, on the other hand, uses the smaller of the two *oova*, "wedding robes," she receives as a means of descending to the underworld after death.

Additionally, Hopi oral narratives include at least four other devices for magic flight. In the present collection, in the stories "The Yaya't and Their Feats" and "How the Pöqangw Brothers Found Their Father," the Yaya't use a spinning piki tray vehicle and a flying burden basket, and the sun transports the brothers on a "spinning device." Elsewhere, a young girl is taken away by a kachina to the Land of the Cloud People in an unspecified round craft that makes a roaring, hissing sound (Courlander 1982: 202).

It comes as no surprise that the sense of dissociation experienced during deep trance is alluded to also in the context of Hopi witchcraft lore, especially in the many references to the sorcerer's ability to fly. Notably among the animal familiars employed to this end are crows, owls, eagles, bats, and skeleton flies. The standard device of metamorphosing into one of them is somersaulting over the *ngöla*, "hoop," which itself may well be a symbolic act for entering an altered state (Malotki 1993: 165–66).

Lewis-Williams (1995: 15), in connection with his three-stage neuropsychological model of altered states of consciousness, points to laboratory research showing that trance subjects frequently enter the third or deepest stage via a vortex or tunnel into which they feel themselves drawn. According to Dronfield (1996: 41), clinically and cross-culturally, this vortical experience occurs graphically in the form of spirals and similar concentric designs. The circular Hopi *ngöla* could thus be seen as a conceptual analog for the endogenously generated vortex or tunnel, and it may be regarded as indirect evidence for the familiarity and use of trance in Hopi culture.

Tunnel and vortex sensations may ultimately be responsible for the Hopi belief in an underworld. Also, the recurring Orpheus motif of Hopi visits to Maski in search of a deceased relative may be reflective of deep-trance hallucinations in the course of which the shaman enters the dimension of the spirit world. Noteworthy in this connection is the Hopi association of a spiral petroglyph at Pictograph Point in Mesa Verde National Park with the Sipaapuni, the place at which the Pueblo people emerged from the earth (the Grand Canyon) (Petroglyph Trail Guide, no date: 10). The Hopi emergence from the netherworld could, in the light of this exegesis, be regarded as a tunnel experience of mythic proportion.

Finally, bird symbolism, and especially the shaman's ability to transform into a bird as his alter ego, is a common characteristic of shamanism. The concept of ecstatic flight or soul loss may also be reflected in the complex of ornithomorphic symbolism that pervades Hopi culture. For example, birds figure prominently in Hopi emergence myths in that they help the people escape from the chaotic conditions in the underworld by finding a passage for them to the upper world. Many birds—eagles, hawks, owls, crows, ducks, parrots, and others—appear as deified personages in the Hopi kachina pantheon. Messengers to the sky gods, they may have had their origin as shamanic spirit helpers. In the present collection of stories, in "An Oraibi Boy's Visit to Maski, Home of the Dead," the dead boy returns as a messenger from the underworld in the form of a snipe to ask his family not to grieve too long for him. Their excessive grief is holding him back from reaching his final destination in Maski. Additionally, the spiritual power of birds and their connection to ancient shamanistic practices may still be lingering in the many uses of feathers in Hopi ritual. Among other uses, they decorate kachina masks, top the headdresses of social dancers, and are found attached to prayer sticks and planted on altars. In Hopi oral literature, the bird as psychopomp is included in stories like those of the present collection, where in "The Man Who Traveled to Maski, Home of the Dead, to Bring Back His Wife," the man journeys partway there on the back of a talking owl, and in "An Oraibi Boy's Visit to Maski, Home of the Dead," the boy returns partway to the world of the living on the back of an eagle.

In addition to these aspects of shamanism reflected in Hopi culture, there are at least eight other classic elements of shamanism that have their counterparts in the Hopi world, beginning with themes of shamanic initiation. Perhaps paramount among these is the "traditional schema of . . . suffering, death, resurrection" (Eliade 1964: 33), often involving "a mysterious illness" or a "dismemberment of the body and renewal of the organs" (Eliade 1964: 53). This is typified in stories such as "The Boy Who Wanted to Be a Medicine Man" in the present collection, in which a young man who wishes to become a medicine man is whipped by kachinas until there is nothing left of him but a pile of bones and flesh. Under the direction of his "father" (a bear), the kachinas dance him back to life. In a similar story, a young man who wants to be a medicine man is taken to Toko'navi, Navajo Mountain, where a group of ancient men break all his bones and reconstitute him (Courlander 1982: 194). Also, one of the feats in "The Yaya't and Their Feats" in the present collection is the dismemberment, cooking, and reconstitution of the Yaya' chief's body. Finally, in a general sense, there is a possible shamanic linkage in this area for the important Hopi god Maasaw, who is sometimes characterized as a skeleton, since as Vitebsky (1995: 18) notes, shamans are "commonly drawn as skeletons, representing their ritual dismemberment during the process of initiation." The fact that Maasaw is said to exist both in a skeletonized or corpselike state and as a handsome (reconstituted?) young man may also lend some credence to this interpretation.

Some form of ascent to the sky is also frequently part of shamanic initiation or practice. In Eliade's (1964: 133) view, such stories "refer to a time when communication between heaven and earth was possible; in consequence of a certain event or a ritual fault, the communication was broken off; but heroes and medicine men are nevertheless able to re-establish it." Those forms of ascent that have a particular Hopi resonance are ascent by rainbow or sunlight and by ladder. In Hopi oral literature, Pavayoykyasi and his son ride a rainbow to Nuvatukya'ovi, the San Francisco Peaks (Malotki 1993: 345); a girl and her suitor, who is actually a Ka'nas kachina, travel great distances on a rainbow that the suitor pulls from his pouch and hurls forward (Malotki 1987: 27); and a boy and girl with supernatural powers but born to an ordinary couple slide down a shaft of sunlight and dangle from the rays (Malotki 1998: 395). Additionally, in Hopi dance paraphernalia such as tabletas, clowns can be seen riding rainbows.

One actual ritualized form of symbolic ascent to the sky in Hopi culture could be the Ladder dance, said to have taken place at the now-extinct village of Pivanhonkyapi. In this dance, seemingly symbolic of free ascent to and movement about the sky, four tall poles of pine or spruce were erected in holes on a rocky shelf near a cliff edge. The kachinas would come out and dance in the plaza, then climb the poles two at a time, where they danced on top of them, dangled downward from the top and swung out over the mesa edge, jumped from pole to pole, and did all kinds of acrobatic feats, all to the sound of rattles, drums, and rasps (Malotki 1993: 189–95). Similar feats are also related in Courlander (1971: 127–32), where it is called the Spruce Tree Dance, and in O'Kane (1950: 162–65) and Nequatewa (1967: 115-20).

"Shamans, like the dead, must cross a bridge in the course of their journey to the underworld," says Eliade (1964: 482), either as a form of initiation or to carry out a particular task. According to La Barre (1970: 126), this Orpheus-like legend "of the shaman's descent to the underworld is widespread in North America, as well as in Eurasia." Orpheus "went to the underworld to retrieve the soul of someone who had died young. This type of journey involved typical shamanic themes of overcoming guardians and obstacles and negotiating with the king of the underworld" (Vitebsky 1995: 51). Here again, only shamans can now do (while still alive) what everyone could do "*in illo tempore*, in the paradisal time of humanity" (Eliade 1964: 483) when a bridge connected heaven and earth. Typically the way is difficult, and the shaman or hero finds himself up against obstacles and ordeals such as a passage in a rock wall that is open for just an instant, millstones that are constantly moving, two rocks that clash together, and monsters that block the path.

Hopi oral literature contains just such obstacles, and marvelously also includes the Symplagades motif from Greek mythology alluded to by Eliade above. Furst (1976: 215) sees the clashing gateway motif, named for a pair of islands that block the entrance to the Black Sea, as "a common theme in shamanic, heroic, initiatory, and funerary mythology and folk tales the world over." In the present collection of stories, in "The Man Who Traveled to Maski, Home of the Dead, to Bring Back His Wife," not only is the man's way blocked by a huge rattlesnake, a giant bear, a mountain lion, and Paalölöqangw, but he must make his way between two gargantuan rock cliffs in the water that open and close with great force. With great skill and exquisite timing, he manages to just make it through without being smashed and arrives in the underworld. While there, he undertakes a form of negotiation to get his beautiful young wife back consisting of further tests of restraint and forbearance set by the chief of the kiva where his wife is held. Also in the present collection, in the story "How the Pöqangw Brothers Found Their Father," the brothers find their way blocked by a huge mountain lion and rattlesnake, whom they defeat by chewing and spraying out medicine given them by Old Spider Woman.

A factor connected with shamanic initiation and practice is the concept of "magical heat" and insensitivity to heat. Winkelman (1992: 30) lists fire immunity as one of the special abilities of the shaman; and often the shamanic ecstasy is not attained until after the shaman is "heated" (Eliade 1964: 476). Mastery over fire and an insensibility to heat indicates that the shaman has passed beyond the laws of the natural world and has entered the world of spirits (Eliade 1964: 335). Two examples of this sort of heat are included in Hopi oral literature; in each case the newly initiated shaman is very hot following his dismemberment and resurrection. These episodes are contained in Courlander (1982: 194) and in "The Boy Who Wanted to Be a Medicine Man" in the present collection. In the latter, the boy looks around among the kachinas who have danced him back to life and exclaims "Oh boy, is it hot."

Eliade (1964: 474) states, however, that the idea of "mystical heat" is not an exclusive possession of shamanism; it is a widespread idea, wherein magico-religious power is often expressed as being "burning" or "hot." From the discussion of Hopi magic below it is apparent that a primary feature of the magic of the Yaya't is the handling of fire and imperviousness to flame. In addition, in the story "How the Pöqangw Brothers Found Their Father" in the present collection, the two brothers must undergo two ordeals by fire to prove their legitimacy as sons of the sun: enduring the flames and suffocating heat of hot rocks, and resisting the effect of sitting on top of a giant pile of burning pinyon.

The shaman operates in a cosmology in which the universe has three cosmic zones or levels—the sky, the earth, and the underworld—that can be successively traversed because they are connected by a central axis. Usually this axis passes through an opening or hole, but sometimes there are other conceptions of the center in the sense of a breakthrough in a plane (Eliade 1964: 259). Connected with these concepts is that of the world tree, which connects the three cosmic regions and can represent the universe in continual regeneration (Eliade 1964: 270–71), and the idea of the cosmic mountain that makes connection between the earth and sky possible (Eliade 1964: 266). This framework can be readily applied to the Hopi world. Geertz (1987: 100 n. 11) does so in this fashion:

I consider the Hopi six-directional system, which I have called the "astrosphere orientation," as relying upon certain fundamental elements in Hopi cosmography. In the first place, the idea of an *axis mundi*, a world axis, is introduced in the form of a gigantic reed plant in the Emergence myth, which connects at least two worlds, if not four. This axis is also used in what I call the Fertility Myths, concerning the home of Muy'ingwa at Tuuwanasavi, and in what I call the Solar Myths—where we find the Sun using two entrances and exits between the Upperworld and the Underworld during his daily route. In these same myths one finds the idea of world centers and opposite worlds, all of which are implicit in astrosphere cosmology.

Thus, a pine tree, a giant reed, or a sunflower, successively tried by the Hopi in Voth's (1905: 10) version of the emergence story, can be considered a metaphor for the "world tree" or *axis mundi*, and the Sipaapuni for the "hole" or "opening." Tuuwanasavi, where there is an opening leading downward through successive levels to the paradisal world of Muy'ingwa, or even Apoonivi, where there is a break in the plane of existence between the mundane surface world of the living and the underworld of the dead, can be the "world center." In a sense, in every version of the well-known Hopi emergence myth, the "tree" upon which they climb to a new world is a means of regeneration and rebirth after the degeneration of the previous world.

The Hopi cosmic mountain par excellence is Nuvatukya'ovi, the San Francisco Peaks, where the earth meets the sky. It is the home of many kachinas, the eminent location of powerful beings, the location of shrines, and the source of wind, clouds, and rain. In "Yaapontsa, the Wind God" from the present collection of stories, the Pöqangw brothers aid the village chief of Shungopavi by taking his *pahos* to the kiva of the rain located there, and they also visit the ice cave of Yaapontsa, who controls the wind that is drying out the crops. In other stories, two scolded children go to live permanently at the antelope kiva on the San Francisco Peaks (Malotki 1998: 386); a gambling boy receives a new life as a healer in the bear kiva there ("The Gambling Boy Who Married a Bear Girl" in the present collection); and the Ka'nas kachina takes his bride back to his kiva on top of the mountains (Malotki 1987: 32).

Tuuwanasavi, literally "sand middle," said to be both an actual place southwest of Kykotsmovi (Malotki 1997: 373) and a metaphorical "earth center," plays the latter part in a story of famine and renewal that appears both in Voth (1905: 169) and in Malotki (1996: 16), making possible the movement between successive cosmic realms. In this story a hummingbird made from sunflower stalk marrow comes alive and goes to beseech Muy'ingwa to make the earth green and fertile again. The hummingbird flies to Tuuwanasavi, marked by a wretched prickly pear cactus, and alights on its single flower. This opens the way down to Muy'ingwa, through kivas on four successive levels, where the bird convinces the deity to come to the earth's surface.

Apoonivi, another metaphorical location for the "center," figures in at least two stories in the present collection, "How Coyote Came to Visit Maski, Home of the Dead," and "An Oraibi Boy's Visit to Maski, Home of the Dead." There, on a promontory, sits a small house-like structure through which one passes and descends a stairway to the plain below. The house forms a dividing line between the world of the living and the world of the dead.

In general, the underworld is conceived by many shamanic traditions as a region where everything "takes place as it does here, but in reverse. When it is day on earth, it is night in the beyond . . . the summer of the living corresponds to winter in the land of the dead" (Eliade 1964: 205). This is certainly true for the Hopi, as reflected in their concept of the year's duality and the characteristics of the dead. One of these is the concept of "a dual division of time and space between the upper world of the living and the lower world of the dead" (Titiev 1944: 173–78) so that when it is day in the surface world, it is night down below. Similarly, when it is winter in the upper world, it is summer in the lower. This inversion or duality has a profound effect on the structure of the ritual cycle due to the fact that "life in the other world is supposed to reflect life on earth so exactly that corresponding ceremonies are performed simultaneously (with the seasons reversed) in the two spheres" (Titiev 1944: 173–78). Also, among many other inversions that could be mentioned, the dead eat only the essence or odor of food, not its material form (Voth 1905: 116), and when they see a live person in the underworld, the children there remark upon them as "skeletons" (Voth 1905: 118).

Finally, one of the operative concepts of the Hopi underworld is that "a person who dies on earth 'becomes like a baby' in the other world, and that spirits of the dead become embodied in children born on earth" (Titiev 1944: 176, quoting Parsons 1925: 75–76, n. 121). An example of this is contained in a story in the present collection, "How Coyote Came to Visit Maski, Home of the Dead." Here the storyteller observes, after Coyote comes across nothing but frolicking children there, "Apparently, when a Hopi dies, he becomes like a child again and for that reason, there were nothing but children there. No matter how much anyone suffers in life, upon their arrival in Maski, they are in perfect health again."

In the view of Eliade (1964: 182), "It is always the shaman who conducts the dead person's soul to the underworld, for he is the psychopomp par excellence . . . because his soul can safely abandon his body and roam at vast distances, can penetrate the underworld and rise to the sky." In Hopi oral literature, this role is often filled by Kwaakwant (One Horn) and Aa'alt (Two Horn) priests, who guide travelers on their perilous journey to Maski, separate the good from the evil, and carry out judgment on the wicked. Geertz (1987: 122) summarizes the role of the One Horn priests thus: "The most important part of their guardian nature is the role they play during an individual's journey to the land of the dead. . . . It is the spirit of Kwan members who not only keep watch over the paths of the dead, thus serving as psychopomps, but also act in judgment over the souls of the dead." This role forms a central theme in two stories in the present collection, "An Oraibi Boy's Visit to Maski, Home of the Dead" and "How Coyote Came to Visit Maski, Home of the Dead," and elsewhere, in the story "A Journey to the Skeleton House" (Voth 1905: 109). These themes are echoed in a delirium vision that Don Talayesva had when sick in the autobiography *Sun Chief* (Simmons 1942: 121–27).

In Hopi ritual practice, other than the kachinas, who are the prototypical journeyers between cosmic zones, Hopi clowns can also be seen as guides or conductors between worlds. In the underworld, "every attribute is reversed, which may account for the clowns saying the opposite of what they mean, for their association with the dead, and for their coming over the clouds to the villages. As inhabitants of both worlds, the clowns also become the caretakers, or 'fathers,' of the kachinas, able to announce their arrival, albeit in an obverse manner, care for their appearance as they dance, and serve as interpreters between the two worlds" (Wright 1994: 4). And "in the manner of a shaman, the clown becomes one with his patron and uses that being's powers to accomplish his ends. In the manner of a priest, the clown makes manifest the needs of both the Underworld and the villagers of the Upper World" (Wright 1994: 7).

Akin to the shaman's role as psychopomp is that of "sacred politician," a political intermediary between this world and the underworld or sky. This is exemplified in a story in which a shaman negotiates a way out of a predicament for the villagers of Shungopavi, who have engaged in an ill-considered pact with the Water Serpents who live underground (Malotki 1993: 35).

A final property often associated with shamanism is androgyny, one more reflection of the shaman's ability to bring about the dissolution of worldly distinctions, return to the state of original unity, and attain balance once again (Halifax 1979: 22). Here, Hopi practice may be vestigial at best, but several facts point in this direction. A notable example is that female kachina deities are always impersonated by men. Stephen (1929: 34) notes that Hehey'a kachinas are industrious but *siwahova*, "bachelors," with the implication that no one will marry them because they are hermaphrodites. Hopis also believe that "twisting together" two children in the womb into one gives the survivor special power to heal others, such as in the case of Don Talayesva—though there is no evidence that his wombmate was female (Simmons 1942: 25). And in at least one example from Hopi oral literature, the initiating figure, a bear, for a new shaman was alternately male and female (Courlander 1982: 193).

Geertz (1996: 56–57) suggests that the Third Mesa germination god Muy'ingwa "is a male deity with androgynous characteristics in a role normally assigned to female deities." This "fusion of gender," in the personage of Muy'ingwa, he claims, is indicated by the fact that he wears a female wedding blanket (Voth 1901: plate 57) and is referred to as both Muy'ingwtaqa, "Muy'ingw Man" and Muy'ingwwuuti, "Muy'ingw Woman" (Fewkes 1896: 350 n. 1).

Magic

Magic is sometimes narrowly defined as the art of producing effects beyond natural human power by means of supernatural forces or through command of the hidden forces of nature. For the purposes of the present collection of narratives, the word applies in its broader sense, as any mysterious or extraordinary power or influence—in short, anything that has a supernatural explanation. It is not surprising then, the nature of Hopi stories being what it is, for magic to appear quite frequently in them and for there to have been a society, the Yaya't, now extinct, known for its conspicuous acts of magic.

Perhaps best rendered as "magicians," the Yaya't are characterized by Stephen (1936: 1008–9) as a "phallic, wizard society," and he claims that they were like a "brother" to the "sister" society of the O'waqölt, a minor women's society that, like the Yaya't, typically conducted its annual public performance in the fall. Apart from sharing this scheduling aspect in the Hopi ceremonial year, present-day Hopi consultants were not able to comment on any ritualistic similarities between the two societies. Nor were they able to shed light on any alleged phallic associations with the Yaya't.

It has been argued (Levy, Neutra, and Parker 1987: 28, 171) that the Yaya't were an eighteenth-century import from Zuni. This contention certainly seems to be borne out by the foreign, non-Hopi ring of the society's appellation as well as the fact that they are also referred to as Si'oyaya't, "Zuni Yaya't" (Stephen 1936: 343; Curtis [1922] 1970: 190). Untranslatable, at least from a Hopi linguistic perspective, the etymon of the term is ultimately supposed to be of Keresan origin, specifically from the New Mexico pueblo of Cochiti, and denotes "mother" in reference to "the corn fetishes of the medicine societies" (Lange 1968: 258). It is possible, then, that the term traveled to Hopi from Cochiti via Zuni. Known collectively as Yaya'wimi, individual initiated members were referred to as Yaya' or Yaya'wimkya, with Yaya't or Yaya'wiwimkyam constituting the respective plural forms.

In light of the narratives collected by Voth and Curtis, the Yaya't affiliation with Hopi may actually be of greater antiquity than suggested by Levy, Neutra, and Parker. According to Voth (1905: 41–46), the Yaya't originated long ago when a hawk in the form of a man took a group of thieving young boys and initiated them by throwing them bodily into an oven, covering them, and singing a song over their bodies. At the end of their initiation, the boys performed such tricks as whitewashing a cliff from a distance of about ten miles. In the story related by Curtis ([1922] 1970: 190), the Yaya't are portrayed as having a hand in the process of the creation of game animals by Tiikuywuuti, "Mother of Game Animals." In this story, they were living in Oraibi, so long ago that the people depended on mice and rats for their meat. The warrior chief there was thinking that it might be a good idea for Maasaw (god of fire and death, lord of the underworld, and owner of the surface world) and Tiikuywuuti to become husband and wife, so that large game animals could come into existence. The people and the Yaya't fashioned animal effigies from *toosi* (sweet cornmeal), and covering them with a ceremonial robe, the Yaya't sang over them all night in the kiva, trying to bring them to life, but without success. Finally, they took the effigies to a shrine for Tiikuywuuti, and on the fifth day they began to see large wild animals wandering about. Tiikuywuuti herself came into the village and told them that she had created them, all the animals from the rabbit up to the deer and antelope, and that she was going to take the animals away into the wild country, where there was good grazing. Maasaw, she said, had agreed to be their father.

Said to have "worked independently of the ordinary religious and curing societies" (Beaglehole and Beaglehole 1935: 10), the Yaya't, in their medicinal obligations, were primarily responsible for healing sore eyes (Titiev 1972: 367) and were able to cure burns (Parsons [1939] 1996: 869). In this role they appear to have been closely linked with the Somaykoli, a "blind" kachina curing society that practiced in the Tewa village of Hano on First Mesa. The Somaykoli, too, treated eye problems and apparently had strong ties with Zuni and Rio Grande pueblos (Stephen 1936: 818–23).

Essentially employing trickery, the hallmark ingredient of shamanistic practice, the shamanic core of the Yaya't is still evident in the tricks-of-the-trade repertoire that they drew upon in the course of public performances. As Vitebsky (1995: 88) has pointed out, the purpose of such tricks is to make others aware, through an outward expression, of the shaman's inner power. Thus, besides the typical tricks reported in the stories in the present collection, those of jumping into a pit oven and later appearing unharmed, producing live rabbits from a pile of bones left over from rabbit stew, and whitewashing a cliff from a distance, Curtis ([1922] 1970: 160–65) reports the Yaya't at Walpi

> producing a talking and singing skull
> turning belts and knee garters into snakes
> calling Salt Woman from the Zuni Salt Lake
> dancing barefoot on burning embers
> leaping over the side of the mesa and returning unharmed
> calling a deer from the mountains to the foot of the mesa
> transforming a long line of meal into a cotton string
> removing their limbs and fastening legs to shoulders and arms to hips
> sailing through the air on a circular shield
> washing hands and arms in fire that streams from a pot like liquid

Finally, however, their powers apparently began to wane. The last Yaya' ceremony at Walpi took place about 1860 (Curtis [1922] 1970: 160–65), and the ceremonies of the Yaya't began to die after one of their tricks went wrong and the villagers decreed that there would never be another public performance of Yaya' magic. By 1905 at Oraibi, the fraternity of the Yaya't was dead (Voth 1905: 41), though the altar paraphernalia were still maintained, and in 1907 a man named Naka died in Walpi and the *tiiponi* of the Yaya'wimi, required for ceremonial performance, was buried with him. Shortly thereafter, in 1908, the last member who understood how the magic was accomplished also died (Curtis [1922] 1970: 160–65).

In the 123 stories analyzed for shamanistic content, we noted 84 instances of magic "medicine," magic acts, and magical devices and objects. Sometimes the magic is used in the service of witchcraft; sometimes it is related to shamanic acts or themes; and sometimes it is central to the story.

The use of magic medicine is especially prevalent, and the medicine is frequently concocted by Old Spider Woman to aid someone who might otherwise not make it through a particular ordeal. In the present collection, in the story "The Creation of the Morning and Evening Stars," Old Spider Woman sprays mica with magic medicine, kneads the mica into shiny balls, and places them in the sky as stars; and in "How the Pöqangw Brothers Found Their Father," the brothers use medicine given them by the old woman to defeat such ordeals as a huge mountain lion and rattlesnake, suffocatingly hot rocks, and the flames of a giant stack of pinyon wood. In a story regarding the destruction of the village of Palatkwapi (Courlander 1982: 32), the village chief dresses his son in four kachina masks and gives him medicine so that he can breathe fire to frighten the villagers into better behavior. Old Spider Woman makes medicine to lengthen a maiden's hair to make her more desirable (Malotki 1997: 123) and also makes medicine to rub on a runner's legs so that he can win for his village against another village that had spurned the old woman (Courlander 1982: 81). Using medicine she has prepared, Old Spider Woman turns a boy back into a human after he was tricked by a witch into changing himself into a coyote (Wallis 1936: 60–68), and she tames the avian monster Kwaatoko by having a brave youth spray some of her medicine on his ashes after she had tricked the monster into incinerating himself (Stephen 1929: 24).

Acts of magic are frequent in the stories, and Old Spider Woman often plays a role. The quintessential magic act, appearing over and over again in Hopi stories, comes when the old woman directs those who want her help to grind their heel in her tiny spider hole, enlarging it so that they may bodily enter her underground kiva (see Malotki 1997: 243). In "How the Zunis Killed the Hehey'a Kachinas" from the present collection, in a particularly poetic act of magic, Hahay'iwuuti has kachina girls grind corn first into coarse hailstones and rain to wreak vengeance on the Zunis when they ignorantly refuse her help, and then she has them grind it extremely fine into soft gentle rain to help them recover from famine. Elsewhere, Old Spider Woman makes lightning split a stump when men shoot arrows at it in a gambling contest with a Spaniard for cattle (Courlander 1982: 91), and she weaves her web between two arrows (fletched with red-shafted flicker feathers) plunged into the ground, providing a barrier to save the village of Oraibi from destruction by fire (Malotki 1993: 115; Courlander 1982: 77). In other magic acts, the Sparrow Girls throw their eyeballs up into the trees and catch them when they fall back down to fool Coyote into doing the same and going blind (Wallis 1936: 57), and Owl blows exploding puffs of smoke down on his pursuers (Courlander 1982: 175).

Magic objects and devices are also encountered, both in the service of evil and against it. There are magic feathers that dive into the ground as an aid in healing ("The Boy Who Wanted to Be a Medicine Man" in the present collection); magic fast-growing corn kernels (Malotki 1993: 321); the image of a cougar, which comes to life and is used to free a youth's hand from the grip of a sorcerer rabbit (Curtis [1922] 1970: 200–201); a gourd that is turned into a *löwa* by the Kwan chief so that the men can satisfy themselves sexually (Malotki 1997: 137); a bone whistle capable of calling Sootukwnangw down from the sky (Voth 1905: 126–31); a swarm of magic flies that is used to spy on witches who have stolen a young man's sister so they can have sex with her (Voth 1905: 126–31); and from the present collection, a magic rabbit stick that pursues and kills rabbits all by itself ("The Snake Clan Boy and the Sorcerers"). Finally, and most powerfully, there is the use of crystals and various forms of flying devices discussed in the section on shamanism.

This brief discussion and analysis of witchcraft, shamanism, and magic in the Hopi oral tradition is, to the best of our knowledge, the first of its kind for a Puebloan society in the American Southwest. Accordingly, though we surveyed a fairly extensive range of Hopi stories, including those that form this collection, we make no claim to having conducted an exhaustive search of all existing examples of Hopi oral literature for references, either direct or indirect, to witchcraft, shamanism, and magic. Nor did we make a study of all recorded ethnographic accounts of Hopi religious practices reminiscent of these motifs. Such studies, if carried out, could be expected to result in an entire volume of its own.

Nevertheless, we believe our observations constitute definite evidence that witchcraft, shamanism, and magic once played major roles in Hopi culture. We also believe they demonstrate that shamanism, in particular, was a Hopi cultural component of long standing, not a late innovation. Collectively, this discussion and the stories that follow should give the reader a good appreciation for these three elemental forces and for their place in the Hopi psyche. It is important to preserve the accompanying examples of the Hopi oral legacy for posterity; but beyond that, the stories provide a unique glimpse into the Hopi collective consciousness, vividly capture intrinsic values of Hopi social and spiritual life, and entertainingly demonstrate elements of the human condition, such as humor, pathos and tragedy, that are common to us all.

References

Beaglehole, Ernest, and Pearl Beaglehole. 1935. Hopi of the Second Mesa. *Memoirs of the American Anthropological Association* 44: 5–65.

Bean, Lowell J., and S. Brakke Vane. 1978. Shamanism: An introduction. In *Art of the Huichol Indians*, edited by Kathleen Berrin, 118–28. New York: Abrams.

Bourguignon, Erika. 1974. Cross-cultural perspectives on the religious uses of altered states of consciousness. In *Religious Movements in Contemporary America*, edited by Irving Zaretsky and Mark Leone, 228–43. Princeton: Princeton University Press.

Brown, Donald E. 1991. *Human Universals*. Philadelphia: Temple University Press.

Colton, Harold S. 1959. *Hopi Kachina Dolls with a Key to their Identification*. Albuquerque: University of New Mexico Press.

Courlander, Harold. 1970. *People of the Short Blue Corn: Tales and Legends of the Hopi Indians*. New York: Harcourt Brace.

———. 1971. *The Fourth World of the Hopis: The Epic Story of the Hopi Indians As Preserved in Their Legends and Traditions*. Albuquerque: University of New Mexico Press.

———. 1982. *Hopi Voices: Recollections, Traditions, and Narratives of the Hopi Indians*. Albuquerque: University of New Mexico Press.

Curtis, Edward S. [1922] 1970. *The Hopi*. Vol. 12 of *The North American Indian*. Reprint, New York: Johnson Reprint.

Dobkin de Rios, Marlene, and Michael Winkelman. 1989. Shamanism and altered states of consciousness: An introduction. *Journal of Psychoactive Drugs* 21 (1): 1–7.

Dronfield, Jeremy. 1996. Entering alternative realities: Cognition, art and architecture in Irish passage-tombs. *Cambridge Archaeological Journal* 6 (1): 37–72.

Eliade, Mircea. 1964. *Shamanism: Archaic Techniques of Ecstasy.* Princeton: Princeton University Press.

Fewkes, Jesse W. 1896. Hopi shrines near the East Mesa, Arizona. *American Anthropologist* 8: 346–75.

Furst, Peter T. 1976. *Hallucinogens and Culture.* Novato, CA: Chandler and Sharp.

Geertz, Armin W., and Michael Lomatuway'ma. 1987. *Children of Cottonwood: Piety and Ceremonialism in Hopi Indian Puppetry.* Lincoln: University of Nebraska Press.

———. 1996. Structural elements in Uto-Aztecan mythology: Hopi gender and cosmology. *Method and Theory in the Study of Religion* 8 (1): 51–64.

Halifax, Joan. 1979. *Shamanic Voices: A Survey of Visionary Narratives.* New York: Dutton.

Hodge, Frederick Webb. [1910] 1969. *Handbook of American Indians North of Mexico.* Smithsonian Institution Bureau of American Ethnology Bulletin 30. 2 vols. Reprint, New York: Greenwood Press.

Jorgensen, Joseph G. 1980. *Western Indians.* San Francisco: Freeman.

La Barre, Weston. 1970. *The Ghost Dance: Origins of Religion.* Garden City: Doubleday.

———. 1972. Hallucinogens and the shamanic origins of religion. In *Flesh of the Gods: The Ritual Use of Hallucinogens,* edited by Peter Furst, 261–78. New York: Praeger.

———. 1980. Anthropological perspectives on hallucination, hallucinogens, and the shamanic origins of religion. In *Culture in Context: Selected Writings of Weston La Barre,* 37–92. Durham, NC: Duke University Press.

Lange, Charles H. 1968. *Cochiti: A New Mexico Pueblo, Past and Present.* Carbondale: Southern Illinois University Press.

Levy, Jerrold E. 1994. Hopi shamanism: A reappraisal. In *North American Indian Anthropology: Essays on Society and Culture,* edited by Raymond J. DeMallie and Alfonso Ortiz, 307–27. Norman: University of Oklahoma Press.

Levy, Jerrold E., Raymond Neutra, and Dennis Parker. 1987. *Hand Trembling, Frenzy Witchcraft, and Moth Madness: A Study of Navajo Seizure Disorders.* Tucson: University of Arizona Press.

Lewis-Williams, J. David. 1995. Seeing and construing: The making and "meaning" of a southern African rock art motif. *Cambridge Archaeological Journal* 5 (1): 3–23.

———. 1996. Light and darkness: Earliest rock art evidence for an archetypal metaphor. *Bolletino del Centro Camuno di Studi Preistorici* 29: 125–32.

Malotki, Ekkehart. 1983a. *Hopi Time: A Linguistic Analysis of the Temporal Concepts in the Hopi Language.* Trends in Linguistics, Studies and Monographs 20. Berlin: Mouton.

———. 1983b. The story of the "Tsimonmamant" or Jimson Weed Girls: A Hopi narrative featuring the motif of the vagina dentata. In *Smoothing the Ground: Essays on Native American Literature,* edited by Brian Swann. Berkeley: University of California Press.

————. 1985. *Gullible Coyote/Ina'ihu: A Bilingual Collection of Hopi Coyote Stories.* Tucson: University of Arizona Press.

————. 1987. *Earth Fire: A Hopi Legend of the Sunset Crater Eruption.* Flagstaff: Northland Press.

————. 1993. *Hopi Ruin Legends. Kiqötutuwutsi.* Narrated by Michael Lomatuway'ma, Lorena Lomatuway'ma, and Sidney Namingha Jr. Collected, translated, and edited by Ekkehart Malotki. Lincoln: University of Nebraska Press.

————. 1996. *The Magic Hummingbird: A Hopi Folktale.* Narrated by Michael Lomatuway'ma. Illustrated by Michael Lacapa. Santa Fe: Kiva.

————. 1997. *The Bedbugs' Night Dance and Other Hopi Tales of Sexual Encounter.* Narrated by Michael Lomatuway'ma, Lorena Lomatuway'ma, and Sidney Namingha Jr. Collected, translated, and edited by Ekkehart Malotki. Lincoln: University of Nebraska Press.

————. 1998. *Hopi Animal Tales.* Narrated by Michael Lomatuway'ma, Lorena Lomatuway'ma, and Sidney Namingha Jr. Collected, translated, and edited by Ekkehart Malotki. Lincoln: University of Nebraska Press.

Malotki, Ekkehart, and Michael Lomatuway'ma. 1987. *Maasaw: Profile of a Hopi God.* Lincoln: University of Nebraska Press.

Millspaugh, C. F. 1974. *American Medical Plants.* New York: Dover.

Nequatewa, Edmund. 1967. *Truth of a Hopi: Stories Relating to the Origin, Myths and Clan Histories of the Hopi.* Flagstaff: Northland Press.

O'Kane, Walter Collins. 1950. *Sun in the Sky: The Hopi Indians of the Arizona Mesa Lands.* Norman: University of Oklahoma Press.

Parsons, Elsie Clews. 1925. *A Pueblo Indian Journal.* American Anthropological Association Memoirs 32. Menaha, WI: American Anthropological Association.

————. [1939] 1996. *Pueblo Indian Religion.* 2 vols. Reprint, Lincoln: University of Nebraska Press.

Petroglyph Trail Guide. No date. Mesa Verde Museum Association.

Simmons, Leo W. 1942. *Sun Chief: The Autobiography of a Hopi Indian.* New Haven: Yale University Press.

Smith, Noel W. 1992. *An Analysis of Ice Age Art: Its Psychology and Belief System.* New York: Lang.

Stephen, Alexander. 1894. The Po-voc-tu among the Hopi. *American Antiquarian* 16: 212–14.

————. 1929. Hopi Tales. Journal of American Folk-Lore 42 (163): 1–75.

————. 1936. *Hopi Journal.* Edited by Elsie Clews Parsons. 2 vols. Columbia University Contributions to Anthropology 23.

Stevenson, Matilda Coxe. [1904] 1985. *The Zuni Indians. 23rd Annual Report 1901–02, Bureau of American Ethnology.* Reprint, Glorieta, NM: Rio Grande Press.

Stone, Eric. 1932. *Medicine Among the American Indians.* New York: AMS Press.

Titiev, Mischa. 1942. Notes on Hopi witchcraft. *Papers of the Michigan Academy of Science, Arts, and Letters* 29: 425–37.

————. 1944. Old Oraibi: A study of the Hopi Indians of Third Mesa. *Papers of the Peabody Museum of Archaeology and Ethnology* 22(1). Cambridge, MA: Peabody Museum and Columbia University Press.

———. 1956. Shamans, witches and chiefs among the Hopi. *Tomorrow* 4 (3): 51–56.

———. 1972. *The Hopi Indians of Old Oraibi: Change and Continuity.* Ann Arbor: University of Michigan Press.

Turpin, Solveig A. 1994. On a wing and a prayer: Flight metaphor in Pecos River rock art. In *Shamanism and Rock Art in North America*, edited by Solveig A. Turpin, 73–102. Special Publications 1. San Antonio, TX: Rock Art Foundation.

Vitebsky, Piers. 1995. *The Shaman.* London: Duncan Baird.

Voth, H. R. 1901. The Oraibi Powamu ceremony. *Field Columbian Museum Publications* (Anthropological Series) 61: 60–158.

———. 1905. The traditions of the Hopi. *Field Columbian Museum Publications* (Anthropological Series) 96: 1–319.

Wallis, Wilson D. 1936. Folk tales from Shumopavi, Second Mesa. *Journal of American Folk-Lore* 49 (191–92): 1–68.

Whiting, Alfred F. 1966. *Ethnobotany of the Hopi.* Flagstaff: Northland Press.

Whitley, David. 1996. *A Guide to Rock Art Sites: Southern California and Southern Nevada.* Missoula, MT: Mountain Press.

———. 1998. Meaning and metaphor in the Coso petroglyphs: Understanding Great Basin rock art. In *Coso Rock Art: A New Perspective*, edited by Elva Younkin, 109–74. Ridgecrest, CA: Maturango Press.

Wilbert, Johannes. 1994. The cultural significance of tobacco use in South America. In *Ancient Traditions: Shamanism in Central Asia and the Americas*, edited by Gary Seaman and Jane S. Day, 47–76. Niwot, CO: University Press of Colorado.

Winkelman, Michael James. 1992. Shamans, priests and witches: A cross-cultural study of magico-religious practitioners. *Arizona State University Anthropological Research Papers* 44. Tempe: Arizona State University.

Wright, Barton. 1973. *Kachinas: A Hopi Artist's Documentary.* Flagstaff: Northland Press.

———. 1994. *Clowns of the Hopi: Tradition Keepers and Delight Makers.* Flagstaff: Northland.

Hopi Stories of Witchcraft, Shamanism, and Magic

The Boy Who Encountered the Jimsonweed and Four O'Clock Girls

Aliksa'i. They were living at Oraibi long ago, and lots of people made their home there. The boys and men were accustomed to going out hunting. One of their frequent destinations was near a spring called Hotvela. However, people in the village began to notice that every now and then a hunter failed to come back, especially when he went near this spring. In fact, quite a few had never returned.

Among the Oraibi villagers was a couple with three children, two girls and a boy. They too had heard that hunters heading toward Hotvela frequently never came back, so they expressly forbade their son to go hunting there.

Of course the boy was curious as to why he was not allowed to go there. "It can't be that dangerous," he kept thinking. Finally, he just could not control his desire to go there. "Nothing will happen to me," he said to himself, full of confidence.

And so, disregarding his parents' orders, he set out from Oraibi, eventually reaching Hotvela. Once there, he continued down the juniper slope toward the northeast, where Yantukya'ovi is located. There he began hunting cottontails. Whenever he flushed one, it would duck into a burrow, and he would then have to dig it out. He spent the day this way, digging out one cottontail after another, until he had bagged five of them, and flushed a sixth. As he dug into the rabbit's burrow, he thought, "When I get this one, I'll have enough. Then I'll go home."

He was still busy scooping out sand when someone approached, though he was so busy he didn't notice. He pulled out the rabbit, struck it across the neck to kill it, and threw it aside for a moment. As he did, he looked up and saw a girl standing there. "Have a seat, stranger," he greeted her.

"Thanks," she said. "I came here just for you."

"Is that so?" said the boy. "For what reason?"

"Well," she said, "I just came to fetch you, because I want you to come sleep with me."

"I can't go with you," the boy replied. "I was just getting ready to go back home after digging out this last rabbit here."

"But you must come with me," insisted the girl.

The boy was completely at a loss, but not knowing what else to do, he gave in. After all, the girl was stunningly beautiful. After stringing all his rabbits on a line, he said, "Very well, let's go. I'll go along with you."

So the two of them started off, heading in a northeasterly direction, skirting Yantukya'ovi on its southeastern side. There is also another hill named Yantukya'ovi, which people refer to as the northeastern Yantukya'ovi, and they were nearing this hill when the boy said to the girl, "I have to go relieve myself. Let me do that first, and then we can continue on. Please stay here and wait for a while."

With that, he put his line of rabbits down on the ground and stepped over a ways, to a small depression in the ground. He had just disappeared from the girl's view and squatted down comfortably, when a voice said, "My dear young man, go a little farther away!"

He looked about, but could not see anybody. "There's no one

here," he thought, and began to strain.

He heard the voice again. "For shame, young man! Step a little aside from here."

As he scanned the area again, he finally noticed a tiny hole directly underneath himself. Next to it, all balled up, sat a tiny spider. "Did you speak to me?" asked the boy.

"Yes, that was me. Please go a bit farther away and do your business there. Then come back here."

The boy obeyed and walked a little ways off. There he relieved himself and then returned to where the spider was. She invited him in, but he protested, "How on earth can I enter this tiny hole? It's far too small for me!"

"Just twist your heel in it and it will get larger," came the reply.

The boy again did as he was told and ground his heel in the hole. Sure enough, an opening the size of a kiva hatch appeared. Once he was down inside, he was invited to have a seat. The spider, of course, was Old Spider Woman, his grandmother. "My poor boy," she said, "if you're not careful, you may spend your last days in this area."

"How is that?" he asked in surprise.

"That girl you met is one of a group who kidnaps careless boys like you," she explained. "That's why your parents warned you not to come around here, but you wouldn't listen, would you? Nevertheless, I felt sorry for you and caused you to come near my kiva. I'll do my best to help you."

With that, she disappeared into a back room, and when she reemerged a little later, she held a small bundle in her hands. "Take this with you," she said. "If we're lucky it will help. And take this too," she added, handing him another small object. "Now let me tell you what will happen to you. This girl will lead you to her house, and when you lie down to sleep, she will make advances to you. When she does, tell her you must go out to urinate. When you're done with that, you can then make use of what's inside the bundle I gave you. If you survive the ordeal that is waiting for you, you can revenge yourself with the second item that I gave you." These were her instructions. "So go now. The girl is waiting for you."

The boy thanked Old Spider Woman and returned to the girl. "You've come?" she said.

"Yes, I'm done."

"Well then, let's go." With the girl in the lead, the two now headed northwest, in the direction of Paaqapa. There, on the southwest side, the girls all had their home near a large boulder. Before long, they had reached their destination, and much to the boy's surprise, he saw a kiva there. When they had arrived, the girl called down, "How about some inviting words of welcome!"

A chorus of voices shouted back, "Come on down! Please, come in!"

The two climbed down the entrance ladder, first the girl, then the boy. Sure enough, there were many people inside the kiva, and as the boy looked around he saw nothing but girls. There was not a single man in sight. After the two had entered, the girls busied themselves with setting out food on the floor. "All right, let's eat," they said.

So they all sat down to the food. The girls had made a delicious meal—somiviki and bean soup. Everyone really enjoyed their supper, and when everyone was satisfied, the dishes were cleared away.

It had been late evening by the time the boy and the girl had arrived at the kiva, and after they finished supper and sat around for a while, night fell. The boy was in no hurry to go anywhere, and kept staring at the beautiful girls. He kept wondering who they were. Finally, he turned to the girl who had brought him there and asked, "Who are you? I had no idea people were living at this place."

"Well, we're the Jimsonweed Girls and the Four O'Clock Girls," she said. "This is where we live."

A little later, all the girls disappeared into the back room. And when they filed back in, they came as ravishing beauties, dressed in their finest clothes and with their hair done up in butterfly whorls, indicating their readiness to marry. Into the whorls they had inserted the blossoms of jimsonweed and four o'clocks. Their dresses were ceremonial capes embroidered on the top and bottom borders. The boy thought they must be rich to own such fine garments.

When they had all come out, they stood in a line and began to dance. They were dancing solely for the boy, and when they had finished, they filed back into the inner chamber, returning a little later dressed in a different manner. One of them said, "It's dark now, and time to go to bed. We have things to do tomorrow."

With that, they began making their beds, placing all their bed rolls in a row in the corner area northwest of the fire pit. Next to this row, they made two separate beds for the boy and the girl who had led him there. Then one of them put out the fire and it became pitch black. Everybody, including the boy, bedded down and no sooner had the boy lain down than the girl began feeling for him in a flirting way. Finally she urged him, "Come on, sleep with me. In fact, you can have all of us tonight if you wish."

"Wait," replied the boy, "I need to go urinate first."

With this excuse, he climbed the ladder out of the kiva. "Don't run away!" the girl shouted after him.

"Don't worry, I won't," replied the boy. He was following Old Spider Woman's instructions, of course, so he urinated somewhere outside the kiva and unwrapped the small bundle. "I wonder what my grandmother put in here," he thought. To his great surprise he found an artificial penis that she had carved for him, with a piece of line attached to it that he used to fasten it in place. The penis was made of cottonwood, and was just the right size for him. "I wonder how the old woman knew that?" he thought.

After fastening the artificial penis to his groin, the boy returned to his bed. This time, when the girl began touching him, he was ready and willing. Climbing on top of her, he inserted his cottonwood penis. He noticed right away that there were teeth in the girl's vagina that began grinding back and forth on it, but of course, it did not hurt him. The girl was none the wiser, and commanded him, "All right, now do it with the others. Be generous with them."

The boy obeyed and had sex with them all, using the cottonwood member. The girls were all alike; each of their vaginas was studded with gnawing teeth. He moved from one to the other there in the dark until he was finished. The girls were astounded that he had survived the intended ordeal. "My, you're powerful! Who are you? You don't seem to be harmed in any way," they exclaimed, for they were accustomed to killing the boys who slept with them. Nobody had ever been able to sleep with them all without dying. In this way they had murdered any number of young hunters from Oraibi.

Staring at the boy in amazement, all they could say was, "How strong you are!" Everyone then bedded down again, and the boy slept with the first girl again, using the real thing, for the cottonwood member had ground down the teeth inside her.

The following morning, all the girls were up early, rolling up their bedding and fixing breakfast. When the boy was full, he moved away from the food area and leaned against the wall. Suddenly he was aware of an itching behind his ear. As he reached to scratch, a voice whispered, "Don't do that!" Evidently Old Spider Woman was back. "I've come to instruct you further. You did everything right. Thanks. That's the reason you're still alive."

Then the old woman filled him in. "They'll tempt you again with all their might, and then they'll let you go. They'll line up in front of you and tell you to identify the girl who brought you here. If you can do that, you may take her home with you. They will put corn flour on a plaque for you. When you go out of the kiva, carry this plaque with you, and the girl will follow. When she is out of the kiva, give the corn flour to her and ask her to walk ahead of you. Then you must use the other thing I gave you. Chew it, then trample down the plants around the kiva, the jimsonweed and the four o'clock, and then spray what you've chewed on them. That's how you will revenge yourself." With those instructions, Old Spider Woman quickly crawled out of his ear. "I'll be off now," she said.

As predicted, it was not long after Old Spider Woman's departure that the girls lined up in front of the boy, inside the kiva. "Now, find the girl who brought you here," they said. "If you pick the right one, you can take her with you. If not, you'll have to bear the consequences."

With some concern, the boy looked up and down the line of girls. Concentrating on the girl in question, he stepped up to the line and pulled her out of it. "She's the one," he said. And indeed, all the other girls had to admit that she was indeed the right one.

"All right, you may take her with you," they said, and with that, they heaped corn flour on a plaque for him. As he went out with it, his girlfriend was right behind him, and as they reached the roof, he told her, "Here, carry this and go on ahead of me."

There, on both sides of the kiva, huge plants were growing; jimsonweed on one side and four o'clock on the other. First, he tore out all the jimsonweed plants by their roots, and threw them to the side. Next, he began to chew the magic medicine Old Spider Woman had given him and went to the other side where the four o'clock plants grew and uprooted all of them. Then he sprayed the medicine he was chewing down through the hatch and into the kiva. Anything and anybody inside was turned to stone. "This serves you right," he yelled, "now you will never again kidnap and kill the young men of Oraibi! He then descended from the roof of the kiva and caught up with his girlfriend. "All right, let's go," he said.

As the two of them neared Old Spider Woman's abode near the northeastern Yantukya'ovi, the boy said, "Let's rest here for a while. I need to go relieve myself." He walked off and looked for a secluded area, but instead of actually relieving himself, he thought he'd look for a present for his grandmother. He looked around a bit, and since there were lots of rabbits there, it didn't take long for him to bag one. Before long, he had flushed another one, and killed it too. He took these two rabbits to Old Spider Woman and she was elated. "Thanks. It's so good to see you unhurt. And how considerate of you to bring me these rabbits!"

"Yes," the boy replied and went back out to his girlfriend, where he said to her, "All right, let's go. I'm done."

So the two started out again, but after a while he had another thought. "I really would like to bring home some meat. You wait for me here while I quickly look for something."

He went off, and before long he had killed six rabbits, for there were many around there, and it was easy. After returning to the girl, they traveled on, tracing the same route on which he had originally come, first past Yantukya'ovi, and then on by Hotvela, where they stopped for a drink. Then, skirting along Qöya'oytuyqa, they reached Qöma'wa. In this way they returned to Oraibi. The boy's parents were overjoyed to see him back unharmed, and bringing home such a beautiful girl besides. The two got married and are probably still living there.

And here the story ends.

2

The Man Who Was Buried Alive

Aliksa'i. People were living in Oraibi, including a couple who lived in a house north of the plaza. They had one daughter, who was exceptionally beautiful. All the young men wanted to marry her and kept calling on her at night. She didn't really love anyone, however. In addition, the girl's father had made a stipulation that if anyone married his daughter, and either one of them died, both would be buried together. This is how the father decreed it to be.

The young men all knew this, but still they kept coming to her house every night. One day a young man who was really serious about marrying her said, "I am going to marry you." The girl readily accepted the proposal but reiterated her father's condition. "Yes," the young man replied, "I know that. Nevertheless, I really love you and want to live with you."

"All right," the girl replied.

And indeed, it was not long before they were husband and wife. Eventually they had been married for a long time, and still did not have any children. One day the wife got sick and looked as if she was not going to make it. Not long after, she died.

Right away, the woman's father came and said to the husband, "Very well, you remember the condition that I laid out for my daughter. If either she or you should die, then the other must also be buried alive."

"Yes," the husband replied, "I accepted your condition, and so now you must bury me together with her."

So, the father and some others set out to bury them. First they dug a large hole for both of them, placed the wife in first, and then had the man get in beside her. When they were both in the grave, they closed it over them.

So now the man lay there with his dead wife, all covered up. Of course, he could not see and couldn't tell how much time had passed because he couldn't see the sun and had no idea whether it was day or night. He lay there, worrying and thinking about many things. "What a fool I was," he thought, "to marry her when I knew that condition!"

He grew steadily weaker and got hungry and thirsty, for they had not placed any food or water in the grave. He was reflecting on these things when something peeked out of a hole, like a mousehole, in the corner. It was not a mouse, but he couldn't figure out what it was. It would peek out, then withdraw into the hole again.

Finally, it came out of the hole and he saw that it was a bullsnake. He watched it crawl toward his wife and do something on her body. This made him very angry. He had been wearing a knife when he was buried, so he grabbed the snake and cut it into three pieces.

He was looking at the severed snake, and then at his wife, when another bullsnake peeked out of the hole. This snake inspected the pieces of the dead snake and disappeared back into the hole. Before long it came back out again, carrying something in its mouth, something that looked like a leaf, and headed for the pieces of the dead snake.

It placed the leaflike thing on one of the sections of the dead snake, then left and came back two more times, placing another leaflike thing on the other two sections. As the man watched, the three sections of the dead snake joined themselves together again and the snake came back to life. As it did so, the leaflike things fell away, and the two snakes then disappeared back into the hole in the corner.

This amazed the man, so he took a closer look at these leaflike things and thought, "I wonder if these things could revive my wife, just as they did that snake?" He picked up the objects and placed one on each of her eyes. The third he laid on her chest.

He waited and watched, and before much time had passed, his wife started to stir. As he watched her, she came back to life. He was beside himself with joy! When his wife became fully conscious she recognized him and burst into tears. When she was able to stop crying, they began to dig themselves out of the grave. The man now carefully picked up the leaflike objects and tucked them away. Eventually, they broke through to the outside world, into the sunlight, and climbed out and made their way to the house of the girl's parents.

When they entered the house, the parents were speechless. They just kept staring at the couple in disbelief, finally breaking down and crying with happiness. When everyone had finally calmed down, the husband told the parents how he had killed the bullsnake, how another snake had revived it, and how he had brought his wife back to life in the same way. "I'm certainly going to keep these leaflike things in a safe place now," he told them.

So, from that time on things pretty much got back to normal. However, one day a neighbor's child fell from the housetop and died instantly. When the man heard about this, he went to the little boy's parents and offered his help, "If you want, I'll take a look at your son." They agreed.

Taking out his leaflike things, he did exactly as he had done to bring his wife back to life. He placed them on the eyes and the chest of the little boy, then waited. Indeed, after a short time, the little boy was alive again!

When he accomplished this deed, the people in the village all talked about how he could actually bring someone back from the dead. He became a powerful medicine man, saving many people. He is probably still a medicine man somewhere.

And here the story ends.

3

How Old Spider Woman Came to the Rescue of the Yaya't

Aliksa'i. People were living at Mishongnovi. Once, long ago, the Zuni Yaya't were staging a dance at this village. Having decided to show the people one of their feats, they constructed an earth oven just for the occasion. When the pit oven was finished, they prepared a huge stack of dry sticks for fuel. This they set ablaze.

When noon came, they were busy at the pit oven again. They dug up the corn they were roasting and feasted on it. Whatever was left over, they distributed among the audience. Next, they replenished the fuel in their pit oven, relit it, and began chasing each other around. At one point they caught their chief. He looked into the pit and saw the glow of red embers. He called to the spectators and said, "All right, watch what we'll be doing now." With that, he ran around the pit four times and said, "Watch me closely now." Once more he ran off and then jumped right into the fiery pit. Sparks flew and the smell of burning flesh hung in the air. As his companions looked in they said, "I guess he's cooked now. Looks like he's all done." Next they spread a wedding robe on the ground, and with repeated shouts of "It's hot, it's hot," took the meat out of the oven. It was indeed well cooked. Then they gathered up the wedding robe and went to their kiva. Holding the robe on all four sides, they chanted "Ahoo, ahoo, ahoo," and then scattered its contents inside the kiva. They then went back over to their pit oven, with their chief right on their heels. They had thrown him, all cooked, into the kiva, and here he was with not a hair on his head burned.

"All right, watch me carefully now," the chief said again. Circling the pit oven four times as before, he suddenly hurled himself down onto the glowing coals. Just as the first time, sparks shot up into the air and there was the awful stench of burning flesh. His companions were still staring into the oven after him when someone stepped up to them. He also looked in and asked them, "Is he cooked yet?" Lo and behold, it was the Yaya' chief! Again he was all right and in good health. After all, he was a Yaya'!

After repeating this feat for a third time, the Yaya' chief said, "We'll kill the fire now, so go fetch water."

His companions rushed off in all directions to do as ordered. In the old days, water was carried in gourds, so these they emptied into the fiery pit. But pour as they might, he fire did not go out. Once more they ran off to fetch water, again with the same results. The flames did not die down. On the contrary, the pit oven became really hot and, one after the other, its walls collapsed. Meanwhile, flames were shooting out of the oven, and even though the Yaya't poured gourds and gourds of water on them, they would not subside.

The spectators began muttering out of concern. The pit was getting ever larger. The Yaya't circled around it, but they didn't know what to do. "How are we going to kill this fire?" they kept saying.

Suddenly, one of their members, who had only been inducted into the Yaya' society a year before, cried, "I remember you told me during my initiation that if I ever had a problem I could not solve, I could ask Old Spider Woman for help. So, I suggest we call upon her. Maybe she can put out the flames for us."

The Yaya' chief replied, "Very well, we did indeed mention this during your initiation. Why on earth didn't we think of that before?" With that, he said to the young initiate, "Run to the southeastern point of the mesa. That's where Old Spider Woman lives. Tell her that we can't extinguish this fire. Maybe she'll pity us and put it out. It's burning out of control and is about to reach our kiva. If it manages to reach it, we could lose it."

The initiate rushed off and soon arrived at Old Spider Woman's abode. He quickly filled her in on what was happening. She exclaimed, "Oh dear. I'm just a poor dirty spider. I can't do anything. Nevertheless, I'll give it a try. You Yaya't are dear to my soul. We spiders are faring well because of you, so I'll come and try to help you. However, I'm weak and can't walk fast, so place me on your ear, and we'll be there in no time. I'm sure you're a good runner."

The boy did as bidden, placing the spider on top of his ear, and rushed off. Arriving at the kiva, he saw that his fellow Yaya' members were still fighting the flames, emptying their water-filled gourds on the fire. By now, the spectators were also coming to their aid and hauling water. The fire, however, was still blazing as high as ever. "You've come?" they cried, when they saw the boy return. "What news do you bring from Old Spider Woman?"

"I've returned with her," he replied.

"Oh good, thanks," they exclaimed in unison.

The boy placed Old Spider woman on the ground. "Here she is, all balled up," he said. "Look how tiny she is."

"All right, why do you want my help?" asked Old Spider Woman.

The Yaya' chief replied, "We were showing off our magic art to these people when our pit oven failed to go out. We've been pouring water on it, and the fire is still spreading. Even the spectators here have been assisting us by bringing water, still without any success. Meanwhile, the flames have almost reached our kiva. That's why we called upon you. Maybe you have a solution."

Old Spider Woman replied, "This fire is really powerful. No one can stand up against it, but I can at least give it a try. If I'm lucky, I just may succeed." With that she crawled toward the fire. The heat was radiating from the pit. "All right, let me warn you now," she said as she turned to the chief, "tell all these people not to look in my direction. Everybody must turn around and look away. When nobody is watching me, I may be able to kill the fire for you."

So the chief did as he was told and made this announcement, "You people, don't look this way. Face the other direction. Otherwise we won't be able to get rid of the fire. It will burn us all. We called upon Old Spider Woman to help us in our need. For her to succeed, no one must look at her."

All the people obeyed. Old Spider Woman then crawled over to the pit oven and placed herself at its northwest end. Then she pulled up her dress, spread her legs wide apart, and urinated directly into the fiery oven. There were sizzling noises, and the flames appeared to be dying down. This procedure she repeated on the other three sides of the oven. Slowly, the flames subsided and went out.

"There now," said Old Spider Woman, "that's better." She had simply urinated into the pit oven when no one was looking. In this fashion, she came to the rescue of the Yaya't and extinguished the fire for them.

So this is what people say: "Whenever the members of the Yaya' society can't control the fire, Old Spider Woman extinguishes it for them."

And here the story ends.

4

The Boy Who Wanted to Be a Medicine Man

Aliksa'i. They were living in Oraibi. A lot of people were living there, among them an elderly couple who had one son. He was a grown-up boy, but he was in no way thinking of getting married. He wanted to be a medicine man, and his mind was always on what he must do to become one. All his thinking was focused on that.

Now he also frequently went hunting, and one day he went hunting again north of Oraibi, most likely toward Hotevilla. At that time Hotevilla did not exist, or rather, no one was living in Hotevilla yet. While he was hunting around, his thoughts were once again on his favorite topic of being a medicine man. In due course he came upon a deer and shot it. Then he went to it and purposely broke the deer's leg, and then he started working on the leg he had broken, trying to heal it again.

After he had spent a considerable length of time on it someone came up to him without him noticing it. Not until that person started speaking to him did he notice his presence. A man was standing by him. The man standing there asked him, "What are you doing?"

"Yes," he replied, "I have always had the wish to be a medicine man. So I broke this deer's leg and was now trying to fix it again."

"Oh yes?" the stranger replied.

"Yes," answered the boy.

"And is that really your desire?"

"Yes, it is."

"Well, actually, I heard you and because I pitied you I came. So if you are serious about being a medicine man, come back here four days from now. Then I will tell you something else. And if you don't really want it I know you will not come," the man said.

"Very well," the boy said. He was happy. "I will definitely return on that day."

"All right," said the man. "So now don't mess around with this any more but go on home."

So then the boy went home with his prey over his shoulder. When he reached home his parents were glad. From then on he eagerly awaited that fourth day. On the third day he said to his parents, "Tomorrow I'll go hunting again but I won't be back the same day. I'll stay overnight."

"Very good," his parents replied, "we won't be expecting you then."

This is what he announced to his parents. Then on the morning of the following day he dressed and prepared for the hunt. When he was finished he started out into the area north of Oraibi. He knew, of course, where the man had met him. So he headed straight to where he had killed the deer. He was not in a hurry. Just when it was getting to be evening he arrived at his destination. The man was not there yet. So he sat down under a tree and waited for the stranger. The sun was about to set when someone came to him. It was that man again. The man said to the boy, "You have come then?"

"Yes," he replied.

"All right then, let's go. We should hurry, it's far."

So they got under way. They went westward. They had covered a considerable distance when the man said to the boy, "Stay here for the time being, while I go shit," he said.

"That's fine with me," the boy answered in turn.

The man disappeared into the forest. It was not long before the boy heard a rustling noise. What appeared in his view was not a man. It was a bear that came out toward him. The boy got frightened, but then the bear spoke to him, "Don't be afraid, it's me," the bear said to the boy. "From now on you can ride on me, because it's still far. If we travel on foot we won't reach our destination early. So climb up on me."

So the boy went up to him and climbed on him. "Now then, let's go," the bear said and started running. A bear can run extremely fast. Now they were really making some headway. In this fashion they got close to their goal. Then the bear stopped. "All right, climb down. From here on we will walk again. We are getting close."

So then the boy got down and the bear disappeared into the forest. When he appeared again he was back in his human shape. "Well, let's go," he said.

Then they got going again. Finally they arrived at a place that was lit by a fire. Evidently they had arrived at a kiva. They climbed on the roof, and the man shouted down inside the kiva. "It's customary to welcome someone."

They were then welcomed by some voices that hollered, "Come in please. We are grateful you have come." Evidently they had been waiting for them. So then they climbed in, the man first and the boy after him.

When they had entered, those inside greeted them. "All right, have a seat. We've been waiting for you."

Many people were there, all men. They made the boy sit down north of the fire pit. Then they smoked. One of the men, most likely the chief, looked out at the sky, and when he came back in he said, "Now, I guess it's about time. So I suggest that you, the father-to-be, ask once more whether he still wants it."

"Very well," the father-to-be said. He went to the boy and asked him again, "Well now, are you still certain you want to be a medicine man?"

"Yes," the boy replied.

"It is settled then," said his future ceremonial father. "Take all your clothes off. When you've done that, come here."

The boy undressed, and his father-to-be spread a wedding dress out right in the center of the kiva. "Now, come here," he told the boy. The boy obeyed and then he said to him, "Sit down here," and he indicated that he meant the center of the wedding robe. So the boy sat down there. "Well," he said to him, "you really want it."

"Yes, by all means," the boy answered.

"It won't be long before they will come," he said.

So then he sat there and waited. And, true enough, it did not take long before some beings with their accompanying noises approached. Meanwhile these beings climbed on top of the roof. Apparently they were kachinas. Then there was actually one that was saying something. Upon entering, it turned out to be Hahay'iwuuti. All kinds of kachinas came in behind her. There were many. Hahay'iwuuti stepped up to the boy, and upon reaching him, said to the kachinas, "Now, use all your energy." This is how Hahay'iwuuti put strength into the kachinas. Then the kachina that was in front went to the boy. He and all the other kachinas were carrying yucca whips. One after the other those kachinas whipped the boy with their whips. Not all of them had beaten him yet when he was already cut up into pieces. Blood was flowing all over his body and after a while he was no longer aware of what was happening to him. Now the kachinas hacked the boy into pieces. Nothing on the boy, neither his flesh nor his bones, was still in one piece. When all the kachinas were finished, the boy was nothing but a pile of meat.

Then the future father of the boy said, "Thank you for being done. So don't tarry now." He then covered the boy, or rather the meat pile, with another wedding robe. Then the kachinas started dancing toward the pile. Without letup they were dancing toward what was covered up there. While they were doing this it looked as if the boy was going to come back to life. Once in a while the pile stirred a little. Then the kachinas really put all their efforts into their dancing. In this way the boy finally began to move quite strongly and eventually uncovered himself. Looking around among the kachinas he exclaimed, "Oh boy, is it hot." He was sweating.

"That's for sure," the men that were sitting there replied. "We are grateful we brought this to a successful end and you've come back to life."

"Yes," he answered. At that he got up. He was the actual boy again and nothing was wrong with him. The kachinas, who had finished dancing, filed out again.

When they had all left, his father-to-be went to him and said, "Come back here," signaling to the northern side of the fire pit. So the boy sat down there and his father said, "Now, this is the way we learn this. You have acquired this knowledge and therefore you must now be there for the people. It was your wish to be this so now you must devote yourself to this task. You will care for the people, not in return for any payments, but only for food."

"Yes, for sure," he replied to his father.

This is how his father instructed him. "Remember these instructions I have given you. Now you can dress. We must go back now. If we leave right away we'll just get back in time."

The boy dressed again and they started out. His father again changed into a bear, and the boy rode on him from there. The sun had not risen yet when they reached their original starting place. There his father changed back to a man and said, "So if you intend to treat someone one day, you must always step out of the house first and call me. I will always hear you."

"Very well," the boy said to his father.

"And always remember what I have told you. I will go back now. Your parents are probably waiting for you."

So then they parted and went their way. The boy went home to Oraibi and his father went also to his house. Shortly thereafter the boy killed a deer and carried it home on his back. And indeed when he returned his parents were happy to see him.

So there he was living now. And so it happened one day that a boy fell from a horse and broke both his legs. When the boy heard about this he said to his parents, "Why don't I go there and see what I can do?"

The parents replied to the son, "No, that's out, you don't know anything about this business."

"But I would like to try at least."

So his parents gave their permission, and he went to the home of the little boy. When he arrived the poor little fellow was lying there crying. He said to the little fellow's parents, "Let me try it."

"All right," the little boy's parents answered.

The boy, recalling his instructions, first stepped outside and called his father. No sooner had he called him than something drove into the ground right next to him. It was the wing of something, or rather, a feather. Then he thought, "This is evidently my father." So he pulled it out and put it into something. Then he went back into the house to the little boy. He sat down by him and inspected his legs. It was clear where they were broken. It seemed to him as if he was actually seeing it, that's how clear it was. So then he put the little boy's legs back together, fixing his legs on both sides. After this he went home.

And the next day, while he was sitting outside his house, some children were playing. Among them was the little boy whose legs he had fixed just the night before. He had evidently completely re-attached and healed his legs. They had apparently healed that same night.

This is how he became a medicine man. As soon as he treated anyone they got well again right there and then. When the people heard this they came only to him when they needed a medicine man. He was a most excellent medicine man. And he had to be there for the people, for at any given time someone might come and get him. I guess he's still taking care of people in Oraibi somewhere. And also whenever someone wants to pay him for his services he refuses. He only accepts food. Thanks to him the Oraibi people are still doing pretty well.

And here the story ends.

5

The Tsa'kwayna Death Spirits

Aliksa'i. They were living at Oraibi. All across the land there were settlements, at Mishongnovi, Walpi, and Shungopavi. Oraibi had a large population, and its villagers were there doing all sorts of things. To entertain themselves they organized social dances once in a while.

One day, the men were planning such an event, so they brought girls to the kiva to rehearse for the dance. When the other people learned of this, they waited for the appointed time when the dancers would emerge from the kivas to dance in the plaza. They failed to come, however, and continued rehearsing inside the kiva.

Apparently, the dancers in the kiva were enjoying themselves, so when other women got word of this, they also started going to the kiva to join in. Even those with little children went. Soon all these women wanted to do was go to the kiva. Then, the men also invited girls and women to the other kivas and started entertaining each other with different dance groups. Before long, the women of the village got so involved in dancing that they came home only to eat and rush off to the kivas again. Dancing was all they could think of. They were oblivious to everything else. After a while, this had been going on for quite some time, and there was no sign that they would ever dance in the plaza.

As the days went by, the boys and men in the kivas were beginning to enjoy the girls and women even more, so when one of the men coveted a woman, he simply had intercourse with her. The women did not resist the men's advances and agreed right away. In this fashion, their lives were soon becoming dissolute and immoral.

The village chief of Oraibi was married, and the couple had a baby daughter who was still nursing. The chief's partner, the village crier, was also married.

At one point during this dance craze, the village chief's wife also began to participate. Soon she was so involved in the activities that she was constantly at the kiva. At first, she still came home to her husband to cook his meals, but as soon as she was done preparing the food, she ran off again. The chief now had to take care of their little baby daughter himself, and did not have any time to see to his other duties. He could not just leave the baby alone. So he decided to take the child over to his younger sister and ask her to baby-sit her. He asked her, "Why don't you watch her while I go hoeing weeds? I'd like to go down to the field for a while." His sister agreed to help out. Each time the baby demanded to be breastfed, she had to take the baby to her mother in the kiva. At the hatchway in the roof she had to keep calling for the baby's mother, but because they were carrying on so wildly inside, they did not always hear her right away. They were dancing with complete abandon and not taking any breaks.

As the dancing craze became worse and worse, the village chief got sick and tired of it. It looked as if the dancing would never cease. Also, he resented having to take care of his little daughter. Eventually, he had enough and called his partner, the village crier. He, in turn, had his helpers come, and they all gathered at night in the village chief's house.

The village crier asked, "What is it that you want us for so urgent-ly?"

"Well, I need your advice. As you know, they've been practicing for the social dance in the kiva for some time, but now they're indulg-ing in other immoral practices so much that they're hardly even danc-ing anymore. Recently, my wife began to take part. She's so involved that she doesn't even cook for us anymore. She's completely aban-doned us, and we're suffering at home. Your wife's the same. She also joined in, so I wonder what you think."

"True, they shouldn't be like that, but what can we do? You must have something in mind that you brought us here to talk about."

"I'm thinking of calling upon the Tsa'kwayna Death Spirits. If they came, they could purify the hearts of that wild lot."

"All right, you do that," the village crier and his assistants agreed. "When will this happen?" one of them asked.

"First I need to make sure that my younger sister will take care of my little daughter. If she consents, I'll let you know. By then I'll have everything ready that we need to succeed."

"All right. You do that. That'll cleanse their hearts for sure." With that the village crier and his assistants departed and went to bed.

The village chief and his little daughter now went to bed too. When she became hungry some time later, he took her to the kiva. He was forced to shout for his wife at the top of his lungs until someone heard him. He told his wife to come out and nurse the baby, but no sooner than she was done, she was back down in the kiva. The danc-ers did not feel like sleeping yet, even though the night was black. They just didn't go to bed anymore.

The next morning, the village chief went in search of material for making pahos. As on previous occasions, he entrusted his daughter to his younger sister. He took a knife to cut the material for making pahos and descended to the plain below. He searched for the proper sticks in the vicinity of Leenangwva, and when he had found enough he went home again. Next, he made string for the prayer feathers. Since he was out of wool, he got some cotton and carded it. Then he started spinning it. After a while he decided to go get his child again. After bringing her home, he put her to bed and continued spinning. By the time he was finished, his daughter was sound asleep, so he made his bed beside her and also went to sleep.

The following day, he ate breakfast at his sister's house again. She had made dumplings out of blue corn flour. Before he left his daughter with her, he said, "I'd like to ask you a favor."

"All right, what is it?"

"I want you to make some piki for me, if you don't have other plans for today."

"No I don't. Our supply of piki is getting low anyway, so I thought I'd make some. I'll light the fire under the piki griddle as soon as we're done eating."

"Yes, and when you're finished with the piki, also make me four miniature flour tortillas, please."

"Of course," his sister replied, "I'd be happy to do that for you."

At noon, when his daughter got hungry, he decided not to take her to her aunt. Instead, he dunked some piki into salt water for her. He poured some water into a little bowl, placed the child on his lap, and the two ate. He was glad that he would no longer need to take the child over to her mother every time she needed to eat.

At night, the village chief took the child back to his sister, asking her to baby-sit for a while. "I have to take care of some business," he explained.

"Just leave her with me. Nothing will happen to her. She will surely go to sleep."

"Also, did you make those flour tortillas for me?"

"Yes, I made them a while ago," she said, and handed them to him wrapped in a bundle.

Happily the chief carried the bundle home and placed it by the fire pit. Then he began working on his pahos once more. Before he started, however, he smoked a pipeful of tobacco. When he was finished with the pahos, he was a bit tired. Still, he went outside, and as he stood there, he scanned the sky above. The moon was shining brightly, and the stars were clear. The night was well advanced, but even so, he could hear the boisterous laughter in the kiva. There was shouting, and they were obviously having fun. So he went back inside again, sat down near the fire pit, and bundled everything up. He tied the bundle up, slung it over his shoulder, and went back outside.

He headed out across the plaza to a point in the southeast. None of the dancers saw him as he passed their kiva, so involved were they in their dancing. He had nearly crossed the village when he turned in a northeasterly direction. As he reached the mesa edge he descended the trail there. At the bottom, after reaching Kwitanono'qa, he stopped to tie his bundle to his waist, for he did not intend to walk any further. He obviously had knowledge of magic, for he chewed a special medicine, spit it into his palms, and rubbed it all over his body. The moment he finished doing this, he was transformed into an eagle. Flapping his wings a few times, he lifted himself into the air and flew off.

He flew in a southeasterly direction. The eagle, of course, is a powerful bird, so he was soon far away. Heading straight for his destination, he quickly arrived near the village of Zuni. Instead of landing right in the village, though, he continued on to the buttes just northwest of it, where he landed next to one of them. As he perched on a small ledge, he scanned the area. "I guess it must be here somewhere," he thought as he looked along the cliff.

By this time, the chief had changed back into his human form again. Descending from the ledge, he took off his paho bundle and went in search of firewood. When he had gathered a good amount, he returned to his paho bundle, stacked up the dry sticks, and lit a fire, feeding it with the sticks one at a time. When it started dying down he added the branches of a nearby saltbush and kept the fire going.

The chief now untied his bundle and stuck the pahos into the ground, some distance from the fire, in accordance with the four directions, beginning at the northwest and ending at the northeast. When he was finished with this, he deposited the four miniature flour tortillas in front of the pahos. Then he returned to his fire, took out his tobacco pouch, and filled his pipe. Placing it next to the fire, he bent over it, and resting his hands on his knees, began chanting a song. This is what he sang:

Iya hiya hiya hiyama
Yohokwi, Yohokwi
Iya hiya hiya hiyama
Yohokwi, Yohokwi
Yoyatsa'a, Yohokwi, Yohokwi
Yoyatsa'a, Yohokwi, Yohokwi.

This is the spot where Yoyatsa'a and Yohokwi lived. They were among several people who had perished there, and it was their spirits he was now calling. That's why he mentioned them in his song.

As soon as he was done chanting, there was a groaning noise just northwest of him. Wailing terribly, a man moved toward him. The man had not fully reached the chief when he halted by the pahos, somersaulted over them, and landed on the other side. Next, he perched on top of the pahos and quickly ate some of the miniature flour tortillas. He then flung himself off the pahos, and crawled toward the chief on all fours. "You've come?" the chief said.

"Yes," replied the stranger.

"All right, have a seat. I'm glad you were willing to come."

"So, why do you want us so quickly?" he asked.

"Well, my children at Oraibi have fallen into bad ways. They're obsessed with dancing night and day. First, the boys and men asked only the girls to participate. Then they also included married women with little children. So carried away are these women that they have more or less abandoned their families. I have decided that this craze must be stopped somehow. They shouldn't be dancing, and yet they keep it up night after night. They're enjoying themselves so much that they don't even want to go to bed anymore. Now all they want is each other. Some of us with wives must somehow get along without them and even take care of our children. This cannot go on any longer—that's why I sought you out. Maybe you can visit them and bring them to their senses. The dancing must stop."

"Very well, we will go to them. You can rely on that," the man replied. "Let me call the others also." With that, he called them. Like the village chief, he placed his hands on both knees as he did so. He had died long ago and the flesh on his body had so shriveled away that he was nothing but skin and bones. As he sat there stooped over, he was like a skeleton. He too now began to chant:

Tii tii waawa, waawayi
Tii tii waawa, waawayi
Hi'aa, hi'a, hi'aa, hi'a
Awoo.

Now a groaning and wailing began in the southwest, southeast, and northeast, and it was moving toward the chief and the spirit. These death spirits also alighted on the pahos and also ate some of the miniature flour tortillas. Then they somersaulted off to land in front of them. When all were assembled they asked, "All right, why do you need us so quickly?"

The death spirit next to the chief replied, "This man here is the village leader at Oraibi. His children are out of control, so he came to seek our help. We are supposed to cleanse their hearts. I agreed and that is the reason I called you, to see what you think."

"Sure, we have no problem doing that. We're glad someone called for our help. We promise to go to Oraibi."

The village chief was elated to hear their consent. He now lit the pipe he had prepared before he called upon them and shared it with them. When they had all finished smoking, the first spirit said, "All right, now go on ahead of us. We'll catch up with you later."

"Thanks so much for answering my plea," said the chief. He then stepped aside a little ways, changed back into an eagle, and flew toward Oraibi.

Although the death spirits followed the village chief on foot, they quickly caught up with him. As he looked back, he clearly noticed a line of fires, moving rapidly in a zigzag motion. It was the death spirits moving toward him and there were lots of them. The chief flapped his wings harder, trying to increase his speed, but in vain. He was not able to outdistance them. Just a little while later, he glanced over his shoulder again, and they were right behind him. Since they were nothing but skin and bones, the chief could clearly hear their rattling as they came.

Eventually, the chief made it back to Oraibi, happy that the death spirits were still following him. Flying past Oraibi on the northwest side, he aimed straight for his destination. He landed right at the spot where he had originally transformed himself into an eagle and changed back into human form. Then he ran toward the village. After climbing to the mesa top on the northeast side, he halted at the edge and looked back. The death spirits were right behind him and now they ascended the mesa after him.

The chief ran straight to his house and rushed inside. He stopped there, looked around and saw that no one seemed to be following him. Evidently, the Tsa'kwayna Death Spirits had already entered the village and were heading toward the kiva.

A boy who was stooped over at the kiva hatch, looking in on the dancers, spotted them first. This boy happened to be one who remained righteous and good at heart and had never joined in the dancing. He just stared at the newcomers. Some of the dancers, overheated, had just emerged from the kiva to cool off, so he shouted to them, "Look, there are strangers coming!" Sure enough, there they were, still moving in a zigzag line. Each of them wore a glowing bark bundle, which was a strange sight in the dark.

When the dancers who were cooling themselves off spotted the arriving strangers, they called down into the kiva, "Hey, stop. There are people coming we don't know." Nobody heard them though. Even when they shouted at the top of their lungs, no one listened. They were all too wrapped up in their dancing and could be heard bursting out in laughter.

The dancers on top of the kiva roof were frightened and ran off. By now the death spirits were getting closer, and it had become very quiet on the kiva roof. Someone who sat on the raised women's area inside the kiva became aware of this silence and shouted to the others, "Hey, stop. There are people entering."

Now, finally, the dancing ceased, and everybody stood up on the stone benches along the wall. They stood there, married and unmarried women among them, awaiting the newly arrived guests.

Finally, the noise of approaching feet could be heard. The revelers were still not worried in the least, for every now and then other dance groups had visited them at night. A few said, "They are most likely kachinas. We can hear their tortoise shell rattles." Now the entire group of Tsa'kwayna Death Spirits shook their rattles, and the dancers down below cried, "Come on in, strangers. Don't delay."

The first one of the Tsa'kwayna Death Spirits to enter did not climb down the ladder, but slid down it, made a big jump, and loudly stomped to the northwest end of the kiva. He was barely inside when the dancers caught a better look at him and were frozen with fright. The stranger was repulsively grotesque. All those standing on the benches, one after the other, simply fell down on the floor of the kiva. The rest of the newcomers now started filing in, but before they had all entered, all the rest of the dancers inside the kiva had fainted and were lying around in piles. By the time all the Tsa'kwayna Death Spirits entered, no one was left standing. Only a moment ago they were welcoming the spirits and now they had all passed out.

The death spirits now began a dance of their own, though there was no audience and no one to urge them on. This is how their song went:

Tii tii waawa, waawayi
Tii tii waawa, waawayi
Hi'aa, hi'a, hiaa, hi'a
Awoo.

They only sang their song once and then filed out of the kiva again. They headed in a southwesterly direction, once again going along in a zigzag fashion. They skirted the mesa edge until they reached a point at the northeast end, where they then descended to the plain below. At Kwitanono'qa they met the chief again. "Thank you for coming," he said to them.

"Sure," their leader replied. "We have finished our work and will return home now."

"Thanks indeed. I'm so glad you were willing to come and bring my children back to their senses." With those words, the chief untied his paho bag and handed pahos to each of them. Then, laying out a cornmeal path for them, he said, "Go now, back to your home, happily." So the Tsa'kwayna Death Spirits started forth, zigzagging along as before, for that is the way death spirits travel. With their glowing bark bundles they looked terrifying. For a while the village chief looked after them, and then they disappeared over the horizon.

The chief now turned around and returned to the village. Back home, he filled his pipe, and when he had finished smoking, he bedded down and slept.

The following morning, some of the dancers came to again, but not all regained consciousness. A few had gotten so frightened that they died of shock. Those who were conscious again now spread the word of this event throughout the village. So many people came to check on their relatives that the commotion was unspeakable. The village chief himself did not get his wife back. Also, an elder daughter of his, one of the first to participate in the dancing, did not survive. Thus he lost two members of his family. The Oraibis had to bury many people that day. All day long they kept carrying the dead to the graveyard.

In this way the Oraibi chief brought the dancing villagers to their senses. Some of them died, but life had to go on. Never again did they dance with such abandon. Soon life became normal again.

And here the story ends.

6

The Fate of Pongoktsina and His Wife

Aliksa'i. People were settled at Oraibi and in many other areas across the land. Long ago, the pueblo of Oraibi was heavily populated. Among the residents was a couple who lived on the east side of the village. This pair was blessed with a teenaged daughter who was endowed with great beauty. The young men of the village were aware of this, and they longed to have her, so they frequently visited her house. Each night they went there to court her, but alas, she had no desire for any of them and paid no attention to their efforts. She never gave in to anyone's wishes, nor spoke to any of them. The youths tried various approaches, but it was apparent that no one would win her heart.

North of Oraibi, at a place known as Pongopsö, lived a kachina by the name of Pongoktsina, whose only relative was an old grandmother. On any given day the kachina would visit Oraibi to stage a dance at different sites in the village. Since he made these appearances on a regular basis, the inhabitants of Oraibi were familiar with him. Every time he went there, he would first perform on the north side of the plaza. Concluding his dance there, he would move onto the plaza itself. After leaving this location, he would repeat his act at five additional spots before finally arriving at the girl's house. There, at a place below her home, he would perform his dance once again and then usually return home. In this way Pongoktsina delighted the people of Oraibi. They, in turn, were happy whenever he showed up, especially the children, who were most pleased about his coming. The children went with him on his rounds, watching every one of his dances at the various stops throughout the village. And it was only when he departed for his home in the north that they ceased following him. In this manner the kachina made his regular appearances there.

Pongoktsina knew full well that the Oraibi girl did not care for any of the young men, but he also knew that they kept flocking to her home. He had gazed upon the girl's face once and, indeed, it was true, she was very lovely and he, like the others, wanted her for his wife. He had first caught a glimpse of her during one of his performances in Oraibi. It had happened while he had been performing his ritual outside her home, and for this reason he now regularly stopped there to dance. Upon his arrival back home he would think of her and picture her face in his mind. He was considering visiting her some night, but he had also learned that all the youths from Oraibi, and even some from other villages who went to pay her a visit, did so to no avail. She had never yet succumbed to any man's wooing, so he concluded that there was no chance of meeting her and therefore did not make an attempt of his own.

One day Pongoktsina dropped by Oraibi again, to make another one of his appearances. Having made his regular stops, he once more arrived at the girl's home, and while he danced there, he sang the following song:

Aahaha ahaa ahaahaayaayaayaa,
Towiiwii liyooyoo'oo'ookaa.
Aahaha ahaa ahaahaayaayaayaa,
Towiiwii liyooyoo'oo'ookaa.
Oosara soo'oo'ootikiinii poolaaynaa.
Aah liyooyoo'ooka.

After finishing his dance, the kachina was about to depart when, much to his surprise, the girl walked up to him and asked, "Are you leaving for home?"

"Yes," the kachina replied.

"Very well, go with a happy heart." Only these few words she spoke to him, whereupon Pongoktsina set out for home. He was elated that the girl had initiated the conversation, and because he knew that she had never before spoken with any young man, he felt flattered and proud.

Back home, Pongoktsina related everything to his grandmother. "Grandmother! Can you imagine, the girl from Oraibi spoke to me!" he exclaimed.

The old woman was delighted for her grandson and remarked, "I'm glad, indeed."

Whereupon the kachina replied, "When I go there tomorrow, I'm going to tell her of my intentions. Then we'll see what she has to say." His grandmother did not object.

That very evening Pongoktsina went to bed early but did not fall asleep immediately. He mulled over what he would say to the girl, and it was not until late that he finally dozed off. Looking forward to the next day, he restlessly tossed and turned all night. Eventually, as he became quite tired, he settled down into a slumber. The next morning after waking up, he eagerly waited for the arrival of evening, which seemed to be approaching at a very slow pace. Finally, evening fell and the time of his usual departure for Oraibi was at hand.

And so the kachina set out toward the village once more. Upon reaching Oraibi, he danced at his customary stops. As before, he came to the girl's house and there, too, he danced. Then he finished his ritual. As it turned out, the girl was also present to witness his performance. Therefore, as he was about to depart, he strode up to her and said, "Young girl, I've come for you. I'm going to take you home with me," he proclaimed.

"Not so fast! Wait until I've sought permission from my parents. If they approve of your wishes, I promise to come along. I have yet to find out what their decision will be," she explained.

"All right, very well," Pongoktsina agreed.

With that the girl ran into her house; soon she reemerged and headed straight toward the kachina, carrying something in a bundle. Upon reaching Pongoktsina she handed him the bundle and said, "Here, take this along with you. When you get home, you can snack on it." That was the extent of her conversation. She said nothing about going along with him.

Pongoktsina accepted the girl's gift, expressing his gratitude. "All right. Thank you very much, indeed." This is all he said and then he started home. Back home he opened the bundle without delay, and to his amazement found that the girl had given him some of her piki rolls. Overjoyed, he showed off the gift to his old grandmother, whose heart was also gladdened at the sight. In this way the two first came to eat the girl's food.

The next day the kachina returned to Oraibi and once more embarked on the same dance circuit. Finishing his performance at the girl's home, he approached her and asked, "All right, what did you find out?"

The girl replied, "My parents have granted me permission to go with you, if that is my heart's wish."

When the kachina heard this news, he was overjoyed. "Very well," he replied, "four days from now I'll come again and take you back with me." To this the girl consented, and the kachina returned home again.

Now that Pongoktsina had shared his intentions with the girl and had departed, the girl knelt down behind her grinding bin and began to grind corn in preparation for the day when she would go to her lover's home. She kept grinding day after day and also through the nights. Of course, she had also informed her parents, who were now looking forward to the arrival of the date the kachina had set. Pongoktsina, after his return home, likewise related these events to his grandmother. She, too, felt happy that her grandson had received such a favorable response. She was looking forward to having a granddaughter-in-law. After this time Pongoktsina stopped making his appearances in Oraibi.

On the agreed day the kachina headed over to Oraibi again, but he did not immediately go to the girl's home. After all, he was certain that he was going to take her with him that day. Rather, he went through his usual dance ritual and reached his future bride's house just at sunset. Once more he danced as he had been wont to do and when he was through, he went to the girl's house. She apparently had prepared what she was planning to take along and was waiting for him when he arrived. "Haw! I've come to fetch your daughter!" he shouted into the house.

The girl's parents responded by saying, "Very well, she's ready and is on her way out to meet you."

It was not long before the girl emerged from the house. With her she brought the ground corn flour. As she stepped up to Pongoktsina, he relieved her of her burden, and the two set out together for his home. Upon arriving at their destination, the kachina called down into the kiva to notify his grandmother. "Haw! Let's hear some words of welcome. I'm not alone!"

Sure enough, Pongoktsina's grandmother bid them enter. "Come on in!" she cried from down below. With that the two made their entrance. The boy's grandmother made the girl welcome. "All right, have a seat. How nice, you truly are a girl of great beauty! And how amazing that he was able to win you over! When I heard that you had never given in to any boy before, I didn't have any faith in my grandson. But apparently you succumbed to his desires, and so I'm happy for him," the old woman said, lavishing praises upon the girl. Having made her feel at home in this manner, she picked up the girl's flour and stored it away. Now the girl could begin her marriage ceremony there.

From what the girl could gather, Pongoktsina and his grandmother lived all by themselves. Consequently, when she cooked her first meal for the three of them, she prepared only a small amount. She readied only as much as she thought would be needed to satisfy their appetites. When the youth's grandmother noticed this, she advised the girl, "Daughter-in-law, prepare a lot of food. To be true, we may be alone here, but don't let that concern you. In the future I want you always to cook large meals."

The girl did as bidden and from that time on always prepared great amounts of food. However, where the food disappeared to she had no idea. After all, no one else resided there with them. But someone had to be consuming it since it kept vanishing at a fast pace. Only the day before she had fixed an enormous quantity of food, but the following day it was all gone. And the old woman was definitely not just throwing it away. Because the girl did not know what to make of it, she kept silent.

Furthermore, since the three of them were there alone, nobody seemed to be engaged in making any of the items necessary for the bride. This much she knew for certain, that lots of people participate during a wedding party, but not one soul ever entered their house. No one seemed to be weaving any wedding garments for her. All this she noticed but she never raised a question about it.

A few days later the old woman turned to her grandson and said, "Well, perhaps they've completed their tasks by now. Therefore I'd like for you to go west from here to Nuvatukya'ovi and find out what your uncles have in store for you. I also want you to ask them for one of their animals. You'll have to kill it and bring it back here. So that's what you must seek from them," she directed him.

"Very well, I'll start out early tomorrow morning," the kachina youth replied, consenting to his grandmother's bidding.

The next day Pongoktsina rose at the crack of dawn, prepared some journey food, and set out toward Nuvatukya'ovi in search of his uncles. He knew where they lived so he headed straight in that direction. When he arrived at his destination, he announced his presence, and some voices from within the underground abode invited him in. When he entered, the people there were delighted to see him and heartily welcomed him. "You are about?" they inquired.

"Yes," he answered.

"All right, have a seat," one of the elders exclaimed. Then he added, "Now, surely you're here for some purpose."

"Oh yes. My grandmother sent me on this errand and so I came to carry out her bidding. She told me to come here for one of your pets."

"Is that a fact? So that's what you're after! Very well, I'm sure we can grant you your wish." With that the elder got up and bade the boy follow him. With the elder leading, they went to the north end of the kiva. The elder opened a door, and the kachina saw, much to his surprise, that it led to an inner room of gigantic proportions. The old man beckoned the youth inside. The youth was amazed to discover that this inner room consisted of a vast stretch of land just as one would find outdoors. The land was covered with green grass as far as the eye could see. Grazing across the green fields were large numbers of all the big game animals, such as antelope, deer, and elk. At this point the man, supposedly an uncle of Pongoktsina, said "All right, take a good look at all the roaming animals and choose the one you desire. After you've made your choice, go ahead and kill it."

As he stood there, Pongoktsina carefully scanned the herd. At last he made his choice. He selected a huge buck from among the deer. He informed the uncle of his selection, whereupon the latter told him that he could have the one he had singled out. The kachina had of course come for this very purpose, and had brought along his hunting gear when he entered the inner room after his uncle. Pongoktsina now walked up to the deer, which made no attempt to evade him, and shot it. Next, he skinned the carcass and after butchering it stuffed the meat into the hide and explained to his uncle that he would carry the meat in this fashion. When the two of them re-emerged, the other uncles were happy that the youth had succeeded in killing his prey. Pongoktsina in turn thanked them for giving up one of their animals, thereby making it possible to bag one without any hardship. Lugging the meat, he then set out for home. The buck he had slain had been huge, however, and had yielded so much meat that the poor boy was barely able to carry it. It slowed him down considerably.

It was late that evening when Pongoktsina finally reached home, loaded down with the huge supply of meat. His grandmother was full of praise. "Thanks! I'm so glad your uncles live there, for in this way you did not have to suffer much hardship to get your game."

Meanwhile, it was time for the bride and groom to have their hair washed to symbolize their marriage. The old woman, therefore, awakened the two somewhat earlier than they usually arose. Then she took the girl aside and prepared her with great care. She then began stewing the meat that her grandson had brought home. And since he had killed such a big meaty buck, she had a large quantity of stew boiling. The moment the sun peeked over the horizon, the old woman stepped outside and shouted out an announcement. "I guess you, my relatives, are out there somewhere. I want you to gather here and wash the hair of our daughter-in-law!" This is what the old woman proclaimed before she reentered the house.

When she came back in she asked the young couple to accompany her outdoors. When they were all outside the old woman had Pongoktsina and his bride stand side by side on top of the kiva roof just south of the hatchway. Then the old woman stood next to them, and no sooner were they all standing there than the light of the day began to fade. From out of nowhere dense masses of clouds had gathered above them. The clouds had barely converged when raindrops started to fall on the three of them. At this point the old woman bade the couple lower their heads. Just as they did, a fine drizzling rain descended upon them. These clouds were apparently the relatives the old woman had summoned. They had shown up to wash the hair of their daughter-in-law. After shedding their rain, the clouds departed again, while the old lady expressed her appreciation for their coming. After escorting the couple back into the house, the old woman herself now washed their hair. When she was finished, she exclaimed, "That's it. I'm grateful I was not alone in performing the hair washing ritual." She was happy to have completed this rite.

With this task out of the way, the old woman reemerged from her home and made another announcement. This time she shouted out an invitation for people to come and feast. "I guess you, my relatives, are out there. Come over to our house to eat!"

Back inside she, along with her new daughter-in-law, began setting out the food. Shortly after they were done, people started coming to eat, and kept coming in great numbers. At this point the girl realized that she had married into a family with numerous relatives. Also, the youth's uncles had prepared a complete wedding outfit for her. They brought in the various items as they arrived. Whatever item a person had made, he presented to the girl. One brought the large wedding robe for her, while another came with the smaller one. Someone else handed her the wedding sash, another came bearing the wedding boots. Nothing was missing. The garments were beautifully woven. Obviously, Pongoktsina had many uncles skilled in weaving. The boots had been fashioned from the deer hide he had brought home, for they were large. The bootmaker was the last to arrive. He had to be carried in on someone's back. The one who carried the bootmaker in on piggyback took him down to the lower part of the kiva and set him down. Only then did he hand over the boots to the bride. He appeared to be paralyzed from the waist down. In this manner the relatives had made every item necessary for their inlaw and personally presented them to her. The bride was overjoyed to receive these gifts and profusely thanked each and every one of them.

Now the feast got under way. Whenever guests had satisfied their appetites, they tried to leave. The bride, however, kept up her friendly urging. "Keep on eating," she would repeat without letting up. And each time someone got up to leave, she would say, "Take some food with you. There's still plenty." And so everyone helped himself to some extra food and then made his departure. Fortunately, the girl had again prepared large quantities of food the day before, and there was enough to go around. She also had had the foresight to prepare a good amount of tsukuviki.

As the visitors made their way out, the old woman, too, thanked them and at the same time reminded them, "Come back tonight. I want you to entertain our in-law one last time before she returns to her home."

There was no hesitation on the part of the guests. "All right, we'll definitely come," they kept replying as they left.

Eventually they had all satisfied their hunger and when everyone had departed, the old woman and the girl cleared the area where the meal had been set out. Astoundingly, every bit of the girl's cooking had been consumed. Not everything had been eaten there; some of the food had been taken home by the guests, but all the food had disappeared. Only a little stew remained. The girl was happy, for not a morsel of what she had prepared had been wasted. When the task of cleaning up was completed, the couple and the old woman relaxed and rested. They did nothing for the remainder of the day.

Finally, evening came and then, later, night fell. The three knew full well that their relatives would make another appearance, so they awaited their arrival. Darkness had just come over the land when voices could clearly be heard approaching. The girl listened and recognized these beings right away. They were kachinas who, while converging at the kiva, gave their particular calls. Upon ascending to the kiva roof they shook their rattles to announce their presence and the old woman bade them enter. As they filed in, they brought large amounts of food as gifts. The bride was seated beside the old woman north of the fire pit, and as the kachinas set foot in the kiva, they handed their presents only to her. Ahead of time, the old woman had spread out a piece of cloth right in front of the girl so that the gifts could be deposited there. By now Pongoktsina's wife had received a large quantity of gifts. Piled before her, in a huge mound, was a great variety of delicious foods: squash, muskmelons, watermelons, and long ears of corn, both boiled and oven baked. As the girl watched the dancing, she munched on these things. At times she became so engrossed in the kachinas' performance that she would not eat for a spell. All night long the kachinas kept up this entertainment. Finally, daylight approached, but so much did the girl enjoy herself that she was not the least bit tired. Just before daybreak the kachinas made their exit again to return to their homes. In this manner they had provided some pleasure for their new in-law.

This day the old woman was also going to send her in-law back home to Oraibi. That same morning she once more washed the girl's hair, this time all by herself, and then garbed her in the clothes a bride customarily wears when she leaves the home of her new in-laws. Then she ushered her out to speak a morning prayer to the newly risen sun. After taking care of her in-law in this way she told the newlyweds to follow her outside. Upon reaching a place slightly south of their abode, where the old woman was going to leave them, she said to them, "All right, go on now. From here on you can return to your home alone. Be happy as you live there together. But from time to time I want you to come and look in on me." With these words she sprinkled a path of cornmeal on the ground for her daughter-in-law, on which she began her journey homeward. Her husband followed, carrying a large amount of meat for her. Since he also took along what she had received on the previous night, he was toting quite a load. But he did not take everything that day. His wife had gotten so many gifts that that was impossible. He knew it would probably take three more trips to transport it all to Oraibi.

The villagers of Oraibi still had not heard who had taken the girl away. The young men were asking one another what had happened to her, but no one seemed to know. They were missing her. Some fortunate man had probably won her over and taken her away. These were the only thoughts that kept coming to their minds.

Now, in earlier times it was customary for boys and men to sit on the rooftops very early in the morning. While sitting there they were generally singing songs. That morning when the girl was returning home accompanied by her husband, one young man who lived at the north end of Oraibi spotted them as they neared the village. The newlywed woman, costumed in her bridal outfit, first appeared only as a white object in the distance due to the fact that wedding garments are predominantly white. Keeping a close eye on the couple, the young man shouted to a neighbor of his, "Hey, look to the north. There's something white approaching." So his neighbor strained his eyes in that direction. Unmistakably, someone was bearing toward the village. This fellow now passed on the news to another who, after looking in that direction, conveyed the same information to someone else. In this way the news spread among the men and boys. Soon they all knew of the sighting and were focusing their attention in that direction.

It appeared that two people were headed toward the village. It was not long before they arrived. The moment the couple entered the village all the men and boys recognized the girl. They could see that she wore a bridal outfit and was bringing someone with her. Passing below some of the men on the roofs, the two disappeared into the girl's house. The reaction of the young men was anger, and they grew even more furious when they discovered that it was Pongoktsina who was trailing the bride. It was obvious now that they had lost the girl to this man.

When the newlyweds entered the girl's home, her parents were pleased to have their daughter back. Pongoktsina presented his mother-in-law with the meat and said, "I brought this for you. Make a stew of it and invite the people of the village to come feast on it. All those who have no animosity toward me may come and eat. There's enough food to feed everybody and some will be left over for us."

Pongoktsina's mother-in-law readily agreed and thanked him. "Yes, indeed, I'll do that. It's most fortunate that you came with so much meat," she exclaimed.

She then recruited the aid of her daughter and together they chopped the meat into bits and stewed it. By evening, when it was tender, the girl's mother went about the village inviting people to the feast. Her father, in addition, shouted out the same announcement from the rooftop. "I guess you people are out there somewhere. I want all of you to come and eat at our place. This morning our new son-in-law brought our daughter home. He also arrived with a great deal of meat and that's what you'll have to eat. Come with joyous hearts!" Upon hearing this those people who held no grudge against Pongoktsina came to eat. They ate until they were full, and they were grateful to the kachina for this opportunity to eat so well. But none of the young unmarried men attended the feast. Even some of the married men declined to join in the festive occasion.

From this time on Pongoktsina lived there in his new role of son-in-law. His wife's father owned a plot of land west of Oraibi, which he farmed. But because he was getting on in age, he no longer had the physical strength he had once possessed. Thus, once in a while when he went out to his field, he would spend the night there and return the following day. He observed this routine until he acquired Pongoktsina as his son-in-law. Now, after his marriage to the man's daughter, Pongoktsina told his father-in-law to stay at home and let him go to the field. Therefore Pongoktsina began going out to the farmland on a regular basis. And although he also engaged in various other activities, he had time for everything. He was endowed with a great amount of stamina. He would rise early in the morning, run to the field, and finish all the hoeing before noon. Then, returning to the house into which he had married, he would pursue other matters that needed his attention. He was extremely diligent, which pleased his father-in-law. As his burden had been alleviated due to the young man's efforts, he was gratified to have such a son-in-law.

After about three years had passed, Pongoktsina's wife became pregnant and gave birth to a son. Two years later she delivered another boy. Life went on, but as it turned out, these two boys were to be their only offspring.

The kachina continued his regular treks to the fields. The children, meanwhile, were growing older and were already engaged in childhood games. Their mother, in turn, carried out her grinding chores. Whenever the time neared midday, she would stop and go relieve herself. To do so she headed out to the east side of the village. Returning to the mesa top, she usually rested somewhere before returning home. East of Oraibi, right at the edge of the village, stood a lone house, and upon reaching this building she would sit there and relax awhile. As she sat there, she usually unfastened her dress at the shoulder and let it slide down. In doing this she revealed her breast, of course. Then she took the piece of cloth which she had normally draped about her back and fanned herself with it. Finally then, when she felt fresh and cooled off again, she continued home. This routine became a habit of hers.

Apparently, a man had spotted the woman there and kept spying on her. One day as she was getting ready to go to relieve herself again, her children came home earlier than usual. Since they were in the house, she said to them as she was leaving, "Don't go anywhere, because we'll be having lunch when your father comes home." With that she went out the door. Once more she headed out to the village edge to defecate and when she was done, she returned to the top and stopped at her usual resting place. As on the previous occasions she let her dress down, and with her breast bared, fanned herself. When she was ready to go home, she began fixing her dress. While doing this she did not notice that someone had stepped up to her. She was still fastening her dress when a voice addressed her. Startled, she looked up to see who it was. "Are you sitting here?" a man inquired.

As she perked up her head, she found a stranger standing before her. He wore a beautiful indigo-hued shirt and had an eagle plume tied to the top of his head. In his hand he carried a bunch of arrows. Once more he spoke to her, "I spotted you here and have been watching you every day. Now I've come to take you with me," he informed her.

The woman, however, declined to accompany him. "I won't go with you," she protested.

The stranger did not heed her words and continued, "You will come with me, for I came here with the intention of taking you along."

The poor woman had no desire to be taken anywhere, but the man was very persistent. Finally, he simply grabbed her tightly by the wrist and jerked her toward him. Now she was compelled to accompany him. He led her to the north side of Patangvostuyqa, where he halted. Then he said, "Wait! From here on we won't be traveling by foot anymore." With that he pulled something out from under a bush. Apparently he had hidden this thing here before he had headed over to Oraibi. When the woman took a closer look, she noticed that the object was a magic shield. The young man explained, "We'll travel on this shield, for we are not yet at our destination. The place where we are headed is far away. By using this device we'll be able to move very rapidly. So let's both get on it."

And so the two boarded the flying shield, the youth still holding the woman firmly by her wrist. Not once had he let go of her during all this time. The moment they were aboard, the shield began rotating. Eventually it rose into the air and flew off exactly due east. The man had come from a place called Kiisiwu in quest of the woman; thus, the flying object was taking them back to this location. They arrived there in a matter of minutes. In this fashion Pongoktsina's wife was kidnapped and transported to Kiisiwu.

That noon when Pongoktsina came to have lunch, he entered his wife's house and found her gone. Only the two small boys were there. When he asked them where their mother was, they told him that she had gone out to relieve herself but had not returned.

All three of them now waited for her arrival, but after a good amount of time had passed and she still had not returned, the father turned to his sons and said, "Your mother is not coming back. So get dressed and then we'll go north to your great-grandmother's house."

After putting on their clothes, all three of them headed over to Pongoktsina's home. There Pongoktsina related to his grandmother what had happened. She was glad to see them, but at the same time she was unhappy that they had arrived without their mother. And when she learned what had happened she was disheartened. "Oh my poor grandchildren," she exclaimed, "I'm sure your mother will not return. So you'll have to live here with me. I'm sure we'll manage somehow."

From that day on Pongoktsina and his two sons lived with their grandmother. While they were staying there, the old woman composed a song especially for them and sang it to them. There was a reason behind the song. The youngsters, however, were unaware of its intent and danced to its tune until eventually they came to know it by heart. Somewhat later Pongoktsina said to his sons, "In four days we'll go in search of your mother."

The children were elated and were looking forward to the trip. As they were still quite young, they needed their mother, and were longing for her. Thus they anxiously awaited the fourth day, the day of their departure. Their great-grandmother, meanwhile, gathered the appropriate clothes for each child. The morning on which they were going to start out, she boiled some corn for them, which they were to take along and use as gifts. Then she washed the boys' hair and also gave them a bath. Finally, she painted their bodies, matching their father's body decoration, and dressed them in the same costume that their father used to wear. The sun was already dipping toward the western horizon when the old woman did this. When she had finished dressing all of them, she said, "All right, be on your way now. It's a long way to your destination." With that she handed the father and his two sons the boiled corn, which she had strung into strands for easier carrying.

The three now started toward Oraibi. There they went about the village dancing in the same places where their father had performed. How cute the little Pongoktsinas were! They all danced beautifully, and in each hand they carried a large amount of the boiled corn.

At first they performed on the north side of the plaza. Upon concluding their dance their father announced, "All right, if there is a woman who has faith in us, I'd like her to step forward and suckle these boys. In return she will receive all our presents." Then they waited, but no one approached them. This procedure they repeated at each customary place. Not a soul came forth. Eventually they reached the house in which Pongoktsina had been married. Once more they staged their performance and when they were done, the boys' father again notified the audience of his wishes. But as before, no one responded. At this point Pongoktsina became quite depressed. The poor little boys just stood there with tears rolling down their cheeks, aimlessly clutching their strands of corn in their hands.

Under these disheartening circumstances the Pongoktsinas were just about to leave when a woman came running toward them. "Wait, don't go yet," she yelled while scurrying along. No sooner had she come up to them than she knelt down before the two youngsters and exposed her breasts. Without delay the two boys began to nurse. The wretched things were so starved for milk that they suckled from the woman's breast with great zest. Not until they had slaked their thirst did they release the woman. In return the boys' father bestowed all of their food gifts on her.

With that the three Pongoktsinas departed. They descended the south slope of Oraibi and pressed on in the direction of Shungopavi. At one point before reaching this village, they came upon a recess at the foot of the mesa through which they climbed to the top. From there they headed in an easterly direction, skirting the north side of Mishongnovi. Soon the younger of the two boys became tired and began to whimper. Tagging along, he fell farther and farther behind. Since his older brother managed to keep up with his father, every so often these two had to stop and wait for the small boy to catch up. As soon as he caught up with them they would continue again. In this manner the three Pongoktsinas proceeded on their journey.

Eventually, they reached a location far to the east, where night came upon them. Once again, the first two decided to pause for a while because the younger boy lagged behind. While resting there, the father heard a noise and listened. However, he did not say anything to his older son, and as soon as the little boy had caught up with them, they moved on. In trekking further east they finally came upon a lone butte at whose base, much to their amazement, they saw light shining from inside a kiva. As it was dark by now, the boys' father led his sons to the kiva, for this was also the source of the noise. Someone was apparently singing. Upon reaching the kiva, the boys' father climbed up on its roof and peered in. Lo and behold, Hahay'iwuuti was in there. From what Pongoktsina could tell, she was busy preparing somiviki and was taking it out of a vessel and putting it somewhere. While engaged in this work, she was singing happily.

The moment Pongoktsina peeked in, the woman raised her head in his direction and said, "All right, come on in. I've been awaiting your arrival for some time. So don't linger and come on down," she said invitingly.

When Pongoktsina entered the kiva with his sons, Hahay'iwuuti was elated to see them. Apparently she already knew that they were out in search of their mother. For this reason she had been waiting for the three of them. Addressing the small children she exclaimed, "My poor grandchildren! Not too long ago your mother was taken east along this route." Obviously, she was well aware that they would come this way. That's why she was also busy making fresh somiviki. Turning to all of them now she said, "Don't feel pressed to rush on. These boys must be exhausted and they're bound to be hungry. Therefore I've been preparing this food. Your destination is still far away, so there's no need to try and reach it now. Rather I want you to spend the night here, and then you can go after your mother again." With that she set out some food for her visitors. When everybody had satisfied his hunger and was finished eating, Hahay'iwuuti cleared the food away. Then she rolled out some bedding for her guests on which they lay down and promptly fell asleep.

The following morning, the old grandmother once more fed the Pongoktsinas. During the meal she gave Pongoktsina some instructions. This was what she said to him: "This wife of yours, the boys' mother, our in-law, is at a place far away from here. You can reach this location by the time the sun is low in the sky. Tonight the people who live there are going to have a dance. I want you and your sons to participate. You will be the last group to perform, after everyone else is through. So when you get there, don't go right into the village. Make camp at some spot along its edge. You'll know when it's going to be your turn. At that time you must perform your dance for them. I'm sure your mother will recognize you before you finish. She will then want to breast-feed you, but you will refuse. She will also wish to go along with you, but you will turn her down. At that point the man tending to the kachinas, the one exhorting the dancers, will tell all those who gave a performance to return the next day. Since he really wants that, he will also ask you to reappear. Agree readily to the invitation and show your willingness to dance once more. Then return to the site where you costumed yourselves and retire for the night. The next day, after all the others have finished performing, I want you to have your turn again. As you end your dance, your mother will approach you and ask the children to nurse. This time they may suckle from her. What's more, she will insist on returning home with you. Let her come with you without protesting. By all means, bring her along. On your way back, darkness will fall once more. Then you will have to stop and rest so that you can continue the following day. After you've settled down and the children are asleep, your wife will indicate a desire to have intercourse with you. Again, give in and comply with her wishes. She will immediately doze off, and when she is sound asleep, sprinkle this into her vulva." With that she handed Pongoktsina something in a small pouch.

Following their breakfast, Hahay'iwuuti said to all of them, "All right, it's time for you to leave now. It's already midmorning and you have quite a distance to go." Knowing full well what was going to happen now, the three set out in search of their wife and mother and in anticipation of the dance.

Just before the father and the two boys left, Hahay'iwuuti furnished them some journey food, which the father accepted. Wrapping it up, he tied it about his waist and thanked her. After these preparations, they emerged from the kiva and headed once again in an easterly direction. After a long trip, they reached Kiisiw, a large village. The sun was already nearing the horizon when the Pongoktsinas arrived. Heeding the instructions given to them by Hahay'iwuuti, they did not enter the village but instead sought out an open stone enclosure and waited. As soon as darkness fell, the dances got under way. That night a multitude of kachinas appeared to entertain the villagers in the various kivas. Whenever one group completed its performance, another took its place. This went on and on.

Finally, after considerable time had passed, the village fell silent. From this the Pongoktsinas concluded that the kachinas had finished their ceremonies, so they proceeded to one of the kivas. The kiva they headed for was the one in which the boys' mother was watching the dances. No one had yet left for home. All the spectators were still inside when the three Pongoktsinas ascended to the kiva top. There the boys' father shook his rattle to announce their presence. Upon hearing the rattle, the man attending the kachinas shouted out, "Come on in. I guess someone is still about. So come on down. I'm glad you've come to look in on us."

The Pongoktsinas entered. Right away the man exhorting the dancers fed the newcomers ceremonially by sprinkling sacred corn-meal on them. After that the three began their dance, chanting the following song:

Aahaha ahaa ahaahaayaayaayaa,
Towiiwii liyooyoo'oo'ookaa.
Aahaha ahaa ahaahaayaayaayaa,
Towiiwii liyooyoo'oo'ookaa.
Oosara soo'oo'ootikiinii poolaaynaa.
Aah liyooyoo'ooka.

This was their song, and each time they concluded their dance, the boys' father cried out, "Kooway kaakuuruu'aa'ay," really drawing the words out. The song had of course been composed for them by their grandmother. In this fashion the Pongoktsinas staged their performance. The boys' mother recognized her children right away. And so, even before the presentation was over, she went out ahead of her family and waited for them on top of the kiva. By coming out ahead of the others, she intended to approach them as soon as they emerged. When the three completed their dance, the man filling the role of the kachina father urged them to return once more the following day. With that, he put a pinch of sacred cornmeal in Pongoktsina's palm. Pongoktsina, once again going by the instructions of Hahay'iwuuti, accepted the cornmeal, thereby agreeing to the invitation.

Following this ritual, the Pongoktsinas left the kiva and headed back to the west side of the village. However, they had not gone far when the boys' mother approached them, praising them for their performance. "How nice! Did you also come with the other kachinas?" she exclaimed.

"Yes," was the only word with which the boys' father replied.

Now the woman turned to her children and said, "Come here to me. I'm going to nurse you. You poor things, you must be starving for your mother's milk."

But both of the boys declined her offer, the older of the two saying, "We're not hungry. Besides, we have to go."

"Then let me come along," the woman pleaded.

"We're not leaving yet," Pongoktsina replied. "We won't be departing until tomorrow." The woman relented and retreated, while the remainder of the family went on. They returned to the enclosure where they had made their first stop upon arriving at the village.

The next day the Pongoktsinas rose early again. After having some of their journey food for breakfast, they waited. By the time the sun appeared over the horizon, the kachinas could already be seen scurrying back and forth near their enclosure. Again, they had returned in great numbers. Apparently, the man entrusted with the role of the kachina father had requested all of them to return, and evidently they had all accepted his appeal, for they were going toward the plaza as if they were vying for a time slot. All day long they kept coming and going. Every so often the spectators requested an encore from a group. In this manner the performances continued well into the evening. It was already pretty late when finally it appeared to be the Pongoktsinas' turn. They proceeded to the plaza, where they entertained the people. The villagers were so delighted with their performance that they asked them to repeat it. The Pongoktsinas did as bidden, and when they finished, the festivities of the day were over. Once again they had been the final dance group. The kachina father now bestowed prayer feathers on each of them and sprinkled them with cornmeal as he bade them farewell. Once more he thanked them for their return and for entertaining the people with such enthusiasm. After these words he sent the Pongoktsinas off. They then left the plaza and headed toward the western edge of the village.

As on the night before, the children's mother was waiting for their arrival, and when the three neared her she again came up to them. She stopped them and said, "Come to me. I'm going to nurse you." This time the boys ran up to her without hesitation, and at long last were able to suckle from their own mother. After quenching their thirst, they returned to their father's side and stood there. Once more the woman pleaded, "May I come with you?"

No one objected, and Pongoktsina said to his wife, "Very well, let's all go together." With that the whole family set out for home. The woman was grateful that her husband did not make a big thing of the incident. She was happy that they were all united again. Joyfully the woman went along, frolicking with the two youngsters.

The Pongoktsina family was still traveling along when once more night came upon them. The younger of the boys was quite tired by now and began whimpering. At this point the father suggested that they halt and make camp, which they did. They built a fire, and after they had eaten some supper, the boys were so exhausted that they lay down on the ground right then and there. The parents quickly prepared a place for them to sleep and then bedded them down. They were sound asleep in no time. Next the two adults fixed another site for themselves where they lay down. It was not too long after when, according to Hahay'iwuuti's prediction, Pongoktsina's wife expressed a desire to have intercourse with him. Pongoktsina did as instructed and readily agreed. "All right, I'll do it," he yielded, where-upon he moved toward his wife and made love to her.

Pongoktsina kept a close eye on his wife. Shortly afterwards she lay there, breathing like one in a deep sleep. He now went over to his children and woke them up, though the hour was late. So stealthily did he perform this task that the two made no noise upon waking. He then instructed them, "I want you to go ahead of me. Don't slow down to wait for me, but run as fast as you can. Take refuge at our grandmother's house, you remember, the place where we rested two nights ago. You'll be able to find it. I'll catch up with you in a while. So, get your clothes on and run along without delay." The brothers hastened to do as their father asked, and as soon as they were dressed, they took off.

After sending off his sons, Pongoktsina returned to his wife. Standing next to her, he looked her over and found that she was still sound asleep. He then knelt down at her side and carefully shifted up her dress. Taking the small pouch his grandmother had given him the night before last, he took a pinch of powder from it and sprinkled it into his wife's vulva. As a result, the woman sank into an even deeper sleep. Pongoktsina now straddled the woman and unsheathed his knife. The woman was completely unaware of what was going on. Straddling her, Pongoktsina then plunged the knife into her throat. As he removed his weapon, blood spewed from the wound. To avoid the gushing blood he leapt from the woman's body and dashed off to follow his sons. In this manner Pongoktsina slew his wife.

Convinced that he was well away from the scene of his crime, Pongoktsina began to slow down. Walking at a fast pace now, he looked over his shoulder for some reason, and much to his surprise, spotted a creature moving toward him. At once he realized that the creature pursuing him was his dead wife. He increased his speed again and once more began to sprint along. By the time he neared his grandmother's home he still had not caught up with his sons. From this he concluded that they had already arrived and were safely inside her house. So, instead of heading to her place, he bypassed it and continued west. He ran as fast as his legs would carry him, but amazingly the thing pursuing him was coming just as fast as before. Meanwhile, he had already put quite a distance between himself and his grandmother's house. Eventually he reached a ridge, which he ascended. Standing on top of it, he scanned the surrounding area. The creature he was fleeing seemed to be nowhere in sight. But as he took another look behind him, he noticed that it was approaching from the east. Once more he cast his eyes about, and this time he spotted a glow of light just south of where he stood. As soon as he discovered the light, he hurried down the sand dune in this new direction, with his legs wobbling in an uncontrollable manner.

Sure enough, when Pongoktsina arrived at the place where the light glowed, he found an inhabited kiva. He ascended to the roof and scrambled down through the entrance hatch without a word of warning. There were people inside the kiva playing the guessing game sosotukwpi. Once inside, he was panting heavily, but when he caught his breath a little, he pleaded with the people, "Have pity on me and hide me. There's a being chasing me!"

Pongoktsina's wish was granted at once. One of the group approached him, spat into his hands and rolled Pongoktsina tightly between his palms until he became quite tiny. Then he took him and concealed him under one of their hollowed-out gaming pieces. He was still hiding there when a thud was heard on the roof. The men down in the kiva waited. Then a voice asked, "Didn't my husband come to this place?"

"No, no one has been around," they replied.

"Oh yes, he's down there. His footprints end here," the voice protested.

"But we told you, no one has entered this place."

The creature did not believe a word, so she abruptly entered the kiva and closely inspected its occupants. "His tracks stop at this place. He's got to be here," she insisted, approaching the players. With that she strode along knocking their gaming pieces over. She had not yet discovered Pongoktsina, but was already nearing him when suddenly he leaped out from under the piece that had harbored him, hastily clambered out of the kiva, and once more fled from the woman. Choosing a route to the west, he focused his eyes in that direction. Just as before, he sighted a place from which the glow of a fire could be seen radiating, so he decided to seek sanctuary there. In the meantime his wife had also emerged from the kiva and resumed pursuing him.

By now Pongoktsina had progressed a little further west. No doubt, there was a light shining. Its source was a kiva slightly west of Walpi. The kiva housed some beings bearing striking similarities to kachinas who were in the midst of rehearsing a dance. Pongoktsina entered and begged them, crying, "Hide me, please. A creature is chasing after me!" They also readily consented. The first dancer in the line placed Pongoktsina directly behind him. Since he bore some semblance to the dancers, he blended in with them and was not easily discernible.

No sooner did the dancing resume than a thud was heard on the kiva roof. Apparently, Pongoktsina's wife had arrived again. She had tracked her husband to this place. Shouting down into the kiva she asked, "Hasn't my spouse come here?"

"No, no one has shown up here at any time," one of the kachinas replied.

"Of course he did, for I trailed him here. He must be down there," the woman insisted. And abruptly, just as before, she entered the kiva. Scrutinizing the dancers who were lined up rehearsing their ritual, she walked to the north side of the kiva. Her husband, of course, was standing at the western end of the kiva at the front of the line. As she went along now and closed in on Pongoktsina, he quickly burst out from among the dancers and dashed up the ladder.

Once outside he scanned the area. "I wonder which way I should go," he pondered as he looked around. Much to his surprise he spotted another light in the west. So heading in this direction, he sped off once more. As it turned out, the light was coming from Qa'ötukwi, which is in the vicinity of the village of Mishongnovi. At this place the Flute society was conducting its esoteric rites. The Flute initiates were sitting at the base of their altar and had a fire burning in the fire pit. This was the source of light Pongoktsina had spotted. When he arrived there and entered, he pleaded with the Flute members and they agreed to help him. One of the participants took Pongoktsina and somehow, miraculously, placed him inside his flute. The Flute members were men endowed with magic skills which enabled them to accomplish this feat. And despite the fact that Pongoktsina was hidden inside the flute, the person playing it played as beautifully as the others.

Pongoktsina's wife once again tracked her husband to this place by following his footprints. Inquiring whether he had arrived there, she was told no, but as on the previous occasions she entered without invitation. She proceeded to search for her husband, evidently knowing where to look. Thus she went from man to man looking into each of their flutes. By now she was drawing closer to the Flute member concealing her husband. He was already pondering how best to get out of the flute when the person playing it simply pointed his instrument up toward the kiva hatch and quickly blew into it. As a result, Pongoktsina was immediately propelled outside. Outside he once again scouted the area, and this time detected a light coming from a point just west of Shungopavi, so he fled in that direction. Upon reaching his destination, Pongoktsina entered the kiva and found that the Gray Flute members were holding their secret ritual there. He entreated them for help and they in turn concealed him, but not without first giving him certain instructions to follow.

Once again the woman had discovered her husband's tracks. It was not long before she arrived and began asking for him. She received the same answer as at the other places, but she did not believe the Gray Flute members either and quickly entered their kiva. Standing at the south end of the subterranean abode she looked around. North of the fire pit was a pool of water in the midst of which grew a tall sunflower. In looking at its stalk she noticed that Pongoktsina's footprints led to the water. Also, there were rings in the water, still spreading in each direction. The woman immediately realized that her husband had hidden himself somewhere in this place. So she headed toward the pond. Upon stepping into the water she inspected the sunflower, but could not find her spouse. He had obviously concealed himself there, but she had no idea that he had climbed the plant and was sitting inside the blossom. Pongoktsina actually peered down at her as she stood there in the water. That very moment she also looked into the pool and saw her husband's reflection looking up at her from the pond. As soon as she saw him she lunged at him, but instead of grabbing hold of him, she began to sink and finally disappeared into the pool. The water was apparently very deep there, but Pongoktsina had somehow managed not to go under when he first entered. At long last he was rid of her.

The headman of the Flutes now said to him, "All right, come down." Pongoktsina complied and descended from the sunflower.

Pongoktsina now expressed his gratitude to the Flute initiates for saving his life. "Thank you! I was fortunate to find you here. Thank you for helping me. She had been after me for quite a while and I was sure she would soon catch up with me; but then I came upon you. People tried to hide me at various other places, but she always managed to find me," Pongoktsina explained. And then he went on relating to them in detail all that had happened before, beginning with how he had gotten married into the girl's family at Oraibi.

Now, since the Flute members had been in seclusion conducting their secret rites when Pongoktsina entered, it was impossible for him to leave. He had no choice but to remain there with them. During his confinement there he suddenly heard some strange noises. Something beneath them kept making thumping sounds. It appeared that the others paid no attention to the noise, but continued to sit about their altar chanting sacred songs. From the day he entered their kiva they spent four more days in seclusion. Early in the morning on that fourth day, just about the time when people go out to greet the sun in prayer, some beings began to emerge from the pool of water, one after another. At this time the light within the kiva was still so dim that he was unable to tell who was coming out of the water. Later, as the light grew brighter, he recognized them as other members of the Flute society. Also, they seemed to be escorting someone as they came out of the pond. He strained his eyes to make out this person's identity. Suddenly it dawned on him. It was his wife who had come out with them at this moment. Evidently she had somehow succeeded in transforming herself back into her normal self so that she was no longer the grotesque creature of before. As a terrifying death spirit she had pursued her husband. Now she had assumed the shape of a beautiful woman again and as such emerged from the pool of water along with the others.

Apparently the Flute members were now going to costume both Pongoktsina and his wife. Consequently they washed their hair, and when that was done, they first garbed the man in the guise of a Flute member. Next they dressed his wife in the fashion of a female member of the Flute society. Then the couple was ushered outdoors to a place on the south side of the kiva. Upon their arrival there, the leader of the Flutes drew a path of sacred cornmeal on the ground pointing north to Oraibi. Over this path he laid out four more lines crosswise. After completing this task he instructed the couple to follow his path. "As you start out, you Pongoktsina will precede your wife. For some time you must not look back at her. If you get to the end of the four lines without looking back, things will be all right for you. But if you can't control yourself and look back at her, evil will befall both of you. Well then, follow each other along this path now." The couple did as bidden and proceeded north along the trail. As advised, Pongoktsina went first and his wife followed. Stepping along the line, the two had not yet reached the final marker, when he looked back and his eyes fell on his spouse.

The instant Pongoktsina did so, the leader of the Flutes caught him and shouted, "Alas, you did not do as I instructed!" And, turning to Pongoktsina's wife, he commanded, "Go on, now it's your turn to run!" No sooner had he spoken than the woman dashed off—never again to stop running. Now it was Pongoktsina who set out in pursuit of his wife. In this manner the two Pongoktsinas carried on. First they headed in the general direction of Oraibi, but instead of entering the village they bypassed it and then disappeared. "You'll have to do this now for the rest of your days. You did not follow my advice and thereby did wrong to your wife," the Flute society leader yelled after Pongoktsina. When the two had disappeared over the horizon, the Flute members returned to their kiva.

The people of Oraibi never did find out what happened to the Pongoktsina couple. When and where they had vanished remained a mystery. Only the two children returned to Oraibi some time later, and since they came without their parents, they went to their grandmother's house. From that time on the boys lived in the village without a father or a mother.

Now it was Pongoktsina who kept running after his wife, but the poor man was unable to catch up with her. Then for some reason the two were transformed into stars. They ascended into the sky where they became stellar beings with the name Nangöysohut, which is "The two stars that are chasing one another." They truly travel about the heavens in this manner. They are two heavenly bodies roaming about chasing one another. People say these stars represent that couple, Pongoktsina and his wife. To this day Pongoktsina is still chasing after his wife.

And here the story ends.

The Man Who Traveled to Maski, Home of the Dead, to Bring Back His Wife

Aliksa'i. They were living at Oraibi. Many people were at home there, among them also a young man who had just gotten married to a beautiful girl. The two were very much in love and were grateful to have each other. One day, not long after the couple's wedding, the woman became so ill that she died soon thereafter.

The woman's husband, poor thing, was terribly distraught about the loss of his wife and became very lonesome for her. His longing for her became so strong that he began to visit her at the place where she lay buried. Before long, he was at her gravesite every night, and each time he sat there he kept asking why she had died. The man's relatives assured him that his wife had gone to Maski. But even though they told him that, they were not familiar with the way to that place. The man, however, said, "I'll go after her. I'll follow her regardless of the consequences for myself. Perhaps there does exist a road somewhere to Maski. Maybe if I pray for this, someone will have pity on me and reveal to me where the road goes that I need to travel." With thoughts like these on his mind, the man kept visiting his wife's grave.

When he visited, he usually lay there embracing the grave mound under which his wife was buried. One night, when he was there again, he heard the hooting of an owl, just northwest of him. This hooting had been happening each time when he was at her grave. As he began to wonder about this, it suddenly struck him, "Maybe this owl took pity on me and wants to show me the road so that I can go after my wife."

Sure enough, the next day when he went to his wife's grave, the owl was there. When it began to hoot, he said to himself, "Let me go to him. Maybe he really intends to tell me something, and here I lie just wasting my time."

So the man headed over to the owl. Sure enough, there he was, perched on a tree. And then the owl reproached him, "You're a tardy one. You wanted to go to Maski, so I took pity on you and sought you out. Your destination is far away, but I felt sorry for you, so here I am. I want you to go home and prepare a few things. First of all, water and toosi, sweet corn flour. That mixture is very fortifying. Next, put on moccasins that have thick cowhide soles. You'll also need some weapons, your bow and arrows and a knife. Bring all these things here four days from now, at night. We will then travel together."

"Agreed," said the man, "you can rely on me being here. I'm so sick with longing, I don't even eat anymore. I already contemplated opening this grave, lying down inside, and dying in it so that I might follow my wife. I'm so grateful you felt pity for me, so I'm still alive."

"Don't worry," the owl replied. "Simply go home now and prepare your things, and don't visit this place for a while. Instead, try and get a lot of sleep. If you're well rested and strong, you'll travel better. The road to Maski is a long one."

The man did as bidden. The next morning, after a good night's sleep, he told his parents about his plans. "That's impossible," they exclaimed. "You'll never make it. You're too exhausted from your longing. You've not been eating and look sicker every day. You don't appear to be your usual self anymore. Still, his mother said, "I'll prepare you some journey food so that you can eat on your way."

"And I'll make you some weapons and new moccasins," his father added. "Also, when you leave in four days time, I'll have some pahos ready for your guide."

The man now no longer sought out his wife's grave. Instead, he slept a lot. Still, he kept wondering what he could possibly do to reach his destination faster. Sure enough, on the fourth day, his father had fashioned everything he had promised his son, including the pahos. So, when night fell, the man headed out to the graveyard again. As he arrived, the owl was already there, hooting. "You've come?" he greeted the man.

"Yes," the man replied, "and I brought you this." With that, he bestowed the pahos on the bird.

The owl was elated. "Thanks," he cried, "no one has ever given such a gift to me. But you brought me these pahos, just what I hoped you'd give me when I felt sorry for you and agreed to help. Thank you so much. All right, then, let's be on our way. Let's go over here to the northwest side."

So they both headed over to that side of the graveyard, and then the owl said, "Now, lie on top of me. Maski is far away, but I can at least show you the way to your destination and get you closer to it."

The man obeyed and lay down on top of the bird. The owl then rose into the air with the man on his back and before long, they had covered a great distance.

"All right," the owl finally said, "this is as far as I am going to take you. From here on you have to walk. Unfortunately, the road is barely visible. You're bound to see it, though. Be prepared for many obstacles along the way. Normally, no living human beings go along here. Only the dead are permitted. They are the ones who will challenge you. So, be on your guard. All right, go now with a happy heart. If you're lucky, you'll get to meet your wife." With that warning, the owl flew off and the man embarked on the rest of his journey.

Somewhere along the way, the man felt like defecating. He stepped behind a bush and was about to squat down, when suddenly he heard a voice. "Yuck," the voice said, "move a little farther away, my grandchild!" Right below where he squatted he noticed a tiny hole. Evidently Old Spider Woman was living there. The man stepped aside and when he was done, went back to the hole. "Twist your heel over the hole and it will get larger," the voice now said.

True enough, the hole became as large as the hatchway of a kiva, and the man entered. "Here, have a seat," Old Spider Woman welcomed him. "I felt pity for you, so I've been waiting here for you. You're on your way to a dangerous place. That's why I'm here. Handing him a deerskin she said, "I felt sorry for you because you have nothing to protect yourself. Wrap this around your legs." The man tore it in half and covered both his legs. "Well, now you can go on," she said. "I'll be waiting for you somewhere else. It'll be at a place where you'll need to relieve yourself again. If you're lucky, you'll get there without suffering too many hardships."

With that the man left Old Spider Woman's abode and started out once more on the trail to Maski. It really was difficult to see. Before long he entered an area that was dry and bleak. Looking about the man noticed some huge prickly pear cactuses. At one place they were growing so thick that he had no idea how to get through them. In the end, he managed to make it by cutting them off with his knife. The deerskin he had received from the old woman and wrapped around his legs also came in handy. The prickly pears had sharp spines, but they failed to penetrate the leather.

Soon he was able to advance more rapidly again, but then he found himself confronted by a new obstacle. These were cholla cactuses, similar to the prickly pear but more cylindrical in shape. The had extremely long spines, but in the end he succeeded in crossing this cactus belt. After stepping lively for a while he neared a hilly region. Just about that time, the white dawn appeared, and then the yellow dawn, and finally it was full sunrise.

The man was still walking along there when suddenly he heard a noise right by his side. As he looked about, he spotted a huge rattlesnake. The snake, standing almost as high as his thighs, spoke to him. "You're going somewhere?"

"Well, yes," the man said. "Just recently my wife passed away. I began to miss her so much that I fell sick, so I decided to follow her to wherever she now makes her home."

"That's too bad," the rattlesnake replied, "but I can't allow you through here. You mortals have no right to travel along here, and you can never get used to this place. I won't let you pass."

With those words, the rattlesnake struck out at the man, meaning to bite him. However, the man remembered his weapons. Quickly he drew an arrow from his quiver and shot it at the beast. The old woman had warned him that it would come to this. After killing the snake, he was supposed to make a medicine from it, which he did. This he then rubbed on his body to gain a brave and strong heart.

After this ordeal, the man continued on his journey. A while later, he encountered another creature standing in his path, all stooped over. At first, he had no idea what it was, but as he drew closer, he realized that it was a large bear. He seemed to be in a ferocious mood, for he was flinging the sand in front of him to the left and right. As the man stepped up to the bear, it growled, "You're going somewhere?"

"Yes," the man explained. "Just recently my wife died. I missed her so much that I got sick. So much did I wish to come to Maski, that an owl pitied me and sent me along this trail. That's why you find me here."

"That's too bad," the bear replied. "I can't allow that. Be grateful you're not dead yet. Turn around and go back. I won't let you pass. That's the reason I've been waiting here for you. Your relatives didn't want you to come here, either. Anyway, I won't permit it."

Angrily, the man pulled another arrow from his quiver and, as before, shot the animal dead. He also made a medicine from the bear's body and pressed on.

After a while the man reached a river, where he felt the urge to defecate again. As before, he stepped behind a bush and just wanted to relieve himself, when he found Old Spider Woman waiting there for him again. She welcomed him inside her underground abode and said, "Have a seat. I've been expecting you. You certainly took your time getting here! There's another challenge in store for you. Look, there's water here. So, I have a boat ready that you can use. Listen carefully to my instructions. As you look over there, you can see some cliffs side by side. Aim straight for them. As you approach them, you will notice that they draw apart and then close again. Watch them carefully. If you're lucky they won't smash together with you in between them. As soon as they open up for the third time, row through the gap. Otherwise, you'll never make it to Maski. So watch out and be on your guard. I'll accompany you as far as the edge of the water." With this warning, Old Spider Woman climbed on top of the man's ear.

The two now started out. Sure enough, the man found a boat

stashed away at the bank of the river. "Get in," the old woman said. "Then use this stick to push the water on both sides. That will propel you forward."

The man obeyed and climbed aboard. "Go with a happy heart, my grandchild," Old Spider Woman said.

So now the man traveled along by boat. After a good length of time he spotted the cliffs. They stood indeed as one, but then they opened up as he drew nearer. After gaping fully open they suddenly snapped shut again. The man counted carefully, and the third time they gaped open, he rushed between them. He had just reached the other side when they slammed together behind him. Having gotten through just in time, he breathed a sigh of relief. Upon reaching the shore of the river, he hid the boat there and continued on his way.

Once again the man felt like relieving himself, and as before, the old woman was waiting for him. "All right, have a seat," she cried. "The appointed time of your arrival in Maski is nearing. The time will be tonight. Again, there will be tests in store for you. The first person revealing himself to you will be Maasaw. I'll give you this medicine. I want you to chew it, and the moment he comes up to you and reaches out for you, just spray it on him with your mouth. That will weaken his power. When he regains his strength, he's bound to chase you. As soon as he does that, climb on the roof of the kiva there. Someone else will be lying in wait for you there, a mountain lion in fact. Mountain lions can take huge leaps and only need to grab someone with their paws to kill him. The animal is bound to be angry when you come, but don't waste any time; chew your medicine again and spit it on him. That will make him gentle and meek. Then you can enter the kiva through the hatch in the roof."

The old woman went on, "Inside you will find a large group of people, all of whom will welcome you. Then look about and you will find the kiva chief sitting at the northwest end of the floor. On his left your wife will be seated. Since she just arrived there, that's her proper place. Wait a little while and then say something to her. The people there will be most friendly and polite to you, and their chief will invite you to sit next to him.

"You must refuse his offer," the old woman warned him. "Tell him that you can't do that. Just say that you came to fetch your wife and that you want to sit by her side. Four times he will ask you to sit next to him, but you must remain steadfast in your refusal. He will then let you sit down, but he will try to persuade you in another way.

When he does so, tell him that you need to relieve yourself. I'll be waiting for you as soon as you come out of the kiva.

"One more thing," Old Spider Woman said, "when you sit down at your wife's side, don't embrace her for a while, even though you've missed her so much. And if she wants to touch you, don't let her do so."

So the man started forth again and soon came to a structure that resembled a kiva. He was on the point of passing it by, when a gigantic being rose from the ground in front of it. The head of the being was so enormous that the man became frightened. This was Maasaw, of course, who now let out his wail. The man was scared out of his wits. His entire body became numb, almost paralyzed. As Maasaw strode toward him and reached out for him, he remembered his medicine and quickly chewed it. He sprayed it from his mouth all over Maasaw. As a result, the god became limp and fell full length upon the ground. Soon, however, he sat up and, shaking his head, rose to his feet. He stepped up to the man and said "My, stranger, you're really strong. You're as courageous and stouthearted as I am. I had no intentions of letting you stay here, but you have beaten me. So be it then; let me take you to your wife."

With Maasaw leading, the two now climbed up on the kiva roof. Sure enough, the mountain lion was there, snarling viciously. He was getting ready to pounce when the man recalled his medicine. He quickly ground it up with his teeth and sprayed it on the lion. Immediately the cat's anger subsided and he settled down. "He'll leave us in peace now," Maasaw declared. "Your wife lives right here. Come on in. Her place is on the left side of the chief. I'm sure you'll recognize her."

Once inside, the man looked around and as expected, found a large group of people there. "Have a seat, stranger," they greeted him. The chief said, "I guess you've come then. We were just about to get started, so sit by my side."

"No, I can't do that," replied the man.

"Sure you can," said the chief. "That's the proper place for a newcomer. So please, sit down."

But the man remained firm. "No, I won't," he said.

Four times the chief urged him in the same way, but the man was not persuaded. In the end he said, "I'd like to sit next to my wife."

"All right," the chief consented.

With that, the man sat down at his wife's side. His wife stretched out her hands for him, but he motioned them aside. As much as he longed for her, and wanted to touch her, he remembered that Old Spider Woman had expressly warned him not to do so. "If I recall rightly, I am not supposed to touch her," he thought to himself and refrained from doing so. He now looked around and saw that he knew some of the people there. They had all died long ago. It now dawned on him that there really existed a road to Maski. Suddenly he recalled that the old woman had told him to find an excuse to go relieve himself. "Wait a minute," he said, "since my departure I haven't relieved myself. I need to go."

"All right," the chief replied. "Go ahead, and when you're back, we'll get started."

The man left the kiva and was relieving himself, when the old woman appeared again, bidding him to enter her abode. "Have a seat," she said. "I'm so glad you showed up. They will now get under way, so let me fill you in on what's going to happen. Your wife is a newcomer, so the chief will first want to have intercourse with her. You must look on without getting upset. You've come this far, so don't spoil everything. Just watch him having intercourse next to you. When he is done, your wife will come back to you.

"Next, they will try to tempt you with your first girlfriend. The chief will say, 'It's your turn now to have intercourse. That's how we do it here.' A girl will get up—you know her of course—she's a real beauty. You'll remember that she died about a year ago and that you really mourned losing her. Anyway, they'll tempt you with her. She'll lie down right in front of you, and the others will urge you to sleep with her. You must not give in. Four times they will urge you, but only if you refuse will you survive the test. And if you beat them at their game, you will succeed in winning your wife back. The chief will then allow you to lead away your wife. As soon as you leave the kiva, come and see me again. I'll be expecting you as before."

The man did exactly as he was told. Just as the old chief was about to start having intercourse with the man's wife, the chief said to her, "All right, lie down here. Let's do it."

Obediently, the woman lay down next to her husband. The chief stepped up to her and raised up her dress. How light-complected her skin was, as she lay there stark naked! The chief now loosened his kilt and, even though he was an old man, displayed an erect penis of enormous size. Then he spread-eagled himself on top of the woman. The man was furious and he felt like his heart would break. He felt like rushing over to the old chief and murdering him. But then he remembered, "I was not supposed to get upset. I came here to find my wife." So he had no choice but to suffer this outrageous act in silence.

Finally, the chief was done and rose to his feet. "All right, now it's your turn," he cried, calling upon the man's first girlfriend. Just as foretold by Old Spider Woman, she bedded down in front of him. As he looked at her, he saw that she was exceedingly beautiful and sexual desire arose in him. As he continued staring at her, he got an erection, but at the last moment he remembered the old woman's warning not to give in.

Four times the chief urged him on. "Come on, you're tardy. It's daylight soon."

But the man kept refusing and after the fourth refusal, the chief declared, "You have really beaten us. You must be incredibly powerful. No wonder you succeeded in coming here and gaining back your wife. She's truly yours now. So be on your way, both of you. I assume you know the way."

So the man departed with his wife. After leaving the kiva they went to its northwestern side, where the man excused himself and went to relieve himself. As before, Old Spider Woman was waiting for him. "Thanks," she cried, "you prevailed in your pursuit."

"Yes," the man replied.

"Well, then let me counsel you again. As you leave here you'll reach the river again. Get aboard the boat. This time the clashing rock cliffs won't be there. Instead, a Paalölöqangw will stand in your way. Don't be afraid of him. Of course, he'll challenge you as you approach him, but that's why I gave you the medicine. As soon as you spray that on the horned serpent, he will calm down. Then I'll be expecting you both again on the other side of the river. She then wished them well. "All right, my grandchildren, go now. If you follow my instructions you won't fail."

So the man took his wife, and soon they came to the boat. They climbed in and rowed off. Sure enough, the cliffs had disappeared, and in their place stood a huge creature that was swaying back and forth. No doubt, that was Paalölöqangw, the horned water serpent. As the two came closer, the water began to churn. The serpent rose up in the air so that their boat was bouncing around. The man remembered his medicine, however, and sprayed it on the serpent. Immediately, the Paalölöqangw was gone from sight, and the man and his wife got through the ordeal. They soon reached the other bank of the river, where the old woman was waiting for them.

"You've come!" she cried.

"Yes," the two replied.

"Well, from here on you will go straight home. It will take you several days," said Old Spider Woman. And then she specifically warned the man, "When you go to bed at night, show no desire for your wife. Don't sleep with her under any circumstances. Not before you reach the village may you engage in intercourse with her. If you follow these instructions, you will have truly won her back. However, if you sleep with her before you arrive back there, you will lose her."

Keeping these instructions in mind, the two traveled on, night after night. And although his wife wanted to make love to him, the man did not forget Old Spider Woman's warning.

Finally, the last night of travel came and went, and the next morning they arrived near the village about dawn. This time, when the woman touched him, the man gave in to her. He was very tempted to take her in his arms. "How great," he thought, "we're home and I have her with me. Nothing can happen to us now." He began to have intercourse with her, and he was still engaged in the act when suddenly his wife started to struggle. A moment later she slipped out from underneath him, hovered in the air in the shape of an owl, and flew away, all the way back to the graveyard. Angry with himself, the man started crying. "Why did I disregard the old woman's instructions? Well, it can't be helped now. I've lost her for good. No one is going to help me any more. Evidently, my wife wanted me for herself and showed me the way to Maski. But I had to do wrong! With that he also headed over to the graveyard. When he arrived he found a hole where his wife had been buried. Apparently, she had left the grave and was on her way back to Maski. In this manner he failed to bring back his wife. By desiring her sexually he had lost her.

And here the story ends.

8

The Yaya't and Their Feats

Once the Zuni Yaya't were staging a dance at Mishongnovi. Skilled in various ways and endowed with special knowledge, they were extremely powerful. In the eyes of the Hopis they were magicians or wizards. During their dances they showed off their magic art to the people, as they did on this occasion.

They were exhibiting their feats around noontime, and at one point, the Yaya't were digging up a buried string, with the last Yaya' in the group following along behind rolling it up. Eventually, the string led into a house where all sorts of delicious foods were stored—watermelons, muskmelons, peaches, pumpkins—and all the other things Hopis really like to eat. The Yaya't brought this food out and threw it to the spectators. The Yaya' women tried to prevent them from doing this, running up to the men and starting to beat them up.

Yaya't are lusty by nature and preoccupied with sex all the time. They are interested in reproducing and want lots of offspring. Their main concern is for the population to increase. Because of this, they will sometimes grab a woman and simulate sex by making pelvic thrusts at her. That's what they did now with the Yaya' women.

When the Yaya't were done with this demonstration, they just lolled about for a while. Now, there is a butte southwest of Mishongnovi called Hooyapi, which the white man calls Little Giant's Chair. When the Yaya't had assembled again, their chief announced to the audience, "All right, now watch this. We're going to whitewash Hooyapi with kaolin."

The Yaya't were carrying around huge pottery bowls filled with the white clay. "All right, let's start," they all cried, and got out bunches of sheep's wool, which was typically used in the old days to plaster the walls of houses. The Yaya' chief dipped the wool into the kaolin and then moved it back and forth in the air, as if whitewashing something.

Incredibly, the upper end of Hooyapi immediately turned white. All the other Yaya' members now joined in, dipping their wool in the clay, and before long, the butte had become completely white. No question about it, the Hopi spectators clearly saw the butte as all white.

"All right," the chief proclaimed, "let's wash it off again." With all the spectators watching closely, one of the Yaya't went to fetch some water, with which they removed the kaolin from the butte, by making washing motions in the air. Immediately Hooyapi stood there again in its natural black color.

The following year, the Yaya't performed another feat, this time at night, on the eve of a ceremony the next day. First they practiced when no one was around, because they wanted to see if their trick would really work.

On the southwest side of Mishongnovi is the projecting point of a mesa called Huk'ovi. Long ago there used to be a Kwan kiva somewhere in the vicinity. To this kiva the Yaya't wanted to transport one of their initiates. First, they chose a wicker piki tray for a vehicle. They set a Yaya' on top of it and gave it a spin. Perched on this tray, the man rode off in the direction of the kiva. Now, a wicker piki tray is very strongly woven, so it held the man up and he flew straight along. However, instead of landing right at his destination, he sailed on by.

So the Yaya't tried once more, this time with a burden basket. They gave it a push and it rose nicely into the air, flew straight to the kiva and entered it, exactly as planned. "Thanks!" exclaimed the Yaya' chief. "That's the way it was supposed to work!"

The next day, after gathering the people together at noontime, the Yaya' chief announced, "All right, let's do it again." With that, the Yaya't heaved one of their men into the burden basket and gave it a big push. With this shove, it rose up into the air, flew away, reached the kiva, and entered it. A little later, it came out again with the Yaya' man still inside it. "That's the way!" cried the chief. In this way the Yaya't showed off their feats there.

On another occasion, the Yaya't performed in Shungopavi. There, on the northeast end of the Wuwtsim kiva, they staged their dances. After throwing all kinds of gifts to the audience, they went to a pit oven they had made. A fire was burning in it and glowing embers could be seen. Next to the oven was a stack of wood, all of which they threw into the oven, with the result that shimmering heat waves were soon radiating from it.

Milling about, the Yaya't suddenly grabbed their chief, and carrying him by his hands and feet, hauled him to the oven. There, they repeatedly threw him up in the air, chanting "Aaho!" Four times they threw him into the air, and then they flung him bodily into the fiery pit. Sparks flew when they did this, as the inside was glowing hot. Then they brought out a wedding robe, which they spread on the ground. One of the Yaya't reached into the oven and pulled out a hand. It was thoroughly cooked. Others reached in, pulling out various parts of the chief's body. The last thing they pulled out was the chief's head. When they had loaded all the chief's parts on the robe, they folded it up, went to their kiva, and dumped them all inside through the hatch.

Next, looking for another victim, they chased after one of the Yaya' initiates. While they were busy doing this, the chief suddenly reappeared and joined in the pursuit. When they finally caught him, they gave him the same treatment as they had the chief. They cooked all of their initiates in this way, but each of them emerged alive again.

On another occasion, at Shungopavi, a large number of Yaya't were assembled in their own kiva. The Yaya' kiva was located right by the Wuwtsim kiva. Many visitors from other villages had come to see their feats. At one point the Yaya' chief emerged from the kiva with a bowl in his hands. It apparently contained stew, made with hominy and rabbit meat. As he carried this bowl among the crowd, he said, "Eat this stew, but please save the bones. I'll be back later to collect them."

The visitors gathered around the bowl and helped themselves to the stew. They soon ate it all up and carefully put aside the bones. Before long, the Yaya' chief returned and collected them. Dropping them at a clear space on the ground, he covered them with a wedding robe. The Yaya' initiates began to dance around it, reaching down under the robe every now and then. Suddenly, as they were doing this, the Yaya' chief said, "All right, I guess that's enough." With that announcement, he jerked away the robe.

There sat dozens of little live cottontails! The bones had evidently been transformed into real rabbits. The little creatures became frightened and dashed off, trying to escape. "All right," the chief yelled, "anyone who wants a cottontail may try to catch him!"

The visitors did not hesitate and chased after them. In this manner the Yaya't displayed their magic skills once again.

One day, when the Yaya't were performing their magic art at Mishongnovi again, their chief volunteered to do something. He carried a sword-shaped batten, used for weaving, that he began to put in his mouth. Further and further he slid it in, until it had completely disappeared. He now asked his companions to find some more battens, all of which he stuck down his throat, until he had swallowed eight in all. He showed no sign that it bothered him, and as he walked about, the spectators watched him in amazement. After all, he was full of battens! After a while, he stepped aside, bent over at the waist, and seemed to be really straining. Then, one after the other, the battens started falling to the ground. To everyone's surprise, the man did not seem to have suffered any ill effects. With this fantastic feat the Yaya' chief entertained the audience there. The Yaya't are really incredible magicians.

9

An Oraibi Boy's Visit to Maski, Home of the Dead

Aliksa'i. People were living in Oraibi and various other settlements across the land. In Oraibi, there lived a boy named Honanyestiwa, along with his parents and a younger sister. They all resided at the far northeastern edge of Oraibi. Thus, when the sun came up in the morning, the inside of their home was the first to be lit by its rays.

Also along the northeastern side of Oraibi was a graveyard. Day in and day out, as the boy went to greet the sun in a morning prayer, he passed by this graveyard. In the beginning, he did not give much thought to it. As time went on, however, his curiosity about the place increased, and he thought, "I wonder if it's really true that upon one's death one goes somewhere. Does one really travel to some paradise? How could I go about reaching such a place and find out about it with my own eyes?" Each time while going by this location these thoughts were on his mind. However, he never confided his thoughts to his parents. Most likely they would harshly berate him for this, for no one in his right mind would willingly choose death. For this reason he never brought up the subject in front of his parents.

But as time passed, he became more and more determined to seek out this place. So he decided, "The next time I go and pray to the sun, I'll ask for guidance on how I may reach this place. People say that the sun goes along picking up everyone's wishes, even the bad intentions of those who are evil."

With this in mind, the following morning when he went to pray, he begged the sun to somehow arrange for him to visit the place where the dead go. Each morning now he made this desire known to the sun.

On the fourth morning, just as he turned back toward the village, someone spoke to him. "Wait a minute," the voice said.

Much to his surprise, when he looked back he saw a stranger standing behind him. It was a man, very handsome in appearance. He was dressed most beautifully and covered with colorful body paint. Each time he moved, bright light reflected from him. In addition, his breath exuded warmth. The boy, staring at the stranger in wonderment, did not respond immediately. At last he asked, "Are you the one who spoke to me?"

"Yes, I came just to see you," he replied.

From all appearances, it was the sun, so the boy asked, "Very well, what do you want?"

"I'm sure you recognize me," Sun continued.

"Yes, it's clear who you are by your costume and your breath," the boy answered.

"I suppose that is so. But you have come to pray several times in the morning now and begged for something that is not pleasant. In your village all the young people your age lead happy lives. They have no desire to die just yet. Why on earth you want this is beyond me," Sun said to the boy.

"Indeed, for a long time I've had this curiosity about where people go after they pass on. Not that I wish to go there permanently. If only I could somehow find the way there, I could go there and see for myself. I'd very much like to learn what life is like there," the boy confessed.

"Is that right? Very well, then," Sun replied. "If you truly want this, you must follow my instructions. You must do exactly as I say," he warned the boy.

"All right, that's fine. I promise to do that, for I really do want to see this place," the boy said.

With that, Sun instructed the boy as follows. "For four full days I want you to make prayer sticks and prayer feathers. Make four of the double male and female prayer sticks that are painted black and green. The rest must be prayer feathers without the breath strand. Make plenty of these, to present to the dead as you go along. They will lack breath strands because the dead no longer have any breath. The morning after you have completed this task, return here and I will give you additional instructions." The boy took his eyes off Sun for just a second, and when he looked again, he was gone.

So the boy returned home. Upon his arrival, he decided not to inform his mother and father about this, for he was sure that they would be very upset with him. They would not want this for their son, so he said nothing to them, quickly ate his breakfast, and then left. He took along all the various materials that he would need to make the prayer items, and grabbed his tobacco pouch and pipe. It was his intention to seek out a place where he would be undetected, so he first went to a point southwest of the village and then descended to the foot of the mesa. As he reached a place directly below Pöqangwwawarpi, he stopped and carefully scanned the cliff there. There was a rock overhang there that was quite deep. He chose this place, for apparently no one ever came through that area. So he began to work on his pahos, and continued until evening. Then he stopped, and heaped all the ones he had made onto a tray and smoked upon them. After completing this ritual smoke, he bundled up the finished prayer items, carefully hid them in a crevice, and sealed the opening with a large rock. Then he headed home.

His family was already having their supper when he arrived. They asked him where he had been because he had been gone so long. "We were waiting for you to come, but when you did not show up, we went ahead and started eating. Your father was hungry when he came home, so we started supper without you," his mother explained.

"You did the right thing. It was my own fault that I didn't come home at an earlier hour. I was out hunting and didn't realize how far I had wandered out, so that's why I was late." This was all the boy had to say for himself as he joined the others at their supper.

He did not eat much as he had plans to go on a journey. He had no fear, but rather looked forward to it. So he ate just a little and after leaving the area where the food was laid out, he went out and climbed up to the second story. There he sat on his bedroll and pondered the matter. "I wonder what I'll see. Perhaps I'll see people I know." These and other thoughts occupied his mind, so he failed to notice that the hour had gotten late.

So he spread out his bedroll and lay down. As he was lying there, he continued to think about these things and did not fall asleep for a long while. But finally he became so tired that he fell asleep without realizing it. The following morning, when it was time to go out and pray to the sun, he realized what had happened and with a start jumped up from his bed. He quickly grabbed his pouch of sacred cornmeal, dashed down from the upper story of their home, and headed out to the northeast side of Oraibi. He took his usual route when he went out to pray, and prayed again that he might be shown how to get to Maski. When he was done, he headed back home.

This time, no one approached him, and nobody spoke with him before his ascent to the mesa top. As soon as he had eaten breakfast, he departed again without informing his parents of his plans. He headed back to the same overhang where he had been the day before making the pahos. Without delay he retrieved his bundle from the place where he had hidden it and again started working. He followed the same routine as the day before. He worked all day without even stopping at noon to eat. When the sun was low on the western horizon, he smoked over the products of his labor and carefully wrapped everything up into a bundle. Once again, he hid it in the crevice and returned home.

His family was already at supper when he entered. This time they didn't pry into what he had been up to, but only invited him to join them. Just as before, he did not fill himself too full before getting up. Again he climbed to the upper level of the house and sat there, mulling things over. When night fell, he bedded down and this time fell asleep a little earlier. This was the routine he followed for four days.

On the evening of the fourth day the boy took all the pahos he had made home with him. This time he arrived back at the village during the night and hid the prayer items in the house. When he entered the living quarters, he saw that his family had already eaten their evening meal and were putting the leftovers away, so he ate alone. Neither his mother nor his father said anything to him for being late.

The moment he had finished eating he was gone again. He climbed to the upper story of the house, took out his bundle, and unwrapped the pahos. Then he smoked over them. After finishing this ritual, he spread out his bed and lay down. He never fell into a deep sleep that night, and when the dawn came he noticed it right away. Quickly he rose and went out for his morning prayers. This time Sun was there waiting for him. "You have come, then?" he inquired.

"Yes," the boy replied.

"Very well. And are you willing to make this journey?"

"Yes, I am. That's why I followed your instructions."

"All right then. You will depart tonight. But you must tell one person what you intend to do. This person will be your younger sister. There will be an opportunity for the two of you to be alone, and then you can tell her. When you start out, you will first head in the direction of Apoonivi. From there you will go on to Awat'ovi. As you reach Apoonivi you will pass through a house. Exiting it on the northwest side, you will descend some stairs and then travel across the plain below to Awat'ovi. From there you will go to Hootatsomi, where I'll be waiting for you. Mark my words now. If you follow my instructions, no harm will befall you prior to reaching me. Some of the dead have not yet reached that place and still have a long way to go. Some died long ago but because of their wrongdoings are traveling at a slow pace. You're bound to come upon more than a few of these wretched ones. As you encounter them, they will speak to you and ask you for something. You must not heed their pleas, though. That's all I want to tell you now. And tonight when you are about to go to sleep, I want you to eat this." With that, Sun handed him something resembling a sweet corn cake wrapped in cornhusk. "As soon as you taste this, your soul will depart from your body. At that moment you will embark on your journey. Also, you must tell your sister that no one is to bother you the next day. No one must take away your death shroud nor touch your body. You will probably be back by the time it gets noon." That's all Sun said before disappearing.

The boy now headed straight home and ate with his family. He then ascended to the upper story to ready the things he would take along. It was not yet noon when he finished with his preparations. After lunch he returned to the upper story and waited for the proper time. He was so anxious that the passage of time seemed painfully slow. When evening finally came and it was time for them to eat, his mother came and invited him down to supper. This time he did not feel like returning to the upper story, so he remained there with them. To while away the time he taught his younger sister how to play cat's cradle. They played for several hours until it was dark outside. At one point the girl said to him, "My brother, please go with me to relieve myself. I'm afraid to go out by myself."

"Sure, I'll go with you," he readily agreed.

The two walked out of the door and headed northeast to the mesa edge. At the spot where the girl was relieving herself, the boy told his sister of his intentions. He revealed all of his plans to her and told her that he would be departing that night. Upon hearing this, the poor girl burst into tears. Her brother tried to calm her down. "That's enough. Don't worry too much. I will return." With that, his sister's crying abated somewhat. He then added, "There's one thing I need to tell you though. Tomorrow someone is bound to find my lifeless body. I am telling you this because I want you to rise early, so that when someone comes to move my body you can prevent them from doing that. Tell them exactly what I told you. And especially remember this one thing: When the sun is high in the sky, I am supposed to come back to life." His sister agreed to carry out his instructions, and with that, the two returned to the house.

As soon as the boy had escorted his sister back home, he told her that he was going to bed. He climbed up to the second story, opened the bundle of pahos, and smoked over them once more. Then he carefully wrapped it shut again and tied it to his waist. Next, he spread out his bedroll and lay down and covered himself. He then ate the entire piece of the qömi-like paste the Sun had given him and immediately fell into a deep sleep. From all appearances he was dead. He became aware of how his soul was departing from his body. Before long, his soul had completely separated. He glanced back now and saw his body lying there.

He looked at it for a long while, but then went on his way, for surely there was someone out there waiting for him. Quickly he descended from his house and headed in a northwesterly direction.

Weightless, he was able to move along rapidly. On his way he came across an old woman he had known who had passed away long ago. And yet here she was, so close to the village still. As he came up to here, she greeted him. "You are also going along here?"

"Yes," he replied.

"Please, have pity on me. Load me on your back and carry me at least four steps along your path. Then you can put me down again," she pleaded.

The boy's reply was brief. "I don't think I can do that. I'm in a great hurry."

That's all he said and then continued on his way. As he was leaving, though, the poor old woman began to weep. It was then that he remembered his bundle of pahos, so he turned around and returned to her, opened his bundle, and gave her one of the prayer feathers. She was elated about the gift and thanked him profusely. Then he went on his way again.

Eventually, the boy came to the crest of Awat'ovi. He had just passed this landmark when, much to his surprise, he found another woman sitting there, crying. As he strode by her, she beseeched him like the old woman before. The plea she uttered was similar, but his reaction was the same. He rejected her plea and gave her one of his pahos instead. Then he pressed on. He did not encounter anyone else as he descended the northwestern slope of Awat'ovi and reached Hootatsomi. Upon his arrival there Sun was already waiting for him. "You have come?" he inquired.

"Yes," the boy replied.

"Very well. Let's not be tardy then, for daylight comes quickly this time of the year. Come here," he ordered the boy. Obediently, the boy stood next to him. Sun now spread something out before them. Evidently it was a plain white ceremonial kilt. He told the boy, "All right, climb aboard this with me. The least I can do is to get you closer to your destination. It's quite a distance to where you're going." The boy did as bidden and squatted down on the garment. Just as Sun climbed aboard, the kilt rose gently up into the air and flew off with the two.

As the magic kilt made its flight, it finally neared a large pool. The edges of this pool were flanked with a great many burden baskets filled to the brim with small pebbles. At this point Sun said to the boy, "Some of the people who are on their way to Maski carry these baskets on their backs. Here is the place where the baskets are selected and put on their backs. For that purpose they are set out there, ready to be picked up."

A short distance later Sun spoke again. "Young man, look down below. The people moving that way have been traveling for a long, long time, yet they have only come this far. A person who dies without any sin reaches his destination without delay, but those who have done wrong in their lifetime are burdened down with heavy loads. Witches especially are forced to go at a very slow pace. Anyone who acquires the knowledge of sorcery and then dies is permitted only one step a year. So, although some of these people died long ago, they have not advanced farther than this. In addition, those witches are surrounded by a stone wall as they move along. Whenever one who is pure of heart passes them by, they beg them for a drink of water. When their plea is denied, they say, 'At least spit into my mouth.' But their request is never granted. It is their own fault that they suffer so severely as they journey along."

The boy stared at all this in great amazement. For truly, countless people were moving along there. Some of the women and men were traveling with burden baskets on their backs. The baskets were filled with large amounts of pebbles so that they, poor things, were burdened down with them. The women had to carry their loads with the straps that were designed for men. They deeply gouged their foreheads and caused excruciating pain. The men, on the other hand, carried their baskets by means of cords that women use to tie their hair. These people are known as Wiiwintses. Whenever an unmarried man weds a married woman, he supposedly must have one of these baskets. The same applies to unwed women who marry married men. He also saw women walking along with large strands of penises about their necks. Then also there were men who had dangling from their necks large strands made up of vulvas. These were women and men who had married more than once.

As the two continued their journey on the flying kilt, they arrived at a place where a man was removing the clothing of some women. The boy didn't know what to make of this, so he asked the Sun, "Why is he taking away the clothing of those women?"

"Well, some of those women were married several times. When a woman marries only once, all the items her husband makes for her belong to her. Occasionally, for one reason or another, a woman will have more than one husband. When she marries a man who had a wife prior to her marriage, and he makes a piece of clothing for her, it really belongs to the first wife. It does not properly belong to the woman he is living with at that time. Therefore, when she arrives here wearing that apparel, that man down there takes it away from her," he explained.

All these things the boy observed as he traveled along accompanied by Sun. He was familiar with some of the men and knew that they had been married more than once. The same was true for some of the women.

Much to his surprise he also noticed that there were mules among the people. Struck by this oddity, he pondered it but didn't know what to make of it. Eventually, he couldn't help himself any longer and blurted out to Sun, "Why are there mules going alongside the people? I thought it was only humans that entered Maski."

Sun snickered and replied, "That's right, those mules are part of the crowd. In truth, they are Hopis. They are the ones who took a Zuni spouse. Whenever a Hopi marries someone from that tribe, he is transformed into a mule. Therefore the elders warn against marriages with Zunis." He did not mention marrying members of other tribes.

After flying over all these beings, the two finally landed. Sun said to the boy, "Now, this is as far as I will go with you. From here on you will have to travel alone for a while. You will soon meet someone else who will assist you. Remember, though, not to help anyone along your way. There will be people pleading with you for a favor. But do not give in to any of them, he instructed the boy. With that, he let him off the flying kilt.

Thoughtful as he was, the boy now handed Sun one of the multihued pahos that he had made. What joy this brought to Sun! "Thank you so much. This is what I desire most from all people, but they so seldom make them for me. I'm grateful you made enough pahos so there is one to spare for me. Don't tarry now, but hurry on, for morning comes quickly." With this advice Sun left him there.

The boy now journeyed on alone. The trail was clearly marked, and people could be seen traveling along this route. At one place he came upon an elderly woman enclosed by a stone wall. She begged him, "Young man, please give me a drink. I'm very thirsty." However, the boy refused, telling her that he was in a rush. At this, the old woman reworded her plea. "Then at least spit into my mouth," she asked. He remained steadfast. He only gave her one of his pahos and continued on. And sure enough, each time he overtook a person, some sort of favor was sought of him. But he acted according to Sun's instructions and did not grant anyone any favors.

Once again, he covered quite a distance before he arrived at a pile of ashes and trash. Much to his amazement, there were some children playing there. He was still a good ways off when they noticed him, and said to one another, "Someone else is coming." That's all they said, staring at him as he went by. Not a single word did they say to him, apparently enjoying themselves. A woman with a burden basket on her back followed right behind the boy. As the children spotted her they exclaimed, "Look, someone else is coming!" As before, they closely eyed the oncoming woman. As she drew closer, they noticed the basket on her back. "How awful, there's a Wiiwintse coming," the children yelled and scattered to hide. Anyone with such a load on their back was known as a Wiiwintse.

Pressing on past this place, the boy continued at a rapid pace, overtaking lots of people. Each time he passed a person, he bestowed one of his prayer feathers on them.

After a while he reached a place where he heard a strange noise. Halting in his tracks, he listened. It was a clacking noise he heard. As he went on, he aimed his steps toward the origin of the noise. As he drew nearer, he saw that it was a man who was walking around there, all garbed in white.

When he stepped up to the man, he realized that he was an Aala'ytaqa, a member of the Two Horn society. At least he was dressed much like the initiates of the Oraibi Two Horn society. He wore two horns that were painted white and had a large piece of buckskin draped about his shoulders. Around his waist he had a ceremonial kilt. And just like the Oraibi Two Horns, he was barefoot.

The man's body was not painted; instead, white kaolin dots ran down from the top of his shoulders to his waist on both sides. To these dots adhered bits of eagle fluff. From his knees down to his feet he was decorated in exactly the same manner. In his left hand he held a mongko, a stick denoting his affiliation with the Two Horn society. His right hand was free. In addition, he wore turtle shell rattles on both legs. They were what was producing the clacking noise the boy had heard as the Aala'ytaqa strode back and forth.

The spot where he was walking to and fro was right along the edge of a cliff. As the boy glanced down, he found that it was a sheer drop-off. "You are just going along here?" the Two Horn man asked the boy.

"Yes," he answered. "Are you waiting for me?"

"Indeed I am. But let's not waste time, for it will soon be daylight. I am to take you down this cliff, for that's the task assigned to me. I must take down whoever arrives at this place."

With that, he too spread out something before them and instructed the boy. "All right, climb on this thing with me. We'll use it to descend the cliff. There is no trail down this place, so no one can go down without my aid," he explained. The boy did as bidden and stepped on the thing after the Two Horn man.

No sooner had the two climbed aboard than the thing rose off the ground. It first took them a little ways beyond the rim of the cliff, and then began its descent with both of them aboard. It was such a long cliff that it took them a while to reach the ground below.

After getting off the magic flier, the boy looked around. The area was covered with blooming flowers as far as the eye could see. The Two Horn man said to the boy, "All right, from here on you must continue on your own. Soon, however, you will meet someone else who will help you." With that, he ascended the cliff using the magic flier.

So the boy started out again. It was easy to see where the trail was leading. After a good length of time he came to an area studded with many rock spires. The spires stood quite tall, and as he walked among them, he suddenly heard a voice. He was not sure where the voice was coming from, nor could he make out what it said, so he paused and strained his ears. Apparently, the voice came from one of the rock spires. There, at the top, sat a man, who had spoken to him. Once more he repeated his words, "Young man, how fortunate to see you this far along! Have pity on me and help me down from here."

But the boy turned a deaf ear. He was probably up there for a reason, so the boy merely said, "I don't think I can help you. I'm in a great hurry." That was all he said, and then he went on.

As he continued his trek he realized that numerous people were perched on top of these rock towers. They all pleaded with the boy to help them down, but he refused, and he finally left the area behind. The people sitting atop these pillars apparently were evil. They too had approached the Aala'ytaqa, but since he recognized their evil nature, he merely pretended to help them down into the abyss. Instead of flying them down, he would take them directly to one of the pillars, where he abandoned them. In this way, they were paying for their wrongdoings.

Once more the boy pressed on, and it was not long before he

clearly heard the ringing of a bell. Without stopping, he headed straight toward the sound. This time he encountered a Kwaani'ytaqa, a member of the Kwan or One Horn society. The Kwan man greeted him and said, "You've arrived?"

"Yes, I have. Are you waiting for me?" the boy inquired.

"Yes, indeed. But let's be on our way, for the morning light comes quickly. I will personally lead you for a ways," he said, and took the boy by the hand.

Together they went on and had not traveled very far when they came upon a fork in the road. There the Kwan man said, "All right, this is as far as I can accompany you. But I will show you which road to choose. One of them leads directly to your destination, the other does not. Onto that road I usher all the evil ones. You must take the other road. Also, you will meet someone else who will lead you to your next station. Make sure you don't stray off this trail, though." The Kwan man showed him the right trail to take and left him standing there.

Once more the boy set out alone. As he went on his way, he kept an eye on the other trail. Sure enough, there were people on it, and like some of the others, they were burdened by such things as baskets, vulvas, or penises. No doubt, those were evil people. Their road was rough and strewn with rocks. Plants with burrs or thorns grew in its midst, and tall cacti grew on both sides of it. While not so thick that they prevented seeing the other road, the cacti still prevented anyone from switching from one trail to the other. So those poor souls had to keep to that road.

At some point along his way, the boy heard the ringing of a bell again. This meant that he must be nearing his next station. So, without stopping, he briskly moved along. Sure enough, he found himself confronted by another member of the Kwan society, who had obviously been waiting for him there. "You've arrived?" the man inquired.

"Yes," the boy replied.

"All right, I'm glad you've made it. I've been waiting for you for quite some time, so come with me. It's been some time since you left your body. This time of the year, morning comes quickly. Let's not tarry, but press on." With that he grasped the boy's wrist and led the way. Soon the two came to a kiva. "We need to stop here first," he told the boy. At the kiva top he took the boy on his back and in this manner entered the kiva with him. Inside, he let the boy down to the right of the entrance ladder. At first the boy had difficulty making out the interior of the kiva. All he could see was the glow from the fire pit. As his eyes became accustomed to the dark and he scanned his surroundings, he realized they had entered a real kiva. Right underneath the entrance ladder was a fire pit around which some elderly men were squatting. No one had yet spoken a word to them. They were still engaged in their ritual smoking. Eventually, one of the men asked, "Have you brought him?"

"Yes," the Kwan man replied, "he's standing here alongside me." He spoke in such a low tone that the boy was barely able to discern his words.

The old men were all clad in old, worn kilts. The downy feathers adorning their hair were equally ragged. As the boy looked at their faces, he seemed to recognize some of them. One of the old men he knew for sure. He was the former village chief of Oraibi, who had been dead for seven years. According to the Oraibi people he had truly been a good leader. Under his leadership the Oraibis had not quarreled with one another, nor had they lacked anything. Apparently, only old Kwan society leaders occupied this place around the fire pit.

Their voices were low as they spoke to one another. No one used a strident tone. That's the way it was in the main kivas of the Hopi villages. Finally, one of the old-timers said to the boy, "All right, come down and have a seat here in front of us."

With that, the man at the extreme southwestern end took his pipe and filled it with tobacco. Then they all started smoking, handing the pipe from one person to the next. By the time it reached the last man, the tobacco in the pipe was almost gone. When he was finished, he passed the pipe back to the one who had lit it. He, in turn, smoked up the rest and then said, "All right, I hope they caught the fragrance." The others now picked up their rattles and, shaking them, commenced to chant.

The person at the extreme southwestern end now took the boy by the hand and led him to a spot northwest of the fire pit. There he ordered him to stoop over. He was still bent forward when a cumulus cloud floated into the kiva and hovered directly above the boy. Next, there was a loud thunderclap and then rain began to pour from the cloud. Apparently the old men meant to wash the boy's hair and they did this with the help of the rain. Next, they had the boy stand in front of them so that they could smoke over him. When they had finished, the old man said to him, "All right, there is still another place you need to visit. So don't waste any time, hurry on. At your home far away, dawn is nearing. This man here will lead you. So go with strength." With that, the boy and his guide left the kiva.

This time, the boy was not carried piggyback. As the two made their exit, they headed in a new direction. Before long they neared a place from where a glow of light came. Upon reaching the place, it turned out to be a pit oven in the middle of nowhere. Beside it squatted a person who was stoking the fire inside. Huge flames were leaping up from the oven, and the heat from it was tremendous. The two stopped, and soon eight people appeared from out of nowhere, headed for the fire pit. They positioned themselves, two each at the four directions, one behind the other, facing the pit.

The boy didn't know what to make of this. He had no idea what they were up to, nor did he bother to ask his guide. On the northwest side a man stood in the front position. On the southwest side, a woman was in this position. On the southeast, a man was at the front again, and on the northeast a woman was at the front. Those standing in the front were stark naked. After a while the person in charge of tending the fire said, "All right, when I give the word, you on the northwest begin. Next, it will be the turn of the one on the southwest, then that of the one on the southeast, and finally yours on the northeast." Suddenly, he commanded, "Now, throw them in!" At this, the designated people took their turns pushing their victims into the burning pit, beginning with the one on the northwest side and continuing around the pit. All this the boy witnessed there. Whenever one was cast in, a large puff of smoke rose from the oven.

After they had performed this, the Kwan man said to the boy, "All right, come over here and take a look into this pit." The boy did as bidden and stepped up to the edge of the pit. There, at its very bottom, he saw a black stinkbug, scurrying about. But he found no trace of a human being inside the pit, nor did he spot any bones or other remains. Now the Kwan man explained, "Those people who were thrown into the pit were evil. They practiced sorcery while alive. Those who flung them in were the ones who died an early death because of them. It was not yet their time to die, but they were killed by those witches. The witches prolonged their lives by killing those people. If anyone with such great powers wants to get out of the burning pit, he transforms himself into a creature such as a fly or a stinkbug. Of course, a stinkbug is of no use for anything," he said.

"Now, there is yet another place you need to see." Billowing smoke was still coming out of the pit oven and the entire area was filled with smoke. They had no choice but to go through it. So again the Kwan man took the boy by the hand and guided him along.

After their departure, new groups of people were herded to the pit. But the boy did not bother to look over his shoulder. He knew that they would meet the same fate as the others. As they passed through the smoke, the Kwan man explained that it stemmed from the burned bodies of the evil ones, which gave off an unusual amount of smoke. So much smoke filled the air that no light shone for quite a distance.

Soon thereafter they emerged from the darkness into the light again. Once more the air was clear, and as the boy looked about, he saw flowering fields in every direction. As they walked through them, all sorts of winged creatures flew about. There were the various songbirds, chirping their particular melodies, and there were butterflies and hummingbirds fluttering about amid the flowers. The hummingbirds were hovering, happily humming and sucking the nectar of the flowers. Cicadas could be heard chirping all over. The weather was so nice and warm that life there was pleasant. It was like the middle of summer except that it was not so humid.

Then, as the two traveled on, they came upon a field in which were growing large amounts of many different plants. The boy had never seen any field quite like this before. Everything imaginable was growing there. He saw watermelons and muskmelons and their vines were spread out all around. There were also squashes growing there, their round shapes jutting up through the vines. The stalks of corn stood tall, with tassels at their tops and long ears protruding from their leaves. Different kinds of beans, too, were there in large amounts. How he wanted to have such a marvelous field of his own! Surprisingly, there were no weeds visible among these plants. The field was so huge that it took them quite a while to traverse it. When they had, they came to a village.

It turned out to be a very large settlement, and as they approached it, the Kwan man said to the boy, "You can stay here for four days. During this time you'll be able to realize all your dreams of what life is like here. Back at your home white dawn has not yet appeared over the horizon. You will have four days here, before the sun rises there. So don't be bashful, go about and talk to the villagers as much as you'd like. They are not evil and will not ask you to do anything improper. I have to go now. So enter the village and enjoy yourself. Don't let anything trouble you. You won't come out of your death before you return. So don't worry about things back at home while you are here." That's all he told him, and then he departed.

On his own initiative, the boy now entered the village and walked about among the homes. The place was teeming with people. Every time someone came toward him, they would gaze at him, but no one had recognized him yet. Since they did not know him, they simply greeted him by saying, "You have just arrived? Fine, settle down like the rest of us and be happy here." That's all they ever said. He soon discovered that the people there were most cordial. Outside of the houses the children were playing. Some of them were snacking on such delicious things as freshly roasted corn, corn baked in pit ovens, boiled corn, muskmelons, watermelons, and the other crops harvested by people there. As he continued through the village, he encountered an old woman. "How nice to see you here," she exclaimed.

"Yes," the boy replied.

"Haven't you met anyone yet that you know?"

"No," he answered, but then he recognized her. It had not been a year since she had died. The old woman further questioned him, "That's odd. How is it that you're walking about here without a prayer feather adorning your hair?"

The boy was perplexed. "What could she mean by asking about this?" he wondered. "Am I supposed to be wearing something in my hair?" he inquired.

"Well, when a person dies, his relatives usually make a prayer feather for the deceased before they bury him," she explained.

The boy was familiar with this custom, but had never given it any thought. It was only now, when she asked him, that he thought about it. So he replied, "I'm going to return back home soon." And then he related to her how he used to go out and greet the sun with his fervent wish and how the sun had helped him to make this journey possible.

"Is that how it is?" the old woman asked. "Very well, then. And you haven't yet met an acquaintance?"

"No, you're the only one I've recognized so far."

The woman next inquired which village he was from, so he explained that he was from Oraibi. She then began questioning him as to who his parents and relatives were, and this he also let her know.

"I see. In that case, I'll escort you to your grandmother's home. She lives with your grandfather only a short way from here. I'm sure you don't know them. I don't believe you were born yet when they died, one right after the other. Your grandfather passed away first, and your grandmother, who missed him, followed soon thereafter. Come on, I'll take you to them," she said and led him off.

Soon they came to a house. Leading the boy, the old woman entered without announcing their coming. They were warmly welcomed by another old woman. "All right, have a seat. I'm surprised to see that you have someone with you."

"That's right, I came upon him northeast of here. He is your daughter's son. I pointed out to him that he was lacking the feather in his hair. But he tells me that he will be returning to the land of the living."

No sooner had the other old woman heard this than she embraced the boy, expressing her happiness. Right away she entered a back room, and came out with an old man. When she told him who the boy was, he too greeted him happily.

The boy still had not given away all his prayer feathers, so he gave one to the old woman who had brought him to his grandparents. Delighted with the precious gift, she took her leave.

The boy's grandparents now began to set out food for their grandchild. They brought out many things and placed them before him. They were an old couple, but they did not appear to live in want. So the boy sat down and started eating. He was anxious to sample all the foods, so he took a little bit of everything. To him it seemed a little wasteful, but in this manner he ate his fill. When he was finished, his grandparents asked him about life in Oraibi. They also wanted to know if he had any siblings, so he mentioned his younger sister. They kept plying him with all sorts of questions. In this way the boy came to know his grandmother and grandfather.

While he stayed with his grandparents, he would go out every so often and tour the village. What he discovered was awesome. He found that the people there were living a good life and that they were always happy. They also treated one another with respect and kindness, and whenever two people met, they had something polite to say to each other.

Every time he went about and met someone, he was asked which village he was from. When people found out that he was from Oraibi, they would inquire about those they had known and how they were faring. Others who had known him as a baby greeted him with great joy.

The fields there, full of lushly growing crops, made him envious as he explored them. They provided an ample food supply, so everybody had plenty to eat. From the crops he moved on to a huge field of sunflowers. He noticed that children were playing in it and having a good time. They kept climbing up and down on the stalks. As he stood there observing them, one of the children approached the boy and asked him to join them in their play. He declined the offer, but the child was so persistent that he finally gave in. He went up to them and at first only watched. Then another child prompted him, "Now, you have a turn."

Deciding to take a chance, no matter what happened, he tried to climb the sunflower, but it would not support him. Once more he tried, but again it could not bear his weight and collapsed. The children kept laughing at his futile attempts, but eventually they said, "You'll never be able to climb on that. We were merely teasing you when we urged you on. Only we who live here can climb these sunflowers because we are only souls and weigh nothing. That's also the reason why the ladders at our village are made from sunflower stalks."

Early in the morning on the fourth day of his stay there, the boy's grandparents said to him, "All right, you must get up and start back. At your home they are getting restless because they cannot revive you. You'll have to go without breakfast." So the boy had no choice but to get out of bed and get dressed.

His heart was not set on returning at all. He had gotten used to the good life there. But since they only allotted him four days, he obeyed and started out without eating. He had barely gone beyond the village boundary when he encountered the Kwan man again. He said to the boy, "I've been waiting for you for quite some time. You are late. The sun is probably just rising at your home, and people there are anxiously awaiting your return." Unfortunately, this time I can't escort you back myself. You'll have to go alone for a while. But you'll meet the person who will get you to the top of the cliff. Make sure you don't get tempted by anything as you leave. I know you haven't eaten yet and must be hungry, but if you eat anything on your way home, you won't live long after your return. That's why your grandparents did not feed you before they sent you off this morning." The Kwan man then urged, "All right, then, go without delay," whereupon the boy dashed off as fast as he could run.

By the time he reached the village fields, his hunger got the best of him. At first he tried not to pay any attention to the crops, but he saw so many delicious and appealing things that he craved food. He had the best intentions, but when he came to the melon patch he couldn't hold back any longer. He broke one off the vine, opened it, and feasted on it.

Then he continued his journey home. Now that he had some food in his stomach, he felt stronger. He had not forgotten the route he had traveled, so when he reached the place that was filled with smoke, he managed to get to the other side without any difficulty, even though he could barely see. As he ran past the fiery pit oven, there were still evil people being hurled into the flames. However, he pressed on without stopping.

Before long he came to the kiva. This time he did not enter, but continued right along. Eventually, he came to a group of children who asked him where he was going. He told them that he was returning home, but they replied that that would be impossible. The boy paid no heed to their warnings and ran on. Finally, he reached the place of the rock pillars. Just as before, there were Hopis perched on top of them. Once more they shouted their pleas to him, but without listening to them, he passed on by. At long last he stood in front of the precipitous cliff.

The person who had helped him down was expecting him. "You've returned?" he greeted the boy. "I've been waiting for you for quite a while. At your home they have found your corpse. Your sister told them exactly what you instructed her to say, but they don't believe her. So let's not waste any more time, because there's another person waiting for you up above. Come on, hurry. Your sister is anxious for you to return."

Once again the man spread out his flying thing, which flew them up the cliff. As they arrived at the top, Sun was already waiting for the boy. "You've brought him back then?" he asked the One Horn man.

"Yes, so you two hurry on, for the boy's relatives are getting nervous," he replied to Sun.

"That's true, it's already late in the morning. I thought he'd get here sooner. That's why I came much earlier. So let's be on our way," he said, whereupon the boy climbed aboard Sun's flier.

They rose into the air and flew off toward Apoonivi. Looking down, the boy could still see the people traveling this route. Some were hauling burden baskets and appeared not to be making much headway. At Apoonivi they passed again through the house on top and then headed in the direction of Oraibi. Sun let the boy off at the northwestern edge of the village. Then he said, "All right, you have had your wish fulfilled. You wanted this, so we have helped you realize your dream. From here on you must go by yourself. It's late in the morning and you've not yet returned. Your sister is unable to control your relatives any longer. They are eager to pull away your shroud." With that, Sun departed, and the boy hurried on toward the village. His greatest desire had now been achieved, and he had experienced many wondrous things.

As soon as he arrived at his home, he rushed up to the upper story. As he entered he found his relatives assembled there, crying. His sister was still trying to impress upon them what he had told her. "He definitely told me to wait and not to uncover him. He said he would come back to life on his own. He was very firm when he gave me these instructions last night." She repeated this over and over, but by now they were almost beyond restraint. He had been lying there without moving for much too long.

The boy now quickly slipped under his cover and began to stir. One of his family noticed this and cried out, "Look, I think he moved a little bit!"

Sure enough, all eyes were upon him as he began to stir. "Maybe he's not quite dead yet," someone said.

With that, they removed his death shroud. No sooner had they lifted it than the boy started getting up. "Thank goodness, we have you back," his father cried. "We were just about to go and bury you. I guess you had left instructions with your sister, but her story sounded so incredible that we didn't believe it. I'm so glad you did not journey there for good." He embraced his son, and now everybody else came toward him, weeping tears of joy.

After they all recovered, they fixed the boy a meal that he devoured with great appetite. Even though he had eaten the melon, he woke up with a craving for food.

The boy now told his parents and relatives, in great detail, about his adventure. They listened attentively to the wondrous tale he had brought back. Then the other villagers learned of this, and they too came flocking to the boy's home. They were curious, of course, whether he had by chance met any of their loved ones. If that was the case and he had indeed conversed with any of them, he let the inquirer know, without having to lie, that the person was doing well. He also mentioned that people were all very happy in the land of the dead. There was no need, he said, to worry about a deceased person who had been good. On the other hand, if he found that the person in question was an evildoer, he made an excuse and pretended not to have seen him. Eventually, people stopped coming to the boy's home and life went on as before.

Then one day the poor boy really died. Of course, the Kwan man had warned him specifically not to eat any fruit from the field or he would not have long to live. This turned out to be true. Now his family really had to bury him. Four days later, when he regained consciousness, he found himself inside a small chamber. He was all curled up with his knees flexed to his chest in a fetal position. As he looked about, he saw a ladder sticking out of the top of the chamber. Climbing up it, he emerged from his grave and scanned the surrounding area. Nearby, there were other ladders in the same position. He departed and headed directly northwest. He knew where Oraibi was, but he passed it by and soon came to Apoonivi. As before, he entered the house on top and then made his exit on the northwest end. From there he continued on toward Awat'ovi. At some point along his journey he thought, "Perhaps I'm going back to my grandmother and grandfather, for this is the same route I traveled before. Also, I remember that a good person, who dies without sin, gets to that place without delay." He had not encountered anyone prior to reaching the Two Horn man, who then helped him make his descent down the steep cliff. It now appeared to him as if he was not moving very rapidly, but he did not let it worry him. After all, this time he was on his own, so his progress was naturally much slower. Not once did he stop to rest, because he wanted to arrive quickly at his destination.

After a while, it struck him that he was indeed not moving very fast. He tried to increase his pace, but to no avail, so he had no choice but to go at the speed permitted to him. Once in a while he was overtaken by someone advancing much more swiftly. He attempted to stop one of these people by shouting at him, but in vain. No one even paused for him. Perhaps they thought of him as being evil; after all, he was moving along at a slow pace. In turn, when he overtook another person and was asked for a favor, he simply ignored the plea and pressed on.

Meanwhile, the boy became tired. He thought of stopping and resting for a while, but then reconsidered. "Why waste my time resting here? Who knows, if I stop here, that stop may become permanent." These and other thoughts crossed his mind.

Eventually, he reached the large pond with the many burden baskets filled to the brim with pebbles. He was aware, of course, that as an unmarried man, he did not have to fear this place.

It had been quite some time since his arrival there. At least seven days had gone by since his death, perhaps more. On his journey with Sun this place had not seemed to be far from Oraibi. Knowing that he had still a long way to go, he hurried on. Soon he began overtaking people with burden baskets on their backs. Then there were the men with vulvas and the women with penises hanging around their necks. Now and then he also passed a mule. By the time he reached the huge cliff, twenty days had passed. As he was drawing nearer, he could clearly hear the turtle shell rattle of the Two Horn man and the clacking noise he was making. Apparently, he already knew of the boy's return and had been expecting him for some time. "You've come?" he asked.

"Yes, I had a hard time getting here. I didn't think it would take this long. I have no idea what has been slowing me down," the boy replied.

"Well, your own relatives can do that to you," the Two Horn man explained.

The boy didn't know what he meant, so he asked, "Really? Why is that?"

"Because you were still young when you died, they won't forget you so soon. It was their crying that slowed you down. Not until they stop lamenting your death will you reach your destination. But that's the way people are. When they lose a loved one and cry over his loss all the time, they hold him back after death," he explained.

"Is that right? What a shame. Couldn't I go back perhaps and make them aware of this?" he asked.

"Yes, we may let you do this, since you died pure of heart. Wait here for me while I go to find out what the others think of this idea." With that, the Two Horn man descended the cliff.

Before long he reappeared and said to the boy, "All right, this man here will be your guide and accompany you back. I must still help others down this cliff. That's why I can't go with you. Now, call your transportation," he ordered the guide.

This guide was about the same age as the boy. He had a small pouch hanging from his waist from which he took a whistle. He blew it and before long a large bird was winging toward them. When it got closer, he could see that it was an enormous eagle. "Come on," the guide said to the boy. "We'll use this bird. He'll take us back in a short time. With that they both climbed on the eagle and sat down, one behind the other. Next, the guide commanded the eagle, "Go!" and the bird took off, carrying both of them aloft.

The eagle was so strong that he easily carried the two passengers. While they were flying along, the guide instructed the boy what to do when they arrived at Oraibi. The boy listened carefully to his instructions. Soon they were nearing Apoonivi. The boy had focused all his attention on what the guide was telling him and didn't notice where they were traveling. According to the guide, they were back at Apoonivi already, but they were not moving as fast as on Sun's magic vehicle.

Flying directly over Apoonivi, they headed straight southeast and then landed at a field near Oraibi. The guide said to the boy, "This is as far as I'm taking you. Now you must go on your own. If you follow my instructions, you'll be back right away." With that, he flew off in a northwesterly direction. As the boy looked after him, the guide on his eagle quickly disappeared over the northwest side of Apoonivi.

As instructed, the boy did not enter the village, but instead went first to check on his father's field. His father would probably be there, trying to put the death of his son out of his mind by hoeing weeds.

At one point along the way, he looked at himself and saw that he had grown feathers and wings. He had actually been transformed into a snipe. His guide had informed him that he could not appear in front of his father in human form. So now he flew to his father's field. Sure enough, once he alighted at the edge of the field, he spotted his father working there. He appeared to be troubled, for he went about his work in complete silence. The boy knew that it was his nature to always sing as he did his chores.

When the boy realized this he felt sorry for him, so he approached his father and scurried back and forth right next to him. His father, however, whose mind was filled with other thoughts, paid no attention to the bird. When he saw this, the boy began to chirp and kept chirping until his father noticed. At first he only stared at the bird, but then he said "You are hopping around here with a happy heart? All right, go ahead. I won't bother you. You don't need to be afraid of me."

Now the boy ceased fluttering around and replied, "My father, it is I, your son." The man immediately ceased his work, but didn't say anything. "Father, it is I, Honanyestiwa. I came back to tell you something, so don't interrupt. Listen carefully to me."

With that, he explained how he had been slowed down on his way to the Maski because they were crying over his death. "So when you get home, inform the others not to weep anymore. The sooner I get to my destination, the happier I'll be. I know you all miss me, but somehow I'll come back and check in on you from time to time. We're all going there eventually. So never let thoughts about me trouble you, and live harmonious lives. If you do that, then one day we'll all meet again." That's all the boy said, and then he flew off.

That day, after the father told the others what he had learned, they did not weep as much as before. The boy then began to advance much faster. Thus, it was only a short time before he arrived at his destination. He sought out his grandmother and grandfather, who were overjoyed to have him back. They sympathized with the boy's parents and relatives but were glad because they were no longer alone. From that time on, the boy stayed there permanently.

At Oraibi, the boy's relatives put him out of their minds and carried on with their lives. Perhaps they still live there. This was how the boy learned about the road to the Maski and how he returned to it after his death.

And here the story ends.

10

The Snake Clan Boy and the Sorcerers

Aliksa'i. People were living somewhere near Shungopavi. The village chief there had one daughter who was extremely beautiful. So beautiful was she, in fact, that young men came from all over to woo her. As a rule, the wooers, who came late at night, had to hold their blankets in their teeth to keep their hands free while climbing up to the second story where the girl ground corn. She was usually so annoyed with the intruders that she scared them into climbing back down again.

One of the ways the wooers whiled away the time while hanging around the girl's house in the evening was by playing a shooting game with arrows. The players would insert bones upright in sand heaps that they constructed at each end of the playing field and then use these bones as targets. Generally, two groups competed against each other. For stakes, they put up all sorts of things, even their own shirts or anything else of value. The winners took all the stakes, of course.

Among the wooers was a boy who didn't know what to put up as stakes. "I have nothing to put up," he said. "Oh, come on," the others said, "you must have something. Go to your house and get something there."

So the boy ran home to his grandmother, and when he arrived there, he said, "Grandma, I want to play arrows with the others, but I don't have anything to put up for stakes. Is there something upstairs that I can take?"

"Is that so?" she replied. "I can't think of anything." But then she stepped into the back room, and when she came out again, she held a parrot feather ornament in her hand, the kind that is typically worn on top of a dancer's mask. It was all bunched up, but its feathers were long and it was in good condition. "Why don't you take this? It's the only thing I can think of."

The boy ran back with this beautiful ornament. A few of the players, who did not own such a ceremonial item, exclaimed, "You really brought something precious there!"

The game then got underway, but no one was able to beat the boy. No one managed to win the parrot head ornament. In fact, the boy started to beat the others, and actually won a nice shirt. He was elated about this, and garbed in his new shirt, decided to try his luck at wooing the girl. He announced to the others, "I'll climb up to her now, and maybe she'll sleep with me, though she doesn't seem to love anybody."

The others laughed at him. "You fool, she won't fall for a homely guy like you!"

"Well, I'll just look in on her through the vent hole in the wall, anyway. She's grinding corn in her room." He grabbed his blanket in his teeth and climbed to the upper story. Standing outside her room, he called, "Hey!"

Hearing him, the girl asked, "Who are you?"

"It's me," the boy replied.

"So, who are you?"

"As I said, it's me." That's all he would say.

"Well," the girl then asked, "where do you live?"

Not knowing exactly how to answer this, he finally said, "I live on the northeast side of the village, where the trash dump and toilet area is."

"Oh, you're from there?" the girl asked, surprised. Then she quickly added, "All right, come on in." Much to the boy's surprise, she took him to her bed and slept with him that night.

When he left her house the next morning, the other boys who lived in the village noticed that the girl had apparently allowed him in. This made them furious. Twice more the boy visited the girl at night, and then she agreed to marry him. When she was ready to go to the boy's house to begin the wedding ceremony, her mother filled a tray full of blue corn flour to take with her, and her father encouraged her to take good care of her in-laws.

When they were ready to go, the boy loaded the flour on his back and they set off to his home to start the wedding ceremony. When they reached the kiva where he lived, the boy called down through the hatchway, "Hey! How about some words of welcome! I have someone with me."

"Come on in," an old woman yelled back from within the kiva. The two entered and the old granny took the flour from the boy and stashed it away. She asked the girl to have a seat, and when the three of them had sat there for a good long time, the boy said, "Let's go to bed."

Right away, his old grandmother rolled out two sleeping skins, for herself and the girl. Puzzled, the boy demanded, "Where am I going to sleep?"

"You'll have to sleep by yourself for the time being. When a girl goes to her groom's house to start the wedding ceremony, she always sleeps alone."

The boy protested. "But I thought I would share her bed!" Nevertheless, he had no choice but to roll out his bedding away from the two of them and sleep alone.

The next day, the new daughter-in-law began to grind corn for the old woman. She did this until the fourth day, when the boy's and the girl's hair was to be washed as part of the ritual. Soon, relatives of the boy and his grandmother started arriving. All of them were members of the Snake clan. They all washed the bride's hair, and then the parents of the bride washed the hair of the groom.

The appropriate meal at a wedding, of course, is meat and hominy stew. Since the boy's grandmother had no meat, she wrapped up some qömi, a sweet cake made from finely ground corn flour, and asked him to take it to his uncle. "You're sure to find him," she said. "He lives near a little cliff."

When the boy arrived at the uncle's place, he found some ropes hanging there, and he saw a head sticking out of a hole. "Are you my uncle?" asked the boy.

"Yes, I suppose that's me," was the reply.

"Well, I brought home a girl that I intend to marry, and she would like to offer a meat and hominy stew to our guests. That's why I came here. Maybe you could stalk a deer for me. If you should bag one, I will carry it home to her."

"Is that so? Well, I suppose I could give it a try." With that, the uncle stashed the qömi the boy had brought him and started off. He slid out of the hole he was in and, taking a rope along, climbed to the top of the cliff. From there he hunted downhill until he came across a herd of deer. Selecting a buck, he captured it by winding the rope round and round its neck until there was no way it could get loose. He then killed the animal and hauled it back to the boy. "You've come!" exclaimed the boy. "Thanks!"

"Yes, and I managed to bring back a little something with me." Then the two of them cut open the deer's stomach and removed the entrails. The boy loaded the animal on his back and trekked toward home. Along the way, some sorcerers, also known as the Turds, happened to spot him. "Look," they exclaimed, "there's the little rascal lugging a deer on his back. Someone must have killed it for him. He couldn't have done that, he's such a weakling."

After the boy's return home, other uncles of his, who were all members of the Snake clan, skinned the animal in no time, then sliced up the meat and cooked it. The following morning they had the feast. Thus the boy and his granny were able to feed her daughter-in-law and guests.

Four days after that, the old woman said to the boy, "All right, now you can sleep with the bride. The time has come." So, that night the groom finally got to sleep with his bride, and the next morning it was the appointed time for the couple to return home to the bride's place to live. Lots of people were in the procession, and they came loaded down with gifts and foods such as corn, beans, and salt. After the gifts were placed in the bride's home, her parents expressed their gratitude.

Meanwhile, the boy went out to find the men who were to provide the wedding garments. The uncles whom he had in mind for these tasks lived on the southwest side of Pa'utsvi. They were all snakes—bullsnakes, rattlesnakes, whipsnakes, and others. As he got near where they lived, he saw a ladder standing up, which he used to enter their abode. "Well, you're about? You must have a reason for coming," they greeted him.

"Yes, indeed I do. I came to ask you to weave my wife's wedding robes."

"Is that right? Okay, you can rely on us. We'll make the dress," they replied. They had plenty of wool stored there, so they immediately set up the loom. They strung the yarn for the weft, and then it was the whipsnake's special job to slide back and forth, doing the actual weaving.

After he left there, the boy said to himself, "Now I must find another uncle who makes wedding boots." There was one who lived not far away in a canyon. When the boy arrived at the canyon, he found someone just sitting there, all stooped over. It was a sagebrush lizard, doing his usual push-ups. He paused when he saw the boy and said, "Have a seat, stranger."

"I came looking for you, uncle," the boy replied. "I understand that you are an expert moccasin maker. I have a bride at home, and since you have all sorts of deerskins, I thought that you could make the wedding boots for her."

"Is that so?" the lizard said, looking a bit reluctant. Now it just so happened that the boy had brought some rolled piki with him in a bundle, which he now offered to the uncle. The lizard was delighted and agreed, saying "All right, you can rely on me. The boots will be finished in a day or two. By then the two wedding robes should also be done."

Happy to have all this arranged, the boy returned home and told his grandmother about his successful mission. "Those are truly my uncles who live there. They promised to do everything in a day or two."

Two days later, the boy returned to where the uncles lived. As before, he took with him a bundle of rolled piki, which he distributed among them upon his arrival. They were overjoyed, and they gave him the wedding robes they had completed. Taking his leave, he continued on to his other uncle, the sagebrush lizard. He had finished the wedding boots as promised, and they were beautiful. Tying the robes and moccasins together in a bundle, he slung it over his shoulder and headed for home.

The Turds, meanwhile, were not happy at all about the boy and his beautiful new wife and began to plot how to take her away. "Let's all meet at the kiva tonight," one of them said, "and discuss a plan I have that's bound to succeed. One of us should tell the village crier to announce a rabbit hunt, with the following little additional provision. There'll be a race after the hunt. All those with lots of rabbits will compete, carrying the rabbits on their backs, and whoever arrives back at the village first will be entitled to the young man's wife."

One of the younger Turds volunteered and sought out the crier, who made the announcement as specified, also mentioning the area where it would take place, an area to the south of Pa'utsvi.

The poor young groom was desperate; he didn't even own a rabbit stick. When he told his grandmother, she advised him to again seek out another one of his uncles. "He is a hawk," she advised him, "and he lives on top of a little butte. He has clubs and hunting sticks in great supply. He's also an excellent hunter."

After breakfast, the boy set out, and sure enough he eventually came upon a hawk perched high up on a butte. "Are you my uncle?" he inquired. "It's me. If you are, please come down."

The hawk flew down from the butte, and the young man gave him the qömi he had brought as a gift. "Thanks," the hawk cried, "this is a delicacy I really enjoy!"

The boy now explained the reason for his coming. "Those Turds are going to test me during a rabbit hunt. Whoever bags the most rabbits and wins a race carrying them on his back can take my wife away from me. I don't even own a rabbit stick, so I came to borrow one from you. I hear you have a lot of them."

"Of course I do," answered the hawk. "I have plenty of them." The two then entered the hawk's abode. The hawk picked up a bunch of rabbit sticks and held them out to the boy, saying "Here, choose one." The boy inspected them, noticing that some of them were still new, and that a couple of them had been wrapped with sinew because they were cracked. "Now be sure and select the best one!" prompted the hawk. The boy studied the weapons some more.

Finally he said, "I'll take this one," picking one with sinew wrapping.

"You made the right choice!" the hawk declared, then added, "When they begin to test your hunting skills, don't use this one at first. Use another one. Take this one out after you reach the turnaround point in the hunt. With it, you can kill as many rabbits as you want. This is my stick, and it pursues cottontails and jackrabbits all by itself. You'll kill so many that you will probably have to hand some of them to your father and your wife's father when you get too loaded down. They can carry them on home ahead of you. You can also throw some out to the other people, even the Turds."

The young groom did exactly as told. It was incredible! All he had to do was throw the stick in the general direction of a rabbit, and it would fly straight at it and strike down, no matter how the rabbit zigged. He killed so many he tied them up in lots of four.

When the hunt was done, the race began. Once again, the hawk was there to help. He swooped down, landed on top of the boy's head, and in no time the two flew so far ahead that the rest of the contestants had no chance of catching up with them. As soon as the two reached the foot of the mesa, the hawk let go and the boy dashed up the staircase to the top. There stood his wife, beautifully dressed. Her hair was newly braided, and she wore a black manta and her beautiful new wedding boots. Over her shoulders she wore an atö'ö, a white cape with red borders. "Thanks for coming up so quickly," she greeted her husband, "you've won me."

That evening the Turds again assembled in their kiva. "What a shame!" they cried. "None of us killed as many rabbits as he did, and we lost the race. Let's meet again late tonight and plan some more." So, after supper they met in their kiva, as it was the custom for men to do long ago. "All right, maybe one of you men has an idea of how we can test him next," said their leader.

"I know," one of them suggested, "we can compete in a kicking stone race. As you all know, in this kind of race, the participants flick the kicking stone along a course with their feet. From wherever the stone rests at the end of the race, all the participants will have to run up the mesa to the boy's wife. Whoever reaches her first wins her."

As before, the village crier announced the event, then went around from kiva to kiva, instructing the men to paint their bodies with mud wash. "All right," he said, "daub yourselves with mud and then go out to the meeting place." Soon the men were all filing out of the kivas, teasing each other for being tardy.

Once more the boy decided to seek help from one of his uncles, this time the sand rattler. This snake can quickly burrow into the ground or disappear in the sand. He is also very strong. The boy took his time heading out to the assembly point for the race. "What's keeping him?" the others complained. "Well, he's probably late because he's a weakling," one of them said.

Finally the boy was in sight. Unknown to the others, the sand rattler had burrowed into the sand and hid himself under the boy's toes with only his long nose sticking out as they moved along together. "There he is," someone yelled, "and he is bringing his own kicking stone." As the racers lined up at the start, the others could see the boy bending down, apparently to pray to his kicking stone. "Look," they laughed and taunted him, "he's praying to his kicking stone!"

Then the race was on, and they all dashed off, flicking their stones forward with their feet. The boy didn't do too well at first, and all the others were soon far ahead. "Oh dear," he cried.

But then the sand rattler peeked out from under the boy's toes, slid under the stone nodule with his nose and flung it with all his might. It landed far ahead of them, and in this manner the boy and his uncle the snake soon caught up with the rest. "Oh dear, here he comes," they yelled. "Come on, give it your all!" But the boy's stone was flicked with such force by the snake as they moved along together that the boy soon overtook all the others and arrived at the finish line first.

"All right," the sand rattler said quickly, "this is as far as I can help you! I'll come out now." And with that, the snake slid out from under the boy's toes and out of the way, saying as he went, "All right now, exert yourself! They're all behind us."

"Thanks, my uncle," the boy said, "I'll race on to the top now by myself." He raced off, looking over his shoulders, and saw that he had left all the others far behind. When he reached the stairs to the mesa top, he dashed up, taking two or three steps at a time. At the top stood his wife again, still beautifully dressed. "Thanks, you're up first!" she exclaimed. "You won me." With that, the young groom led his wife home.

The rest of the racers were mortified. They had failed miserably. "What will we do now? We had no chance against him!" they lamented.

"Just gather at the kiva again tonight," said the chief of the sorcerers. "We'll hatch another plan. Let's try one more time at least."

When it was dark, the sorcerers met in their kiva again. "Darn it! We may not be able to take his wife away after all," the chief groaned, "unless one of you boys has a good idea."

One of them replied, "I do. Let's require him to go to the southwest side of Pa'utsvi and bring us the giant rattlesnake that lives there. If he manages to do that, which I doubt, *then* he can keep his wife."

"That's a great idea!" the other sorcerers chimed in together. With that, they all set to making pahos. It was their intention to put a charm on the snake, but the pahos they made were not pretty at all.

The next morning, when they called the boy to their kiva, they gave him the prayer sticks. "All right, take these pahos to the giant rattlesnake. We made them especially for him. So go with a happy heart."

The boy did as bidden and headed toward Pa'utsvi. There, in the southwest, stands a butte called Höövatuyqa. That's where the giant rattlesnake lives. As the boy arrived there, the snake rose up in all his might, shaking his rattle menacingly. He was enormous!

"Calm down," the boy said. "You are my uncle. I came just to see you. Don't do me any harm."

The giant rattler then settled down, and the boy handed him the pahos. The snake just stared at them. "These are sloppily made," he muttered, casting them aside disdainfully.

"Well, those are the ones I was asked to bring to you."

The rattler was furious. "Come on, let's go to my kiva in the southwest. That's where all the snakes live."

Inside the rattler's kiva, there was a shelf that held large vessels filled with venom. Some of them were huge. The giant rattler took one of them and drank all the contents, then took another and drank it also. When he was done he said, "So it was their fervent wish to have me, was it!"

The boy then picked up his uncle the giant rattler and, slinging him around his neck, headed for home. He soon reached the stairs to the mesa top and climbed up.

It was late evening by the time he arrived, so the boy made straight for the kiva of the Turds, the giant rattler draped over him. The sorcerers had already gathered. The boy stood at the hatch opening of the kiva and shouted, "Hey! Here's the snake you wanted so badly!"

No one replied.

"Hey!" he yelled again. "Isn't anybody in there? I brought you the giant rattlesnake you asked for. Come up and relieve me of my load."

Again there was no reply, just silence.

Now the giant rattlesnake said, "Just put me down and go on home to your wife. Then tell all your relatives who are members of the Snake clan to go over to your grandmother's place at the dump. When you've all gathered there, I'll meet you, and we'll go and seal this kiva up tightly. I'll do the rest."

The boy did as his uncle asked him—went home to his wife and headed over to his grandmother's place with her. When all of his Snake clan relatives had gathered there, the place was really crowded. When the giant rattlesnake met them there, they all went to the sorcerers' kiva and tightly closed the hatch opening in the roof. When they were sure that none of the sorcerers could escape, the rattlesnake got up the nerve to do his part.

Sliding up to the hatch, he lifted the cover a bit and sprayed down all the venom he had drunk. The stench from the poison was overwhelming. After a while, he looked inside and saw them all, prostrate on the floor. He had killed them all.

The giant rattler now moved from kiva to kiva in the village, spraying his venom inside, and all the men in them perished too. In this way, he killed all the men, for they had participated in the schemes of the sorcerers.

After this, life went on again, but the boy and his relatives really were not happy with their lives there, and felt they could no longer stay. So, one morning they packed up their belongings and set out for Oraibi.

When they arrived there, however, they did not enter the village, but settled down at a place southwest of it. From there they approached the village chief and asked him for permission to come live in Oraibi. The chief refused. Four times the boy and his relatives asked to join the Oraibis. "We are members of the Snake clan," he said. "We're bringing with us the Snake religion and many other things that could be of benefit to you and your people. In summer, when watermelons and muskmelons ripen, we stage our ceremony. With this ceremony we can aid you ritually."

The chief just sat there, deep in thought. Finally, he said, "All right. I'm glad you mentioned your ceremony. You can indeed help us in that way. So tell all your people, and tomorrow you can move up here to the top of the mesa. You can then select your living area and begin building your homes wherever you like."

Happy with this favorable response, the boy returned to the plains below, conveying the chief's decision to the people. So, the next morning, they gathered their belongings and made the ascent to Oraibi.

In this way, the Snake clan members became part of the Oraibi people. They had come with their Snake ceremony, which they now introduced to the residents there. Every summer, when the melons ripened, they performed their Snake dance. In this way they helped the Oraibi village chief.

And here the story ends.

11

The Man Who Was Married to a Witch

Aliksa'i. People were living in Oraibi, and all across Hopiland there were people living in other villages.

At Oraibi a young couple had made its home. The man's wife was well versed in witchcraft, completely without the knowledge of her husband. It never even occurred to him that she might be a witch.

One night when the two of them went to bed, the woman made plans to go out, so she only pretended to be asleep. Her husband was not aware of her intentions, so he was soon sound asleep. This was the moment his wife had been waiting for, so she quickly got up and sneaked out of the house, past her sleeping husband. He never heard a thing.

Once she saw that she could get away like this, she began going out at night on a regular basis. One night, however, the man woke up for some reason, and as he glanced over to his wife's place, found it empty. He did not give it much thought, however, because he figured that she had just gotten up to go relieve herself. He went back to sleep right away and never noticed that his wife did not return until just before daybreak. They woke up together as usual.

A few days later, the woman again decided to leave in the middle of the night. Her husband woke up and did not see his wife at his side, but soon he was sleeping soundly again. However, when he woke up a second time and still found her absent, he grew a little concerned. Nevertheless, he didn't think too much about it and quickly went back to sleep. They both woke up together in the morning, as usual, and so he did not ask her why she was gone so long during the night.

As his wife's absence began to occur more often, the husband finally began to worry. "I wonder where she's going at night and why she returns just before daybreak?" he asked himself. So, he made up his mind that he would follow her the next time and find out.

That night the man pretended to be asleep. As usual, his wife watched him carefully, and when he seemed to be in a deep sleep, she got up from her bed. He heard her rummaging around in the house, and then he saw her preparing herself with great care, fixing her hair nicely and putting on a beautiful dress. She then quietly slipped out of the house.

This time, he was determined to follow her. Jumping out of bed, he quickly put on his clothes and ran after her. His wife had started out in a northeasterly direction, trying to hide herself by following the shadow of the moon.

He took his time following her. She had not yet come to the northeast edge of Oraibi when she met a man, one the husband had never seen before. His wife stopped and spoke to the man briefly, but he couldn't make out her words. Soon, his wife and the strange man continued on, the man leading the way, and he trailed them, just far enough away to avoid being detected.

When his wife and the man reached the mesa edge, they turned toward the northwest, skirted the edge, and changed direction again to the northeast. Finally, the two appeared to have arrived at their destination, a kiva with firelight shining from the hatchway. Without hesitation, the two climbed up on the roof and called down.

Immediately, voices invited them in. "Come on in. Enter right there," they said.

The husband, who had observed all this from behind a bush, now crawled up on the kiva roof himself. Lifting the hatch cover slightly, he managed to peek in. Much to his surprise, he found the kiva packed with people. Some of them he knew, and he was sure they were all sorcerers and witches.

He could clearly hear what was being said. An old man, who was seated next to the fire pit, stood up and said to the gathered crowd, "All right, let's get started. It's late already." With that he walked to the northwest end of the kiva and disappeared behind the door to an inner room. A few seconds later, he returned with a hoop in his hands. He placed this hoop in the middle of the floor and said, "Hurry now, because daylight comes quickly at this time of the year."

The whole group now gathered around the hoop. Each person in turn grabbed the hoop, sent it rolling toward the northwest side of the kiva, and then ran after it, somersaulting over it as it rolled. Each person was transformed into an animal upon landing on the other side of the hoop: coyotes, ravens, owls, wolves.

It was now the wife's turn. As she stepped up to grab the hoop, the din down below in the kiva was incredible! The noise was deafening, with all the different animals giving their cries at once. As the man's wife landed on the other side of the rolling hoop, she was unchanged, still in human form. Something had gone wrong!

The chief of the sorcerers got up and said, "Something is wrong. I'll bet someone is spying on us, that's what happened. Or maybe you made a mistake. Try again."

The woman made another attempt, but as before, nothing happened. The chief was sure now, "Somebody must be watching, that's why it didn't work. I want some of you strong ones to go out and look around. Maybe you'll find someone."

A few men who had changed into flies went out and flew around the kiva, but found no one. The husband had heard the chief order the search and quickly ran away and hid in the dark. When the flies reported to the chief, he ordered, "Okay, then, someone else have a go at it. Maybe I was mistaken."

One of the sorcerers now somersaulted over the hoop, but also landed on the other side, still in human form. Once again the chief complained, "Darn it! Someone must be looking in on us. Go out again and search!"

The flies did as they were told and buzzed out the hatch. They flew so quickly that this time the husband had no time to hide. To try to avoid being detected, he tightly rolled himself up into a ball in his blanket. This time the flies looked more carefully, however, and soon spotted the intruder.

"He's trying to hide right here," said one fly to the other, "come look."

"Why are you spying on us?" one of the flies asked, as they all buzzed around the man's head. "When an outsider is watching, we can't change our shapes. Since you have found us here, you must now go into the kiva with us." With that, they grabbed the man and led him into the kiva.

The flies took the man over to the chief sorcerer, who asked him, "So you're the culprit! If someone watches us, we can't practice our knowledge. And since you witnessed what we do here, you have no choice but to become one of us. You too will have to learn witchcraft now."

When the man's wife saw him she was very angry but didn't say anything in front of all the other sorcerers gathered there. She felt no pity for him that he would now have to be initiated into the art of witchcraft.

The chief now said to the husband, "You're one of us now, and from now on you must practice witchcraft like the rest of us. So, to start with, you must return to the village and do what I tell you. We have knowledge of many things, and know that your parents are sound asleep, and that you have three younger sisters, one of whom you dearly love. Here is what you must do. You must go to that sister and while she sleeps, take out her heart. Use this for that purpose."

The chief then handed him something that looked like a spindle, except that it was quite a bit shorter and lacked the wheel that is typically part of a regular spindle. After handing him this instrument, the chief explained how it worked. "Your sister is sleeping on her back. Step up to her and place one end of this thing on her chest and make it spin. If you do it right, it will instantly extract her heart. Bring it back here to me."

The poor man didn't know what to do, but he had to carry out the chief's instructions or forfeit his own life. So he left with the spindle thing and returned to Oraibi, heading straight to his parent's house. He entered the house without arousing anyone, as they were truly all sound asleep. There was the sister that he loved so much, lying on her back, with the other two sisters nearby. He looked at them in anguish, wondering how he could possibly remove the heart of any of them. Finally, he just couldn't take it any longer and burst into tears. He simply couldn't do it! So with tears streaming down his cheeks, he left the house and headed out to the southeast edge of the village, and paced back and forth there, racking his brain what to do.

Then it dawned on him what he might do. It so happened that many people in Oraibi kept turkeys as pets, and some belonging to his parents were in pens right near him. As he approached the pen, the turkeys made no noise, for they knew him well. After looking them over, he selected a large tom that did not resist him when he grabbed it.

He thought, "I'll use this one. He is also dear to me, but they won't know the difference when I bring his heart." With that, he placed the spindle thing on the turkey's breast and made it spin. Instantly, the tom's heart came out, and the poor bird fell dead.

With the turkey heart in his hand, the man returned to the sorcerers' kiva. They were expecting him, so he went in without any announcement. "You've come already? You're back quickly. Thanks." He then turned to the others and said, "All right, do it again. I'm sure it will work this time. Once more they all somersaulted over the hoop, one after the other, and were instantly transformed into various animals.

When they had all finished, the chief turned to the man and said, "Okay, now it's your turn. When you're done, we can proceed with our business. I don't know, though, who you want as your father, your animal helper?" The man didn't know either, but he felt that he had no choice but to carry out the chief's orders. He flung himself over the rolling hoop, and the instant he landed on his feet, he found himself transformed into a turkey!

Now, all the sorcerers and witches filed out, for the chief had told them all to meet at another location. The man was also told to go along. As he came out of the kiva, his wife was waiting and she was furious with him! "Why did you choose a turkey for a father? That's a weak creature." As they went along, he was quite slow, and his wife kept herding him along and scolding him all along the way. Most of the others had animal helpers that were strong and brave and quickly reached their destination.

Abusing her husband for his slow pace, the wife continued to herd him along. Apparently all the sorcerers and witches were headed for Palangw, the place where all those versed in witchcraft gather. Palangw lies somewhere far in the northeast, in the vicinity of a large canyon.

By the time the wife and her husband finally arrived, the others were already lined up, waiting their turn to enter. There was such a multitude of people gathered there, it was simply unbelievable. The man could hardly believe his eyes, it was such a fantastic sight.

Apparently, the sorcerers were going to stage a dance. When all of them were assembled in a line, they began to dance, all of them transformed into their particular animal shapes. They had a song to go with the dance:

> There's no light
> For my blue-green face paint,
> There's no light.
> Shine firelight on it.

That's all they chanted. The song was completely monotonous and never changed, and they gestured with the bones and skulls of babies in their hands. They had evidently murdered their own nephews and nieces and were using their bones to dance with. They had murdered them to extend their own lives, for this is what happens when a sorcerer kills a relative.

Their monotonous song referred to themselves because their face paint was not usually visible. That's why the song said, "Shine firelight on it." Whenever the dancers reached this point in their chant, the one tending the fire stoked it so vigorously that all their faces lit up and became clearly visible and repulsive. They were all dancing as skeletons! All night long they danced in this guise.

When it was finally nearing daylight, someone said, "It's getting light, let's go home." They all then stopped dancing and filed back out of the kiva. The husband had fallen asleep some time before and was unaware that they were leaving, and when those departing noticed that, the sorcerer chief told them, "Don't wake him up yet. Just let him sleep here." His wife had no desire to wake him either, so she and all the other sorcerers and witches left, returning to their various home villages.

When the man woke the next morning, he was no longer in the kiva at Palangw, but lying on a small ledge in the canyon near there. The ledge was so narrow that it was impossible for him to even turn around. It was also far from the ground. If he moved a little too much, he could fall and break his neck. So he held very still, and pressed himself tightly against the cliff wall. "How on earth can I get down from here?" he wondered, as he cringed there. "Nobody ever comes by here."

He lay in this cramped position until evening and still no one had come by so that he could cry for help. Finally it was dark, but he dared not try to sleep for fear of falling. All night long he lay perched on the ledge, trying to keep his eyes open, and by noon the next day he was exhausted from lack of sleep. Every so often his eyes fell shut, but he quickly jerked awake again. Finally, however, sleep overcame him, and he fell asleep without even realizing it.

When he woke up again, the sun was just rising, and he was all confused, for he remembered being awake at noon. As he thought about it, it became clear to him that he had slept all the rest of the previous day and the following night. So deep had he slept that he had never stirred once. When he thought what could have happened while he was asleep, he became frightened. This quickly passed, however, and he realized that he was extremely hungry and thirsty. Inspecting the ledge once more, he saw no hope of getting down the sheer cliff.

He strained to hear if anyone was nearby who could help him, but heard nothing. In desperation he yelled at the top of his voice, "If anyone is around here, please come and help me down!" Nothing. Only silence.

Sometime later, he was just lying there in despair when one of his ears began to itch. Though he was in danger of falling if he tried, he knew he had to scratch it somehow. He finally managed to reach his ear and was about to scratch it, when a voice said, "Careful, young man! Don't scratch your ear; you might hurt me!" He stopped, and the voice continued, "It's your grandmother here. Palöngawhoya, Little Echo, made your voice reach all the way to me, so I learned about your plight and came here to help you. The sorcerers, including your wife, did this to you, when they left you without waking you up. Your wife knows that you are hungry and thirsty, so she will come and tempt you. She will come in a disguise, so don't be fooled. I will not abandon you, so just wait and lie as still as you can. As soon as we have dealt with that evil witch, your wife, we'll get you down from here."

The man was greatly relieved, for he had recognized Old Spider Woman right away. He knew it must be her, because he knew that she has one grandson named Palöngawhoya.

Before long, he heard someone approaching from above and just a little later, a woman appeared, chatting incessantly. "Oh you poor thing," she said. "I came because I felt sorry for you." She then began to sing:

> Aa'aahaahaa ii'iihiihii
> Aa'aahaahaa ii'iihiihii
> Haaya, I'm known as Polimana
> Haaya, you retraced my tracks
> Hee'ee'ew, hee'ew, hee'ew, hee'ew.

Singing this song, she now started dancing. Each time she finished a stanza, she shouted "Hahay'i!" It sounded like the female kachina Hahay'iwuuti had come to him, but it was actually the man's wife who had transformed herself into Hahay'iwuuti and named herself in the song, for her Hopi name was Polimana. He had followed her tracks to the kiva, so that's what she was referring to in the song.

When she quit dancing, she exclaimed, holding out her gourd canteen, "You poor thing! You must be thirsty, so I brought you some water. Open your mouth so I may quench your thirst."

Old Spider Woman, however, had warned the man not to give in to her temptations. This was actually just one of his wife's attempts to make him fall from the ledge, so when she poured out the water, he kept his lips tightly pursed. As a result, the water splashed on his face and ran down the face of the cliff. Hahay'iwuuti was furious at his refusal to drink, but didn't show it. Instead, she said sweetly, "You poor thing. You must be starving, so I brought you some food. I'll throw it down to you. Just reach out for it, and when you catch it, you can satisfy your hunger."

This time she threw somiviki down to him, but Old Spider Woman had warned him to resist grabbing for it, or he would surely fall off the ledge. As hungry as he was, he stayed still. When Hahay'iwuuti saw this, she became even more angry, but still concealed it. "Wait here for us," she said kindly. "I'll get help and then we'll get you down." Then she was gone.

Old Spider Woman then told him, "When they return, they will try to trick you with other gifts to make you fall. Don't reach for these either, or you are lost. Here, I have something for you. Chew it now ahead of time to be prepared for whatever comes. If you spray it on your attackers, I'm bound to know." The man began to chew the medicine.

In just a few minutes, he could hear singing in the distance, accompanied with repeated calls. These calls were being made by kachinas that Hahay'iwuuti had brought back with her. They had brought with them all manner of desirable gifts, which they proceeded to drop down past the ledge, yelling to the man to grab them. But the man, true to Old Spider Woman's instructions, stayed where he was.

As he looked up, he saw a whole line of different kachinas, the ones that typically accompany the staging of the Paalölöqangw or Water Serpent dance. He had seen this ceremony on many occasions and was familiar with all the personages involved.

When the man showed no interest in her gifts, Hahay'iwuuti ordered her helpers to haul the man up to the top of the cliff. "We are going to let something down to you. Grab on to it, so we can bring you up."

She didn't say what they were lowering, however. He thought it might be a rope or something like that. It took all the kachinas to hold it as they slowly lowered it toward him. As it came closer, it appeared to indeed be similar to a rope, but it was huge. Then he recognized it for what it was. It was the Water Serpent itself. What a terrifying creature it was! Repulsive looking, it had a gigantic head and was baring its teeth in a hideous grimace. Its eyes were large and bulging, and a large horn stood on the crown of its head.

The beast came closer and closer and was about to reach him, when Old Spider Woman urged the man to spray his medicine on it. The creature was now hanging right above him, making a thunderous roar. He took a deep breath and, with all his might, sprayed the medicine from his mouth. The instant he did, the giant serpent became slack and heavy and crashed down the precipice. At the same time, this pulled all the kachinas over the cliff and they too fell down, slamming into the ground at the foot of the cliff. The Water Serpent itself had been filled with them, and a wailing and groaning now rose up, for the kachinas had only been evil sorcerers in disguise. When the man realized this, he felt no pity at having destroyed them.

Much to his amazement, several of the sorcerers and witches had survived the fall somehow, though they were severely injured. As they hit the ground, their legs, arms, or heads had been severed. These survivors now groped around for their missing body parts, and since they were anxious to escape, just quickly attached whatever body parts they found.

As a result, some of the men had women's heads, and women

were walking on men's legs. Some of them had legs of uneven length and had to limp along. It was terrible to see them like that, but the man only felt like gloating. "Ouch! Oh!" these sorcerers groaned as they fled. This was the disaster the man had brought down on the sorcerers. He himself, however, was unhurt and still on the ledge.

Finally, it became silent down below. The man was still lying there when he heard a voice. "Who's coming to tempt me this time?" he thought. "What will I do?" Whoever the voice belonged to was climbing up the cliff toward him. The man held his breath, waiting. Closer the noise came, and then, a tree squirrel appeared in front of him. Old Spider Woman greeted the squirrel, "Thanks for coming. Let's get this man down now."

"Wait a minute," the squirrel replied. "This poor fellow must be thirsty and hungry. Let me get him some water and food." The squirrel scampered down the cliff and back up in no time, carrying a pinyon nut and the shell of the nut filled with water. The man did not believe he could quench his thirst from such a tiny container, but he took it and drank it anyway. He also ate the nut, tiny though it was, and was surprised to find that both his hunger and thirst were satisfied.

"Now we can help you down," the squirrel declared. "I'm sure that those evildoers won't bother you anymore. Those who got away are now grotesque creatures, fit only to laugh at."

With that, the squirrel was on his way down the cliff again. When he reappeared, he was pulling a pine tree by its tip, until it had stretched all the way to the ledge. The strength of this small creature was astounding! "All right," he said to the man. "Check this. Shake it with your leg and see if it is strong enough to climb on."

Carefully the man rocked it with his foot. Realizing that it would not yet support the man, the squirrel pulled the tip of the pine tree up higher, and it became taller and stronger. The man tested it again. "I think that will do now," the squirrel concluded.

The pine tree's branches were now stretching out right to the man on the ledge. The squirrel hopped onto one of the branches and instructed the man how to climb down. At first the man was afraid, but as he reached lower and stronger branches, he became more confident and climbed all the way down. In this way, Old Spider Woman and the squirrel rescued the man from the ledge.

At the bottom of the cliff, the bodies of sorcerers and witches were strewn all about. Old Spider Woman now advised the man, "All right, you'll have to go on home by yourself. You should be able to get there without any problems." With those final words, she and the squirrel took their leave.

The man set out for Oraibi and reached the village without further incident. When he finally arrived, he went straight to his house. When he entered, he found his wife waiting there for him! Happily she exclaimed, as if nothing had ever happened, "Where have you been? You were gone so long, I was terribly worried!" The man was seething inside, for his wife knew full well what an ordeal he had just been through. He kept quiet though; not a single word did he speak.

He was so upset to find his wife still alive that he quickly went out and ran over to his parent's place. Overjoyed to see his sisters unharmed, he greeted them happily, and told them in great detail all that he had experienced, including what his own wife had done.

They sympathized with him, but were elated that he had been rescued from the clutches of the sorcerers and witches by Old Spider Woman and the squirrel. The man never returned to his own home after that day, but remained there with his family.

Not long after that, the man's wife died. One of her relatives found her dead when he called on her. She had finally met the same fate as the other sorcerers. The man who had been married to a witch is probably still living there at Oraibi.

And here the story ends.

12

How Coyote Came to Visit Maski, Home of the Dead

Aliksa'i. People were living at Oraibi and other villages all across the land. Beyond Hopiland, there lived other Indian tribes, such as the Zunis, Navajos, Apaches, and the Northeastern Pueblos along the Rio Grande River.

Humans, no matter where they are, don't live forever, as we all know, and pass away for various reasons. A person may not recover from an illness and die for that reason. Some Indians also wage war and kill each other. Occasionally, someone who hates another person will use black magic against him if he is versed in this art so that the person dies without any apparent signs of ill health. For all these reasons people don't live forever. Only rarely does a person die of old age.

Not far from Oraibi, at a place called Ismo'wala, Coyote had made his home. He was married, and he and his wife had several children. The children were always hungry, so the coyote couple was constantly on the lookout for food.

Whenever they could, they went out hunting. One day, toward evening, they were roaming the area looking for prey. Since they had not seen any game near their home for quite a while, they had decided to range a bit farther afield. As they reached Qöma'wa, they lucked out and flushed a rabbit. Since it was near twilight and visibility was getting poor, the two could barely make out the terrain, but they pursued the rabbit vigorously. The rabbit zigged and zagged in all directions, suddenly disappearing and then popping up in front of them again. Despite the growing darkness, the couple kept up their pursuit, and the coyote man, determined to capture the rabbit, made an all-out effort.

He was close on the rabbit's heels when they neared the edge of the mesa. The rabbit, who had his burrow near there, was familiar with the lay of the land and, making a sudden sideways leap, hid under a bush. Coyote, right behind him at full speed and intent on catching the rabbit, had not noticed how close they were to the edge. Unable to control his momentum at the last moment, he shot out over the rim of the mesa into thin air.

Coyote's wife had seen the edge of the mesa coming up, and was about to warn her husband when he disappeared out of her sight. It so happened that there was a steep cliff at this point, and Coyote fell with great force, struck the ground below, and was killed instantly.

When Coyote's wife reached the edge, she looked down and saw her husband flattened out down below. She thought perhaps he was just unconscious. She finally found a way down the steep cliff, and when she arrived at her husband's side, she tried to revive him and make him sit up. It was no use, however, for he was dead. Full of grief, she had to trot back to her children without bringing anything to eat.

The little coyotes were inconsolable at the loss of their father. Although they had some leftovers to eat, they were so sad that they didn't feel like eating, and lay around listlessly for the rest of the day. When bedtime came they were still too distraught to go to sleep, and decided to go out the next morning and bury their father. When they finally dozed off, it was nearly daybreak.

While it was still dark and before the children arrived where

Coyote lay, he rose to his feet. Looking around in bewilderment, still searching for the rabbit, he suddenly remembered his accident. He looked around for his wife, but she was nowhere in sight. The moon was shining brightly, and as he glanced back at the place where he had just been, he saw his body lying there. This confused him, for clearly he was standing right there on his own four feet. How could he be seeing himself lying there?

Stepping up to his body, he checked it out. No question about it, the poor thing was as dead as a doornail.

He was completely at a loss. Without giving it any more thought, he started out in a southwesterly direction and soon realized that he was headed directly toward Apoonivi. Strangely, though, as he trotted along he felt weightless, as if something was pushing him along. Although he had no particular desire to climb up to Apoonivi, when he arrived there, he felt something compelling him to climb up to the top of the promontory.

On top of Apoonivi stood a little houselike structure that he passed through before descending the stairway on the other side. When he reached the plain below, he trotted on in a southwesterly direction.

After a while, he encountered a Hopi woman. The woman, not particularly unnerved by seeing a coyote there, nevertheless exclaimed, "How odd. What brings you here?"

"I don't know," said Coyote, "for some reason or other I'm just moving along here." Then he shared with her the events leading up to his death.

"Is that so? Oh my," the woman said, and continued on her way. Coyote followed her and soon overtook her, and she shuffled along behind him.

Before long, he came upon a man, who was astonished by Coyote's presence. "What are you doing here?" he asked, when he caught sight of the animal.

Once again, Coyote explained how he had met his end. The man got amused in his heart and couldn't help laughing. "Old Man Coyote is up to something," he thought, shaking with laughter. "You're not human, yet you travel along here!"

"Why are you laughing at me?" Coyote asked.

"Because of your big necklace. Hasn't your neck grown tired?"

Coyote now looked down at himself and, much to his astonishment, saw a chain of vulvas hanging around his neck. That's what had amused the man so much. When Coyote asked the man about the reason for such a necklace, he pointed out that this was the punishment for men who had lain with several women and had been married to more than one wife. That's why he was burdened down with the vulvas of all his wives.

Not anxious to hear any more, Coyote continued on. He really didn't fully understand the meaning of his necklace. Sure he had died, but why did he have to wear this odd thing?

After a while Coyote came upon a woman who was slowly moving in the same direction. When Coyote caught up with her, she stopped him and cried, "Please, have pity on me and give me something to drink."

"I have no water on me," Coyote said, in truth, "so I cannot help you."

"Well, at least spit into my mouth," the woman persisted. "Maybe that will lessen my thirst."

Without knowing exactly why, Coyote refused and traveled on. Soon he met a man with a burden basket on his back. The man was clearly straining under the load, and when Coyote peeked into the basket, he saw that it was filled with pebbles. So heavy was the burden that the tumpline had made a deep cut in the man's forehead. He also encountered women hauling similar baskets. These basket carriers were people who, as boys or girls, had gotten together with married men or women. They were being punished now by these enormous loads.

Next Coyote spied people who were walking very slowly, only one step per year. These were sorcerers and witches. Some of the men carried large necklaces of vulvas, and then there were women who had penises strung around their necks. These women had had more than one husband when they were alive. In addition, he saw many mules among the travelers. These were those who had married Zunis. These are some of the strange sights Coyote saw as he moved along.

He still had no idea what his destination was, however. He traveled on and eventually came to a fork in the road, with one path leading off to the right, and one to the left. He stopped in his tracks, wondering, "Which is the right trail to take?"

Since he was not sure, he sat down on his haunches to ponder the matter. As he sat there with the vulvas around his neck, he noticed that they were emitting an awful stench. He jerked and jiggled them back and forth, trying to remove them, but they seemed fused to his body. Finally, he gave up. Then he became angry with himself, berating himself for being so lecherous when he was still alive. Each time a person of pure heart passed by where he sat, they laughed at him and his necklace.

As Coyote observed the passers-by, he noticed that those who were moving right along always selected the trail on the right. Apparently, these were those who had not sinned or committed any crimes, so he decided to follow them. He knew he had chosen well when he looked over at the left trail and saw that it was overgrown with thorny cactuses that kept sticking those who traveled along it. In addition, the road was very rough. Coyote even saw some people who had bunches of prickly pear hanging between their thighs. These poor creatures walked along with their legs spread, trying to keep from getting stabbed even more painfully. Why they were afflicted like this, he had no idea.

In due time, he arrived at a pit oven where people were lined up in all four directions. There was a tremendous fire in the pit, and long flames shot out. Though frightened, Coyote stopped to watch what was going on. Both men and women, married and unmarried, stark naked, stood in the lines of the four directions. Not a single child was among them. Nearby stood a Kwan, or One Horn, priest. The Kwan priest commanded, "All right, push them in!" To his horror, Coyote now saw those in the front of each of the lines being flung into the fiery pit, starting at the northwest, continuing around, and ending with those in the northeast line.

Having witnessed this terrible spectacle, Coyote tried to sneak quietly by the people there. Stealthily he crept along, unaware that he was being followed by the Kwan priest. Suddenly, he heard a bell ringing behind him. When he turned to look, he saw the priest coming toward him. "Hold it!" the priest shouted. "What business do you have passing through here?"

Somewhat scared, Coyote replied, "I have no idea why I'm here. Something seems to be compelling me to move along this path. Earlier today I fell off a cliff and thought I had died. But maybe I'm just imagining all this."

"Is that so? Well, I guess that's all right then. It's just that no creature like you, be he coyote, bear, badger, or any other animal for that matter, ever came here after his death. To be sure, there are mules coming along here, but those are really people who've sinned. As a rule, only humans are permitted here. I'm surprised you've been able to come this far. You've almost reached the final destination of all these people, so I won't keep you from going on. Maybe the Creator wants it this way. You will meet him soon enough, and maybe he'll explain what he has in store for you. He may not personally talk to you, but he will probably let you know somehow or other." With that, the Kwan priest returned to his duties at the fiery oven.

As Coyote resumed his journey, he came to the edge of a mesa where a crowd was gathered, waiting. It appeared that they all wanted to descend to the plain below. Then, he noticed that women were sailing down on their wedding robes, and men on their wicker wedding plaques. Unmarried boys and girls were using the blankets and kilts they had received as little children.

The moment Coyote trotted up to the waiting crowd, they all burst out in laughter, for they could see that, being only a coyote, he had nothing to use for transportation to the bottom. He was determined to get down, however, so he asked some of them for help. Strangely enough, they agreed. Women handed the men cords that they use to tie their hair, and when a great pile had been accumulated, the men wound the cords together into a rope. They attached this rope to Coyote's tail and began to lower him down the cliff. As it turned out, however, the rope was not quite long enough to completely reach the ground, so several people waited on tiptoe with their arms stretched out, and after a number of tries, got Coyote down on solid ground, unharmed. Secretly snickering at him, the people watched Coyote go on his way.

From this point on, Coyote encountered no more hardships or obstacles. After traveling quite a distance he reached an area where the land was green with grass, as far as the eye could see. There were numerous cottontails, jackrabbits, and deer on the land. Though he saw them, he felt no desire to stalk them as he normally would, so without molesting them he pressed on.

Further on, the landscape became filled with flowers, all sorts of flowers. The fields were covered in blossoms all the way to the horizon. What a beautiful sight! Before long, he came to a large field of sunflowers. Happy children were playing on them, climbing up and down and greatly enjoying themselves, their laughter ringing out as they played. Some of them climbed to the top of the sunflower stalks, swung about, and climbed down again. Others simply jumped down to the ground. Now and then, a child would simply leap from one flower to the next and continue swinging on it.

Coyote hesitated to walk right up to the children, so he observed them from a hiding place. After crouching there a while, he mustered up his courage and crawled a little closer. Then he sat up and watched them playing.

Without realizing it, he had gotten quite close to them. Suddenly, one of the children spotted him among the sunflowers and shouted, "Look! There's a coyote!"

"Really? Well, let's chase him," the others yelled in unison and ran after him, just for fun. After a bit, they quit chasing him and returned to their play. When Coyote noticed this, he stopped and trotted back to where they were playing. Once more he settled down on his haunches and watched them.

When the children saw that, they began to discuss what to do. They were tired of chasing him. Instead, one of the children suggested, "Let's go find our father. I don't think this creature is supposed to be here, but there he sits. Maybe our father can explain why." So, a couple of the children went off to fetch their father and soon came back to resume their play with the others.

Not long after that, Coyote spotted a man coming his way at a fast pace. He was still so far off that he could not make out his face. Coyote just stayed where he was, as he had no intention of running away. As the man came closer, Coyote noticed that he was gigantic and that he had a most repulsive face. Apparently this was the father that the children had gone to fetch, and as it turned out, it was the god Maasaw, caretaker of Maski and guardian of the children there.

Apparently, when a Hopi dies, he becomes like a child again, and for that reason there were nothing but children there. No matter how much anyone suffers in life, upon their arrival in Maski, they are in perfect health again. That's why all the children Coyote saw were so healthy and happy.

Coyote was astonished that they were willing to accept such an ugly man as their father. So abhorrent was he that Coyote couldn't face him any longer. However, when he tried to run away, his legs felt completely paralyzed. Terrified as he was, he could only make pitiful jerking movements and was frozen to the spot where he stood.

Maasaw was getting closer and closer. Frenetically doubling his efforts, Coyote finally succeeded in dashing off. Immediately Maasaw set off in pursuit of him, taking giant strides as he went, but failing to catch the speeding animal.

Coyote, frightened out of his wits, dashed back to the spot where the people had lowered him down the cliff. There he saw that people were still waiting to descend. He ran up to the cliffs and begged the people above to help him to the top. Without much fuss, they lowered the rope made of hair-tying strings and hauled him up, just as Maasaw appeared. He had escaped Maasaw's clutches just in time! As it turned out, however, Maasaw had not really wanted to catch him, only to scare him.

Still frightened, Coyote now ran back along the way he had originally come. Soon, he came across the Kwan priest again, who greeted him, "You're back?"

"Yes," Coyote replied, all out of breath. "Somebody dreadful was chasing me. I had a terrible time escaping him, that's why I wanted to come back. I don't think I could have stayed there where that monster lives!"

The Kwan priest chuckled and said, "I was going to tell you that Maasaw would never tolerate you in paradise, but I failed to stop you in time. Remember, I warned you that only humans are allowed to travel there. No one like you has ever been admitted, that's why he chased you back here. Also, each time a Hopi dies, the sun in the sky is fueled in its movement by his death, so even a dead person still has some use. Dead humans also visit their relatives in the form of clouds and kachinas and bring them rain. On the other hand, you're nothing but a coyote and are not of any use to anybody. No wonder Maasaw chased you back here. It's time for you to go back now. I'll accompany you for a while and then leave you on your own."

With that speech, the Kwan priest ushered Coyote along. When they had reached Apoonivi, the priest said, "Wait. From here it's not far to the place where you began your journey. You have to go on alone now. You must realize, however, that you really died, and now you must enter your body again. Return to the area where you and your wife usually hang about. How on earth you managed to travel through Maski is a puzzle to me."

The Kwan priest then consecrated the ground by laying down a path of cornmeal for Coyote, and sent the animal on his way. "So now be off," was all he said, whereupon he turned and disappeared.

Without complaint, Coyote started out and soon was at the promontory of Apoonivi. As he ascended it from the northwest, he recognized the way he had come. Going through the small houselike structure at the top, he then descended to the southeast and arrived at the spot where he had perished, finding his body still lying there.

Unsure of what to do, he just stood there by his body, waiting for daylight. After a long while a stranger appeared. "I've come to get you," the stranger said. "It's late already. I came for you a while ago, but you were not back here yet. You should have gone with me when you died, but somehow you got on the road to Maski. I know all about your adventures there. With those words, the stranger led him away.

In this way, Coyote visited Maski, but since he's not really worth anything, he was sent back out again. After returning to his body, he was taken away by the stranger to the place where he should have gone. In this way the coyote family lost their father. I guess they're still living around Ismo'wala somewhere.

And here the story ends.

13

The So'yoko Ogre and His Wife

Aliksa'i. People were living way over at Wupatki. Many of them had their home there. They always did things together and were especially fond of dances, so they led happy and content lives.

One day, they began to notice that the village was getting smaller, not because so many people were dying, but because they simply disappeared. Frequently, when they went planting, hunting, or collecting wood, they just failed to return. Their relatives would go looking for them but never found anything but their tracks. These were clearly visible for a distance, but then suddenly disappeared. Among the human footprints they always noticed those of a giant being, but they had no idea whose footprints they were.

By this time, many people had disappeared and still the Wupatkis had no idea who or what was causing it. They now made it a rule not to go out alone anymore, even in broad daylight. They were so frightened that they only went out in twos and threes, even when they went to relieve themselves. Once in a while, some foolish or brave person would go out alone, never to return.

Among the residents of Wupatki was a boy in his early teens who was quite ugly. His nose was always covered with snot, his body was dirty, and his clothes were tattered. To top it all off, his hair was constantly disheveled. The other children could not stand him, and he had no playmates. In fact, they teased and bullied him every chance they got.

He had tried to court girls on several occasions, but none of them wanted anything to do with him. He did accompany his father to the field, though, and became quite good at farming. As a reward his father, a skilled bowmaker, made him a fine sinew-backed bow and some arrows. Of course the boy now looked forward to going hunting, but his father was too busy with other chores to go with him. The boy understood and laid his bow aside for the time being. A few days later, the boy asked his father again, but he was still busy. So, that night the boy made up his mind to venture out by himself. "No one wants to go hunting with me," he pouted. "They're all mad at me. I'll just go alone then. I'm so ugly that no one is going to bother me. Who would want to kidnap someone like me?" Determined to go on his own, he soon fell asleep.

At white dawn the next morning, he got up and dressed. After preparing a little journey food and getting his canteen, he took his bow and quiver down from where it hung on the wall and walked out of the house. He had decided to head southwest of the village toward Nuvatukya'ovi. There he hunted among the hills, keeping his eyes peeled for the spoor of game animals, but he didn't find a single sign. When it was about noon, he sat down under a ponderosa pine and laid his weapons aside. He had just finished eating and quenching his thirst when someone embraced him tightly from behind. Startled, the boy struggled as hard as he could to free himself, but to no avail, so finally he just stood still. Whoever it was began to tie him up. When he finally succeeded in getting a glance at his attacker, he saw that it was a So'yoko. Immediately he thought, "This ogre must be the one who's been kidnapping our people!" The So'yoko had large feet, which explained the large footprints the villagers found when they searched for those who had disappeared. In addition, the ogre had a large snout and huge buggy eyes. Strands of his wild hair kept falling into his mouth and eyes, and he was constantly blowing and brushing them away in a vain attempt to control it.

When the boy's arms were completely tied, the So'yoko attached a rope to him and jerked him to his feet. Since the boy's legs were not tied, the ogre was able to pull him along like a dog on a leash. For some reason, however, the boy was not afraid, though the ogre kept pestering and teasing him as he stumbled along. In return, the boy would first drag his feet, then when the ogre got closer, he would start running, so that he was causing the So'yoko to stomp along with quick, short steps. Since the ogre wasn't really able to run, he kept flopping on his belly when he tried to keep up with the boy. Each time this happened, the So'yoko was furious, and when he was able to get back on his feet, he would severely scold the boy. In this fashion, the two of them stumbled and fell toward the So'yoko's house.

They still had not reached the ogre's house when the boy turned to him and asked, "Why don't we stop here for a while? I need to relieve myself."

"No!" answered the ogre. "You're just trying to trick me, so you can run away."

"Very well, then," said the boy. "You're probably just going to eat me anyway. So go ahead, eat me now the way I am, even though I haven't relieved myself."

Pondering what the boy had said, the So'yoko reconsidered and allowed him to go relieve himself. The boy, of course, was still at the end of the ogre's rope. It was quite long, so he stepped behind a bush and squatted down. Right away a voice said, "For shame, my grandchild! I live here, so please move aside a little bit. When you're finished I'll untie you. Just tell me when you're done." So the boy moved aside a little and had a big movement.

When he was done, he said, "All right, I'm finished." He had no idea who he was talking to, for he hadn't seen a soul. Much to his surprise, he saw a spider come crawling toward him.

"Oh dear, you poor thing!" said the spider. "I'm the grandmother of all people and I saw you being led through here by this cannibal." It was Old Spider Woman, of course. "That monster is the one who's been stealing people from your village for him and his wife to eat. He plans the same for you. Let me untie you. Then we can enter my house, where he won't be able to find you."

After loosening the ropes tied around his arms, Old Spider Woman instructed the boy, "Now, wrap this rope around your pile of excrement." When he had done that, she added, "All right, now go on ahead of me. I have to do some magic here and I'll follow you shortly."

Old Spider Woman now chewed some medicine and sprayed it on the pile of excrement. She then commanded it, "I want you to answer on behalf of the boy when that So'yoko asks a question. While you do that, we two can hide from him." With that, she caught up with the boy and led him to her house.

Meanwhile, the So'yoko was getting impatient because the boy still had not returned from relieving himself. Finally, he asked, "What's going on out there? Aren't you done yet?"

As commanded, the pile of excrement replied, "No, I'm not finished yet. I won't be long now," in a voice that sounded just like the boy.

This satisfied the ogre for a while, but he became impatient again, and hollered, "Come on, aren't you done yet? You're taking an awfully long time. Maybe you're putting me on." With that, he pulled on the rope, hoping to make the boy hurry up. The boy still did not return. Finally, he became so angry that he thundered, "Come on out! You must be done by now!"

As before, the pile of excrement replied, but now with a straining tone, "I'm just about finished. Just wait a little bit longer. You would not want to eat me the way I am now."

This exchange with the So'yoko went on for quite a while longer, until the So'yoko was so disgusted and angry that he said he was coming to get the boy. At this point, the pile said, "I'm done now, but somehow a branch has snagged my shirt, and I'm stuck here. Give me a pull with the rope and maybe that will free me. Pull with all your strength!"

The So'yoko pulled so forcefully that the excrement, still bound up with the rope, flew toward him and, with a great splat, landed smack in his face. When he realized what had hit him, he stomped around, muttering in disgust. He somehow managed to clean himself up a bit, and went searching for the boy. Night fell and he had not found him, so he abandoned his search, built a fire, and settled down there for the night.

Meanwhile, the boy was comfortably passing the time in Old Spider Woman's house when she said, "It's getting dark and that old ogre will have had to quit looking for you. Run back to the place where you left your bow and quiver and bring them here."

He did so and was back in no time. The old woman greeted him warmly and said, "Thanks for returning so quickly. Put your weapons down and have something to eat. I've set out some real delicacies for you."

The boy settled down on the floor where the food was spread out, but when he took a closer look, it struck him as really meager fare. There was a tiny morsel of hurusuki pudding on a plaque, and next to it something that looked like a tiny roasted bird's thigh. He bit off a little piece of the thigh, and to his great surprise, found that it filled his whole mouth. The same thing happened when he ate the pudding. How sweet it was! Soon, he was full and Old Spider Woman cleared away the food.

"Stay where you are," she said. "I need to go get someone who might be able to counsel us on how to kill that evil ogre." With that, she departed.

The boy now had an opportunity to look around the room. He noticed that pahos were inserted in the ceiling, but that they were old and moth-eaten. "I wonder who made these for her," he thought. Before long, the old woman was back with good news. "Your uncle promised to come and help us!" she cried.

"That's great, I'm glad to hear it," was all the boy could think of to say. As far as he knew, all his relatives lived back at Wupatki, so he was anxious to learn who this uncle might be.

It wasn't long before there was a hissing sound outside, and the ground shook. This frightened the boy, but Old Spider Woman comforted him saying, "Don't be scared. Everything is all right. That's just your uncle and he won't do us any harm. There's really no need to be afraid."

In a moment or two the earth ceased shaking, but the hissing noise continued. There was someone right above them on the roof. The old woman shouted up a greeting, "Thanks for coming so quickly. We've been waiting for you, so come on in."

The entire roof of Old Spider Woman's kiva shook, then the ladder swayed back and forth. The boy looked up and saw a gigantic yellow rattlesnake slide down the ladder. The snake came to rest near the fire pit, coiled up with his head raised. Around his neck he wore a bunch of pahos which, just like the old woman's, were rather tattered and moth-eaten. "Hmm," thought the boy, "I guess nobody makes pahos for these beings. They've been abandoned by the people. No wonder their pahos are so old and worn."

Old Spider Woman now informed the yellow rattlesnake why she had brought the boy here. "I'm glad you agreed to come so quickly. Since you are this boy's uncle, you can help him make a plan to kill that So'yoko monster."

"All right," said the snake. "I'm glad you asked me to come here. I am truly the boy's uncle, and I always bear that in mind. But the people in Wupatki seem to have forgotten me, because they never make any pahos for me anymore. Still, I'll help the boy. After all, he is my nephew."

As it so happened, the boy was a member of the Snake clan, as were most of the Wupatkis. So this is how his uncle, the rattlesnake, decided to come help him. Old Spider Woman now said to the rattlesnake, "Perhaps you came with a plan already in mind. Share it with us, and we will carry it out."

The rattler replied, "Yes, indeed I do have one. Bring out a quiver full of arrows, so that I can treat them with my medicine." The boy fetched his arrows and lay them before the big snake. The snake picked up the arrows, one by one, and spat on each of them. He was greatly endowed with poison sacs, so it was venom that he spat on them. "All right," he said, "that should do the trick. This venom of mine will allow you to kill that ogre instantly. That's all I can do, so I will go home now."

Wishing the boy good luck, his uncle slid out of the kiva. As before, the ladder swayed and the earth shook as he slithered along, hissing loudly. It was not until he was far away that the earth was still again.

Old Spider Woman now said to the boy, "I knew he would assist you. You're bound to be successful now. So, don't worry anymore, and go to bed." With that, she rolled out a sleeping skin for him. He lay down and was soon asleep.

The next morning he awoke to the sound of Old Spider Woman rummaging around. She had already laid out a breakfast of the same foods as before. He ate only some hurusuki pudding and was soon full. Thanking her for the food, he said, "Now it's my turn. I won't forget you and my uncle when I return to Wupatki. I'm grateful you live here and that you came to my rescue. You saved me in the nick of time from that ogre."

"Very well," she said, "you'll be on your own now, but you can be sure you'll kill that So'yoko. Be on your guard, though. So go on, things will work out for you. Here's a little something I prepared for you. When you get hungry, eat some of it." With that, she handed him a tiny bundle and added, "Although that So'yoko is not a very good runner, be careful when you take a rest. Don't stay too long, and sit with your back against something, so that he can't surprise you from behind." Then she, like his uncle, wished him luck.

The boy then departed and began trying to track the ogre. Since the So'yoko had stomped back and forth so much, however, this was no longer possible. So, instead of trying to follow the ogre's footprints, the boy just went searching for him in the pine forest. He searched without rest until it was midday. He was getting hungry, so he looked for a big ponderosa pine to lean against, opened his food bundle, and ate. She had wrapped up some more of the pudding and the tiny roast bird thighs, and his hunger was soon satisfied.

He resumed his search for the So'yoko and soon spotted him, rummaging through the underbrush. He, in turn, had been searching for the boy, and huge boulders were turned upside down here and there. As the boy watched him, he had to laugh. After awhile he began sneaking up from behind, to where the ogre stood, bent over, scrutinizing the ground. With all his might, the boy stuck the end of his bow into the ogre's behind, yelling "Yap pahaha!" and then he jumped back out of sight. He prodded the ogre several times, until he stood up and angrily looked around. "Who had the nerve to do that to me? Wait 'til I catch you. I'll devour you!" he threatened. He turned wildly, looking here and there, but when he failed to see anyone, he continued his search. The boy now prodded the ogre's behind again and again. Soon, the So'yoko was wild with rage. Eventually, however, the boy grew tired of teasing the ogre and just jumped out in front of him. "Here I am, you slowpoke! Try and catch me, you evil monster. Come and eat me, if you can. It was me who was goosing you." The boy almost laughed his head off.

Furious, the ogre stomped awkwardly toward the boy, but his gait was too slow. The boy had plenty of time to nock an arrow and aim it at the So'yoko as he lumbered toward him. Drawing the arrow to its fullest length, he let fly just as the giant was upon him. The shaft flew with great speed and struck the So'yoko right in the heart. He was dead before he even hit the ground, due to the magic medicine his uncle had spat on the arrows. It was incredibly potent. In this way the boy killed the So'yoko with the aid of Old Spider Woman and his rattlesnake uncle.

The corpse of the So'yoko lay there, still handsomely dressed in the clothes he had stolen from the many people he had killed. The boy had been poor all his life and was shabbily dressed, so he thought, "I'll strip him of these things. He can no longer harm me." So, he exchanged his rags for some of the splendid clothes the ogre had on. He looked very attractive now, and feeling very confident, continued his hunt.

However, the So'yoko still had a wife, who had remained at home while her husband went foraging for human prey. He had been gone so long that she began to worry. Finally, she dropped everything and went in search of him.

She started looking in the pine forest near their home, and came across his corpse, sprawled on the ground, stripped of his clothes and belongings. Outraged by this sight, she screamed, "Who did this to you? I swear, I'll look for him, and when I find him, I will revenge you!" She buried her husband, then started out immediately in search of his killer.

She searched all through the pine forest. Nothing. She then decided to head toward Wupatki, eventually coming to the edge of the pine forest, where pinyons and junipers grew. Suddenly, she stopped and listened, sure that she could hear footsteps. Quickly she hid behind a tree.

Sure enough, along came the boy, still looking for game as he headed home. As he walked right past the ogre woman behind the tree, she spotted her husband's clothes on the boy and thought "He must be the one who murdered him!" After the boy had gone some way, she came from behind her tree and followed him.

The boy was unaware that anyone was around until someone tried to trip him by sticking a crook in his path. He deftly jumped over it, and when he turned to see who had done it, saw an ugly monster coming toward him with her hands outstretched. He was so frightened he turned and ran, forgetting all about his bow and the arrows tipped with medicine. Eventually he reached a field near Wupatki, where a man was hoeing weeds. Stammering that a So'yoko woman was chasing him, he headed straight for the farmer's field hut, where he hid himself.

In a few minutes, the ogre woman had tracked the boy to the field. When she saw the farmer, she asked if he had seen a boy running by. The farmer mumbled something in reply, but the ogre woman couldn't really make it out, so she repeated her question. "No," the farmer answered, "and he's not in the field hut either."

"Sure he is!" the ogre woman yelled furiously. "His tracks end here. He must be here somewhere!"

It so happened that the man hoeing weeds there was a Hehey'a kachina. Hehey'a kachinas always say the opposite of what they really mean. The ogre woman didn't know that and was really upset with the farmer, for clearly the boy's tracks stopped there. Muttering angrily under her breath, she resumed her search, heading for the field hut. Just then, however, the boy slipped out the other side of the hut and continued to run.

Soon he came across a gopher and quickly begged for help. "A So'yoko woman is chasing me. Her husband was murdering our people, so I killed him. That's why his wife is after me. Please help me. That farmer over there tried to hide me, but she discovered where I was."

"Don't worry, I'll help you," said the gopher. "I'll open my jaws and you can climb in. She can't find you there." With that, the gopher opened his mouth really wide and the boy jumped in, feeling quite comfortable.

Before long, the So'yoko woman came puffing along, almost out of breath. Right away she asked the gopher, "Has a boy come through here, by any chance? I'm going to eat him when I catch him. I nearly had him a few minutes ago, but he escaped me again."

"No, I didn't see anybody," the gopher replied.

"You're lying! He must have come here, because his footprints end right here in front of you. Why are your cheeks bulging so much? You must have him in your mouth!"

"That's not true," insisted the gopher. "I had a bad toothache last night, and my cheeks are still swollen."

The So'yoko woman didn't believe a word the gopher said. "Let me look inside your mouth!" she demanded.

"Oh no, I can't allow that," said the gopher. "If someone touches me there it really hurts. I was in terrible pain all night long!"

The ogre woman was not convinced, however, and walked up to the gopher. He quickly turned and nonchalantly spat out the boy, who landed running, speeding away with the So'yoko woman right on his heels. She had no intention of giving up. She was just too angry for that, so she redoubled her efforts to catch the boy. In the meantime, the boy was getting exhausted and had to slow down momentarily, but then, spurred by the realization that the ogress could catch him any second, he pressed on.

It was not long before the boy came upon a billy goat. He had long whiskers and was striding back and forth restlessly. Again, the boy explained his problem and pleaded for help. "Sure, I'll help you," said the goat. "Come right into my kiva and sit down in the middle of the floor, in plain view. When that ogre woman comes, I'll kill her for you."

The boy was very relieved to receive such an offer. He climbed down the ladder and sat in the middle of the floor, shaking with fear. The billy goat tried to reassure him. "Don't be afraid," he said. "She can't harm you down here. I just need to think how to handle her." These words calmed the boy down considerably.

The billy goat kept striding forcefully back and forth. When the boy was relaxed enough to size him up more carefully, he noticed that the goat had a large erection and seemed in the throes of strong desire.

Suddenly, the billy goat said to the boy, "Just wait here. I need to go fetch something. That ogress is so slow, she'll take a while to get here."

The billy goat was soon back with sumac berries, which he put to soak in some liquid. Then he said to the boy, "I'm really quite glad the So'yoko woman is chasing you here. I've been without a woman for so long, that I tell you plainly I'm going to couple with her when she gets here. However, I know that her vagina is studded with teeth. That's why I'm soaking these sumac berries. Their juice is so sour, it will dissolve those teeth and make it possible for me to do it without harm."

When the sumac potion was ready, he smeared some on his member and waited. He had just finished his preparations when the So'yoko woman peeked through the hatch of the kiva. She spotted the boy right away, and the billy goat too. "Bring out the boy!" she commanded the goat. "He murdered my husband and I'm going to punish him."

The billy goat only replied, "If you want the boy, come in and get him yourself."

The ogre woman repeated her demand and received the same answer. Apparently she would have to go in and get him herself. So she clambered down the ladder and headed for the boy, her hands menacingly outstretched. The billy goat watched her closely, and when she approached the boy, he knocked her down and began to couple with her. Because of the sumac juice he was able to do it without harm to himself. He was so full of desire that he just kept going, and as a matter of fact, went at it so long that he killed the So'yoko woman in the process.

The boy and the billy goat checked the ogress for any signs of life, but sure enough she was dead, no doubt about it.

The billy goat now disappeared into a back room of the kiva, returning with a blanket. He covered the So'yoko woman's body with the blanket and squatted down by its side. He had a little rattle in his hand that he shook briefly, then he began to chant. As he did, something stirred under the blanket. Finally, he stopped singing and jerked the blanket away. Low and behold, there sat a newborn billy goat, bleating at the top of his lungs! He moved aside and a second one emerged from the So'yoko woman's womb; then two more. And not only billy goats, but she-goats and sheep too. Quite a number came out quickly and it was pandemonium in there, with all the bleating and baaing.

"All right," said the billy goat, "it's time for you to go home. I'm sure your parents are missing you. I'm so happy you came by here with that So'yoko woman. I was getting desperate. In return, I'd like to give you these little ones you see here. You can herd them home with you, and when you get married, you can use them to support your family. You're handsome now, so you're bound to get a girl."

So, without further talk, the boy set out for home, herding along his flock of little goats and sheep. He felt proud, because he had become rich, and because of him, Hopis now had these domestic animals to own and raise.

Sure enough, the boy's parents were anxiously waiting for his return. They hardly recognized the handsome boy, with his beautiful and rich clothes. He told them right away about his adventures, about the So'yoko who had kidnapped all their people, and how he had been assisted in killing the So'yoko and his wife. When he had finished his story, the boy's father said, "You must make pahos for Old Spider Woman and your uncle, the yellow rattlesnake. Their hearts will be gladdened by these offerings. The same holds for the Hehey'a and all the rest."

So, he and his father began working on the pahos. When they were done, the boy once more headed out toward Nuvatukya'ovi, the San Francisco Peaks. There he hunted for songbirds until he had killed a large number. They would provide meat for Old Spider Woman. Then he went from kiva to kiva of those who had helped him, delivering his gifts.

Old Spider Woman, Hehey'a, and his uncle the yellow rattle-snake were elated to receive the pahos, and Old Spider Woman relished the bird meat. For the gopher the boy brought a bag of shelled corn, which he was very glad to get. He brought nothing for the billy goat, however. When he had asked him previously what he really wanted, he had said, "There's nothing that I especially want. Coupling with that ogress was like a gift from you. That was really all I needed." When the boy arrived there, he protested, "I didn't bring you anything, but I feel like I really must do something for you. After all, I owe you my life. And besides, you gave me a large flock of sheep and goats. Because of this wealth I'm now respected in the village, rather than scorned. How about this: When one of the little she-goats is older, I'll bring her over to you. Then you and she can be happy together."

The billy goat thanked him and said, "All right, that's a gift I'd be glad to accept."

In this manner the boy repaid his debt. Because he was now handsome and wealthy, he soon found a sweetheart. He probably still has his girlfriend there somewhere, along with all his animals.

And here the story ends.

14

How Somaykoli Came to Shungopavi

Aliksa'i. They were living at Shungopavi, the old village on the south-east side below the mesa. There, in a wash, the children used to play. They usually did this while guarding the corn plants. Once, when they were playing a game, a stranger came by, limping on his left foot.

He watched them as they slid down the bank of the wash. One of the children, who had not placed his hand properly as he slid down the bank, broke his arm. The stranger called the injured boy over to him, saying "Come here, I can fix it for you."

Though in pain, the little boy climbed out of the gully and went to the man without hesitation. "All you need to do is this," said the man, and quickly gave the arm a jerk, snapping it back into place. He consoled the boy, rubbing the spot where it had been broken. "There, stop your crying, it's all fixed. You can go and play again."

Before long, another child had broken his arm. Once again, the man beckoned him over and healed it. When he was done, he said, "There, that should do it."

The children found this amusing and began breaking their bones intentionally. They broke their arms or legs and the stranger put them back together again. Finally, the children became curious and asked the man how he managed to do this.

"Well, I have this knowledge, that's why," he replied. Then he added, "If you want to learn this skill, I'll teach you. Then you can heal yourselves." Then he asked, "Where do you all live?"

"We live near here, in Shungopavi," they answered.

"Is that so? Well, if you really want to learn my skill, go tell your parents about what happened here. Have them go to your village chief and ask that a Zuni Yaya' ceremony be performed. I will come to you there on the eve of the event. Just wait until I show up. You'll recognize me by my limp. You must then take me to a kiva, where I'll show you how the healing is done." It just so happened that the man who talked to the children in this way was Somaykoli.

The children ran home to tell their parents the news. The parents, in turn, went to the village chief and told him about their children's encounter with the stranger, how he had healed the children's broken bones, and how he had offered to pass on his skill. If they were impressed and wanted to carry on with this skill, then they could do it in the fall when some of the crops mature.

The village chief was very enthusiastic about the prospect of acquiring this skill, so he readily agreed that it was a good idea. He said they could do it in the northwest kiva, the one called Kyar'ovi. There the children could learn Somaykoli's skill. The fathers of the children were all members of the Wuwtsim society, so they could use that kiva for the Yaya' performance.

And so indeed the children gathered at Kyar'ovi, and Somaykoli came to them one night. First, he told them how to costume themselves, then he said, "Invite all the girls to the kiva in the southeast, and when you go from house to house to fetch them, use these as lights." With these words, he handed them torches that he had made that were tightly wound and quite long. After lighting them for the children, he said, "If a torch starts to go out, wave it around and the wind will fan it ablaze again. When we start rehearsing, you must gather all the married men. No one must be allowed to walk around outside the kiva. If you see anyone try to leave, grab him and, without mercy, throw him back down inside. He might get roughed up, but he'll be cured."

The Yaya't now went into session in the kiva. When all the men of the village were assembled in the center of the chamber, Somaykoli announced a series of songs that they would dance to. During the first two rehearsals they learned these songs, and when they had memorized them, he showed them the proper dance steps. "Stand in a circle, with one girl always between you and another man. Then motion like this when you make your ceremonial circuits through the village. When you do that, we Yaya't will enter the kiva. When Somaykoli comes, you will then close us in here, where we'll do the initiation. When we are through with the initiation and come out of the kiva, then you can do your procession throughout the village. That's how we're going to do it."

With those instructions, the Yaya' told the men to start chanting, and the song leaders started to sing. Grabbing hold of each other and forming a circle, they sang together. "Yes, that's the way, that's how you must do it," said the instructing Yaya', "and each time we come in, you must close us in the kiva. When Somaykoli goes out of the kiva, you must move on throughout the village."

The next day, they rehearsed again. On the third day, the Yaya't went out of the kiva, and as they came out, Somaykoli told them, "This is how you must make your calls, 'Aahoo, aahoo,' while waving your torches. And when you arrive at a girl's house, you must say to the people inside, 'Hey, we're coming to fetch your girls.' The girls will surely come out. Do the same at the next house. When you have gathered all the girls, take them to the kiva and usher them inside. Go in behind them. By the time you have performed the correct number of times, it will be well into the night. Bring the girls out then, take them back to their homes, and return here to the kiva. There will be other things for us to do."

And so they continued practicing. When the men being instructed were finished, they all retired for the night. Now the Yaya't saw to their own preparations, for they intended to show off their magic skills to the people.

Finally it was the morning of the Yaya' dance day. The people, meanwhile, had heard that there would be a Somaykoli at Shungopavi. This caused quite a stir, as this personage had never appeared there before, and villagers everywhere made plans to come. On dance day, they came in large numbers from far and wide until there were great crowds of spectators milling about.

At noontime, the Yaya't filed out of the kiva. As they moved along, they pulled a string up from the ground, all the while crying "Aahoo!" With the last one in line winding up the string, they circled the plaza, then ascended to the second story of a house on the northwest side. From there they threw down to the audience all sorts of good things—watermelons, muskmelons, peaches—all the fruits that Hopis enjoy. After this, they told the spectators to assemble on the northeast side of the plaza.

When the people arrived there, they saw that the Yaya't had a fire going in a pit oven and were continuing to throw wood into it, sparks flying up from the glowing embers as they did so.

The Yaya't now reentered their kiva. "All right," announced their chief, Somaykoli, "the time has come. Go to the fire pit and chase each other around until one of you is caught. Grab him by the arms and legs and toss him in the air. After the fourth time, cast him in the fire pit. Then spread a wedding robe on the ground, pluck his body parts out of the oven, and pile them on the robe. Come back and dump them into the kiva. I will then do my magic over them until he is completely restored, whereupon he will come out without a scratch on him. You wanted to learn how this is done, so I will show you."

And so the Yaya't went out. Chasing each other as instructed, they grabbed one of the little Yaya't in the group, threw him into the air four times, then flung him into the blazing hot oven. Sparks flew and steam rose from the oven as they did so, and the spectators gasped! They were sure the child would be burned to death. The other little Yaya't now stepped up to the fiery pit and started pulling chunks of cooked flesh from it. After bundling these chunks up in a wedding robe, they hauled them to the kiva and dumped them down the hatch.

Now they began chasing after a new victim, but while they were engaged in this pursuit, the one they had thrown in earlier appeared, shouting at the top of his lungs. He was completely unhurt. Not a hair on his head was singed! He also joined in the pursuit and when they had caught the new victim, they did the same to him as the first. Each of the Yaya' children were caught and thrown in the roaring pit oven, only to emerge later, unscathed. The spectators were watching all this with their mouths hanging open. How could they survive that fiery pit?

Meanwhile, the women brought food to the Yaya't as required by tradition. Rabbit stew was what they brought. The Yaya't began to eat hungrily and invited the spectators to share in the feast, only asking them to be sure to save all the bones from the stew.

The Yaya't collected up all these rabbit bones and piled them up next to their kiva. They then covered them with a wedding robe and, standing in a circle, chanted over them. Suddenly, something began to stir under the robe, and the Yaya't lifted off the cover. A baby rabbit was there! And another! Simply by singing over the bones, they had transformed them into little jackrabbits and cottontails, which now began scampering in every direction. "Come, catch one and keep him for a pet," yelled the Yaya't. All the children in the crowd then jumped up and chased after them, hoping to catch one.

In this manner, the Yaya't demonstrated their magic art before the people. From that time on, whenever anyone wanted to sponsor a Yaya' dance, he would set a date for some time in the fall, for it was at that season of the year that the Zuni Yaya' ritual was first introduced to the Hopi. However, in Shungopavi the Yaya' tradition is now extinct, following the death of the Yaya' leader.

And here the story ends.

15

The Boy Who Was Born from a Dead Mother

Aliksa'i. People were living over at Zuni. Long ago, people there used to eat all kinds of food, including pinyon nuts. Hopis did the same. They would gather cones filled with the nuts and lay them out on their rooftops. As the cones dried in the sun, they opened up and the nuts popped out.

The Zunis liked pinyon nuts a lot, so one day some boys decided to go pick them at a place high on top of a cliff where there was a large stand of trees. One of the boys had been near there recently and noticed that the trees were heavy with nuts.

This boy had a younger sister, so he also asked her, "Don't you have a friend that you'd like to take along?"

"Sure, I have one," she answered.

"Well, ask her if she wants to come along with us." The sister agreed.

Now, some girls, as well as boys, have not always behaved properly. The sister's friend was one of them, for she was pregnant, probably by a boyfriend of hers. Anyway, the boy's sister invited this girl to come along, and she readily agreed.

Since they were all going to go the very next morning, they immediately began to get the things they needed ready, such as sifter baskets. The sister's friend had lost both her parents and lived with her grandparents, so she told them she was going to harvest pinyon nuts. She also mentioned that the sister's older brother would be coming along.

"All right, be on your way then. If you're able to bring back lots of nuts, we'll have food for some time," said her grandparents, granting her permission to go.

So the group of boys and girls set out. When they arrived at the cliff, they decided to go straight up it instead of trying to find the trail again. They had a number of tumplines along, which they tied together to use as a rope to help them climb. It so happened that a juniper tree was growing above, right on the edge of the cliff, so they decided to secure the tumpline rope to this tree. They threw it up and looped it around the tree. They tested it and it held fast.

They agreed that one of the boys, who was a good climber, should climb up first and pull the rest of them up. "You go first," one of them said to the boy. "Once you're up, you can lower the rope to us. We'll tie the rope around ourselves and you can pull us up."

"All right," the boy agreed, and scaled the cliff using the rope. He was a good climber and managed to reach the top without any trouble. He then proceeded to pull the others up, one by one.

The last one to go up was the pregnant girl. The others, however, did not know of her condition. The boy had almost pulled her to the top of the cliff, when one of the tumplines making up the rope snapped, and the poor girl fell the length of the cliff. The others wanted to climb down to her, but since the rope did not reach to the bottom of the cliff anymore, this was impossible. Frantically, they searched for another way down, and finally found a place, quite a distance from where she fell. By the time they reached the girl, she was dead.

The unhappy group returned home, the trip cut short by this tragedy. They felt they had no choice but to leave the girl's body behind. They just hid her under an overhang and piled rocks around her.

When the group brought the sad news to the grandparents, they broke down and started crying, asking if she was really dead. They didn't feel like they could journey to where she was hidden, so they just accepted it. "Well, I guess there's nothing we can do," they lamented. "We'll just have to live alone now."

Now, unknown to everyone, the girl had somehow given birth right after her fall. This may seem strange, but as we all know, stories are powerful things in which almost anything is possible. So a child was born there, right under the overhang.

Not far from the cliff where the girl had fallen, in a little gulch, lived a rattlesnake. He was an old man who had lived there for a long time. He was just eating breakfast when he heard the sound of a baby crying. Leaving his den, he went searching in the direction of the sound and finally came across the body of the girl. A newborn baby lay beside her, whimpering. He looked her over, saw that she was dead, and picked up the baby.

"You poor thing!" he exclaimed. "What are you doing here all alone?" As he inspected the baby in his arms, he saw that it was a boy.

He carried the little child back to his den and began to take care of him. Periodically, he also checked on the dead mother to prevent anyone from harming her. He also hoped that the milk in her breasts would not dry up, so that he could breastfeed the child. From that time on, every time the little boy cried from hunger, the old man would take him to his dead mother and let him suckle. He kept this up for some time, and the child became bigger and stronger, until one day the mother's milk finally did dry up. When this happened, he boiled fresh corn for him, chewed it up, and fed it into the child's mouth.

By providing for the little boy in this way, the boy continued to grow. Years went by and he was soon a teenager, and old enough to go hunting by himself. Finally the old rattler said to the young man, "You're old enough now to do things for yourself. Therefore, I must tell you that you have grandparents in the village of Zuni, not far from here. That's where your real home is and where all your relatives live. Although I raised you, your real mother fell to her death near here long ago. Your grandparents are still alive, however, so you can't stay here with me for the rest of your life. Besides, my ways are not human ways. If you stay here with me, you'll lead a dull, boring life without any joy. Over there at Zuni the people have all kinds of things to occupy their time and have plenty of diversions and entertainment. So return to your grandparents. They've grown old and need someone to take care of them. I will now teach you a song. When you know it by heart, go out hunting. Then I will have some more to say to you."

"All right," the boy agreed.

So the old rattler composed a song for the young man. It dealt with the dog belonging to the young man's grandparents, a dog named Tirohwa. When the young man had memorized the song, the rattler said, "So, go hunting now. Kill a pronghorn antelope if you can and bring it back here. We will skin it for you to take home to your grandparents."

With that, the old man rattlesnake drew pictures of antelope tracks for the boy and also showed him what the tracks of jackrabbits and cottontails look like. "These are the ones that really taste good," said the rattler, "and the ones the Zunis like to eat. There are other game animals, of course, but the Zunis don't care too much for them. So go hunting now for the ones whose tracks I drew for you. And when you are back home, go hunting for these same animals once in a while, so you and your grandparents will have plenty to eat. They are your responsibility now."

The young man went hunting as he was told, killed a large antelope, and lugged it back to where the rattler lived. There they skinned it and cut the meat up into flat, thin slices, which they hung up to dry. A few days later, when they were cured, they packed them up in a bundle. The old man rattlesnake then said to the young man, "You will have to leave soon, and when you reach Zuni tomorrow morning, your grandparents' dog is bound to hear you." He then described to him exactly how to get there and where he would find his grandparents' house, right at the edge of the village on a little hill.

"Just southeast of it is a ridge," he instructed him. "Stand there and sing the song I taught you. The dog will surely notice you then."

The boy took his leave and in due time reached the ridge as

predicted. Sure enough, as he stood on top of the ridge, he could see a house, out by itself on top of a little hill, and a dog was running around near it. "I guess that's it," he thought. "That's where my grandparents live." He then began to sing the song he had been taught. This is how it went:

Wi'yaa haw haw Tirohwa
Wi'yaa haw haw Tirohwa
Wi'yaaya wi'yaayoowiiyahe
Haw haw Tirohwa
Haw haw Tirohwa
Wi'yaaya wi'yaayoowiiyahe
Hiineeya.

Twice he sang the song, then the dog heard him and came running. When the dog reached the boy, he jumped around him and barked. Then he ran back to the grandparents' house, stopped at the door, and continued barking.

After a while, the old man inside said, "I wonder why our dog is barking. There must be some reason." So he looked out, and at that moment the dog dashed off again toward the ridge, barking excitedly.

"Is there somebody out there? What are you trying to tell me?" he asked the dog. When the old man came out, the dog turned back and jumped up on him. Just as he came out of the house, he heard a voice singing a song that mentioned the dog by name. "Gee, is someone asking for you? Is that why you are barking so much? Let's go find out."

So the old man and the dog headed over to the ridge. Much to his surprise, he found a young man standing on top of it. Climbing up to him, the old man asked, "Are you the one singing my dog's name? And who are you?"

"Yes, I did sing his name," the boy replied, "and I am your grandson."

"Is that so?" exclaimed the old man. "How do you figure that?"

"Well, my mother, who was your daughter, once lived here at Zuni."

The old man looked the boy up and down. "That's impossible! My daughter died a long time ago. She went to harvest pinyon nuts with some friends and fell to her death. She couldn't have a son."

"Well, yes, but it's the truth. I'm her son. I've been living all these years right next to the spot where she died. Not far from there, in the northeast, is a gulch, and in it a cave where old man Rattlesnake raised me. It was he who bade me come here."

"Is that so?" The old man could hardly believe what he heard.

"Yes, it's true. Your daughter was pregnant at the time she fell. I was born right there, and grew up at old man Rattlesnake's place."

Bursting into tears, the old man ran up to his grandson and embraced him. With tears running down his cheeks, he exclaimed, "Thanks! I am really glad that you were found there. What a stroke of luck that you did not die with your mother. And what a good thing that someone rescued you and brought you up. Otherwise, you wouldn't be standing here now. Now you can live with us. Come, let me take you to your grandmother. She's still alive also."

So, the old grandfather led the boy to his house and presented him to his wife. "Look!" he said, "I brought you your grandson."

"How can this stranger be my grandson?" the old woman asked, in surprise.

Her husband then told her what he had just learned. Now she too burst into tears and ran up to her grandson and embraced him. She hugged him and cried for a long time.

This is how the old couple came to have a grandson. He was now of a working age, so he was able to help with many tasks. Whenever the old couple wanted meat, he was able to hunt and bring it home to them. He was a very industrious young man, and the grandparents were well taken care of from then on. They were very grateful for this, though they regretted not having raised him up from a little child.

And here the story ends.

16

Kotsoylaptiyo and the Sorcerers

Aliksa'i. People were living at Shungopavi. The village chief there
had a daughter who did not care for any of the boys who came to
woo her, and she refused all marriage proposals. The girl's parents
had grown old and were hoping for a son-in-law who could help out
with such chores as planting and gathering wood. So, when their
daughter refused all her suitors, they began to worry. After all, there
were no eligible boys left in the village who had not tried to win her.

However, there was still one undesirable boy left, whom she had not met. This boy lived near the dump at the edge of Shungopavi. His name was Kotsoylaptiyo, and one day, he said to his grandmother, "Grandma!"

"Yes, what is it?" she replied.

"You've probably heard of the girl who is so particular that she has refused all of her suitors up to now. Not a single one has been to her liking. There's no one left, except for me, who has not tried to win her. Maybe I ought to go try my luck."

"My dear grandson," exclaimed the old woman. "We live here all by ourselves. As far as the rest of the people in the village are concerned, we don't even exist. Some of the boys who tried were prominent, well known for their skills, and rich besides. Still, she showed no interest in them. You're nothing but a firewood-stoking boy. What makes you think you have a chance?"

"Well, I don't know, but I can give it a try at least!" persisted her grandson.

"All right, I'll do my best to help you. I don't think she'll encourage your courting, but let's just see what happens."

Kotsoylaptiyo, who normally never groomed himself and was constantly disheveled, actually combed his hair for the first time. Also, he usually just hunkered by the fire pit, his face covered with soot and ashes, but now he washed his face and spruced himself up a bit. Finally, he shook the dust out of his kilt and shirt and went out the door, on the way to see the girl.

When he arrived at the girl's house, there were lots of boys climbing down from the second story, where the girl usually ground corn. The suitors burst out laughing when they caught sight of Kotsoylaptiyo. "Ha! Look at that! She won't encourage him. She won't even respond to one of us, much less to the likes of him. He's nothing but a fire stoker!"

Undaunted by the boys' mockery, Kotsoylaptiyo climbed the stairs to the upper story, where the girl was busily grinding corn. Long ago, it was customary that the room where a girl knelt to grind corn had a vent hole nearby. Kotsoylaptiyo stuck his head through this hole and said, "Sh-h-h!" The girl did not hear him, or at least did not react. Once more he said, "Sh-h-h!" but there was no reaction. He did this several more times, and finally she looked up at him and asked, "Who are you?"

"It's me," Kotsoylaptiyo replied.

"Where are you from?" she asked.

"I live here in Shungopavi, on the southeast side of the village."

The girl was now somewhat confused, because she had never seen him before. So she asked him again, "Are you sure you're not lying to me? Where's your home?"

"I told you. I live here on the southeast side."

The girl replied, "Come back again tomorrow."

"All right," agreed Kotsoylaptiyo.

Before he left, the girl quickly wrapped up some of her rolled piki and handed it to him. Full of pride, Kotsoylaptiyo accepted the gift. Only the first visit, and he had already gotten the girl's attention! He jumped off the roof and ran home to tell his grandmother, almost falling down the ladder of their house as he entered. "Grandma!" he shouted.

"What is it?" the old woman asked.

"The girl spoke to me! And on my first visit!"

"I don't believe it," said his grandmother. "You're just a fire stoker. That girl wouldn't speak to a homely fellow like you!"

"But she did, and look, she gave me this," he said, placing the bundle of rolled piki in front of his grandmother.

The old woman was delighted and now believed he told the truth.

"And she invited me back tomorrow," he added.

"All right," she said, "but spruce yourself up a bit first."

So the following day, Kotsoylaptiyo took great care in combing his hair and, when he was done, headed over to the girl's house. Once more she was cordial to him and wrapped up a gift for him before he left. Then she added, "Come back again tomorrow. Then, four days from now, I'll go home with you to start the wedding ceremony." This time, the girl had given him tsukuviki, a crescent-shaped treat made from blue corn flour wrapped in dried corn shucks.

Full of pride, the boy sauntered home with his gift. His grandmother was very pleased when she learned of the wedding plans, and true enough, four days later Kotsoylaptiyo brought his bride home to begin the wedding ceremony. Her main task to start with was to grind plenty of corn.

Now since the boy and his grandmother lived at the edge of the village, many people passed their house on the way to relieve themselves. Early one morning a young girl came by on the way to do so and heard someone grinding corn. The sounds of the grinding were so quick and even, she knew they couldn't be caused by the old woman. Struck by this revelation, she turned around and hurried back to tell her parents. When they heard the news, they and others all headed out to the toilet area to listen. No doubt, someone was grinding corn in that house, and it wasn't the old woman. It had to be someone young.

Of course, there were sorcerers among the other suitors, and when they learned of this, they had to satisfy their curiosity. They decided to do this by sending one of their own to the house under the pretense of borrowing some live coals to start a fire. As a rule, Kotsoylaptiyo and his grandmother were early risers and always had a fire going and live coals available. If indeed there was a young girl grinding corn there, their spy would be able to see who it was.

So, early the next morning one of the sorcerer boys went to the house where Kotsoylaptiyo lived with his grandmother. He yelled out and a voice answered him, "Come in!"

"I came to borrow some live coals. Our fire died down, and we couldn't get it to flame up again. Finally it went out completely, and we began to get really cold."

"Sure, you can have some of ours," replied Kotsoylaptiyo's grandmother. With that she put some glowing coals on the shredded juniper bark the boy had brought with him. Just as he went out the door, he quickly glanced around and sure enough, there was a young girl grinding corn. He could hardly believe his eyes. It was the daughter of the village chief! She was a beautiful girl, and when he realized that she had agreed to become Kotsoylaptiyo's bride, he became very angry. He ran back to tell his fellow kiva members the news. When he arrived at Excrement Kiva, as the kiva of sorcerers and witches is typically called, he didn't even bother to drop the glowing embers into the fire pit. "What's the matter?" his fellow sorcerers asked.

"Well, as you may recall, you told me to go borrow coals at Kotsoylaptiyo's place so I could check on the situation there. I found out that he and his grandmother do indeed have a girl there, who is going through the wedding ceremony. She is the daughter of the village chief!"

"Is that so?" the sorcerers cried in astonishment. They were extremely resentful that a wretch like Kotsoylaptiyo could have taken away from them the most beautiful girl in Shungopavi. The chief of the sorcerers then exclaimed, "There's no way we can let them marry. We must somehow take her away from him. All of you come back here tonight and I'll tell you what to do."

So, that night they all gathered at Excrement Kiva, and their chief began, "All right. I told you she must not marry that boy. I want one of you to volunteer to challenge him. If you volunteer and succeed against Kotsoylaptiyo, you can have the girl."

At first, no one said a word. They all just sat there with their heads down. The chief kept looking at them and waiting, until finally someone said, "I'll do it."

"Very well," the chief continued, "here's my idea. We'll sponsor a hunt four days from now, to stalk deer. I want you all to stay here with me for the time being, so that I can prepare you for this undertaking."

When Kotsoylaptiyo learned of the sorcerers' challenge, he told his grandmother. "I had a feeling it would come to this," she said. "That's why I didn't want you to court that girl in the first place. But it can't be helped now. Let's just wait and see what happens."

Kotsoylaptiyo felt a bit relieved at his grandmother's words, for he knew that she was endowed with extraordinary powers. Three days later, the hunt was publicly announced by the village crier, who explained that they would hunt for big game animals such as deer and pronghorn antelope. He also outlined the area in which the hunt would take place.

Kotsoylaptiyo did not feel like going hunting, but his grandmother said to him, "The hunt has to do with you and your bride. Those Turds have created a pet deer that they will use as their instrument against you, so you must go, whether you want to or not."

On the morning of the appointed day, there was snow on the ground. The boy had never hunted before in his life, so his grandmother had to explain to him what the tracks of big game animals look like. "When they just walk, they look like this, and when they run, they look like that," she instructed him, drawing the tracks in two places. "When you come across these tracks, just follow them. They're bound to lead you to the animal."

Kotsoylaptiyo grabbed his bow and arrows and was on the verge of leaving for the hunt, when his grandmother called him back. "Wait! Take this along." She handed him a little bundle, which he thought contained some journey food. "Tie this to your waist."

He tied it to his waist and headed for the hunting ground. Since it had snowed, it did not take him long to spot the tracks of a deer. They were enormous and clearly stood out among the footprints of the hunters, so he began to follow them. Soon he reached the promontory of Kaktsintuyqa and climbed up to it, following the tracks until he came to the edge of a steep drop-off. Leaning out over the edge, he spotted the deer below, standing on a long, narrow ledge.

Kotsoylaptiyo knew there was no way of getting a shot at the deer from where he stood. He would have to climb down to the ledge. Struggling with the decision, he finally thought, "Well, he is the reason for my coming," and started to climb down. When he had made it down to the narrow ledge, the deer just stood here. Inching closer, Kotsoylaptiyo pulled an arrow from his quiver and nocked it on his bowstring. When he did this, the deer began to move about, as if getting ready to run. He waited. He would shoot as soon as the animal was still again. Kotsoylaptiyo was kneeling there on the narrow ledge, aiming his arrow, when the deer lowered his head and suddenly charged! Scraping the cliff wall with his huge antlers as he came, he aimed straight for the boy!

Flattening himself against the rock face, and with all his might, Kotsoylaptiyo pushed the end of his bow at the animal just as it was upon him. The enormous deer collided with the boy, but the boy remained firmly against the cliff wall. The deer, however, slipped from the ledge and crashed to the ground below. The bundle around the boy's waist had attached itself to the rock face and prevented him from being knocked from the ledge by the charging deer. Instead of journey food, as he thought, his grandmother had packed it full of devil's claw plant, which has tenacious hooks.

Now Kotsoylaptiyo, with great effort and risk to his life, managed to descend to the bottom of the cliff. Here he skinned the deer, gutted it, and slung it across his shoulders. It was very heavy, so it took him all day to reach the village.

The sun was about to set when he finally arrived. He headed straight for the kiva of the sorcerers, and could hear the murmur of their voices as he got close. No one noticed as he stepped onto the roof of the kiva, and he could hear them saying, "Our pet must have destroyed him by now. I'm sure Kotsoylaptiyo fell to his death from that cliff."

The sorcerers were still gloating over his demise when Kotsoylaptiyo dropped the carcass of the deer down the hatch of the kiva. It fell to the floor with a thud, and it became very still inside. The sight of their dead pet deer had utterly silenced them.

With that act, the boy turned on his heels and headed home. The sorcerers had hoped to kill him with their witch deer. Inside the deer had been the sorcerer boy who also wanted the girl and who had volunteered to challenge Kotsoylaptiyo.

The sorcerers were stunned by this turn of events but went about their daily business once more. That was not to be the end of it, however. They intended to challenge Kotsoylaptiyo again, so they began to hatch another scheme. This time, it involved a hunt for cottontails and jackrabbits. The same sorcerer boy volunteered a second time, and this time Kotsoylaptiyo's grandmother had to sketch rabbit tracks for him.

As before, the boy started out early and soon came across the spoor of a jackrabbit in the snow. He followed this until he flushed the rabbit from behind a bush, chasing it until it took refuge in a prairie dog hole. Kotsoylaptiyo decided to dig the rabbit out, but prairie dog holes are deep, so it took a lot of digging. When he thought he must be close to the rabbit, he lay down on his stomach and thrust his arm into the hole. Groping around, he could barely touch the rabbit's fur, so he dug out more of the burrow and reached in once more. This time, he could feel the rabbit's snout, but the moment he tried to grab the rabbit, it bit down on his wrist and held him fast. Try as he might, he could not pull out his hand, so he was forced to lie there all day long. The rabbit simply would not let go.

Meanwhile, the weather was getting colder and colder, and lying there in the snow, he began to freeze. The rabbit showed no signs of ever letting go. "I'll never get him out," he thought, "and I'll never get back to the village in time to keep from freezing."

By now, the wind was beginning to blow harder, and it suddenly got extremely cold. Kotsoylaptiyo was getting desperate, and just then he remembered that he still had the small bundle tied to his waist. He had his right hand down the burrow, so he had to try to untie it with his left. It was tightly fastened, but somehow he managed to undo it. When it was loose, he removed some of the contents and put it in his mouth. He chewed it and sprayed it on the bundle itself. Immediately, there were buzzing sounds and a number of wasps began to swarm around him. He said to them, "Go on now, fly inside the burrow and sting that jackrabbit. And hurry, I'm almost frozen stiff!"

The wasps did the boy's bidding and entered the prairie dog burrow, where they stung the rabbit. Soon, Kotsoylaptiyo could feel the jaws of the jackrabbit begin to relax and finally they released his wrist altogether. He now quickly grabbed the rabbit and pulled him out, killing him by striking him a blow across the neck. Their job done, the wasps flew back into his little bundle.

He wasted no time in heading for home. The sun was just setting when he arrived back at Shungopavi, where as before, he went straight to the Excrement Kiva of the sorcerers. They were all inside, happily talking with one another.

Suddenly, a jackrabbit fell to the floor in front of them. They reacted with stunned silence, just as before. Kotsoylaptiyo simply went home without saying a word to them.

The sorcerer who had been transformed into the jackrabbit resumed his human shape. He just lay there, dejected, for now he knew he would never get that girl.

After these failures, the sorcerers and witches ceased threatening Kotsoylaptiyo for a while. They realized that they could not easily outwit the boy and his powerful grandmother. Both their challenges had gone miserably awry. One day not long after that the sorcerer boy who had volunteered both times went insane and jumped off the mesa on the southeast side of Shungopavi, instantly killing himself.

Kotsoylaptiyo's bride, meanwhile, finished her wedding ceremony. Even though they were poor, somehow Kotsoylaptiyo and his grandmother had managed to obtain the wedding outfit for the bride. So when she and Kotsoylaptiyo were finally married, they both moved in with her parents where they lived as husband and wife.

The Turds, however, were not going to give up so easily. They just could not tolerate the thought of having Kotsoylaptiyo living in their midst happily married. When they assembled in their kiva again, their chief was already sitting by the fire pit hatching a new scheme. It involved Kaatoya, a gigantic snake who lived southeast of Apoonivi near a large butte. An evil creature, he carefully watched all the villages to see what desirable women or girls he could kidnap and take back to his lair. The old chief sorcerer was quite familiar with the giant snake, and when he had finished his smoke, he turned to the assembly and said, "I'd like for one of you strong ones to take my pahos to Kaatoya and ask him something on my behalf."

Kotsoylaptiyo's wife, meanwhile, had become pregnant and her belly was getting big. Every day, it was a little more awkward for her to move around, especially when she needed to relieve herself. When she did, she never went far because of her heavy belly. As a rule, she just went down to a little ledge on the outskirts of the village, a little hidden place just right for that purpose.

The chief of the sorcerers knew this, of course, and it fit right in with his plans. Finally, one boy among the sorcerers who also had coveted Kotsoylaptiyo's wife said to the chief, "I really want her, so I'm ready to volunteer. I'd be most happy to take your pahos to Kaatoya."

That night, the sorcerers worked straight through until morning making pahos. They were just finishing as daylight approached. After heaping the pahos on a tray, they ritually smoked over them. When they were done, the volunteer immediately picked up the tray and headed out toward Apoonivi. As he neared his destination, he spotted Kaatoya coiled up on a stack of wood on top of his kiva. Although the boy was still some distance away, he could hear the rattling of the terrible snake and became too frightened to step any closer. Somehow or other, he regained his courage and moved closer to the giant snake, whereupon it lifted its head and looked around. Silently then, it slid into its kiva, followed by the boy. Much to his surprise, when he came inside, the boy saw a large number of people there. Kaatoya, now in the shape of an old man, was seated by the fire pit. Farther in the background were the women and girls. They all welcomed the boy. "Have a seat, stranger," said the old man. Then he turned to the womenfolk and said, "Feed this boy something. He's come from far away and is probably hungry."

When the boy had satisfied his hunger, the old man smoked a pipe with him. When they were done, he said, "All right, you must have a reason for coming here. No one has sought us out for a long time."

"Yes, that's true," the boy replied. "Our chief sent me, and this is what I brought you," he added, handing the tray of pahos to the old man.

The old man carefully inspected all the pahos and set them aside, after taking some of them for himself. "Thanks!" he exclaimed, "this is exactly what I wanted." He then rose to his feet and shuffled over to the northwest corner of the kiva where an altar was set up. He placed all the rest of the pahos on it, and when they were all arranged just so, returned to his place and sat down next to the boy. "So, what is the purpose of your visit?" he asked.

The boy began to explain, "Well you see, at our village Kotsoy-laptiyo won the most beautiful girl as his wife, and we don't think he's entitled to her. Many of us coveted her when she was still unmarried, but none of us won her heart. We're still interested in her, however, married or not. We were hoping that you would go kidnap her for us. That's why I came; to ask for your help in doing this." The boy then told the old man where the young wife usually went to relieve herself. "She always goes there right at noon," he added.

"Very well. I generally go for a walk at just about that time, so it won't be hard for me to grab her," the old man replied, readily agreeing to the sorcerer's proposition. "I'll keep an eye on her from here, and when I spot her, it won't take me long to reach her." He knew full well that the woman, after relieving herself, would take some time in climbing back up from the ledge.

His mission accomplished, the sorcerers' messenger to Kaatoya returned to Oraibi, where he entered their kiva and conveyed Kaatoya's favorable response to the others. This gave them all great satisfaction.

The next day, Kaatoya made ready to go kidnap Kotsoylaptiyo's wife. Since it was his habit to bask in the sun atop the wood stack on his kiva roof, he could easily watch the womenfolk as they went about their business. Then, as was his habit, he could abduct any that he liked and take them back to his abode, where he could take advantage of them sexually at will. It was also his habit to give his undivided attention to the new ones, and then when he tired of them, to kill them.

It was already midmorning when Kaatoya came out of his abode and watched the women over at Oraibi. Sure enough, it was exactly at noon when he spotted Kotsoylaptiyo's wife coming out to go to relieve herself. At the same moment he saw her squat down, he lunged off the wood stack and headed directly for her. He propelled himself forward by gigantic leaps, and it only took a few of these before he reached Oraibi. Quickly he came up from behind, wrapped himself around her, and made off for his abode, hurling himself forward as before. Miraculously, he left no tracks behind.

When Kotsoylaptiyo's young wife failed to return home, her parents began to worry. "Oh dear," they kept saying, "why isn't she back yet? She went down there quite a while ago." They waited a while longer, but finally her father went out to the toilet area to look for her. He could see that she had been there, but her footprints ended on the way back up from the ledge.

When Kotsoylaptiyo came home that night, he noticed right away that his wife was absent. When he asked her parents, they had to admit there was no trace of her when the father went to see why she had not come back from relieving herself. "Where on earth could she have gone?" her husband exclaimed. "Did you ask around among the villagers?"

"Well, no," they answered. "Since she never goes anywhere, we didn't think to ask."

"Oh, dear!" Kotsoylaptiyo cried. They were all distraught at the young woman's disappearance, but they had no idea what to do or where to search, and it was very dark by then. Kotsoylaptiyo was so unhappy that he didn't feel like eating, so he told his wife's parents that he was going to go over to his grandmother's house. "All right, go ahead," they encouraged him.

So Kotsoylaptiyo headed over to his grandmother's place. He hadn't been to see her since he had gotten married, but he entered without first announcing his arrival, for that is the Hopi way if one arrives alone. The moment he entered her house, his grandmother gave a cry of surprise. "My! What are you doing here this time of night? It's kind of late."

"Yes, I know," replied Kotsoylaptiyo, "but my wife's parents keep telling me that she went to relieve herself at noon and never came back."

"Are those Turds at it again?" said his grandmother. "I was afraid of that. They probably recruited that horrible Kaatoya. He's a really evil creature and probably took great delight in kidnapping your wife. We've got to get her back of course, but just stay here with me for the time being. I know the habits of that monster. Each time he brings back a new victim, he waits until the following day to have sex with her. But once he starts, he won't let go of her for four days in a row. We'll go over there soon, but first we have to gather some materials. First, I want you to go fetch some oak to make a bow. Then we'll need some stems of the Apache plume for arrows. Finally, we'll need some feathers of the mountain bluebird for fletching. These feathers are very powerful."

So Kotsoylaptiyo gathered all these materials, and when the arrows were finished, his grandmother smeared their tips with rattlesnake poison. "All right, that'll do," she said. "We'll get even with that creature in our own way." When everything was done, the two waited, for the next day was the fourth day.

The Turds, meanwhile, waited in their kiva, wondering if Kotsoylaptiyo would somehow find a way to get his wife back. So far, they had no indication that he had even tried. They sat there, gloating in Kotsoylaptiyo's misery, saying things like, "He'll never get her back now. Nobody will want her now that she has been spoiled. What a waste when he married her!" They had nothing but contempt for Kotsoylaptiyo. "Now that Kaatoya has her in his power," they sneered, "Kotsoylaptiyo will have to live the rest of his life without her. The poor fool, he's probably flat on his face with despair at his grandmother's house."

The next morning, Kotsoylaptiyo and his grandmother headed over to Kaatoya's kiva. As they came up the slope leading to it, the sun was already high in the sky, so he was already coiled up on the wood stack, basking in the sun. Since the sun was shining directly on him, he had his head tucked under one of his coils and was sleeping soundly, totally unaware of their approach. The old woman handed her nephew some medicine and instructed him, "Here, chew this and spray it on him. He will then sink into a stupor and will never notice when we get close to him."

Kotsoylaptiyo did as she told him and sprayed the magic medicine over the snake with his mouth. They waited just a bit and then the old woman said, "All right, he's bound to be in a deep sleep by now. Let's get a little closer."

They moved closer and the old woman reassured Kotsoylaptiyo, "He's no risk to us anymore. He can't even hear us when we talk loudly. So, nock an arrow on your bowstring, aim right at his tail, and shoot!"

Kotsoylaptiyo did exactly as she said and aimed an arrow directly at Kaatoya's tail. The instant he let it fly, the monster snake jerked as if startled, and raised his head. Immediately the old woman commanded Kotsoylaptiyo, "Go on, shoot him again! Fire the other three arrows at him!"

Quickly, Kotsoylaptiyo shot another arrow, then another and another. Punctured with the arrows, Kaatoya crashed down the ladder into the kiva, once more trying to raise his head. The poisonous arrows were too much for him, however, and his head dropped back down. Immediately the old woman and Kotsoylaptiyo rushed down into the kiva after him, where people were scrambling off in every direction. By the time they reached him, Kaatoya was completely still.

The girls and women who were confined there were overjoyed to see them and welcomed them effusively. "Yes," said the old woman, "he deserved to die. He was an evil monster who kept you all here against your will and abused you. Where are you from?"

Two of them replied that they were from Mishongnovi and Shungopavi. One was from Matsonpi. Some others were so young when they were kidnapped, they no longer recalled where they came from. "We've been here for many years," they explained, "and we've seen him kill many girls and women. There used to be a lot of us, but each time he got tired of one of us, he simply killed her."

"Well, don't worry any longer," the old woman replied. "He's dead now and we can leave. If you want, you can come to my place in Oraibi, or you can return to your former homes." Then she asked, "By the way, do you know where my daughter-in-law is? She was brought here just recently."

"Oh, yes," one of the women said, "she's still lying in the back room. Each time he brought back a new victim, he kept her in there. When he got aroused, he would go back there."

Kotsoylaptiyo and his grandmother entered the back room and there lay his wife, shivering in the dark. The old woman rushed to her and said, "All right, daughter-in-law, get up! We've come to rescue you."

Right away, Kotsoylaptiyo's wife recognized them and jumped happily to her feet, embracing the old woman. "How wonderful that you found me! I'm so glad to see you. That awful Kaatoya brought me here and showed me no mercy. It was horrible!"

"I'm sure it was," said the old woman. "You can blame those evil sorcerers at the village for this. They asked Kaatoya to kidnap you and he agreed. That's why you had to endure this shame."

The old woman then turned to her nephew and instructed him once more. "Now my nephew, chew some more of the medicine I gave you. Go back in and spray it on the monster's corpse. Then it won't be so heavy anymore, and you can carry it out and put it on the woodpile."

Kotsoylaptiyo did as instructed and dragged the snake out of the kiva by its tail. He and his grandmother then placed the monster on top of the woodpile and lit a fire underneath it. Soon huge flames were leaping up, engulfing the woodpile and the evil snake along with it, causing its flesh to crackle and sizzle. Eventually, the fire spread to Kaatoya's kiva roof and caused it to collapse. They waited for the fire to burn itself out, then filled the kiva hole with dirt and left it there, smoldering.

When they all arrived back at Oraibi, there was great rejoicing.

All the girls and women cried from joy and thanked Kotsoylaptiyo and his grandmother for rescuing them from that horrible creature. Though some of them planned to go on to their homes in other villages, they stayed the night at the old woman's house.

After Kotsoylaptiyo had made his wife safe and comfortable at his grandmother's place, he went over to his in-laws' house to share the good news with them. They too were overjoyed, for she was their only child. "We'll be staying at my grandmother's house for a while," Kotsoylaptiyo explained. "No one can harm us there. But don't worry, we'll come to see you soon."

"Very well, if that is your wish," said the girl's father. "Some of those witch fiends are probably watching us, so it's best if you remain there for the time being. As soon as your wife gives birth to her child, however, you must come back."

And so Kotsoylaptiyo and his wife stayed at his grandmother's place. The next morning the old woman asked the village crier to announce that all the strongmen of the village should meet at her house. And indeed, several who heard the announcement showed up. The old woman was quite familiar with all the men and selected only those who were of good character. These she asked to accompany all the women who wished to go back to their home villages. Soon, they headed out in every direction with the girls and women entrusted to them. A few, however, who had no idea where they originally came from, decided to stay with the old woman.

Meanwhile, the Turds now knew that their plot had failed. They had come to respect the power of the old woman and refrained from any further attempts to harm the young couple.

Some time passed and finally Kotsoylaptiyo's wife gave birth to a baby boy. Life went on, and eventually, some of the girls who had decided to stay with the old woman also got married. Since the old woman had saved their lives, they in effect became her relatives. In this way, she gained lots of male in-laws who were of great assistance to her. They helped make her life quite comfortable, and indeed, she became as wealthy as the other villagers. They're probably still helping her there somewhere.

And here the story ends.

17

How the Snake Ceremony Came to Oraibi

Aliksa'i. People were living at Toko'navi. Among the many who lived
there was a couple with one son. He had a habit of sleeping on the
roof, so he was usually up early in the morning. He would then take
his blanket and head out to a little ridge where he sat watching the
sun come up. It always rose in the east, then traveled across the sky
until it set in the west. After breakfast, he usually busied himself with
chores, but he went about wondering just what kind of place it was
where the sun rose and where it went when it disappeared beyond
the western horizon. This question was constantly on his mind.

Along the northwest side of Toko'navi flowed Pisisvayu, the
Colorado River. The boy enjoyed spending time at the edge of the
plateau high above the river. He would just sit and stare down at it as
it flowed along. The river intrigued him as much as the sun, and he
often wondered where it flowed to and where it ended.

So the sun and the river were always in his thoughts. One morning, when the family was eating breakfast, he said to this father, "Father?"

"Yes, what is it, son?"

"I'd like to ask you a question."

"All right, go ahead," said his father.

"Well, I'm always observing the sun, where it rises and where it sets. I wonder where those places are and what they're like."

"I have no idea," his father replied. "It just comes up and then disappears, but where exactly those places are, I can't tell you."

The boy continued, "I've also been watching and thinking about Pisisvayu, to our northwest. Where, do you think, does it end? Where does all that water flow to?"

Again, his father said, "I'm sorry, I have no idea where all the water goes, and where the river ends."

"Well, I'm asking because these questions are always on my mind. I think I will follow the river downstream and try to find out."

"Is that so?" said his father. "Do you know when you want to go?"

"Yes," said the boy. "I'd like to leave about eight days from now."

"Really? Well, go ahead then. As I told you, I certainly can't help you answer your questions. Why don't you just go ahead and find out for yourself?"

From that time on, the family began to prepare for the boy's departure. The boy's father occupied himself making prayer sticks and prayer feathers for the boy and was usually gone all day. He wanted to have them ready by the night before his son left on the trip. He intended to make lots of them, so he spent every day on this task.

He made four lots of the taqvaho type, and then a whole bunch of regular prayer feathers. Then he made some sakwavaho, again four different lots of them. Finally, he made some of the tsotsokpi type, which have a little perch at the top for the spirit of the deceased. All these he piled on a wicker plaque and ritually smoked over them. When he was done, he wrapped them up in a bundle. He had finished just in time for his son's departure the next morning.

At daybreak the next morning, as the family ate breakfast, the boy's mother got some journey food ready. She gathered pieces of dried meat and ground roasted sweet corn. These she stored in a little buckskin bag, which she tied up tightly and gave to the boy.

When they were finally ready, the boy and his father walked together to the edge of the plateau, and from there they descended all the way to the banks of Pisisvayu. When they arrived there, the father said, "Wait for me here. I'll be right back." He headed upstream and returned a little later with something resembling a drum. It was a sort of floating vessel, and his father had equipped it with a peephole and placed some wooden crosspieces in the center. "Climb in," he told his son, and he instructed him on its use. "Here you can sit, and there you can sleep. And through this opening, you can relieve yourself. Come on, get in."

The boy climbed aboard and his father continued, "If at any point in your journey you don't seem to be moving, look through this peephole. If it looks like you're stuck against something, watch the river carefully. When a wave comes by, push your vessel off with one of these crosspieces. That should get you going again. If that doesn't work, you'll just have to get out and walk."

After these final instructions, the father closed the vessel tightly and pushed it out into the stream. It was soon caught by the current and he was off, floating along nicely. Every now and then he would look through the peephole, especially when he could feel the vessel bouncing through some rapids. Many times his vessel got jammed against the banks, but he was always able to get it unstuck using one of the crosspieces. In this way, the boy journeyed for many days and nights, but still had not reached the end of the river. Eventually, the vessel got caught against the banks again, and when he looked out of the peephole, he saw that he was in a large rapid. Try as he might, though, this time he could not free his vessel, for it was wedged tightly against a large rock. He packed up his food and paho bundle, climbed up from the riverbank, and headed downstream on the plateau above. After a while he reached a ridge and climbed to the top.

When he reached the top, he found himself on a beautiful level expanse covered with green fields. There was a large cornfield there, and the corn looked very healthy. As he was walking along the edge of the cornfield, he saw something in the distance that looked like human beings, so, plunging right into the thick corn plants, he headed toward them. As he got closer, he could see that they were two beautiful girls standing right in the middle of the field. Their hair was done up in large butterfly whorls and they wore nice atö'ö capes and wedding boots. One of them greeted the boy. "So, you've come?" she said.

"Yes," he replied.

"We heard that you were coming," the other one said, "so we've been waiting here for you. Let's go."

With that, the girls headed off, the boy trailing behind them, through the corn plants. When they all reached the field's edge, one of the girls inquired about his destination. He told them that it was his intention to follow the river to its end and find out where the sun went down.

One of them then remarked, "We have no idea about that. Who knows where the sun sets after his journey across the sky? Anyway, not around here. The river, too, just keeps flowing. It certainly doesn't end here."

Suddenly, one of the girls stopped and said, "We can't walk all the way home. It's much too far for that. Wait here a minute." After a few minutes she came back carrying a wide, round thing. It was a *paatuwvota*, a flying shield. "We'll use this," she declared, placing it flat on the ground.

They all stepped aboard the shield. The girl placed a stick under the edge and lifted it up slightly. When she did that, the shield started to spin and rose smoothly into the air. They flew along at great speed for quite some time and, when the sun had almost reached the horizon, landed on top of a kiva.

"Here we are!" the girls announced happily, and they all embarked from the magic shield. Right next to the hatch of the kiva lay a large rattlesnake, all coiled up. The boy was very apprehensive, but the girls were apparently quite familiar with the snake and said, "Don't worry, he won't harm you; just come on in."

The boy entered after them and the snake didn't move. Down below, the kiva was full of men. Every seat was occupied. "So you've come?" they greeted the three of them. "Sit down and make yourselves comfortable. We're glad you're here."

All the men sat with their heads bent. One old man, probably their chief, beckoned the boy to come sit by him. Then he took out his tobacco pouch, filled his pipe, and lit it, and then smoked with the boy. When they were done, he turned to the boy and said, "You've come a long way. Why? No one has ever come this way before."

"Well," the boy replied, "back home, I always sat outside before sunrise, thinking of things, and I couldn't help wondering where the sun rises in the morning and where it sets in the evening after its journey across the sky."

"Is that right?" the old man said. "So that's what you've been thinking. I'm sorry, but I can't help you with that. The sun certainly doesn't set here."

"Well," the boy continued, "then there is also the matter of this river. It just flows and keeps flowing. I would very much like to know where it ends, so I decided to follow its course."

Here again the old man was stumped. "All we know is that it just keeps on flowing. It sure doesn't end here."

By now, food had been served and the boy ate his fill. The girls then cleared away the dishes and everyone got ready for bed. They all unfolded their sleeping skins and bedded down. Soon, everyone was sound asleep.

When the boy awoke the next morning, when it was still white dawn, the old chief said, "All right, let's eat."

Is was then that the boy noticed he was in the midst of a pile of snakes. Around him there were bullsnakes and rattlesnakes, whipsnakes too, on top of each other and coiled up side by side. Apparently, nothing but snakes lived here. Then he noticed that the uprights of the ladder, even its rungs, consisted of snakes. The whole floor of the kiva was teeming with them. All of them were in the process of putting back on their skins, which they had sloughed off during the night. Then they all filed out of the kiva and settling down at the ledge around the kiva entrance, inhaled the power of the early morning light.

The two beautiful girls now said to the boy, "We must go too," and transformed themselves into their rattlesnake shapes. Taking the boy in tow, they led him outside with the others, where they too inhaled the power of the light of the white dawn. When everyone was done, they all entered the kiva again, where the girls announced, "All right, let's eat breakfast!"

Soon, however, it was yellow dawn and the snakes filed out once more and, in reverence, breathed in the light of the yellow dawn. When they had all been infused with it, they slid back down the kiva ladder. They changed back into their human forms and finally sat down to breakfast.

After breakfast the old man said, "The two girls will take you now." Just then, the boy remembered the bundle of pahos his father had given him. "He probably had these people in mind when he made them," he thought, as he reached for it. As he looked around at them, he noticed that some had nothing but the strings of prayer feathers tied to their hair. Others had feathers, but they were ragged and worn clear down to the quill. So, he opened his paho bag and handed the old chief a taqvaho. "Here, I brought this for you," he said.

The old man's face lit up with joy. "Thanks! Because of you, we'll be able to renew our altar. No one has ever made prayer items for us before, that's why ours are so dilapidated." He then distributed the rest, and they used them to replace the tattered pahos on an altar and tied them in their hair. They were elated. Again and again they thanked him, saying "Because of you our lives here have been renewed! No one ever thought of our spiritual needs before; that's why we all look so neglected." Fortunately, the boy's father had made enough pahos for everyone. There was just the right number.

The two girls who were to guide the boy now heaped white cornmeal on little wicker plaques and stowed them away carefully. All three of them then departed, once more climbing onto the flying shield. All day long they were airborne. At one time during the day, they saw a large body of glistening water that stretched all the way to the horizon. It was the ocean. Way off in the southwest, the boy spotted a little black dot, but couldn't tell what it was.

They landed the magic shield right at the seashore and disembarked. "This is as far as we can take you," one of the girls said. "From here on you're on your own. If you return here, we'll be waiting for you. You can count on that."

Then they uncovered the wicker trays of white cornmeal they had brought along and shaped the meal into solid balls, which they flung across the water. As the balls skipped along the water's surface, the ocean suddenly separated, creating a passageway. It led right through the ocean, with a wall of water standing on each side. "All right, go now," they urged the boy.

Utterly amazed, the boy set forth. After he had traveled a short distance, he looked back and saw that the water was closing up behind him. After a long journey through this tunnel of water, he finally came to a structure resembling a kiva. He climbed up on it and entered, whereupon he spotted an old woman. "You've come?" she greeted him.

"Yes, I have," the boy replied.

"Well, your heart has been set on coming, and now you're finally here."

After the two conversed for a while, the old woman said, "It's time for him to come home now. Let me hide you." With that, she took the boy and hid him behind the altar in the northwest corner of the structure. "From here you can see everything that goes on," she said.

The boy flattened himself on the floor behind the altar. Within minutes there was a sharp clattering noise from on top. Tortoise shell rattles were tied to the ends of the ladder poles sticking out through the hatch opening, and it was apparently these that made the sound. Just a moment later, a man came sliding down the ladder. Much to the boy's surprise, he did so on his back, and he held something in both his hands. He was obviously the sun. No sooner had he come to rest on the floor of the kiva-like structure than he faced his grandmother and demanded, "Did you let someone in?"

"No, how could I?" fibbed the old woman.

"Well, I sense the presence of a visitor down here," Sun persisted.

"There's no one here but me," she insisted.

Satisfied for the time being, Sun stepped down to the lower level of the room, holding out pahos and cornmeal that he had collected on his journey that day. "Look here," he said to his grandmother, "Tawvaya is praying to you for food."

"Thank you," the old woman said.

Sun handed her the prayer offerings. The old woman was especially fond of prayers for food and accepted them gladly. She always looked forward to receiving nice thoughts, also. Ugly things and evil thoughts, however, she found repugnant, and when she received them, she immediately discarded them at the base of the ladder. The nice offerings she always placed in front of the altar.

After a while, Sun, still not quite satisfied, said, "I still feel like there is someone here." This time, he thought of looking around, so he walked over to the altar and peeked behind it. "There's someone lying here!" he exclaimed. "I've found you. Come on out."

The boy had no choice now but to get up from the floor and come out of his hiding place. "So, you've come?" said Sun.

"Yes, I have," the boy replied.

"Well, I know you've always wanted to come, and finally, here you are. I guess you saw me coming in?"

The three of them now sat down and ate supper. When that was finished, Sun took a bath and then said to the boy, "There are a few things I need to do. Wait here for a while." With that, Sun went over to the altar and lifted it up. Right underneath was a hole with two ladder poles sticking up, as into the entrance of another kiva. The altar served as the cover to this hole. Sun said, "I have to go now and take care of the people underneath." With those words, he slid down the ladder, whereupon daylight shone up through the hole, and the people down below began their day.

Just then the boy remembered his paho bag again and handed one of the tsotsokpi pahos to the old woman. She was elated at the gift. "Thanks!" she cried. "No one ever thinks about us here, and now because of your gift, our altar has new life again." She was simply overjoyed at receiving the paho.

The boy now went to bed, and while he slept, the sun traveled through the lower world until he rose again in this world. At the place where he rose, everything was the same as here, with a kiva and an old woman.

Sun completed four circuits on his own, and then he was ready to take the boy along with him. "We'll travel together this time," he announced to the boy. "Observe everything you see very carefully. Whenever anything happens on earth, we will be the first to know. The people in the lower world are about to go out and say their prayers to the rising sun. The good ones rise early because they are anxious to pray and scatter sacred cornmeal as an offering. Others don't bother to go out until after noontime. These are the ones with ugly, evil thoughts; that's why they go out so late."

Sun and the boy now traveled along together, picking up the prayer offerings of all these people. There were so many, they had a hard time gathering them all. All day long they traveled until they reached the kiva at the other end, just like the one the boy had originally arrived at, with an old woman living there too. When they arrived, they handed all the prayers they had gathered to the old woman there. With that, Sun and the boy had completed their day's work.

Once again Sun intended to travel by himself. Just prior to his departure, the old woman went up the ladder and attached a gray fox pelt to one of the ladder poles. White dawn appeared. A little while later, she did the same thing with a yellow fox pelt, and yellow dawn could be seen in the sky. Following this, Sun climbed out and completed his circuit from the upper world to the lower world and back again four times, and then told the boy he would return with him to the upper world again. So, they journeyed together for four days, and the boy watched the good people rise early to say their prayers and place their offerings in the palms of the sun. He also saw those with evil thoughts who did not go out to pray until after the sun had reached its peak. Whenever there was fighting, or someone really hurt themselves, Sun was the first to feel it, and some days, after receiving evil thoughts, Sun came home with blood-stained hands. When they had traveled four full days together, Sun returned the boy to the kiva in the ocean where they had first met. The boy spent another four days there.

Soon, it was time for the boy to leave. On the morning of his departure, the old woman packed a few things in his buckskin bag. Tying it tightly, she warned him not to open it until he had returned to his relatives, assembled his uncles, and told them all the adventures of his journey, and only then when the sun was high in the sky.

After these instructions, the two of them climbed out of the kiva. The old woman rolled some white cornmeal into a ball and threw it out onto the water. As before, a passageway opened in the water, with a wall of water on the left and right. "All right, now go with a happy heart. Your relatives are probably anxiously waiting for your return."

So the boy departed, and as before, the waters closed behind him as he went, becoming one body of water again as he stepped ashore at the end of his journey. He was surprised to find the two snake girls there waiting for him. "So, you've returned?" they greeted him. "All right, let's get going." Once again, they traveled on the flying shield to the girls' home, where the boy spent the night.

When he awoke the next morning, he found that he now belonged to the two girls. "They own you now," said the old chief. "They are both your brides, so you must go home with them." The old man also wrapped up something for the boy to take along and warned him, "Don't open this until you're back home and have related all your experiences to your relatives. Also, remember that the sun must be shining."

The old chief instructed the girls, "When you arrive at his village, put your shield back in the water. It will return here on its own." The boy then started out with his two brides. The three of them boarded the magic shield and took off. It was evening before they landed at the river near the boy's village. Here they put their magic vehicle into the river and it was swept away by the current.

Climbing to the plateau above, they soon arrived at the boy's village. He was very happy to be back home, especially since he was bringing two brides with him. His parents were also overjoyed to see him with the two girls, and they all made plans to start the wedding ceremony right away.

When they had all eaten supper, the boy asked all the villagers to gather at his house, where he narrated his adventures. All night long they listened to his story, until daybreak was getting near. When the sun had fully risen, he opened up the two mysterious bundles he had received. Both were packed with turquoise necklaces and earrings, which the boy distributed among his relatives.

That day, his uncles set up a loom and started weaving the required wedding garments for the two brides. When both the small and large wedding robes were finished, the boy went hunting so that meat would be on hand for the hominy stew. In the meantime, the two brides made pik'ami.

That same evening there was a large feast, and everybody ate to his heart's content. The next morning, the boy's mother prepared everything for her son's return to the home of his brides. After their prayer to the rising sun, the three of them set out for the spot where they had landed, near the banks of Pisisvayu. However, as soon as they arrived there, they just turned right around and went back to the village. That's how the boy's mother had arranged things, as the two girls were expected to remain in the boy's village.

After some time, the older of the boy's two wives became pregnant and gave birth to a boy. Shortly after, the other wife also bore a son, who was very handsome.

As the two boys grew, they played with the other children of the village. In the course of their play, these children would sometimes hit one of the boys. The boy would then get angry and bite them in retaliation. As a result, the bites would swell up and cause the children to die.

Since these incidents happened rather frequently, it soon became apparent that the children of the two snake wives could not be tolerated in the village any longer. Now it turned out that the boy had been related to snakes all along, as his father was actually a member of the Snake clan, a fact that he had kept from his son. This was the reason he had been able to make exactly the right number of pahos for his son to give to the Snakes he met on his journey.

So, because of these incidents, the villagers of Toko'navi got fed up with this Snake family and began plotting their deaths, actually setting a date, in four days, to kill them. When the Snake family learned of this, they had no choice but to leave the village. As they wandered along, they stopped at various places for a while, then resumed their trek. One full year they journeyed in this way, always in a southerly direction. Each time they stopped at a place with no water, they planted a spring. At each location where they did this, water flowed right away and kept flowing when they left, as they had the help of Paalölöqangw. He remained behind in each of the springs so it would continue to provide vital moisture for the land.

In this way, the Snake people moved along. Eventually, they reached Qötstuyqa, from where they continued slightly southeast, until they came to Moencopi. They arrived where the road past the present-day village curves. After descending to the area below, they noticed that the Kookop clan and the Bear clan had already passed through, for their emblems were pecked into the rocks. The Snake clan people now did likewise, engraving a rattlesnake on the rock surface.

After staying here for a while, they continued on southward until they reached the area called Wupatki. They settled here for a while but soon learned of people living at Oraibi. So, they turned around and headed back in the direction of this village.

On their journey toward Oraibi, they first came to Söynapi, or Grand Falls, and then to Munaqvi. Here, the elder of the boy's wives became very tired, as she was pregnant and couldn't go on anymore. It was evening when they arrived at Munaqvi, and she said to her husband, "I need to stay here. You can go on without me and make camp further on. Tomorrow morning, you can come back and check on me. I'll be able to give you further instructions then."

So the Snake people went on, making camp at some distance northeast of where they had left her. The following morning, after building a fire and eating breakfast, the boy's father said to the group, "You can start out ahead of me. I'll go back and check."

So the father headed back to where they had left the pregnant woman. When he arrived, she was not there, but he saw her footprints and followed them to the foot of a mesa, off to the northwest. There, much to his surprise, a lot of little jackrabbits and cottontails were hopping around, and little rattlesnakes were zigzagging to and fro among them. Their mother was still giving birth to other animals, and there were little pronghorn antelopes and fawns jumping around. The area around her was teeming with all kinds of other game animals—there was not an animal that the young woman hadn't given birth to. The boy's father was almost speechless. "How cute!" was all he was able to utter.

His daughter-in-law replied, "Let me counsel you now. When you get to Oraibi, ask for admission to the village. Mention our Snake religion in order to gain permission to settle there. Tell the Oraibi leaders that we will perform our ritual near the end of the year, when no other ceremonies are being conducted. At that time, make pahos for me and deposit them anywhere you want. If you think of me when you do this, I'm bound to receive them. And when you set up the effigy of your clan ancestor, hang the necklaces my husband brought back from the ocean around his neck and attach the earrings on him. After you've done that, carry out your ceremony. We're bound to learn of it here."

"Very well," said the father, "we'll do that. And you live happily here." With that, the boy's father left to go follow the others.

They traveled on, and came to Owakw'ovi, where they established a village. There they started their Snake ceremony. All day long they danced. It was an awesome event, and as a result, the rain poured down.

While the Snakes were performing there, the Oraibi village chief sent word, asking them to come, before they even had a chance to ask him. The Snake people replied with a condition, "We'll come if we may hold our ceremony when all the others are finished."

"Very well," the Oraibi chief quickly agreed.

This is how the Snake clan joined the other clans at Oraibi. And when they reached the appointed time for their dance, they set up their tiiponi, or emblem of their clan ancestor, and attached the earrings to it and hung the necklaces on it. Then they conducted their ritual and made prayer feathers for the woman they had left behind. She always receives their offerings, and if the rites are done right, life flourishes and there is plenty of rain.

In this manner, the Snake clan gained admission to Oraibi. The necklaces and earrings they use really came from that place in the ocean, so they are carefully stored away somewhere in the village. They are always used when the Snake clan performs.

And here the story ends.

18

A Flood at Oraibi

Aliksa'i. Long ago, people were living at Oraibi, a great number of them. They were bored, because they didn't have much to do. There were no social dances and no kachinas to entertain them. However, they did enjoy gambling and frequently played sosotukwpi, a guessing game played with cups made of cottonwood. That's about the only thing they had to make themselves happy.

As a rule, some girls and boys gathered in a kiva, divided themselves into two groups, and set up their cups in the middle of the room. One player from each group would squat down by the cups. Then one of them would slowly move his hand over the cups while the rest of the players standing behind the two contestants would begin to sing. When ready to guess, the other squatting player would knock over one of the cups, and if the gaming piece was hidden under it, he or she won a point for their side. Choosing the correct cup on the first try was called *supakoyma*. The losers handed over a few strands from a grass brush to the winners, and these were used to keep score. That's how sosotukwpi was played.

Also, long ago it used to be the girls' duty to grind corn and prepare the various dishes from it. At mealtime, the household members gathered and ate together. When they did, they began to talk about how enjoyable sosotukwpi was and how much fun the players had, and before long, even the married women were attracted to the game. Before long, they became so wrapped up in playing it that they hardly came home anymore, and neglected their daily chores. Finally, many of them became so addicted to the game that they even neglected their infants, and their husbands would have to bring them to their mothers in the kiva to be nursed.

When the husbands had to do this, they usually had to call to their wives repeatedly, because the noise being made by the gamblers drowned out everything else. And to top it all off, when the wives finally responded and came out to nurse the babies, they could hardly wait to get back inside the kiva to continue playing. This state of affairs also meant that wives hardly stopped long enough to cook for their families.

Things really came to a head when the wife of the village chief got involved. He became so disgusted when she failed to return home that he decided to do something about it. He paid a visit to his partner, the village crier, and discussed it with him. "I have to see you," he said, as he entered the crier's house.

"What about?" inquired the village crier.

"Well, our women are so obsessed with sosotukwpi that they don't care for us anymore. As a result, we're really in sad shape."

"That's for sure," the village crier replied.

"I'm fed up with this gambling craze," continued the village chief. "We must do something to bring our children back to their senses."

"Yes, indeed, but that's up to you. What did you have in mind?"

"Well, I have a nephew," answered the village chief. "I've decided to ask a favor of him, and if he's willing to do what I want, I'll let you know."

"That's fine," the village crier agreed. The village chief then took his leave and returned home.

The following night, the village chief sought out his younger sister and asked her to send her son to his house. She agreed. The village chief's sister and the village crier's wife were not yet involved in the gambling craze. When the chief's nephew came round in the evening, the chief explained to him that he was sick and tired of the constant sosotukwpi playing, and that he intended to bring things back to normal somehow.

"Well, what did you want me to do?" asked the nephew.

"I can't tell you just yet. I'm preparing some ceremonial items for you. I'll let you know in four days."

"All right," the nephew replied and went back home.

So the village chief set to work on his preparations. Four days later, when his nephew returned, he told him, "I want you to go hunting for me. I'm hungry for rabbit stew, that's why. Kill one or two jackrabbits, if you can, and beat them to a bloody pulp. I'll use them for something later."

The nephew agreed to do what the chief asked and returned home. The next morning, after breakfast, he descended the Oraibi mesa and headed southeast, looking for jackrabbits. Before long, one sprang up and he brought it down with his rabbit stick. He ran up to it, and following instructions, beat it until it was bloody. He slung it over his shoulder and continued on, spotting a second rabbit a short time later. Unfortunately, this one disappeared into a hole. He began to dig it out and, with a long pointed stick, twisted the skin of the rabbit and pulled it out of the hole. After killing it with a blow across the neck and beating it bloody, he headed straight to his uncle's house. He entered and flung the rabbits on the floor at his feet. "Here you are," he said.

"Thanks!" exclaimed the village chief. "I see you were lucky."

When the boy had left, the village chief skinned the rabbits, drained their blood into a bowl, and stored it away. In the evening, he worked on some other things and then took everything and went to his nephew's house. It had gotten quite dark.

When he arrived there, he greeted his nephew and said, "All right, let's go over to my place. When we get there I'll have further instructions for you."

The nephew and the chief started off, but as they did so, the chief veered off from the way to his house and, bypassing Wupakits'ovi, went down the trail on the southwest side of the mesa. From there they continued in a northwesterly direction, soon arriving at some cliffs that formed a big overhang. Sitting down there with the large bundle he carried, he announced, "All right, I have a costume here for you. I'll help you put it on."

First, the chief fastened a kilt around the boy's waist. Next, he wrapped a tattered woolen manta around his shoulders. Then he placed a mask over his head. Then he put on three more masks, one on top of the other. The outermost one was that of Maasaw, the god of fire and death. When the boy had all the masks on, his uncle poured the rabbit blood over them. "That's it!" he said, satisfied with his work. "I want you to go to Tiposqötö now. Climb up to it from the northeast side where there is a little ledge, and sit down there and wait until it's really dark. Then sing this song that I'll sing for you now. Listen to it carefully and learn it by heart." Then the chief sang this song:

> At Oraibi, at Oraibi
> Something will happen at dusk
> Haa'ay'aa, haa'ay'aa
> Haa'ay'aa, haa'ay'aa
> Anoo.

"As soon as you're through singing, run off toward the village. As you come up the stairs on the southwest side, turn northeast. There, on top of a house, is a little room, the front of which is green. You will find two metates in it, side by side. Climb up there and kneel down by the grinding slab, grab hold of the mano, and make a few grinding motions as if you're grinding corn kernels. Chant these words as you do that:

> Tutaahe, tutaahe
> Tutaahe, tuta wunaahe
> He, he, he.

Then quickly go out of the room and run to the kiva where the gambling is taking place and peek in. Those who see you will take to their heels, frightened by the sight of you. After doing that, come back here again. By then, it will be deep into the night and no one will be out and about, so you won't be in danger of being followed. Skip the second and third nights, but on the fourth night repeat exactly what I just told you. Keep making these appearances, with two days in between, and people will soon become aware of your routine. When that happens, I'll have more instructions for you."

"Very well," the chief's nephew replied, and headed off for Tiposqötö. Sure enough, as he climbed to its top, he found a little ledge there, and he waited until it was dark. When it was time to go, he sang the song his uncle had taught him:

At Oraibi, at Oraibi
Something will happen at dusk
Haa'ay'aa, haa'ay'aa
Haa'ay'aa, haa'ay'aa
Anoo.

Then he ran off. He was a strong runner and extremely fast. At the request of his uncle he had practiced running for several days in a row before he had assigned him this task. Of course, he could not see himself, and had no idea that he looked like a ghost; a fearsome thing, with fiery eyes glowing in his face. Sparks flew from the torch that he carried. After stopping briefly at Masvoksö, he turned around and soon reached Mastanga. There he said a short prayer and headed toward the village. He climbed up the stairs to the mesa top and listened. No one appeared to be about, so he pressed on to the house with the upper story. He dashed up the ladder leaning there and quickly entered the grinding chamber. Making a few strokes on the metate, he sang:

Tutaahe, tutaahe
Tutaahe, tuta wunaahe
He, he, he.

Then he let go of the mano and quickly jumped off the roof. From there he ran to the kiva where the sosotukwpi gamblers were in session. He glanced in briefly and then ran directly northwest through a narrow passageway between buildings. Stopping briefly, he returned to his starting point. No one had seen him.

He sat out two nights as agreed, then repeated his performance. This time, an onlooker seated by the sosotukwpi kiva hatch saw him and immediately ran, screaming to those in the kiva, "Stop, stop! There's a ghost coming!"

But none of the gamblers had heard him, and he continued running. The next evening, when the man went back to the kiva to watch the gamblers, he told some of the other spectators what he had seen. "Something terrible came here last night!"

"What was it?" they inquired.

"I don't know. It was a really repulsive thing, whatever it was. I was just sitting here when I saw it approaching. It climbed up to the second story of a house, where it made some grinding motions on a metate, chanted, and then dashed off again. It was terrible, I can assure you. Why don't you stay here with me tonight? Maybe it will come back."

"All right," the others agreed. "Perhaps we can ambush this ghost."

They waited and waited, but of course nothing happened, as the chief's nephew was taking the night off as instructed. All night they stayed there, but nothing came around. "Perhaps you just thought you saw something," the others said to the man who had first seen the figure.

"But I'm telling you the truth!" shot back the man. "It was a ghostly creature with fiery eyes!" So, the rest of them reluctantly agreed to come back the next night and look for the ghostly figure.

The following evening they all gathered again, but of course nothing appeared. Again they accused the man of lying, and he insisted he told the truth. On the next night, none of the spectators bothered to look for the figure. All their attention was focused on the gamblers once more. They were all intent on the action down below when the man who had first seen the creature cried out, "There's the ghost. Here he comes!"

"Where?" shouted the others.

"There, I just caught a glimpse of him. He's bound to reappear!"

No sooner had he spoken than the ghost materialized, heading straight for them. Suddenly he veered away and ran up the ladder to the grinding room. He was indeed terrifying, and no one had the courage to try to grab him. They were all so scared that they ran, while the figure entered the narrow passageway unhindered and disappeared.

The following evening the men gathered again, berating themselves for their lack of courage. They were determined to try again, so they lay in wait for the ghost once more, and then again, but it did not come. On the third night, however, the monster was back, and they began to notice that he came around the same time of night each time he appeared. They spotted him right away as he was coming up the side of the mesa.

"There he comes!" one of them hollered. "Let's not run away this time!" another beseeched the group. "We can't let him escape this time. Stand fast."

Suddenly the ghost appeared in view, doing everything just as he had on previous occasions. The men had to hold on to each other to keep from falling over. As the ghost jumped off the roof of the grinding room and came toward them, they all lost their nerve and fled. They had failed again!

They gathered together again and discussed another plan. Some had noticed where the ghost came up to the mesa and where he went on his route through the village, and they thought they should station themselves along this route. The ones who were stationed near the mesa edge could holler to alert the rest of his arrival. There were just enough of them to cover all the crucial locations. Somewhere along his route they were bound to be able to ambush him.

By now, they had figured out his routine. "He always misses two days before he reappears," they agreed. "He'll be back the night after tomorrow. We must come out a little earlier and take up our assigned positions."

The evening of the ghost's expected return, they all ate supper earlier than usual, took up their stations along the creature's route, and waited. Before too long, there was a shout from the two men stationed at the mesa edge. "He's coming! I can hear him!" they yelled.

The two men at the mesa edge were hidden behind a large salt bush and a boulder. "All right," they encouraged themselves. "Don't be scared." But when the two saw the dreadful sight of the creature, they ran to the next two men stationed further up the trail. "He's coming!" they shouted, nearly out of breath.

"Why didn't you catch him?" the men reproached the two fugitives. "You were supposed to catch him at the mesa edge!"

Meanwhile, the ghost was fast approaching. When his dreadful face appeared right by their side, and they could hear his laboring breath, they just crouched down and allowed him to pass. The next two, stationed near the grinding room, did not fare any better. They lost all courage to block his way and ran off. The same happened with the fourth pair, who became terrified and took off running. They had failed again!

Three days later, the men all took up their stations again, and resolved to ambush the ghost. Once again, however, the men at the first three stations on his route lost their nerve and ran away. The ghost now entered the narrow passageway where the final two men were waiting. When the creature came out of the tunnel, one of them fainted on the spot. The other, however, was undaunted and grabbed hold of the ghost with all his strength, screaming at the top of his voice, "Hurry! Come here, I've got him!"

The ghost tried to fight his captor off, but to no avail. Two of the men came to help, then a third. Together they surrounded the ghost and finally overpowered him. What a repulsive thing he was! He stood there, breathing hard, but powerless to resist.

"What are we going to do with him?" one of the men asked.

"Kill him! We caught him, so now let's just kill him and dump his body somewhere!" the others all exclaimed.

Now the chief's nephew said, "No, don't kill me. Instead, take me inside the kiva where all the gambling is going on. There you can remove my mask and decide what to do next."

"Very well, if that's your wish," they all agreed. Evidently the ghost was human after all. So they dragged him up to the kiva hatch, and one of his captors shouted down to the gamblers below, "Hold it! Stop gambling for a while. We're bringing someone in."

The gamblers were so involved in their game, however, that they paid no attention, and the men just came on in with their captive. The men were descending the ladder with the ghost when the gamblers finally noticed them. Instantly they stopped and quickly cleared away their gaming pieces, jumping up on the stone benches along the walls, transfixed at the sight of the ghost.

"Here, we brought you this ghost," one of the men said to the man tending the fire. "We were planning to kill him, but he asked us to bring him to the kiva and remove his mask. We have no idea why, or why he's been coming here all this time."

With that, they tore off the ghost's mask, the one with the face of Maasaw. Much to everyone's surprise, there was a second mask underneath, that of the Nuvaktsina. They took that one off, and underneath was a Ngayayataqa, and underneath that the Na'uykuytaqa. And who would have believed it? Underneath everything was the face of the village chief's nephew. "So, it was you!" they all cried, in astonishment.

"Yes," the boy admitted.

"So, what are we going to do with you? We'll definitely have to kill you now."

"All right, you can kill me if you want. My only wish is that afterwards, you throw me into the big gulch nearby, along with my four masks. Four days after, you can come and check on me. Who knows what could be revealed to you then."

"Very well," the men all agreed, and killed the boy right there and then. Then they hauled his body down to the gulch and hurled him in, his four masks with him. After this interruption, the gamblers carried on playing until daylight, but the fun had gone out of their sosotukwpi. So they all went home at daybreak and ate breakfast.

After this event, people didn't go to the kiva to gamble so frequently anymore. They were just not as interested as before, now that the ghost had been caught. Thus, every night, the crowd of players got smaller and smaller. On the fourth day after they had killed the boy, the fire tender reminded everyone, "All right, it's time to go out to the gulch and take a look. Remember, the boy said that something might be revealed to us."

Somebody finally volunteered to go. As he peeked down, he noticed that the boy's body had disappeared, with the exception of a single finger sticking out of the ground. His belongings still lay scattered about. He returned to the kiva and reported what he had seen. "Very well," said the fire tender, "he probably has more in store for us. We'll check again tomorrow."

True enough, when they checked again the next morning, two fingers of the boy's hand were thrusting up from the earth. On the day after there were three fingers, and on the fourth day, four fingers jutted up.

When they found out about this, everyone was wondering what else was going to happen. Not knowing what else to do, they decided to remain in the kiva until evening. Shortly after they ate lunch, the ground began to tremble. As the afternoon wore on, the tremors kept increasing in frequency and force, and just at evening time, there was such a forceful shock that a crack appeared in the plaza. Out of this crack seeped some water. Night fell, and the whole village was rattled by a mighty earthquake. Water began to flow from the crack and was beginning to fill the entire plaza. People were beginning to panic, and, stopping just to grab a bite to eat, they fled the village and scrambled down off the mesa. By midnight the water had inundated most of the village, and every house was deserted.

The following morning there were violent new tremors and aftershocks. Now it so happened that when everyone fled, they left behind a blind man who lived near the plaza. He had saved himself by climbing up on the roof, where he now sat, not knowing what else to do. And it just so happened that, across from him on the other side of the plaza, was another man who was lame. He was perched on a stone bench in front of his house.

When he spotted the man on the roof, he called out to him. "Who are you up there?" There was no answer. Once more he shouted, "Who are you, sitting up there?"

"Who, me?" asked the blind man.

"Yes, you. I'm lame and couldn't run away, but why didn't you run off with the others, away from this dreadful earthquake?"

"To tell you the truth, I was not able to. You see, I'm blind. I simply survived by climbing up here. It was terrible!"

Now the lame man suggested, "Why don't we leave together?"

"How can we?" asked the blind man. "We're both handicapped. I can't see where I'm going and you can't walk. Still, if I could somehow manage to get over to you, we could probably follow the others."

"Yes," said the lame man, "Let me be your eyes. I'll guide you down off the roof. You can then grab some journey food from your house and come over here. You can carry me on your back, and I can do the seeing for you, guiding you each step along the way."

The blind man agreed and with the lame man's help climbed down from the roof. He groped around inside his house and found some leftover piki. He wrapped this up and poured some water into a canteen. He found his way out of the house and called over to the lame man, "All right, which way do I go?"

The lame man talked the blind man over to where he sat. The blind man leaned over and took the lame man on his back. "All right," said the lame man, "from now on I'll be doing the seeing for both of us." They went together inside the lame man's house, where they got some journey food, then headed out of the village.

The village chief was busy making pahos. He placed all the prayer feathers on a wicker tray and went over to the spring on the northeast side of the mesa. Stepping up to the edge of the water, he prayed for an end to the flooding. It was Paalölöqangw, the Water Serpent, of course, that had caused the earthquake and ensuing flood. The chief now begged him to have pity on them and cease his destructive writhing. Some time went by as he prayed, and nothing happened. Then, suddenly, Paalölöqangw rose up from the spring.

Quickly, the chief held out his pahos to him. The gigantic serpent took the offering and sank back into the spring, causing a whirlpool to form. "Thanks for accepting my prayer feathers!" the chief exclaimed. "You have helped bring my children to their senses." With that the chief returned home. There were fewer tremors now, and by nightfall they had ceased altogether.

Meanwhile, the blind man and the lame man had been trekking along without meeting a single soul and were discouraged that they had not caught up with the others. They were exhausted, so they stopped to rest under a ledge. The blind man said to the lame man, "Let's gather some sticks so we can build a fire and spend the night here. We can try to catch up with the rest of the people in the morning."

So, guided by the lame man's directions, the blind man walked about collecting firewood. By the time he had a good-sized pile together, night had fallen, so they built a nice fire and warmed themselves. As they sat there, they heard a noise, like an animal moving through the underbrush. "Listen," said the lame man, "I can hear a rustling sound. An animal must be coming our way."

"Really?" said the blind man. "I can't see it, so I have no idea what it is."

The two were still seated there, trying to figure it out, when an antelope appeared right in front of them. It had enormous horns, and it just stood there staring at them. The lame man said, "Give me my bow and arrows. They're right behind you. There's an antelope right in front of us. I'll shoot it."

The blind man reached behind himself and handed the bow and arrows to the lame man, who quickly nocked an arrow, drew it to the point, aimed, and let go. The poor antelope made one big leap in the air and collapsed on the ground. "I hit it!" exclaimed the lame man. "Let's go get it." He directed the blind man to the antelope carcass, and upon reaching it, the blind man quickly climbed on top of it and patted it on the shoulder. "Thanks! You really killed it!" he said, praising the lame man.

"Sure I did. I knew I couldn't miss," he said.

The blind man now dragged the carcass over to the lame man, and they both began butchering it. When they were done, they cut off the antelope's head. The fire had produced a lot of hot coals, so they dug a pit and buried the head in it to bake. Then they set to cutting the meat into thin slices. They were still doing that when the roasted antelope head exploded with a loud clap! The noise was so loud, with sparks flying in every direction, that the two were startled and jumped to their feet. "Whew! That really scared me!" exclaimed the lame man, who was hopping around like crazy. "Yes, what a scare!" said the blind man, who was so startled when it popped that he opened his eyes. Both of them were so astounded by these miraculous events that they didn't want to go to sleep. The blind man was almost beside himself, seeing the stars in the sky for the first time. He just stared at them, afraid that if he closed his eyes, he might lose his ability to see. The lame man, on the other hand, was so taken with being able to walk that he kept walking to and fro the whole night long. He was afraid that if he sat down, he might suddenly lose his ability to walk again. In this way the two of them spent the entire night.

At dawn, after packing up their meat, they decided to head back to the village. "Now that our handicaps are gone, let's hurry back home," said the formerly blind man. "Yes," said the formerly lame man, "now that we both can walk and see, we should get there in no time."

Before long, they were climbing up the mesa to Oraibi. The earthquake and flood had caused a lot of damage, and the village was a sorry sight.

Now that the earth was still again, the villagers began returning one by one, though some were too scared to ever return. Soon, life was more or less back to normal. Many people, realizing that they might have brought the catastrophe upon themselves by their excessive gambling, began to pursue other, more worthwhile things. The spring, however, completely dried up. Because the Paalölöqangw had accepted the chief's nephew as a sacrifice, it had committed a transgression. So it disappeared from the spring and, as a result, the spring ceased flowing. In this way the Oraibis lost a precious water source. Also, the rocks now lie flat like a slope on the north side of Oraibi near the graveyard. This is because the flood caused the whole cliff to slide down. Anyone who goes there can see the evidence for himself.

And here the story ends.

19

The Boy Who Became a Deer

Aliksa'i. People were living at Oraibi. Long ago, there were so many of them that the village was crowded, and to supplement the food they raised as crops, the men and boys often went hunting.

Mostly they hunted jackrabbits and cottontails in the vicinity of the village, but now and then they got a hankering for the larger game animals, and this meant they had to go much farther afield. Pronghorn antelopes were not too far away, but not until they reached the ponderosa pine forests around Nuvatukya'ovi, the San Francisco Peaks, did they encounter deer and elk. Buffalo were found even farther away, beyond the villages of the Rio Grande Pueblos in the northeast, so the Oraibis never hunted them.

Among the inhabitants of Oraibi was a boy in his early teens who only occasionally was able to bag a rabbit or two. He had yet to go on a hunt for big game.

One day the village crier came around announcing a hunting expedition to the northwest to seek big game. The thoughts of all the hunters of the village then became focused on these animals as they awaited the morning of the appointed departure day.

When he heard the announcement, the boy was really eager to go on this hunt, so he told his parents that he had decided to go. He asked his mother to prepare some food for the journey, and he asked his father to help equip him with the things necessary for such an undertaking.

The boy's parents were very pleased to hear that their son wanted to go and enthusiastically made preparations. His father even made a new bow and arrows for him. "Thanks indeed," they said, "we haven't had any meat from these big game animals, so if you're lucky and kill one, we'll be able to eat their meat just like others around here. We're so glad you're confident enough to go along and that you decided on your own to do this."

Having decided to take part, he rose early every morning and before doing anything else went out to pray to the owner of all the animals. "Please," he implored, "have pity on me and grant me the good fortune to kill one of your big game animals. I'd like to bring one back for my parents." Only after praying would he go home to eat breakfast.

A good hunter, of course, is known for his skill, and people praise him for never failing to bring something back. The boy was eager for such fame, and so he looked forward to the hunt with great anticipation. The evening before their departure, the man in charge of making pahos for the hunters asked the boy, on behalf of everyone, to go deposit them in a shrine northwest of the village.

When he reached this shrine, he prayed, "All right, we will come hunting for you tomorrow, so don't stay out of reach. We'd like to sweeten our mouths with your meat." With that prayer, he deposited the offerings, scattered some sacred cornmeal over them, and headed back to the village.

He had just turned around to go back when he thought he heard voices, so he stopped in his tracks to listen more closely. Sure enough, he did hear voices, and they seemed to be speaking Hopi. He knew he was expected back, so instead of investigating further, he returned to the village and mentioned this experience to the others who planned to go on the hunt the next day. "Maybe they were other Hopis, also out hunting," the boy suggested. Others in the planned hunt, however, said, "Those may have been game animals that you heard, gathered nearby. They may have heard you. They speak Hopi, you know, just like us, so that's probably what you heard."

The next day, the hunters set out and soon reached the hunting ground that had been selected. Game was plentiful there, and before long they had all bagged an animal, including the boy, who bagged a rabbit. They all returned home carrying their kills on their backs, and the boy's parents were overjoyed that their son had brought some rabbit meat.

Encouraged by this success, the boy decided to try his luck again in a few days, this time by himself. He shared his intentions with his parents and they wholeheartedly agreed. "Just make me a little journey food," he asked his mother, "and if I'm lucky, I'll come back with enough meat to last us all winter."

"That's wonderful," said his father. "I'm glad that you intend to go."

The day before his departure, the boy asked his father to make some pahos to deposit in the shrine in the northwest. His father readily agreed. The next morning the boy left early, and upon arriving at the shrine, deposited the pahos and prayed as before.

Again, as on the previous occasion, he heard voices just as he turned to go home. Listening closely, he seemed to hear many voices, based on the amount of noise he was hearing. And indeed, they seemed to be speaking Hopi. He thought, "Maybe those are hunters who have camped there."

He listened more closely, then headed in the direction of the voices, stopped again to listen, and then proceeded once more. In this way, he moved farther and farther from the village without realizing it. After a while, the sun set and it grew dark. Finally becoming conscious of the passage of time, he stopped and looked back. He could no longer see the firelight of the village!

Not knowing what to do, the boy stood still, listening again to the voices, which seemed very close now. "Why don't I just go up to them?" he thought. "They're most likely Hopis and will welcome me." Groping his way through the dark, he moved in the direction of the voices. When he was close enough to see a fire, he saw that many people were crowded around it. They were clearly speaking Hopi. When he took a closer look by the light of the flickering fire, he could see not only men but also women and children.

One of them spotted the boy, jumped to his feet, and shouted, "There's someone coming!"

Another one of them replied, "That's probably the boy who went hunting big game for the first time the other day. Don't frighten him; he'll come closer."

When the boy hesitated, one of them urged him on, saying "Come here. We heard you coming." Only then did the boy walk up to them and sit down by their fire.

"All right, welcome," an old man said. "You must have a reason for being here."

"Yes, I do," said the boy. "I was in a hunt around here a few days ago and really enjoyed it. So I decided to try my luck on my own. If I can bag at least one big game animal and lug it back home, my family will have enough meat to last the entire winter. I'm not really a skilled hunter yet and have only killed a rabbit here and there. Their meat doesn't last very long, however."

The boy now explained that he had heard their voices and headed toward them, straying so far away from Oraibi that he could no longer see its firelight.

The old man who spoke on behalf of all those gathered there now reassured the boy. "Don't worry. Feel free to spend the night with us. We have plenty of food and lots of wood to burn, so you won't get hungry or cold."

The boy readily accepted their offer and said, "Thank you so much for your kind welcome. I'd be glad to stay here with you, because it's too dark to head back home."

The boy was still eating when several of the others got ready to go to bed. When the boy finally seemed satisfied, the old man asked, "Are you full?"

"Yes indeed, I am," replied the boy.

"All right then, let's go to bed. Just lie down here and sleep. I'll be right over there." With that, the boy spread out his sleeping skin and was soon sound asleep.

A little later, while it was still dark, he felt a hand on his shoulder, shaking him. Then a voice said, "Wake up!" When the boy opened his eyes and looked up, he recognized the face of the boy who had first spotted him coming. "Thanks," the boy who first spotted him said, "you belong to me now."

The boy from Oraibi didn't really understand what he meant by that and asked, "Why?"

"Well, when you approached us, I was the first to see you. You wanted to become a great hunter and gain fame through your hunting skills, isn't that right? Wasn't that your deepest wish?"

"Yes, that's true. That's why I came out here."

"Well, I knew that. And now that you're here with us, you've been transformed, so don't think about going home for the time being. You'll be able to go in four days."

"That's fine with me," agreed the boy from Oraibi, still not completely understanding what was going on.

"All right then. Tomorrow my people here will ceremonially wash your hair." With that he left, not saying another word.

Still a little puzzled, the boy became a little frightened and reproached himself for straying so far from Oraibi by himself. He lay awake for a while, pondering his strange experience, but finally tired and fell asleep again.

When he awoke early the next morning, the old man already had a fire going. He was stoking it when he said, "Get up, boy! Remember, we are going to ceremonially wash your hair today."

True enough, the sun had hardly risen when some women arrived with a bowl full of yucca suds. Beckoning the boy to them, they washed his hair, one woman after the other. Then one of the women told him to go out and pray to the sun, and when he had done that, they would serve him breakfast.

When he had finished eating, the boy who had spotted him first and who had said the night before, "You belong to me now," said to him, "All right, you have given yourself to me, and I am now your ceremonial father. Let's go hunting together."

They had just started out when his new father said to him, "Wait a minute. Let's sit down here for a while. I have some things I want to say to you before we go."

After sitting down, he continued, "You see, all pronghorns, deer, and elk have their own scent. If you want to get close enough to them to kill them, you must first obtain their scent and keep it stored away for later use. If you don't do this, you'll never be able to kill any of us. I know this because I myself am a deer. That's what I wanted to tell you and why I brought you here."

The boy from Oraibi now realized for the first time what his ceremonial father was. His father continued, "I also have my own scent. You must take some of it from me and smear it on your body. Then you won't smell like a human anymore, but like one of us, and we won't run away when you approach. If you don't use it, you'll smell like a human, and we'll always run at your approach. So, always bring that scent with you when you go hunting and smear it on your body." With that, the deer boy removed some of his scent and handed it to the boy from Oraibi, who rubbed it all over his body. The two then set out again.

Before long, they encountered a herd of browsing deer. "All right," the boy's father said, "go ahead and sneak up to them."

The boy cautiously proceeded toward the herd. They were in a clearing and spotted him right away, but since he smelled like they did, they just stood there and continued browsing.

The boy's father, who had followed behind him, now prompted the boy, "Well, which one do you like the most? Go ahead and choose one."

Skirting around the herd, the boy looked them over carefully. Finally he chose a large buck. After the boy had killed him, the two of them dragged the carcass aside. After skinning the deer and butchering it, they hauled the meat back to camp, where the girls and women helped cut it up into slices and bundled it up in the skin.

"Tomorrow we'll go to another place," said the father, "but now let's have a bite to eat and get some rest."

Sure enough, the next morning the two set out again and soon reached a ledge above a steep cliff leading down into a canyon. Mountain sheep lived here, and they were cavorting among the rocks. As they watched them, the boy's father reminded him, "You should still have some of that scent I gave you yesterday. Rub some on your body before we climb down here."

The boy did so and the two of them started down into the canyon, closely watching the mountain sheep all the while. The sheep were not disturbed at all by their presence. They had spotted the two of them, but continued about their business, frolicking, jumping from boulder to boulder, and really seeming to enjoy themselves. It was truly amazing that they never made a misstep and fell.

Again, the deer boy urged the boy from Oraibi to select one and kill it. The boy chose the largest ram he could see. His father then said, "Climb a little higher so you can hit him right in the back. If you're lucky, he won't fall into the canyon when he dies. Mountain sheep are powerful and can quickly scamper over the boulders and disappear. That's why you must stand above them. Then you can see where a wounded animal runs."

The Oraibi boy did as he was told, took careful aim and hit the ram in exactly the right spot. It simply collapsed on the very boulder where it had stood. They climbed down to it, skinned it, and cut it in half. The deer boy then said, "Before you load this on your shoulders, scratch your palms and the soles of your feet with his hooves. These mountain sheep are so surefooted that they never fall, even when they run. If you do this, you will have their wonderful climbing skill."

The boy scratched his palms and feet and the two of them climbed back to the top of the ledge and continued back to the animals' camp. All of them were happy to see the Oraibi boy again, and one of the women said, "Thanks, you were lucky. Bring your meat over here, and we'll cut it up into thin slices and hang it out to dry."

On the third day, the Oraibi boy and his father woke early and headed out in a southeasterly direction. After traveling for quite a while, they came upon an open area with grass and a few bushes.

"The animals that live here are the pronghorn antelopes," said the deer boy. "They are the fastest of all game animals, so be very careful when you approach them. Again, select one and kill it. When you've done that, look around for some of their dry, round droppings. Then, when you feel like hunting an antelope, just pulverize some of these droppings and sprinkle the particles on yourself. When antelopes bed down at night, they do so on top of their droppings, to keep warm, and so they come to smell like the droppings. So, if you sprinkle that odor on your body, you'll smell exactly like them and they won't run away when you get close."

So, before approaching the antelopes, the two picked up some of their droppings, crushed them finely, and sprinkled them on themselves. Sure enough, the antelopes were not at all skittish, though one of the large bucks raised his head and watched them closely.

Suddenly, all of the antelopes that had been resting in the grass jumped to their feet and just stood there, motionless. The deer boy said, "I know you also want to become known for your speed, so look at these animals and select the fastest one. If you kill him, you'll acquire his swiftness."

By now, most of the antelopes had returned to browsing, because they could not detect any human scent. Circling around the herd, the Oraibi boy examined them all closely. Then he saw an enormous buck, right in the middle of the herd, that seemed different from the others. His coat was slightly brown. When the boy spotted him, he thought, "That's got to be the one. There's something different about him."

The Oraibi boy now told the deer boy which one he had chosen. "All right," said the deer boy, "I'll go herd them toward you. Stay here and wait until they run past, then shoot the one you want. Aim carefully!"

The antelopes began galloping toward the Oraibi boy, with the chosen buck fourth from the rear of the herd. As the buck went past, the boy drew his arrow, aimed carefully, and shot him right in the heart. The beautiful buck plummeted forward and fell to the ground. Fearing that there was still some fight in him, the boy rushed over and straddled the antelope, grabbing for his horns. He was stone dead, however.

"Thanks," said the deer boy. "You chose the right one. That's the one I set aside for you when we first came upon the herd."

"Is that so? Well, it pleases me that I guessed right. I really did take a fancy to this buck," responded the Oraibi boy.

After that episode, the two of them returned to the camp site with the slain antelope buck. Again, the people welcomed the Oraibi boy, and the women butchered the animal and dried the meat for him.

Later that night, the deer boy and the Oraibi boy headed off to the southwest. Along the way, they met an antelope that had been waiting there for them. "You've come?" he greeted the two.

"Yes," replied the boy and his ceremonial father, the deer boy.

"All right," said the deer boy, "you go on with this antelope. I'll catch up with you later."

So the Oraibi boy and the antelope went off, the deer boy following along behind. Eventually, they reached the place where the boy had killed the antelope buck earlier in the day. Not far from this place, the antelopes had their homes, and when the two of them arrived at the antelope kiva, a good fire was going inside. "How about a welcome! There's someone with me," said the antelope when they had arrived on top.

Right away, they were asked to enter. "Come on in. Looks like you have the boy with you," said a voice from inside.

"Yes, I won him. That's why I led him here," said the antelope, "so let's wash his hair ritually."

An old man in charge of the fire now beckoned to the Oraibi boy to come to his side, and said, "We know full well why you are here."

"Yes, I'm sure you do," said the boy. "I came here for you. I'm sure you know that I want to become a skillful hunter and become famous for my hunting ability."

"Yes, we know. So now your father, who had you brought here, will teach you some things." With that, the old antelope man turned to the deer boy, who had suddenly arrived, and said, "All right, call on our relatives, the kachinas, to come here."

The deer boy went out on the kiva roof and did as he was told. When he came back in he said to his adopted son, "Listen carefully to the songs that I will sing for you now." The Oraibi boy concentrated hard, and since he had a good memory, he quickly had them memorized.

Next his father said, "Pay close attention to the kachinas who are about to arrive. If you ever want to put on a dance like them, tell your kiva mates to dress up just like them."

Very soon thereafter, the calls of the kachinas could be heard on top. They were mountain sheep. "Have a seat," the old man antelope welcomed them. "We can't teach the boy our ceremonial knowledge all by ourselves, so that's why we asked you here. You can dance first."

The mountain sheep agreed. They stood up, got in line, and began to dance, disguised as kachinas. They sang and danced for some time, and by the time they had stopped, the boy knew their songs perfectly.

The old man now said to the Oraibi boy's father, "All right, now go southwest and call a few of our other relatives."

This time, the deer came and danced as kachinas, and by the time they had finished, the Oraibi boy knew their songs by heart.

Next, the old man had the boy's father call upon their relatives in the southeast. In a short time, antelopes came and danced as kachinas. The boy also learned their songs very quickly.

The fourth time, the patriarch of the antelopes asked that relatives from far in the northeast be invited. It took a long while, but finally they could be heard coming. They were strong runners and came galloping along, so forcefully and in such numbers that the ground shook. They came to a halt, snorting, their combined breath sounding like the rushing wind.

When the large group of buffalo had calmed down, they filed into the kiva. They had come from far away; that's why it took so long for them to arrive. "Thanks for coming," the old man said. "You can start your performance right away, so you can return to your homes before daylight. We called you because we wanted to initiate this child of ours from Oraibi. I'm so glad you came, so do your part now."

Now both the antelopes and the buffalo kachinas began to dance and sing their songs. When they were done, the old man said to the Oraibi boy's ceremonial father, "That's not all yet. Go out between the northeast and northwest now, and call our relatives from there." The father went out and did as instructed and sat back down to wait.

Soon, a large number of animal kachinas approached the kiva, so many that the Oraibi boy could not tell them apart. They all had different calls and were all calling at once, making an awful racket. As they grew closer, and the boy could see them better, he realized that it was a mixed group of all the animals he was familiar with, including some elk. There were so many of them that clouds of dust hung in the air behind them.

Before long, they too had entered the kiva and were dancing. The Oraibi boy's father instructed him, "Pay close attention now, and memorize their song. We always dance like this for someone like you who wants to became a great hunter. Take careful note how they're all dressed so you can remember everything when you get back home."

The boy paid close attention, and by the time they finished, all the details of their performance, song, and dress were forever recorded in his memory. He was really impressed with the beauty of their song and the message it conveyed.

When these kachinas had departed, the old patriarch now had the boy's father call one more animal, this time from above. This puzzled the Oraibi boy, because he knew of no game animal that could fly, but he sat there anyway, staring up at the sky, waiting to see what would appear.

Suddenly, a large bald eagle landed right next to the fire. Immediately, he asked, "Why did you call me at this late hour?"

"Well," said the old man, "we have our child here and are gathered to teach him our way of life and our ritual dances and songs.

That's why we called you."

"Is that so? Well then, I understand," the eagle replied.

The patriarch of the antelopes now explained to the boy, "This eagle makes his home high in the sky. In a way, he possesses all of us, for he can see everything that happens as he soars. Because of that ability, he's the best hunter of all. From him you will receive his hunting skill."

"That's fine," said the bald eagle. "I'm glad to know that this boy will also give himself to me, and that I'll have him as my son. Let's teach him my knowledge now."

With these words, the game animals began to chant for the eagle, while he danced. He danced beautifully, so light on his feet that he hardly seemed to touch the ground. Every now and then, at the right place in the song, he flew up a bit and then touched down again. When he was finally done, he exclaimed, "There! That's the way."

Now the old man turned to the Oraibi boy and said, "Now you've seen our way of dancing, and I imagine you've learned our songs, including the song of the eagle. Tomorrow you will go back home, filled with hunting skills and our ceremonial knowledge. Unfortunately, you Hopis are eternally envious of each other and covet each other's skills and possessions. So when you use these skills one day, there will be some who hate you for it. You are no longer just an ordinary person; you are related to powerful people, and if you reveal your ceremonial knowledge, these hateful people will be insanely jealous. Because of the initiation you've just gone through, you are now one of us. If these jealous people ever try to harm you, just come to us. We're your relatives now and will always welcome and protect you."

The boy nodded that he understood everything, then bedded down with his ceremonial father. Shortly after rising the next morning, the deer boy's relatives ritually washed his hair once more and handed him some meat they had packed up for him.

As he was just about to leave, his deer father said to him, "All right, go happily now. Your parents are probably wondering where you've been and are anxiously waiting for you. Be sure not to take this meat off your shoulders anywhere on your journey. If you do, you won't be able to lift it up to your shoulders again." And so the boy took his leave and set out for home.

In Oraibi, meanwhile, the people had realized that the boy had not returned from his hunting excursion. Four days had passed and still there was no sign of him. Some men and boys went out to look for him, finding a place where he had camped, but his fire had long since burned down. They saw that his tracks led off in a northwesterly direction, but there was no trace of him anywhere, so they returned to Oraibi.

When they told the boy's parents that they had failed to find him, they were distraught and began worrying that he might be dead. Negative thoughts crossed their minds, such as "He shouldn't have gone all by himself. Those game animals are powerful and can kill a hunter."

That afternoon, some men were hunting in the area southwest of Oraibi, when one of them saw a figure coming from the northwest, apparently carrying a large load on his back. "That looks like the boy that went out hunting and hasn't returned," exclaimed another one of the hunters. "Someone run to the village and tell the others." Another of the hunters volunteered and set off immediately for Oraibi.

From the messenger's description, the boy's father felt that it must be his son, so he quickly left his house and descended to the plain below. He ran to meet the distant figure, and sure enough, when he got closer, recognized him as his son. The father embraced him and cried, "Thanks, you're back. When you didn't come back from your hunting trip, your mother and I got very worried. Some men and boys searched for you but gave you up as lost and came back. We really began to lose heart then."

"I can understand that," the boy replied, "but while I was gone, I learned many things and obtained a lot of meat. Other than being slowed down with all this weight, I'm just fine."

Back at the village, the boy's mother was also elated to have him back. "Look, mother," he said, "I brought back all this meat. Why don't you make a pot of hominy stew with it and bake a lot of piki? Then we can invite all the people to come and feast with us."

When the boy and his father were alone, he told him everything that had happened, and that he now belonged to the animals. "They specifically instructed me that any hunter who kills one of them must invite all the people to a communal meal. If this is done, they will continue to offer themselves up to be killed the next time the hunter goes out. That's why I told my mother to invite the whole village." Once the food was prepared, the mother heeded her son's wishes and fed all the villagers, who were delighted with the fine stew and piki.

Meanwhile, wintertime had arrived, and it was the month of

Paamuya. At this time of year, kachinas go from kiva to kiva and dance. The boy went to his father's kiva, of course, and the members of this kiva were trying to decide what kachinas they would come as when they entertained the people. Several were suggested, but there was no support for them.

They met three times, and still couldn't come to a consensus, so the boy decided to address them about it. "I've been thinking about a group we could perform," he said.

Surprised, his kiva mates replied, "Really? Tell us who you have in mind, so we can discuss it."

"Well, it occurred to me that we could dance as all the various game animals."

"Is that so? Do you know their song?"

"Yes, as a matter of fact, I know it quite well, so that's not a problem. I'll sing it to you right now and you can decide." Immediately, the boy began to sing, and the song was so beautiful that they agreed to dance as a mixed group of game animals.

On the eve of dance day, they all costumed themselves as various game animals—whatever animal struck each man's fancy. The boy told them exactly what their masks and costumes should look like. That evening, when everyone had finished his own mask, they lined them all up in a row on a shelf. All the big game animals were there: antelope, deer, mountain sheep, elk, buffalo, even the bald eagle.

When everything was ready, the spectators filed into the kivas and the kachinas began to dance. The boy who had suggested they dance as mixed game animals danced as an antelope and was in the leading position in the line. The eagle, guarding them all, danced at the end of the line. When they finished, the kachinas went up the kiva ladder, all uttering their particular calls. The bald eagle, of course, went out last, as much flying as using the rungs of the ladder. The spectators just sat there in stunned silence, staring after them. They had really enjoyed their dancing.

The group went around to the various kivas until there was only one stop left before returning to their home kiva. Now it so happened that this final kiva belonged to the sorcerers of the village, sometimes called the Turds, but the game animal group didn't know this. They just entered the Turds' kiva, did their performance there, and returned to their home kiva. Here they danced one more time, concluding the kachina dances.

The sorcerers, who were still assembled in their kiva, now began to smoke ritually. Their chief then said, "I had a feeling that boy would come back and do something like this, because he was away so long hunting. He could never have brought back so much meat without having special powers, powers that he probably obtained from the game animals that his group just presented to the people. We cannot tolerate anyone with this kind of power. We must kill him!"

However, not all the sorcerers, evil as they were, shared the chief's opinion. Some had greatly enjoyed the feast the boy had treated everyone to. And indeed, he was responsible for this impressive new group of kachinas. Granted, they were envious of the boy, but they didn't necessarily want to see him die. They were content simply to cause him harm.

Meanwhile, tired from the night dances, the boy retired to his kiva. After rolling out his bedroll, lying down, and falling into a deep sleep, he felt someone shaking him and whispering, "My son, follow me!" The boy sat up, immediately recognizing the voice as that of his ceremonial father. "Let's go out to relieve ourselves together," he suggested.

When they had both relieved themselves, the boy's ceremonial father said, "I just learned that the Turds are jealous of you and are planning something bad. You're dear to me, so I've come to alert you. Four days from now, when the sun just peeks over the horizon, they'll come for you, but I'll wake you just before they arrive so you can be ready for them. Gather up all the samples of the game animal droppings that I gave you when you left us and take them with you. You and I will run off together, with me in the form of fog, preceding you." With those instructions, his ceremonial father disappeared.

Sure enough, four days later, early in the morning, he was awakened by his ceremonial father's voice coming from a thick fog. "All right, my son," said his father, "get up! The sorcerers are coming."

Quickly he jumped out of bed and fastened a bag of animal scat to his waist. He was just climbing out of the kiva when the Turds came rushing up with arrows in their hands. They were completely out of control, and, leering with hate, they yelled "We don't want you here! We're going to kill you with our own hands!"

The boy's ceremonial father, who had just then come upon the scene, now transformed himself into a gigantic deer, and, lowering his antlers, charged toward the kiva entrance. Before the sorcerers knew what was happening, the huge buck was goring them and flinging them left and right. Immediately then, the boy and his ceremonial father dashed off toward the southwest, descending to the plain below.

When they had reached Pangwuvi, Bighorn Sheep Point, the boy's father stopped and said, "Wait a minute. Let me change you first, and then we can keep going. Some of us game animals are very swift, so they'll never catch up with us if I do that."

The boy's father chewed some magic medicine, which he then sprayed on his adopted son. Instantly the boy was turned into a deer. "All right," said his father, "with you as a deer, they have no chance of catching us, even though they have powerful helpers." The two then took off again, running much faster than before.

The Turds still pursued the two, but realized they were getting further and further behind. Finally, they concluded that it was pointless to continue pursuing the boy and his father. "We had a feeling that boy had supernatural power," one of them said. "He demonstrated it back at the village, and we could not tolerate that. But now, we'll never be able to catch up with him! Too bad, but it looks like it can't be helped."

Having failed to catch and kill the boy, the Turds returned to the village. When the Oraibis learned of the sorcerers' murderous plot, they all became enraged and called upon the village chief, urging him to banish the sorcerers to a place far away where they could establish their own settlement.

Since this was the will of the villagers, the chief headed over to the Excrement Kiva and chastised the leader of the Turds. He was so upset with them that he spoke in a high-pitched voice. "What you tried to do to that boy was unforgivable! We could have thrived here, relying on his hunting skills and spiritual power, but you had to spoil all that. That boy was no ordinary human; he not only supported us with plenty of meat, but also brought those powerful game animal kachinas to us. You couldn't tolerate his power and tried to kill him, but he bested the lot of you, and now he's gone.

"It's your fault that from now on, we'll only be able to kill these game animals with great effort and luck. That boy is now one of them. Because of your hateful actions he will surely explain to the other game animals what we Hopis are like, and they will learn of our wicked ways. When they do, they will be extremely wary around humans, and no one will ever be able to just walk up to them. Curses on you!"

This is how the Oraibi village chief berated the chief of the sorcerers. Then he continued, "These children of mine, the Oraibi villagers, told me that it is their unanimous wish not to put up with you any more. They hate you, and don't want you living here among them. I certainly share their feelings. So, get out and go settle somewhere else! There you can treat each other as you see fit. You're the bane of this world, and think of nothing but evil. Even some of your own people can't stand the likes of you any longer. So, leave, once and for all!" With these harsh words, the village chief turned on his heel and left. The sorcerers were compelled to leave Oraibi.

Meanwhile, the boy and his ceremonial father had reached the animal range far in the northwest. The boy's relatives were happy to see him back. "Thanks for returning safely. We can all live together happily now," they assured him.

The animal chief now spoke somewhat in the same vein as the Oraibi village chief. He declared that from now on, the Hopis would have to suffer great hardships in order to obtain their meat, and that no game animal would ever freely offer itself to a hunter again. Nevertheless, he said, "Since not all of them tried to murder you, and some of them remained pure of heart, they will not suffer like the rest. If a person has a good heart, he may change our minds when he goes hunting."

He turned to the boy. "We hold you dear, so we rescued you. You are now one of us for good, and will live here with us from now on."

Then he added, "You'll be our protector henceforth. To carry out this duty, you must roam the land and spy on the Hopis. If someone appears in the distance who is out hunting, you must warn us by herding us away from them, so that the hunter does not find us right away. The humans are not supposed to be able to kill us without great difficulty."

From that day on, the Oraibi boy lived there with all the game animals, acting as their lookout. Long ago, antelopes came quite close to the villages, but when the boy became their protector, he immediately herded them away from the village, toward the southwest. He did not quit driving them until they had crossed the Little Colorado River. That's why they can only be found in that area today.

At Pangwuvi, Mountain Sheep Point, the mountain sheep also became extinct, but since they used to roam there, the spring there is named after them.

In this way the sorcerers treated that boy. As a result, he ran away and became one with the game animals. The Turds, in turn, had to leave Oraibi and go into exile. They became scattered all across the land, and Oraibi remained free of them for a long time.

And here the story ends.

20

The Woman Who Gave Birth to the Seeds

Aliksa'i. People were living at Shungopavi, up on top of the mesa, after having abandoned the old village down below.

At the time the village had lots of children who roamed around, playing in every nook and cranny of the village. They also explored the edges of the mesa top. They were sitting on the rim one day with their legs dangling over, when they heard a voice. It seemed to be coming from the southeast. They all stopped talking and strained their ears to listen. No doubt about it, a noise that sounded like crying was coming from a place called Naasiwam, off to the southeast.

Staring hard in that direction, they finally saw a woman slowly coming their way. Curiously, she would walk a short distance and then sit down and rub her belly, crying all the while, and occasionally saying something to no one in particular. She was so far off that the children couldn't understand what she said. After resting a bit, she would get up and walk another short distance, only to stop and cry and rub her belly again.

In this manner, the woman headed straight for the children, but for some reason they were not frightened of her. Soon, she had reached a place directly below them at the foot of the mesa. Once more, she stopped and rubbed her belly, weeping noticeably. This time, the children could hear what she said. "Ouch! My belly hurts. I think I'm about to give birth!" she cried. Wailing like this, she climbed the mesa slope directly toward them.

As the woman came toward them, the children fled back to the village. They dashed from house to house, telling their parents about the woman, and then they all ran back out to where the woman had been climbing up. She was still there and, once again, stopped and massaged her belly, groaning, "Ouch! My belly hurts something awful! I think I'm going to give birth. Somebody please help me; I need a place where I can deliver."

All the people watching her turned around and ran to the village chief to bring him the news. When he learned of the woman, he went out to the mesa edge accompanied by his wife. By the time they got there, the woman had reached the mesa top and sat there on the edge, wailing, "Ouch! My belly really hurts! I think I'm going to give birth any time now. I need a place where I can deliver."

Now everyone saw that she was a young woman, and very beautiful. There was no question that she was pregnant. The village chief stepped up to her and asked, "Who are you?"

"Well, I live here in the southeast all by myself," she answered. "When I became pregnant I had no one to help me, so I thought I could call on you here. I thought that perhaps someone would have pity on me and allow me to use their house to give birth."

"By all means," answered the village chief, "you can come with us." He and his wife led the woman to their house, right by the plaza, and took her inside. Once they had her inside, the chief said, "I think it's best if we find someone who can help you deliver."

The woman agreed and replied that she would prefer a little boy to assist her; any little boy would do. So the chief rushed outside to look for one. Just as he stepped out the door, he saw a little boy playing by himself in a corner of the plaza. He called to the boy, asking him to hurry and come inside his house. The little boy stared at him, thinking, "Why on earth is the village chief telling me to come inside his house?" He was the child of some lower-class people, not born into one of the important clans, so he was a shabbily dressed and homely little thing. When the chief urgently repeated his invitation, the boy finally got up and entered the house.

As soon as the boy was inside, the chief said to him, "Quickly!

Come over here. Stand here and embrace this woman from behind. Then squeeze her as hard as you can. You might be able to help her in this way."

The little boy agreed without hesitation, and, placing his arms around the woman's belly from behind, tightly squeezed her. Groaning intermittently, she finally stopped and said, "Thanks, I think I finally got it out."

Everyone listened closely, expecting to hear the crying of a baby. To everyone's surprise, however, there was not a squawk. They checked underneath the woman, now wondering if perhaps the poor woman had had a stillbirth. When they did, however, there was no baby. The chief then moved the woman aside and inspected the place where she had been kneeling. There was something piled up there, and when he looked at it more closely, he realized that it was a heap of seeds. In the pile were all the different kinds of seeds for plants that Hopis typically eat.

The young woman was very grateful for their help, especially that of the village chief. "Thanks, I did just right," she said, and, motioning to the chief, she continued, "and since you helped me deliver, you're now my father. Make sure you store these seeds away safely and, when the warm season comes, plant them. Now I want you to take me from house to house around the village, so that I may leave these seeds, my children, with other people. Because of me, you and your people will reap great benefits from them."

"Very well," the chief replied. They left the chief's house, taking the little boy along with them. They entered the homes of all the villagers, and each time they did, the woman was pregnant all over again and gave birth to a pile of seeds. Each time the little boy helped with the delivery. The village chief, as the woman's father, impressed on the villagers the importance of the seeds. "She brought these for us, so keep them in a secure place," he admonished them all. "Later, when summer comes, you can put them in the ground." They visited all the houses in the village, without exception, and the men, in every case, safely stored the seeds away.

When the little group had finished these visits, they returned to the house of the ruling clan, that is, the clan of the village chief. The little boy was now ready to leave, so the woman said to him, "Thank you so much. You really were a great help to me. Be strong in your heart and live a long life. Something good is bound to come from what you did for me."

The little boy did not pay too much attention to what she said. All he could think of was that he had accompanied those important people all over the village and had become known to everyone because of that.

When the boy was gone, the woman turned to the chief and said, "As you know, I have nobody and live all by myself. Let me ask you something."

"Sure, what is it?" the chief replied.

"Well, since I live all alone, I wonder, would you be willing to take me into your household?"

The chief immediately consented. "Sure, no problem," he said. "From this day on, you may stay with us."

"Very well, then, but could you do me one favor?" asked the woman. "Go to my house in the southeast, where you'll find two large boulders, side by side. Enter between these boulders, and once inside, you'll see a back room beyond the living room. Enter the back room and look to your right. There should be a bundle lying there. Please bring it here to me."

The chief agreed and turned the woman over to his wife, who treated her the same as any woman going through the purification period following childbirth, even though there was no newborn child. After providing a place for the woman, she went about closing off all openings that would allow light inside. Then after telling his wife what he intended to do, the chief took along some cornmeal and prayer feathers and headed to the woman's house.

After descending the mesa on the southeast side of the village, he soon found the place the woman had described, near Naasiwam. Sure enough, there were two big boulders there, leaning against each other. When he entered between them, he noticed a delicious aroma in the air, as if someone had just ground some corn and then roasted it. The place was very clean and orderly. Then he saw the door to the back room and entered it. It was very dark inside, and when he first entered, he couldn't see anything. He stood for a while, letting his eyes get used to the dark, then started searching for the bundle he had been sent for. Sure enough, there it was over to the right. He walked over, picked it up, and uttered this prayer, "All right, I was sent here to fetch this bundle. The young woman who came to us to give birth gave herself to me as my daughter. She bade me come here, and I brought these." With this, he laid his prayer feathers in place of the bundle and returned home.

Upon his arrival back home, he handed the mysterious bundle over to his new daughter. "Thank you," she said, "this is it; just what I wanted." That's all she said.

From that day on, the beautiful young woman was part of the chief's household. In no time, the twenty days of the postbirth period, during which she was not allowed to see the sun, had passed. As a rule, she slept all by herself, all the way in the rear of the house, with her bundle held tightly in her arms.

One morning the chief's family was up earlier than usual, eating breakfast. The young woman was still in bed, so the chief's wife went to invite her to eat. When she entered the room in the rear, she found the young woman, apparently still asleep, wrapped snugly in her blanket. She leaned over and shook the blanket-covered form, saying, "Get up, we're eating." The young woman did not budge, however.

The chief's wife then pulled the blanket aside. The young woman was not there! In her place was a tiny effigy resembling a child. Immediately, she called her husband, "Come and look at this!" Kneeling down, he looked at the effigy. There was no question—it looked very much like the young woman they had taken in.

The village chief tried to figure out what all this meant. Finally, he could only conclude that the young woman was a supernatural being, and he thought, "She must be very powerful to be able to do this. First, she gave us all those seeds, and now that she has come to live with us, she has changed herself into this." Sharing these thoughts with his wife, he added, "She must have been transformed into this child effigy. We must certainly take care of it. Let's build a shrine for her and she can live there." And so they kept the child there in a shrine and regularly fed her.

Meanwhile, summer grew near, and as customary, the corn planting was first done for the ruling clan, that of the chief. After the appropriate announcement by the village crier, the chief placed a few of the woman's seeds in a bag and headed for his field. When all the men had gathered there, they held a ritual smoke. When this was done, the village chief distributed the seed corn among the men, and since he had only brought a small quantity, passed out just a few to each one.

The chief's field was large and the men thought they would surely run out of seeds before it was fully planted. They said nothing, however, and began to plant. After a while, they had sown a large area, but the quantity of seed corn showed no signs of decreasing. As a matter of fact, it seemed to be increasing. When they had finished planting the field and placed all the remaining seeds in one pile, they found that there was still an abundance of the seed corn left. This was unbelievable!

Seeing what had happened, the chief now said to the men, "Whoever desires some of this seed corn may put some aside for themselves. Take as much as you would like."

Excited, the men helped themselves to the seeds. When everybody had had his turn, the pile was still large, so the chief said, "All right, be sure to take them all." They all took turns again, and finally there was nothing left over.

Now the village chief said, "Go on over and eat at my place now. Go with happy hearts. There's bound to be plenty of food set out for you there." As soon as the men had left for his house, the chief lit a large fire. Long ago, that was the traditional way to signal those cooking the food that the helpers were coming to eat. When the woman who had been watching received this signal, the other women began setting out the various foods for everyone. By the time the planters arrived back in the village, all the food had been served, and they all were soon feasting.

All the helpers who had received these magic seeds now planted their fields. Their plants grew abundantly, and by harvest time, they were able to gather all the crops that Hopis enjoy. Then they all ate heartily, thanks to the woman that the village chief had taken in.

That child effigy still lives in the shrine of the ruling clan, and the village chief still prays to it. It's helping him to reap abundant crops.

And here the story ends.

21

The Creation of the Morning and Evening Star

Aliksa'i. There was no one living on Hopi land yet. In fact, the entire earth was still uninhabited except for Old Spider Woman and her two nephews, Pöqangwhoya and Palöngawhoya.

The sun was already in existence and it lit up the day. At night, there was some light when the moon was up, but as soon as it disappeared, they were in total darkness. Therefore, they decided to create a source of light, at least until the moon came up again. They were tired of walking around so much of the time in total darkness. Also, the two Pöqangw brothers feared for the safety of their old grandmother, who often tripped and stumbled in the dark. When they mentioned this to her she said, "Yes, I have also been giving this some thought. We need to do something. Even a little light would prevent me from going around stumbling all the time. I'm afraid I'm a lot of trouble to you, now that I've gotten old and feeble. I just can't walk long distances with you anymore."

"Yes, that's true," the brothers agreed.

"All right, then," their grandmother said. "Go to a place southwest from here. There is a hill there where some things grow that are about this thick." She showed them the size with her fingers, then continued, "They occur on the side of the hill where you'll see a shiny cliff face. These things give off a light something like firelight. Bring me some pieces of these things. I'd like to use them for something. In four days, we can all check them out, to see if they work."

The Pöqangw brothers started out as they were instructed. What they were going to do was quarry some of that shiny rock face. Naturally, they had to play shinny along the way. So intent were they on their game that they didn't even realize it when they passed by the shiny rock. Finally, the younger brother realized it and said, "Oh my, wait a minute!"

"Why, what for?" Pöqangwhoya demanded.

"I think we just missed our hill," said Palöngawhoya. "Look, it's over there."

So, they turned around and headed back. When they reached the hill, it was indeed apparent that it was covered with this glittery stuff that emitted light. Staring at it, one of them said, "Maybe this is it."

"Yes, I guess this is it," said the other one. "This is the only mountain around here that has any shiny stuff on it."

So they filled a bag with pieces of the shiny material and carried it home. When they arrived, their grandmother inspected it closely, then cried happily. "Yes, thanks! You brought exactly the right thing!" She then stashed it away in the back room of their kiva.

Four days later, just at nightfall, she said to the brothers, "All right, now let's get to it. You must not doze off, because if you do, we won't succeed. Remember what we planned? This is something important—we need to create a little light so that we can walk about safely at night, when the moon is not up."

"Don't worry," the two brothers reassured her. "We won't fall asleep. We all want this, so we'll work hard at your side until it's finished."

Their grandmother was glad to hear this. "Very well, then," she said, "let's get going."

With that, they started working with the glittering material the boys had quarried. "This shiny stuff I had you bring back is called mica," Old Spider Woman explained. "As you can see, it glimmers. Maybe we can somehow attach it to the sky so it will shine light on us when the sun has set. That's what I had in mind when I sent you to get it."

Next she said, "All right, each of you take a sheet of mica and break off some small pieces. Then put them into this basket. Let me know when you have a lot of pieces broken off. I have an idea what we can do with them."

The brothers obediently began pinching off little bits with their fingernails and breaking them into tiny fragments. They dropped these into the woven container and when they had amassed a large number, they said to their grandmother, "Do you want to check, Grandma? Is this enough?"

The old woman took a quick look and decided it was all she needed. "That'll do," she said. With that, she opened her medicine pouch, removed something from it, and chewed it up. She then sprayed the liquid into the basket containing the mica pieces and kneaded the mixture into round shapes the size of a shinny ball. She repeated this process several times. Amazingly, the spheres had fire in them and, just like a fire, gave off sparks and light. "I guess that'll do," the old woman said. "When the sun sets over there, these will illuminate the entire sky. Maybe they'll give off some light, just like a fire produces firelight."

Inspecting her creation, she added, "Yes, that'll do. Now we'll just have to wait until exactly the middle of the night to put them in the sky."

Now as she sat there, Old Spider Woman began to chant something over her creations. What exactly it was, nobody knows, for there were no songs then as we know them now. Nevertheless, she chanted something, turning the round objects over and repeating the chant again. Finally, she ended her singing and proclaimed, "All right, let's go. Now is the time."

All three of them started out and soon came to a big mountain. After they had all climbed to the very top, the old woman declared, "All right, this looks like the spot." With that, she pulled out two of the spheres she had fashioned. Handing the larger one to Pöqangwhoya, she said, "Here, you take this one." The smaller one she gave to his younger brother and said, "Here, this one is for you. As soon as I give the signal, both of you hurl your spheres into the sky. The one that Pöqangwhoya has will be the constellation called Nangöysohut, Two Stars Chasing Each Other. If we do it right, they will perhaps create a little bit of light for us in the night sky. Then we won't have to traipse about in the dark any longer."

Then she continued, "This one, which Palöngawhoya will throw, will be the consecrated cornmeal path. On this path, Hopis will travel to another world when they die. Now I want you to throw the two spheres at exactly the same time. As soon as I say 'Taa,' do it."

Old Spider Woman now took out a bag of shells and once more began to chant. The moment she ended her chant, she cried, "Taa!" Simultaneously, Pöqangwhoya and Palöngawhoya threw the spheres up into the sky. Flying up at great speed, they soon reached the zenith, where they became stars. Immediately, they began to move along their courses, as Nangöysohut, Morning Star and Evening Star. One of the stars quickly moved ahead, leading the other one. It was like a cornmeal path. "That's the way it's going to be!" Old Spider Woman exclaimed.

When the three of them had been standing there a little while it suddenly became light. "Look!" exclaimed the old woman, "there's Nangöysohut. I thought he might place some more stars in the sky for us." As she was speaking, Nangöysohut reappeared, climbing all the way to the highest point in the sky, and the sky became filled with stars. They gave off quite a bit of light, so that it was no longer completely dark.

"That's the way I planned it," the old woman said. "When the moon is down, we'll no longer have to grope around in the dark. Also, one day all the people on the earth will be glad to have this light. Now the star that you created, Palöngawhoya, that is the cornmeal road to Maski. All Hopis will one day go to Maski. By using this road, they can avoid getting lost on their way to Maski, where they will continue to live their lives. That's why we made this path. The Morning Star and the Evening Star, the two stars of Nangöysohut, will chase each other forever, making sure there are always numerous stars to shed their light on us."

In this fashion, Old Spider Woman and her two nephews created Nangöysohut and all the other stars, and for this reason there is starlight when the moon is not up in the sky.

And here the story ends.

22

How the Pöqangw Brothers Stole the Lightning

Aliksa'i. People were living at Shungopavi. Long ago, there were a great number of them. They were industrious and always had bountiful harvests. However, one year they failed to get any rain. No one knew why, but as summer came, there was simply no rain. Nevertheless, the people went ahead and planted their fields, but while the seeds sprouted, they failed to thrive. Everyone kept saying, hopefully, "We're bound to get some rain, sometime," but the days went by without so much as a drop. Finally, without any moisture, the plants just shriveled up and died, and there was nothing to harvest.

The village chief was depressed about the drought and wailed, "Why on earth doesn't it rain?" It soon became apparent that he was going to have to seek help from someone, and after giving the matter a lot of thought, he hit upon the Pöqangw brothers as a possibility.

The brothers lived on the southeast side of Shungopavi, so he thought, "Why don't I go over and consult with them?"

A few days later, in the evening just after supper, he went over to where they lived. When he arrived there, he stomped his foot a few times on the roof of their kiva, right next to the hatch. Someone responded from inside, so he went down the ladder and found Old Spider Woman and her two nephews, Pöqangwhoya and his younger brother Palöngawhoya. The old woman was hunkered down by the fire pit, and the two brothers, as usual, were playing shinny. As soon as the chief entered, the old woman told the two boys to stop playing, but they paid absolutely no attention. They just kept hitting the ball, which bounced off the walls and whizzed past her head.

Old Spider Woman warned them again, "Quit it! We have a visitor," but to no avail. The two snotty-nosed boys just continued to play. Suddenly losing her patience, the old grandmother grabbed a stick and gave them both a good thrashing. Finally, the two halted their game, and the old woman said once more, "There's someone here." Only then did they notice the village chief standing there.

The chief and Old Spider Woman now sat down and exchanged a ritual smoke. When the pipe was empty, the old woman asked him, "Well then, what did you come here for? There must be a reason. None of you has ever called on us before."

"Yes, that's true," the village chief had to admit, "but we have a problem. We Shungopavis planted our crops earlier this summer, but then there were no rains and our plants suffered terribly. No sooner had they sprouted than they quit growing, then wilted, and finally dried up and died. We're certain we won't have anything to harvest this year. That's why I came to ask for help."

"Is that so?" the old woman replied. "Oh my, oh dear, that's truly sad." She really felt sorry for the poor people of Shungopavi.

"Yes, that's why I came," continued the chief. "I was hoping you'd pity us and help us find someone who could send us some moisture."

"Oh my," the old woman cried again, "we can't promise anything, but we can certainly give it a try. We just might succeed in getting water for you and your plants. I know that you and your people are all thirsty, so go home now and make some pahos and prayer feathers for us. Come back here tomorrow at the same time and bring them with you. My nephews will carry them over to Nuvatukya'ovi, the San Francisco Peaks, and we'll see what happens.

That's all we can do for now."

"Very well," replied the chief, encouraged at the reply of Old Spider Woman. He went home feeling a bit relieved, but still lay awake that night for some time, worrying. If he and his people were lucky, Old Spider Woman might persuade those responsible for rain to end the drought.

Right after breakfast early the next morning, the chief began working on the prayer items. He intended to make enough pahos for those living on top of Nuvatukya'ovi, for the sun, for Pöqangwhoya and Palöngawhoya, and for Old Spider Woman. When he had finished that, he got out a piece of buckskin and, of his own free will, made a shinny ball from it for the Pöqangw brothers. These tasks took nearly all day, and when he was finished he stored everything away and waited for nightfall.

Finally, it was time to go. He slung his bundle over his shoulder and headed to the kiva of the two brothers and their grandmother. There he again stomped his foot on the roof and was invited in, finding the old woman sitting near the fire pit, engaged in some task or other. Of course, the two boys were as naughty as ever and continued to play shinny.

Immediately she picked up a stick and struck both the boys right on their shins. "Why don't you hold still for once?" she yelled. "Can't you see that we have a visitor?" Screaming in pain, they both hopped around on one leg.

When the two brothers had finally settled down, she and the chief had a ritual smoke once more. As soon as they were finished, the chief opened his bundle and distributed the gifts he had brought for them. First, he handed the old woman her prayer feathers and the boys the pahos meant for them. They really liked these, but were overjoyed when they saw the shinny ball he had made for them. Next, he gave her the offerings for those who dwelled at Nuvatukya'ovi, and finally the pahos designed for the sun. The old woman was elated at all the gifts. "Thank you! You made exactly the right things!" Seeing how pleased she was, the village chief left for home.

With that, the old woman turned to her nephews and said, "All we can do is give it a try. Tomorrow at daybreak I want you to take these prayer offerings to Nuvatukya'ovi. If we're lucky those in charge of the rain will have pity on us."

The next day, Old Spider Woman carefully instructed her nephews, "Take these offerings over there to the shrine near Nuvatukya-

'ovi. You'll recognize it. Deposit them there and pray to those in charge of the rain. Plead with them not to delay, and urge them to come again and again, without waiting too long between times. Tell them that the people need water and that their plants are dying of thirst. Pray to them on behalf of all living beings. And be sure to humble yourselves."

The two boys agreed and promised to do exactly as they were told. They both then slung their bundles of prayer offerings over their shoulders and set off, traveling in a southwesterly direction. They had to play shinny as they went along, of course, and didn't make much progress. They knocked the ball forwards and then backwards, and occasionally it would wind up hidden in a bush, causing them to waste a lot of time looking for it. Once the ball got caught in a large saltbush, and to retrieve it, Palöngawhoya, the younger of the two, laid down his bundle. He knocked the ball out of the bush with his shinny stick and they were off again as fast as their legs could carry them. Back and forth they played for quite some time, until Pöqangwhoya noticed that his brother had lost his bundle.

Pöqangwhoya was angry at his brother and severely scolded him, but they had no choice but to go back and find it. They followed their footsteps back until they found the bundle, and were soon on their way again. Now they actually paid a little more attention to what they were doing and made some headway. In this manner, they eventually reached the area around Nuvatukya'ovi.

When they got there, they soon spotted a kiva. When they entered it, however, they found no one. They hollered, but there was no answer. Then they saw that there were tunnels leading from the interior of the kiva off into the four directions. They peered into each of them but saw nothing. Not being able to contact anyone, they opened their bundles of prayer offerings and deposited them on the northwest side of the fire pit. Then they prayed as instructed by their grandmother, completing their mission with all the diligence and humility she had directed them to use.

When the two brothers were done they waited, but no one came. Not a single soul was in sight. As the two of them studied the interior of the kiva, they noticed a shelf along the ceiling on which rested a line of big pottery vessels, looking like those used to store water. Curious, they decided to check out their contents, but as usual, they began to argue about it. "Go on," Pöqangwhoya commanded his younger brother, "you climb up and hand one down."

"Why me?" asked Palöngawhoya. "You do it. You're older than me."

After arguing back and forth for a while, Pöqangwhoya, the older of the two, finally agreed to climb up and lift one down. When he had it down on the floor, he lifted the lid to look inside. The instant he did, a blindingly bright blue-green light flashed out, and just as quickly withdrew. "Gee!" exclaimed Pöqangwhoya, and quickly put the vessel back on the shelf. He picked up the one next to it and took it down, lifting the lid as before. The same thing happened, only this time the streak of light was red. Puzzled, the two brothers stared at each other. "Let's take these outside," suggested the older of the two. This was a really mischievous thing to do, really bad.

So they each took one of the vessels and climbed up to the roof of the kiva. Once again, just to see what would happen, Pöqangwhoya lifted the lid of his vessel, and instantly a bolt of blue-green light shot out, struck the earth northwest of the kiva, and disappeared back into the container. Palöngawhoya then opened his vessel, and in a flash a streak of red light shot out, hit the ground southeast of the kiva, and jumped back into the vessel.

Curious as to what might happen with the other containers, they took these back inside the kiva and lugged out two more. The same thing happened with these two vessels, only this time the flash from one hit the ground in the northeast and was all white, and the other was yellow and struck the earth in the southwest, both instantly withdrawing into the vessels again.

Their curiosity satisfied, they took the vessels back inside the kiva and stored them on the shelf. Not knowing what else to do, they felt sort of bored. Nobody had yet shown up, so the older said to the younger, "Let's go. Nobody seems to be around."

They had just come out of the kiva and walked a few steps, when one of them had a thought. "Why don't we just take those wonderful vessels along with us?" he said. "Then we can show them to our grandmother. Who knows what they are?" They both quickly agreed to do so, and entered the kiva once more.

Each of them picked up two vessels. "Let's run straight home with these, for someone might want to take them away from us," said one of them. So they came out of the kiva and ran off, not bothering to stop and play shinny, and were soon nearing their home.

Just as they were approaching the foot of the mesa on the southwest side of Shungopavi, the rains came after them. It was terrible!

Without warning, they unleashed their lightning bolts, which struck with such frequency that the whole sky lit up. Clearly, they were trying to hit the Pöqangw brothers, as they carried the vessels through the pouring rain. Then, large hailstones began pelting them, and icicles too. There was no doubt about it, the rains were attacking them.

It so happened that on the southwest side of Shungopavi there was a straight cliff with a rock shelter. The two brothers sought refuge there from the onslaught of the rains, each of them hunkered down with two pottery vessels in his arms. The lightning bolts struck at them without letup—red, white, blue-green, and yellow. Slowly the cliff wall above the rock shelter began to collapse, and the younger brother became frightened. "They seem to be after these pots!" he yelled. "Let me give them back."

"That's up to you," Pöqangwhoya replied. "I'm not going to part with mine."

So Palöngawhoya held up his vessels to the rains. No sooner had he done so, than two lightning bolts reached into the rock shelter and snatched them away. The lightning, however, continued bombarding the cliff, which was crumbling more and more. Also, the flashing bolts were so hot that they scorched the rock, making things very uncomfortable inside the shelter. Then, large holes started appearing in the searing rock where the hailstones hit it. When this happened, Palöngawhoya yelled to his older brother, "They want your vessels too, that's why they won't leave us alone!"

"I'm not going to give mine back!" Pöqangwhoya stubbornly insisted. Eventually, however, when the lightning strikes continued with ever increasing force, he relented and said, "All right, I suppose I have to give them up. It seems that the clouds are really after us, for they just won't go away." With that, he handed his vessels over to the rains, and just as before, lightning bolts instantly grabbed the pots and shot out of the rock shelter with them. Right away the rain and lightning began to slacken off and finally stopped altogether.

The two boys now left the shelter. What a dreadful experience it had been! Outside, the land was devastated. The entire cliff had collapsed and rock fragments were scattered about in big heaps, shattered by the hailstones and blackened by the searing lightning strikes.

Pöqangwhoya and Palöngawhoya now went home to their grandmother. When they arrived, they told her how they had fared and about everything that had happened. "We walked off with those pots," said the younger brother, "so maybe they came after us because of them."

When Old Spider Woman heard this, she became very angry. "You shouldn't have done that, you disobedient rascals! Those water vessels belonged to the clouds and rains, and you stole them. They wanted them back, so they pursued you until you surrendered them. You were lucky they didn't kill you!"

Because of this event, some of the boulders and rocks on the southwest side of Shungopavi are totally black and full of holes, and the cliff is all broken up. Long ago, this was not the case.

Now that the clouds had returned home, they frequently came and released their moisture on the land. Somehow Old Spider Woman was able to appease the rains, and they calmed down. They could not stay mad about the theft of their lightning bolts by the Pöqangw brothers, for they knew very well the two of them were the culprits, and were quite familiar with their mischievous behavior.

And here the story ends.

23

The Poor Boy Who Wanted a Horse

Aliksa'i. People were living way over at the Pueblo of Laguna. A man and his wife lived there, on the northeast side of the mesa where the road leads up to the village. Though they had a son and a daughter, as a family they led a miserable existence, as they were nearly destitute.

Many of the other villagers, however, were well off, primarily due to the fact that they owned horses. Horses were especially useful when it came to hunting. Not only did they enable the hunters to cover a larger area looking for game, but they made transporting it back home much easier.

The boy of the family usually felt very left out when the others went hunting, for his family had no horse. So the desire for a horse was always on his mind. Every morning before sunup, he would climb to the roof of his house and think about it.

On the days when a hunt was scheduled, the horses could be heard whinnying as they were rounded up. He stood and watched all the preparations, taking everything in. He saw how the harnesses were put on and how the hunters departed from the village, proudly riding their beautiful horses. He would watch them until they all were gone from sight. Then he would follow them on foot, and since his family was so poor, he had nothing to take along to hunt with but a club. When he caught up with the hunting party, he sat down on the fringes of the group, then followed them as they moved on. While the men and boys on horseback were mostly after big game animals, especially deer and elk, he was able to hunt only the smaller animals, like cottontails and jackrabbits, and sometimes even packrats, tree squirrels, and songbirds. Whenever he had a chance, he would hurl his club at them in hopes of killing one. Deep down in his heart, though, he envied the hunters on horseback and passionately wanted to own a horse of his own.

Now, over on the southwest side of the village, right at the edge of the mesa, lived a medicine man. He was rich and owned a variety of domestic animals. The boy had long been thinking of paying the man a visit, so one evening he wrapped himself in his blanket and set out for the medicine man's home. Fortunately, the man had not retired for the night when he arrived there. "Have a seat," said the medicine man. When the boy was comfortably settled, the man said to him, "Well, I imagine you've come to talk to me about something in particular, haven't you? You didn't walk all this way for nothing, right?"

"No indeed, I didn't," answered the boy. "To tell the truth, I've really been quite envious of you and all the others who own horses, especially when I see you going out hunting. I'm poor, but I'd really like nothing better than to own one too. I came here because I thought perhaps you could teach me to heal people. Maybe then I might stand a chance of realizing my dream of owning a horse."

"Is that so?" said the medicine man. "Is that the reason you came? You would like to own a horse."

"Yes," the boy replied.

"Well, it's up to you. If you're really willing to become a medicine man, then I'm certainly willing to show you how."

"I'm ready and willing," the boy assured him. "I want a horse so much that I'd be happy to do whatever it takes."

So the medicine man set a day on which the boy was to return. "On that day, at nighttime, I want you to come back," he told the boy.

The boy was elated that the medicine man had agreed to instruct him in the business of healing, and from that day on eagerly awaited their next meeting. When the day finally arrived and night had fallen, he wrapped himself in his blanket and set out for the medicine man's home. "You've come?" the man greeted him when he arrived.

"Yes," the boy replied.

"All right," the man said, "sit down for a while." The two of them sat there for quite a while, until it was about midnight and pitch black outside. The medicine man went outside and, looking up, saw that Orion was high in the sky. "Well, it's about the right time," he said. "Let's go."

With that, he picked up his wooden planting stick and wrapped himself in his blanket. The boy wrapped his blanket around his shoulders and the two of them went out. One behind the other, they headed to the graveyard. When they reached it, they went from place to place until the medicine man said, "This is it," pointing to a particular grave.

He immediately started digging with the planting stick, throwing dirt left and right until he had excavated it to the desired depth. When he had, he said, "I guess that will do." Motioning to the boy, he continued, "All right, climb in."

As the boy stepped up to the edge of the hole, he noticed that it was quite deep. "All right, get in," urged the medicine man. "I want you to spend the night here. If someone comes to visit you, don't get scared and try to climb out. Remember, it was your wish to learn the business of healing, so you must not run away under any circumstances. Stay in this grave until daylight comes. Then you may come out. When you do, look over there toward the forest. You might see something of interest to you."

The boy did as he was told and climbed into the grave. The medicine man then removed his blanket and covered the gaping hole with it, fastening it down on all sides so that the boy was completely enclosed. That done, he left for home.

So there sat the boy in the reopened grave, waiting. Nothing happened for a long time, then suddenly he heard a rattling noise. It was apparently the resident of the grave, and he was nothing but a jumble of bones. "Come on," urged the bunch of bones, "put me back together. If you can, I'll be able to walk again." The poor thing was simply clattering along, his bones clacking at every move he made. The boy began to put the bones in order, attaching them at what he hoped were the proper places. When he was done, he told the skeleton, "All right, I'm done. I've fixed you back up."

When the skeleton tried to stand up, however, he couldn't. "You didn't put me back together right," he chided the boy. "Try again!"

So, once more the boy took all the bones apart and reattached them. This time he was sure he did it right.

Sure enough, the skeleton was able to rise to his feet. "Thanks!" he cried. "You placed my bones in the correct order!" Without any further comment, he strode away.

Not long after, a second pile of bones came tumbling along, pleading with the boy. "Please fix me. If you do, I too will be able to walk." The boy reassembled the skeleton and it too walked away. Others then presented themselves to him to be fixed, and in this way he spent the entire night, restoring skeletons one after the other, until they were all capable of walking again. Eventually, the sun began to rise, so he lifted the blanket covering and climbed out of the grave. After wrapping himself in his blanket again, he just sat there, staring into the forest nearby. He stared and stared until suddenly he saw a large animal emerge from the trees. It was a horse! It slowly walked around the meadow, grazing on the grass that grew there. Before long, a second horse appeared and it too began to graze. After they had grazed for a while, they both vanished into the forest again. The boy watched them in amazement until they had completely disappeared, and then he headed for home.

The next morning, he went up to his customary spot on the roof of the house. He lay there for a long time, until his mother called him to breakfast. He went down to eat, but his heart was not in it. He just sat there, thinking about the horses. When the family had finished breakfast, his sister carefully washed the dishes, and when she was done, she climbed the ladder to go dump the dirty dishwater. Somehow, she slipped on one of the rungs and fell to the floor, breaking her leg in the process.

The boy and his parents rushed to where she was lying, crying pitifully. There was no doubt that her leg was broken, for she could not stand, and apparently she was in great pain. The parents immediately thought of a neighbor who was a medicine man, so they asked the son to go and fetch him. They were convinced that the neighbor could help her.

The boy refused to go, however. "Let me treat her," he implored them. "I can repair her broken leg."

"But you're not a medicine man," they protested, "you can't fix her leg!"

"Well, at least let me try," he calmly insisted, still refusing to go fetch the medicine man. "Let me treat my sister. I know how to do it."

"All right, go ahead," his parents said, finally giving in, though they were upset by their son's behavior.

The boy quickly sat down by his sister's side and gently felt her leg. Feeling where it was broken, he carefully reset the broken bones, doing everything just right. Soon the girl stopped crying and fell asleep. All the pain was apparently gone, much to his parents' amazement. Not only was the bone set correctly, but it was entirely healed. Before the day was over, the girl was awake and standing up again, able to walk as if nothing had ever happened.

From that day forward, the boy became famous as an extraordinarily talented medicine man. As soon as people learned what he had done for his sister, they started arriving at his door, seeking his help. He became renowned as a one-day medicine man who could see right away what was wrong with his patients and then heal them instantly. People who came to him with broken bones were able to return home completely healed.

One day a man from another village who had heard of the boy's incredible curing power came to fetch him because one of his children had had an accident. When the boy arrived at the patient's house, he quickly set the child's broken bones. The child was seen playing again the following day.

This is how the boy lived now, from day to day, healing people with great skill. He still did not own a horse, however. Then one day, when he and the rest of his family were eating breakfast, he heard a horse whinny just outside their door. "Listen," said the boy, "someone has come." When he went outside to check, there stood a beautiful horse. It was a big pinto stallion, beautifully colored. There was a man leading the stallion who said, "Here, I brought you this horse. If you remember, you treated my child recently, so I brought you this as a reward."

The boy was ecstatic. "Thank you, indeed!" he exclaimed, tying the horse to a post. "We're still eating breakfast, so why don't you come in and eat with us?"

So this is how the boy became the owner of a fine horse. Now he would be able to go along with the others and hunt big game. From that day on the boy became richer and more respected, and I guess he's still there somewhere, a successful healer and hunter.

And here the story ends.

24

How the Pöqangw Brothers Found Their Father

Aliksa'i. People were living in Shungopavi, among them a couple with just one daughter. The girl was exceedingly beautiful, but she was still unmarried. Since her family's water supply was exhausted, she headed down to the spring to fetch water. The spring was located in the recess of a cliff overhang from which moisture was dripping steadily. The droplets were collecting in a pool behind a small earthen dam, and that's where people got their water. As the girl arrived, she stood above the spring and as she squatted down with her ladle to scoop out the water, the droplets dripping from the overhang struck the water and splashed right into her vulva. In this fashion the water had intercourse with the girl.

The girl, unaware of this event, carried the water home in her water jar. Meanwhile, it was getting toward evening, and the sun was slowly setting. As its sinking rays fell on the houses of the villagers, they also entered the home of the girl through a vent hole in the wall. It so happened that at that very moment the girl had lifted up her dress all the way in the front, because she was longing to have sex with a man. When the sun spotted her like this, he penetrated her with his rays and had intercourse with her. Again, the girl was totally unaware of this, but as time went by, she realized that she was pregnant. Soon she had a large belly and before long she gave birth to two little boys. They were the Pöqangw brothers, Pöqangwhoya and Palöngawhoya.

Being endowed with greater than human powers, the two boys grew up rapidly. Quite aggressive by nature, they enjoyed teasing the other children until they cried. Being the supernaturals that they were, they were soon old enough to inquire about their father. "Mother," they asked one day, "who is our father?"

"I truly don't know. I have no idea who your father is," their mother replied.

"Well, in that case we'll just have to go in search of him," the two brothers replied.

"Is that so? Oh my, you can't go anywhere yet. You're too young!" their mother exclaimed in alarm.

"No matter, the least we can do is give it a try," the boys insisted stubbornly.

So their mother gave in and baked some piki as journey food for them. The following day their uncle made a shinny ball for them and two nice sticks to strike the ball. Playing shinny, then, they set out, heading in a northeasterly direction. They really had no idea where to go or where their father lived. But, for some reason, they kept going toward the place of the rising sun.

At some point the brothers felt the need to relieve themselves, so when they reached a little depression with tall snake weed growing in it they said, "Let's stop here for a while and relieve ourselves." They were just squatting down and beginning to strain when a voice protested, "For shame, you boys! Move a little farther away."

The two brothers were confused, for there was no one in sight.

Once more they hunkered down and began to strain, when the voice sounded a second time. This time they looked underneath themselves and spotted a tiny hole in the ground. In it was a spider with her rear end sticking up. It was Old Spider Woman. "My poor grandchildren, where are you headed?" she cried.

"We're on our way to look for our father."

"You'll never get to where he lives," the old woman replied. "Why don't you come in for a little while?"

"How can we? That hole is much too small."

"Simply twist your heels in it and it will widen," the old woman instructed them. "Come on down. There's a ladder there."

The brothers did as told and turned their heels in the tiny hole. Lo and behold, it opened up to a size that allowed them to enter. "My dear grandchildren, you can't just go after your father like this. You'll never make it on your own. Let me go with you to help you find him," Old Spider Woman suggested.

"Really, would you?"

"Yes, I will. Come on, have your older brother place me on one of his ears so I can ride along with him and tell you what to do along the way." With that the old woman got busy filling a bag with a special medicine. Who knows what kind of medicine it was.

As soon as she was done with her preparations, the two brothers climbed out of the subterranean abode and were on their way. As before, they were playing shinny, with Old Spider Woman sitting perched on Pöqangwhoya's ear. At one point they reached an area with large gopher hills. "There must be a gopher here," the boys said when they saw the fresh mounds. Suddenly a voice could be heard. "Have you come?" It was indeed a gopher who greeted them. There he was, peeping out from one of his burrows. "Why don't you come in for a while? I've been expecting you, and you arrived just at the right time."

The Pöqangw brothers accepted the invitation and entered the gopher's den. It too grew larger as they crawled in. "I've been waiting for you," he repeated. "Where are you headed?"

"We're going in search of our father," the brothers replied.

"Is that so? In that case you'd better take me along. I'll accompany you, for I may be able to help you in your endeavor." With that, he handed the boys two hollow reed pieces, the type that serve as mouthpieces for a smoking pipe. "Take these along," the gopher said to them. "Then have your older brother carry me like this," the gopher advised the two.

With that, the Pöqangw brothers left the den of the gopher and continued on their journey, always heading in the direction of the rising sun. After a while Old Spider Woman whispered into Pöqangwhoya's ear, "Careful now, we're nearing a place that is protected by a vicious guard."

Sure enough, it was not long before they could see a ferocious beast striding back and forth. "Here, put this medicine into your mouths and chew it up. When the animal is about to attack, spray it in its face."

The guard beast turned out to be a big mountain lion. What a fearsome creature he was as he paced there to and fro. Obediently chewing their medicine, the Pöqangw brothers stepped up to the huge cat and just when he was set to pounce, they spat their medicine at him. Instantly, the powerful animal fell to the ground and lay still, completely harmless.

"Well done," the old woman exclaimed. "Here, you better chew some more of this medicine ahead of time. This is not the only beast that will obstruct your path."

And so the Pöqangw brothers continued along with Old Spider Woman and the gopher. After some time they approached a kiva with a gigantic creature on its roof moving back and forth. It was a huge rattlesnake. "Now," Old Spider Woman urged the brothers, "spurt out your medicine."

The boys did as told and, as a result of the magic medicine, the rattler lay back down. "Well done," Old Spider Woman exclaimed, "he's in a stupor now. We are safe to go on."

And so they trekked on until they came across a kiva in the ground. This time, there was no guard in sight. "Go on, don't be hesitant about climbing in," the old woman encouraged the boys. Pöqangwhoya entered first, with Palöngawhoya close on his brother's heels. As they stepped off the ladder, they saw an old man seated close to the fire pit. He was all by himself with a smoking pipe by his side. Raising his head to see who the visitors were, he finally said, "Have a seat, strangers."

The boys complied and sat down. By then it was early evening, and as the brothers sat there telling the old man about the purpose of their journey, there was suddenly a muffled swoosh and a man landed in the middle of the room. He was Sun, a handsome man dressed in beautiful clothes. The Pöqangw brothers just stared at him, watching in awe as he began removing his garments. First he took off the sunshield that he always carries on his back and hung it on the wall. Then he took off his clothes. When he was finished, the old man said, "These boys here are looking for their father. Maybe that's you."

"I don't know," Sun replied. "Maybe I am. Let's test their mettle and find out. We'll start by smoking." Sun had a tobacco pouch of enormous size hanging there. In it was a huge pipe with an equally huge mouthpiece.

Now, before the Pöqangw brothers had entered the kiva, they had put the gopher down, at his request. "I'll stay here and dig a tunnel ahead of time, because I know that you will be challenged to a smoking contest. So when something tickles you in your behind, don't stir or move away, for I will be right underneath you, sticking a reed up your bunghole. Later as you inhale the smoke, it can escape through the reeds," he instructed them. "So be sure not to stir."

Sun now took the huge pipe from the pouch and began filling it with tobacco. He kept pinching large amounts of ground tobacco into it, again and again. When he was finally satisfied, he lit it and, holding it out to the boys, said, "All right, if you are truly my children, you will smoke up all the tobacco in this pipe. However, you must swallow the smoke, not exhale it." With that, he handed the pipe to the older of the two brothers.

Pöqangwhoya just sat there, stunned, staring at Sun. Finally he uttered, "My father!"

"I don't know," came the reply. "I really don't know. Maybe I am. Who knows what will be."

As requested, Pöqangwhoya did not exhale the smoke but swallowed it. Then he passed the pipe to his younger brother. He too inhaled all of the smoke and let it escape through the reed in his behind. By now, quite a distance away, down in the depths of a canyon, clouds of smoke could be seen billowing from the gopher's abode. Passing the pipe back and forth between them, the Pöqangw brothers finally consumed all the tobacco. When they handed the empty pipe back to Sun, he did not utter a word. Silently he emptied out the ashes from the bowl. "Gee, you two are powerful." That's all Sun conceded. Then he continued, "But this is not all yet. Come on out with me."

So all three of them climbed out of the kiva. "For a second test I'll put you into this circular hut. There are rocks in there that are glowing hot," he declared.

Immediately Old Spider Woman whispered into Pöqangwhoya's ear, "He will try to kill you by heat suffocation in there, so place this medicine in your mouths ahead of time."

By now they had reached a huge circular structure with a pointed center, similar to a Navajo sweat lodge. In front of it, a large fire was burning, and in it had been placed hard rocks that were red hot. After ushering the boys inside the hut, Sun had them sit down in the middle and said, "All right, you stay right here. If you are stalwart enough, nothing will happen to you. That may prove that you are my offspring." As he said this, Sun heaped the red hot stones next to them.

Before long, the glowing rocks flamed up high, and just as the flames were about to reach their legs, Pöqangwhoya and Palöngawhoya quickly chewed up their medicine and sprayed it on the searing flames. Instantly the temperature inside the hut cooled down. As the fire in each rock was extinguished, the rock rolled aside on its own and came to rest some distance away.

Sun, meanwhile, was waiting outside to see how the boys would fare. When he was convinced that he had killed the two, he went to the enclosure and opened it. Much to his amazement, the Pöqangw brothers were unharmed, sitting where he had left them. "Gee, you are a pair of powerful ones," Sun exclaimed. "I can't believe you survived this ordeal. But this is not the end yet. Come on out, we'll go somewhere else."

With that, Sun led them to a place in the southeast. A huge pile of wood was there, nothing but dried pinyon wood. So huge was the stack that it almost reached the sky. On top of this stack he now placed the two brothers, instructing them as follows, "I will set this wood afire, and if you don't burn to death, you are truly my sons."

Once again the two brothers chewed their medicine. Sun now set the wood ablaze. Being full of pitch, it ignited in no time, and soon large flames were leaping up right next to the boys. As the fire made crackling sounds, they sprayed their medicine on it and instantly the heat began to die down. The burning stack was slowly becoming extinguished. With the boys right in the middle of the stack, it eventually reached the ground, completely burned down to ashes. Once more Sun stepped up to inspect the result. "Gee, you two are something else. Maybe you are indeed my sons. However, there's one more test for you to pass."

Now the three of them headed for Sun's kiva. By the time they reached it, night had fallen. Upon entering, Sun said, "All right, if you don't fall asleep by the time the sun comes up, I will declare you my sons." He was convinced that they would be overcome by tiredness and fall asleep. This time he had them stand up, not sit. At this moment Old Spider Woman spoke into Pöqangwhoya's ear again. "Make sure you and your younger brother stay awake. Keep poking each other into the ribs so you don't feel tempted to doze off."

All night long the Pöqangw brothers stood there. By the time it was getting close to daybreak, they were so dead tired that they were ready to fall asleep. At this point, Old Spider Woman took a couple of short sticks that she had with her and placed them into the boys' eyes to keep them wide open. By then the moment of white dawn was nearing, so Sun took out his gray fox pelt and hung it on one of the ladder poles outside. In doing so he signaled to all the people that the time of the white dawn had arrived. Meanwhile, yellow dawn was approaching. Sun signaled this to the world by attaching a yellow fox pelt on the ladder pole outside.

Then he went to take a look at the two boys. When he saw that they had not succumbed to sleep, he finally acknowledged them as his true sons. "I see, you still stand there where I left you. You must indeed be my offspring. Let me tell you what will happen next. People will now come out of their homes to speak their morning prayers. As they do so they ask for all sorts of things—not to die, to have a good life, to raise large crops, and other such things. Listen carefully to what they have to say, because you can't see them."

By now, sacred cornmeal was falling down on the three of them. People were casting pinches of it out as they were uttering their desires. As the meal piled up on the boys' palms, they filled their cornmeal pouches with it. Several times they had to do this. Finally, the boys' father said, "All right, that's enough. I can see that you are really my sons." With that, he embraced them and presented both of them with a bow and fletched arrows that he had personally made for them, one set for Pöqangwhoya and one for Palöngawhoya.

By now it was time for sunrise, so Sun carefully dressed and said to his sons, "Here, perch on top of this spinner. We'll travel together until we land somewhere."

The two brothers did as bidden and climbed aboard the magic flier. Their father did something to it, whereupon it began to rotate and lifted off. After a short flight they landed again. "We'll stay here for a while," their father announced. By this time all those people who had risen late also went out to speak their morning prayers. They did the same as the early risers. As the sacred cornmeal began falling on Sun and his sons, they filled their cornmeal pouches with it. "You see, these are the latecomers. By praying so late they are delaying my journey," he explained to the boys.

Then they boarded the magic flier again and were soon airborne, traveling along high up in the sky. At some point their father dropped them off again. Here the ground was flat, so the two brothers went rabbit hunting with their new bows and arrows. Exactly at noon they stopped again somewhere and their father said, "All right, let's remain here and rest for a while. After that I will help you back down to earth."

With that, Sun cast a rainbow all the way down to the ground and said, "All right, you can descend on this rainbow. Embrace it tightly, and as you slide along it be sure to keep your eyes shut. As soon as you touch the ground, you may open them again. Then return home to your mother. There's no doubt in my mind that you are my sons."

And so the Pöqangw brothers slid down along the rainbow, embracing it tightly as they went and keeping their eyes shut. Finally, when they didn't move any longer, they opened their eyes again and saw that they had reached solid ground. "We're down," they exclaimed, and instantly the rainbow retracted back into the sky.

From that point on the sun, their father, journeyed on all alone in a southwesterly direction. The Pöqangw brothers, in turn, set out for home and soon neared the village. A few children spotted them and one of them dashed off to notify their mother. Their uncle, too, was there when they arrived. "You've come," he greeted them.

"Yes, we're back," the boys replied.

"And did you find your father?"

"Yes, we found him. He's the sun." That's all they said.

So life went on again for the Pöqangw brothers, but at least they knew the identity of their father now.

It so happened that at that time somewhere northeast of the village of Shungopavi, in the vicinity of a great lake, a gigantic So'yoko monster was killing people. He had made it a habit of carrying them home after kidnapping them and keeping them there imprisoned without feeding them until they perished. He also stripped them of all their belongings, especially any jewelry they were wearing.

The Pöqangw brothers had been warned by their grandparents

never to go into that region, but the two disregarded the warning. "Let's go anyway. Nothing can harm us." So, one day, as they were roaming the area, they decided to head straight northeast to the forbidden lake. There they hunted for birds along its shoreline. Right at the edge of the lake stood a gigantic ponderosa with branches reaching way into the sky. The two brothers were still busy hunting around when suddenly they heard a shout. When they looked for its source, they spotted a huge creature approaching them from the northeast. What was so amazing was that the whole thing was glittering and sparkling with light. As it came closer it became obvious to the boys that what they saw was the So'yoko who had been kidnapping the people there. Unfazed, the brothers stood their ground. "He can't hurt us," they kept saying to each other.

However, when the monster was nearly upon them, they ran off and quickly scrambled up the pine tree. They were now perched at its very top. When the So'yoko reached the place where he had seen the boys he began searching for them. "Where on earth did they go?" he kept muttering to himself.

"Where on earth did they go?" the brothers on top of the tree repeated his question, teasing him. Now So'yoko spotted them. Staring up at them he commanded, "Climb down, the two of you." But the brothers just snickered and did not reply.

So the So'yoko took the big knife that he carried with him and started cutting into the trunk of the tree. The Pöqangw brothers, clinging to the branches at the top, were unconcerned. Meanwhile, the So'yoko continued chopping, and the tree began to make snapping sounds. Finally, it broke through and with a mighty crash fell into the middle of the lake, dunking the Pöqangw brothers in the process. The minute they emerged from the water, the So'yoko was upon them and, grabbing hold of them, said, "You two are something else. You should have been killed by that tree. Let's have a contest and see who is the stronger."

"Do you mean it?" the two brothers exclaimed in surprise.

"Yes, we'll compete with one another. You go first."

"No way, you go first, because you wanted this contest," the brothers protested.

The So'yoko gave in and started off. He took about twenty giant strides, then stopped and brandished his knife. "As soon as he hurls his knife, let's jump aside just when it is about to strike us," Pöqangwhoya suggested. Carefully they observed the giant as he kept swinging the weapon. Suddenly he let go of it. Whew, how it spun! At the last moment, just when it was about to hit them, the two brothers jumped aside and the knife landed where they had stood. The So'yoko couldn't believe it. "Gee, you two are just as brave as me," he admitted.

"No, we're not. We're no match for you," the Pöqangw brothers assured him.

"All right, it's your turn now," the So'yoko insisted.

The Pöqangw brothers stationed the monster some twenty strides away from themselves. They intended to use the bows and arrows that their father, the sun, had made for them. "All right, let's aim carefully," Pöqangwhoya said to Palöngawhoya. "Let's take careful aim and kill him dead." Nocking their arrows and drawing their bows, they shot. The So'yoko too tried to step aside, but he was much too slow and clumsy. As a result, one of the arrows pierced him right through the heart, and he just flopped to the ground. "There, that'll teach him," the two brothers shouted, running up to him and trampling him with their feet. They now noticed that his entire body was made of quartz crystals. That explained the sparkling when he walked along. What a wild creature he was! His eyes were huge.

The Pöqangw brothers had little knives on them that they took from their belts and used to begin flaying the monster. When they had skinned him completely, they tucked away their knives again. The So'yoko had been reduced to a lump of red meat lying there. Next, the brothers went into the forest where they stripped bark off the trees. Large loads of this bark they carried back to the place where they had slain the So'yoko. Stuffing the bark into his skin, they sewed it up with yucca. Then they fashioned a rope of yucca, tied it to themselves, and also slung it around the monster's neck. Then they started off, dragging the stuffed skin as they went.

As they neared the village, some of the children spotted them. "Look, the Pöqangw brothers are coming, pursued by the So'yoko." By pulling the dead body between them, it appeared as if So'yoko was chasing them. Eventually, the brothers reached the village and dragged the stuffed corpse to the plaza. By then a crowd of people had gathered there. "Look, we killed this kidnapper and butcher of our people," the two brothers proudly exclaimed. "So tomorrow you can all go to the place where he lived."

I don't know what the Shungopavis did with the So'yoko skin that had been filled with the bark. Maybe they burned it. At any rate, the following morning the villagers who had had a relative kidnapped by the monster went over to his living quarters. It was located in a cave along a cliff. Upon entering, they found a few poor souls still alive. Those who had died had simply been thrown into the canyon below. So they brought out the ones who were still alive. They also retrieved all kinds of possessions, such as necklaces. Whoever recognized one as belonging to him or her took it along.

"Well, we got rid of this monster," the Pöqangw brothers kept saying. "He won't molest anybody anymore." They had of course dispatched the So'yoko with the arrows their father had made for them.

And here the story ends.

25

The Water Vessel Boy

Aliksa'i. They say Walpi was inhabited, and many people living there were always making pottery. One of them, a girl who had just recently reached childbearing age, also was versed in this skill. Indeed, this was all she was good for, making pottery.

One day she and her girlfriend were going to get some clay, for they intended to fashion a bowl from it. Upon bringing the clay home they first soaked it in water. When it was nice and wet, they kneaded it, but because it was still quite hard, they took off their moccasins and together crushed the wet clay with their bare feet. When the clay became the right consistency, the two quit trampling it. Then they began fashioning the pottery bowl.

Some time after this event, one of them found that she was pregnant. Her friend inquired about the father of the child. "I have no idea," she replied. "You know me. I haven't been together with any man. Neither of us has ever been with a man, so I'm at a loss as to who it could be."

The two girls thought and thought. "Maybe once, when we were both asleep alone, some man secretly came to visit us at night," the one girl suggested to her friend. However, she could not think of anyone who would have done that. Then, suddenly, it occurred to her, "It doesn't seem possible, but remember some time back when we wanted to make a pottery bowl? Our clay was so hard that we had to grind it underfoot. The moment I stamped down on it, water splashed up right into my löwa. It seems to me that this must have caused me to have this child," she said.

"Yes indeed, that must be the reason you got pregnant," agreed her friend.

And so the days went by. Meanwhile, the girl's belly got quite large. Then, one day, she began to feel labor pains. The time had come for her to give birth. Eventually she gave birth, but it was not a child she delivered. Something else fell on the ground next to her. Much to her surprise, she discovered that it was a tiny water jar. She had given birth to a water jar, but just as she would with a real child, she took care of it on a regular basis.

As time passed the little jar grew bigger, and whenever it went somewhere it simply did so by rolling along. Amazingly, it also began to speak a little bit of Hopi and whenever it talked, it talked exactly like a little boy. Evidently it was a little boy.

Every so often mother and child would go somewhere. As a rule, the mother simply carried the little jar on her back.

As it grew older, she would set it down where the ground was even, and it would roll back and forth all over the place. The two also had a cornfield somewhere, and each time they went there, the little jar would tumble along on the ground.

One day the mother decided to look for wood with her son. It was in the fall, and every so often the days would get quite cold, so collecting fuel was going to be the purpose of their outing. As it was, the whole family was going to go. It was their intention to head to the wooded area northwest of Walpi, and naturally, the little jar also wanted to come along. At first his grandfather objected to this. "Why don't you stay here with your mother? Your grandmother and I will go alone," he said. "After all, if we get too far away, you might not be able to catch up with us."

But the little jar's mother said she would also like to come along. This was nothing extraordinary. Long ago women were quite strong and were good at doing some of the men's tasks. And because she was still quite young, she easily persuaded her father to consent to her wishes. She told him that she would take her son along. "He's not very heavy, and when he gets tired I can always carry him on my back. Otherwise, who will be here with him? Who will watch him?" This was enough for her mother to side with her, and so her father agreed.

By this time the child had grown much older, and it was his habit to roll along at great speed. Also, he had become constantly stronger, and so he went along like that as the family set out for wood. He kept tumbling along right beside his mother, chattering incessantly as he did.

It so happened that a rock lay in his way. The little jar bumped right into it and, alas, cracked instantly. The poor thing split all the way apart. He was trailing behind his mother as this happened, so when he screamed "Ouch!" she quickly looked back at him. What had happened that he should start screaming in pain all of a sudden? As she looked over her shoulder, she could hardly believe her eyes, for a beautiful little boy was sitting there. That beautiful little boy had apparently been inside the jar.

No sooner had the mother seen the human child than she ran up to him, snatched him up, and with words of gratitude hugged and embraced him. The girl's parents did the same. So they all went for wood in a happy mood. When the wood was gathered, they each carried their part of the load. The little boy was quite strong and hauled almost the same weight as the others. In this way they got a real little boy.

From then on the girl had a real human child to care for. He grew quickly, and as he did, he turned out to be skilled and apt in many ways. Eventually he reached the age where he would go off on his own. Once in a while he even went hunting and returned home with a big game animal for his mother. For some strange reason he always kept to himself on these outings. The people were not surprised, for they knew that he was no ordinary human being.

One day the boy went hunting but had not yet come home when clouds gathered in the sky. The sky became more and more overcast until the rain began to fall. It was a real downpour and continued all day. The clouds covered the entire sky, and not once did the rain let up. On that occasion it rained all night long.

It had been raining for several days, and still the boy had not returned. His relatives worried, of course. He was the only boy they had, and for that reason they really treasured him. He still failed to come home, so the boy's uncles and his grandmother said to his mother, "We really must talk to you about this. As you know, the boy doesn't have a Hopi father. He is the son of some superhuman being and came to us in an extraordinary manner. But even though you bore him for someone other than a Hopi man, we dearly love him and he means a lot to us. However, as we thought of this, it occurred to us that you were impregnated by clay and water. Thus he must be a child of the clouds, and the clouds must have come to fetch their child. Only this could account for the fact that they caused it to rain so hard. Don't worry about him anymore. He will surely come to see you when the clouds gather and it starts to rain. In this way he will keep you from crying. So don't take it too hard. We should be glad and grateful that he will help us in this way. No doubt, you must have raised that boy for the clouds." This is what they said to the boy's mother.

Now the girl did not have the boy anymore. His fathers must have wanted to have him back and so they arranged for it to rain all night long. And as it began to rain that day, the boy showed no desire whatsoever to seek shelter; instead, he continued walking about in the rain. Since he had been fashioned from the clay, after walking in the rain for a good length of time he began to melt. Before long he was melted to the ground, and since the boy also consisted of water, this element represented his breath. In this way his fathers got him back.

So, somewhat later, when the sun began to shine again, he was changed into fog, which then ascended to the sky, the home of his fathers. From that day on, whenever he set out in the company of the other clouds to let it rain, he never failed to water the plants of his mother and her relatives. In this way he helped them a great deal, even though he no longer resided with them.

And here the story ends.

26

A Famine at Oraibi

Aliksa'i. Long ago, people were living at Oraibi, and throughout the year, they conducted their rituals and ceremonies. They performed these properly, in accordance with tradition, and every summer they succeeded in raising bountiful crops. At harvest time in the fall, they were able to reap and set aside large amounts of food, and they always had plenty to eat.

As time went on, however, something happened. Their plants began to dry up and they harvested less than normal. Each year they sowed again but harvested less than the year before. Finally, one year their plants just refused to grow at all, and the crop was a complete failure. The Oraibis felt that they must have done something wrong, but if so, they were unaware of what it might be.

Bit by bit, the food the people had set aside began to run out, and many of them abandoned the village. They went wherever they might find something to eat, and over time they dispersed all over the land, stopping for a while wherever they found something. One group of the Oraibis found some wild potatoes and lived on those for a while before moving on. They ate the potatoes mixed with potato clay, a kind of salty yellow clay they used for seasoning. Other Orai-bis came across some Jerusalem artichokes, so they stopped and ate those. In this way the people scattered all over, eating anything they could find.

Still living at the northwest corner of the plaza was a couple with two children, a daughter and a son. The son was quite a bit younger than his sister. When the couple finally began to suffer from the famine, they left their home, just like the other villagers. Alas, they felt they would be burdened by traveling with their children, so they left them behind.

Left to themselves, the two children did the best they could. The sister was old enough to be familiar with her household duties and she tried her best to provide for both of them. Their life was wretched, however. To hunt for food, they would descend to the plain below and search the fields for forgotten ears of corn, some-times finding three or four. They also dug through the refuse dump, occasionally finding some beans. She would shell the corn and parch it, and when enough beans had been collected, she would make bean soup.

This is how the two stayed alive, sometimes devouring whatever meager morsels they could find, but frequently having nothing what-soever to eat. Then one day, a boy they did not know came up to them. He was a little older than the girl and had a little sister. They had also been left behind by their parents. When they met each other, the boy said, "Are you also living here all alone?"

"Yes," said the girl. "Our parents left us here, so we've been going from field to field and rummaging through the refuse heaps, trying to find something to eat."

"May we stay here with you?" asked the boy.

"Sure, why not. I know how to cook, so I can fix things for us, if we can find anything to eat."

"Well, we are in the same predicament. If we team up, maybe we can help each other."

So the four of them now lived there together and jointly roamed the area in search of food. The two younger children, however, tired easily and often fussed, and the two older ones felt hindered by them. Consequently, they decided to leave them in the village while they went foraging. They were sure no one would harm them. The two little ones cried all day long in their absence, but there was nothing they could do about it.

Once, when the older boy and girl were returning from one of their foraging excursions, the boy cut a piece from a corn stalk and took it with him. That night he busied himself making something with the piece of stalk, but he wouldn't say what. The next morning, before heading out in search of food once again, he brought out what he had created. It was a tiny songbird, which he gave to the younger children to entertain them while they were alone. The tiny bird could fly very nicely. They would let it go in a slight breeze, and since it was very light, it glided along smoothly on its cornhusk wings. Playing like this, the two would laugh and forget about being all alone.

Once, when they were playing with their bird, they threw it up into the air and, much to their delight, it flew away. When it failed to come back, though, they began crying inconsolably and were still crying when the older two returned. When the older boy asked them what was wrong, they explained that the toy bird they loved so much had flown away and was still gone.

The next day, just when they were all about to go search for food, the tiny bird came back, alighting in a storage niche in the wall. When they looked, there was a large pile of shelled corn next to where the bird perched. Apparently, the bird had collected these kernels for the children and had been flying back and forth to deposit them there. Now the children had food to eat, thanks to the tiny bird. He kept up this routine for almost a year, until one day he declared that he was done. He said, however, that someone else would come to help. With this assurance, he flew off, never to return.

Once again, the children had to fend for themselves. They had depended on the bird for so long, and the fields were picked so clean of corn, that they didn't know what to do but wait for the one who supposedly would come to help them. So, they were again reduced to rummaging through the refuse heaps in hopes of finding something they had overlooked before.

Once, when they were at the refuse heaps, they heard a voice. It sounded like someone was coming up the northeast side of the mesa, and the little ones were so frightened they started running toward the house. The two older ones were more curious than frightened and dragged the two younger ones back. Soon, a strange figure appeared on the trail, yelling, "Wa, wa, wa, wa, waa!" Now unsure, the children all moved away from him, but he placed a sifter basket on the ground in front of him and shouted, "Don't run away! Look, I brought you this."

The older boy stopped, then the others. As they all stood there looking over their shoulders, they could now see a repulsive-looking creature with an enormous head. He had hollow sockets for eyes, and something they did not recognize stuck up from behind his skull. His clothes were nothing but tattered rags. Frozen in place by fright, they saw that the sifter basket was filled with things. When he put the basket down, he rose up and started to dance and sing. This is how his song went:

> Kitanoo, kitanopo,
> Kitanoo, kitanopo.
> Kyaynaa, kyaynaawe, kyaynaawe,
> Kyaynaa, kyaynaawe, kyaynaawe.
> Kitsilili, katsililika
> Katonkiwaki mashikiwaki,
> Koki, kokiikiw mashishiwmaa,
> Himaalawmaa, hopee.

When he ended his song, he dumped the contents of the sifter basket at their feet and shuffled off again, disappearing down the southeast side of the mesa. When the children looked, they found parched corn scattered all over. They immediately began picking up the kernels. When they had collected them all, they carried them home and were able to once again eat without great hardship.

By the next morning, they had eaten all the parched corn and once again went rummaging in the refuse heaps. The ugly stranger again popped up right in front of them, yelling "Wa, wa, wa, wa, waa!" He startled them by suddenly jumping up like that, and at first they ran off a little ways but then halted and watched.

The stranger went through the same performance as the day before, with the same dance and song. When he finished he again dumped the contents of his basket on the ground and disappeared below the mesa. Once more the children ran up to the spot where he had emptied the basket and there were many corn kernels, enough to eat for another day.

The next day, they set out for the refuse heaps, more or less expecting to see the stranger there. And sure enough, he came and did his dance and song. They were getting used to him and hardly showed any fear, only moving a few steps away when he appeared. Once again he left food, and in this way they continued to receive food every day. Once in a while, in addition to the corn kernels, he also brought them some somiviki, boiled greens, cooked bee weed, or saltbush greens.

As it turned out, it was a Masawkatsina that brought them this food, and it was thanks to him that they managed to survive there in Oraibi. They were doing all right, whereas all the other Oraibis were still roaming about, eking out a miserable existence.

In this manner, the years went by. Both the older boy and the older girl reached marriageable age, so one day the girl said to the boy, "Why don't we get married? Then we can raise our younger siblings, and when they are old enough, they too can live together."

The boy agreed without a moment's hesitation. "All right, let's do that," he said. "Somehow we'll survive." And so they lived together and raised the two younger kids. The Masawkatsina kept bringing them food just as always, and they never wanted.

When summer came, the kachina brought the boy an ear of corn and said, "Take this to your wife and have her shell it. Then, go down below the mesa and clean the field of weeds and get it ready for planting. If you plant these kernels, keep your field free of weeds, and work hard, you should harvest a good crop of corn in the fall. That will tide you over the wintertime." Then he explained to the boy, in great detail, how to properly plant the corn kernels.

When the weather turned warm, the boy planted the corn as instructed. He planted in three separate places in all. Soon, the rains came and the plants really started to grow. Day after day he went out to his field, hoeing weeds and never allowing them to spread. He was a truly industrious young man who never tired of his work.

Since the corn plants were not yet mature, the Masawkatsina continued caring for the four of them by bringing them food. In addition to encouraging the young man in his work in the fields, he showed his young wife how to fix various kinds of dishes, and she learned many good recipes from him. In turn, she taught her husband's young sister how to cook, and she also soon became very good at cooking and helping out. Likewise, the husband took his wife's young brother along to the fields with him and taught him the art of farming. He too never seemed to tire of helping out in the fields. Since the young husband and his wife's brother were so hard working, their plants grew very well and bore abundantly. So the four of them recovered from the crisis of the famine and lived pretty well after that.

Eventually, word got around the land that there was now food available at Oraibi, and many of the people who had left started returning. Each time some of them came back, they asked the four young people for permission to join them once more. Permission was always granted, and in addition, Masawkatsina decreed that the four young ones should give the returnees small handfuls of corn, so that they could then plant and have their own livelihood once again.

Slowly the population of Oraibi began to increase again, and many of its former residents returned to their homes, after receiving permission to resettle. And so, some time passed, with various groups returning, until one day an old couple showed up. When they arrived all they could say, over and over, was, "How miraculous! You've recovered from the famine?"

"Yes, have a seat, strangers," answered the young wife. The old couple then revealed who they really were—the parents of the young wife and her brother. "We used to live here," they explained.

"Is that a fact?" the young wife coolly replied. Parents or not, that's all she said to them, for she was furious at suddenly seeing the parents who had abandoned them as children. They had caused them enormous suffering, and here they were asking to come back as if nothing had ever happened. When she thought about all the hardships she and her little brother had experienced all alone, she really grew angry.

The poor things were nothing but skin and bones and had aged beyond their years. When they begged for food, she cut open a watermelon. With great anticipation her wretched parents waited to eat. "How wonderful that you have made such a splendid recovery," they said, "so we can have something to eat!"

Their daughter, still seething with anger, cut off a piece of the watermelon and held it out to them. They reached out to take some, but before they could get even a bit, she silently let it fall into the dirt in front of them. The old couple began to weep, the old woman wailing, "Why do you treat us so meanly?"

"Well," the young wife spat back at her, "you caused us a great deal of pain. You left us to live in the most miserable way, and now you're back here begging. Why didn't you take us with you when you left? We had to suffer here all alone until we found a way to make a living. We're still alive, no thanks to you!" The girl really lashed out at her parents, who just sat there sobbing.

The girl and her brother continued, "You did that to us, so we don't want you in this house. Find your own place. We don't care where it is, just go and live out your lives there. Later, we'll give you some seed corn so you can plant and raise some food for yourselves.

But we'll never allow you to live here with us!"

"How dreadful! We thought we'd live here with you!"

"Never!" cried the girl. "Go and live somewhere else. We grew up without your help, so you can grow old without ours! I had a hard time raising my brother and he knows that's why he survived, so he won't allow you here either. So, make your fire somewhere else. I don't care where. There are several empty houses in the village, so you can move into one of those."

The old couple was crushed, but had no choice but to get up and leave. Still crying, they went out to look for a place to live by themselves.

In due time, the young married couple had their own children. And when their two younger siblings were old enough, they married each other and also had children. They established their own households and since they were skilled in many ways, they took good care of their offspring. In all respects they lived a good life.

All the other Oraibis who, thanks to the young couple, had not perished, enjoyed a pleasant life again, and the village grew in population once more. Because the Oraibis owed so much to the husband, they appointed him village chief. As more and more former residents drifted back, they asked him for permission to rejoin the village, and he usually granted it. His wife's brother was assigned the role of village crier. Thus the two young men became important village leaders.

Whenever there was a problem, these were the two the villagers consulted. The rains came frequently once again and soon everyone was harvesting bumper crops. Each fall, they filled their storage rooms, so they had plenty to eat and were happy and content. When warm weather came, the land was green and covered with flowers all the way to the horizon. Since the two leaders were pure in heart, the lives of all the people were good and harmonious. Once more, life was good in Oraibi. They never forgot, though, that they had recovered from the famine and received all these benefits through the generosity of the Masawkatsina.

And here the story ends.

27

How the Zunis Killed the Hehey'a Kachinas

Aliksa'i. People were living at the pueblo of Zuni. During this time the Zunis had a famine. No one knows exactly why. Perhaps they committed some transgression or crime and brought it upon themselves, as the Hopis had done before. This famine at Zuni became so severe that the people soon had nothing at all to eat.

Far away from Zuni lived the kachinas, at a place called Kiisiw. It was their custom to travel from village to village across the land in the shape of clouds. In this manner they visited the people to see how they were getting along. Thus, when people were suffering, they knew it right away. So of course they knew the Zunis were starving, and they took pity on them.

Hahay'iwuuti, who was in charge of them, told her grandchildren to go to Zuni and do something to gladden their hearts and help them with their problem. She selected the Hehey'a kachinas to go. Obediently, they prepared all kinds of gifts to take with them. To console the people there, they planned to stage a dance and bestow a great variety of gifts on them afterwards.

Now, it so happened that the villagers at Zuni had never seen kachinas before, so they were not familiar with these beings. The Zunis did hold social dances, though, and they entertained themselves in this way every now and then.

So, the starving Zunis did not really expect any visitors from outside the village. They were half crazy from the stress of the famine when the Hehey'as arrived there, out of the blue. Since they had no idea what a kachina was, when the Hehey'as first appeared, they thought they must be enemies. Without waiting to find out who the strangers were, the Zunis immediately attacked them. The Zunis, of course, acted out of ignorance. They just didn't know any better. As soon as they spied the Hehey'as, they ran into their houses and, grabbing whatever weapons were at hand, dashed back out in pursuit of them.

When the Hehey'as realized what was happening, they fled. They had intended only to deliver presents that would help the Zunis recover from the famine, but here they were being chased away, in danger of being killed!

The Zunis chased the Hehey'as in a northeasterly direction through an area with big buttes where there happened to be a rock shelter. The Zunis intended to herd them into this shelter and kill them there. The Hehey'a kachinas did not know what the Zunis intended to do, so as they fled, they headed straight for the shelter to seek refuge in it.

They found the rock shelter and were hiding in it when the Zuni men caught up with them. The Zunis had brought along with them some chile peppers, which they now set ablaze and hurled into the shelter, along with dead branches and other things that would quickly catch fire. The Hehey'as, trapped in the shelter, choked on the acrid smoke and burned to death.

The Hehey'as could be heard screaming inside as they died. They cried, "Ahiiniiya, ahiiniiyaa'a!" so these are the words that they now typically use to end their songs. In this gruesome way the Zunis murdered the Hehey'a kachinas.

When the Zunis had finished killing this presumed enemy, they turned and left. One of the Hehey'as, however, had crawled far to the rear of the shelter and had not perished. He had suffered terribly, and his hair was singed, but he had somehow survived the ordeal. So after a while, when he was sure it was safe, he emerged from the shelter, and with tears running down his face, looked around at his dead comrades. He soon realized that he was the only one left alive.

Devastated by this tragedy, he started for home. Heading straight for Kiisiw, he sang this song as he dragged himself along:

Teneyoo, teneyoo, teneyoo, teneyoo tayoo hatii'ii.
Teneyoo, teneyoo, teneyoo, teneyoo tayoo hatii'ii.
Naa'aa'aa'aahoototo pee'elaka shiwana, towii towii ahhaa'ihii.
Towiiwikaa liyooyokaanaa'a'ay ahaa'ihii.
Towiiwikaa liyooyokaanaa'a'ay ahaa'ihii
Hih, hih, hih.

Crying like this from pain and sorrow, the surviving Hehey'a neared Kiisiw. It so happened that just below their village, the kachinas had some cornfields, and one Hehey'a was out there hoeing weeds. He was one of the Kuwanhehey'as, or Beautiful Hehey'as. When the crying Hehey'a came up to him, he asked, "What's the matter? Why are you wailing like that?"

"Well," said the crying Hehey'a, "early this morning we traveled over to the village of Zuni to entertain the people there, but they trapped us in a shelter and set us on fire. I'm the only one that survived. I was only burned a little. Just my hair got singed." True enough, all of the poor kachina's hair was singed, causing it to curl up. "Otherwise I'm unhurt," he continued, "and so I came home."

"How terrible! I'm sorry indeed. Why on earth did they treat you like that!"

"I have no idea. All I know is that they attacked us and killed everyone but me."

When the Kuwanhehey'a fully realized what a massacre there had been, he too began to cry, and they both stood there together, crying. This is how they wept:

Wutsiitamo, iiyaawa, iiyaawa.
Iniiniyaa, iihihi'iw hi'iw hi'iw
Hih, hik, hik.

"Come on, let's go home," said the one who had been hoeing weeds. "I wouldn't be able to enjoy my work now anyway. We'll go together." And so they both went off, climbing up to the village.

The surviving Hehey'a finally stopped crying, but he had been crying so long and so much that his mouth would no longer straighten out. It was set in its twisted shape. When the two of them arrived at the village, though, they began crying all over again. Hahay-'iwuuti, who heard them coming, asked, "Why are you crying like that?"

The Hehey'a then related to her how he and his comrades were treated at Zuni, and that he was the only survivor.

"How dreadful!" Hahay'iwuuti cried. "Why did they do that to you?"

"I don't know," he said, "but this is what happened to us, so I came back alone."

"That's awful! Believe me, we'll get even with those Zunis! All of you, drop what you're doing!" she commanded her grandchildren, the kachinas, of which there were a great number.

The kachinas also had many younger sisters, and to these Hahay-'iwuuti said, "Go to your grinding bins! I want you to grind some of the white corn, but not too fine. Leave it coarse."

The kachina girls knelt down in front of their metates and started grinding, doing as Hahay'iwuuti ordered. Since they were strong young girls, they had the corn broken into coarse bits in no time, heaping it into containers. It was just shortly after noon when they had finally amassed a large quantity of the coarsely ground corn, which they put to soak in boiling water. When the mixture was ready, they molded it into large balls. These were to be transformed into hailstones. "Don't hold back," said Hahay'iwuuti, "make them really large. We must have revenge!"

When the kachina girls were done, the kachinas departed for Zuni as clouds, carrying huge loads of these hailstones in their arms. It was late afternoon by the time they arrived there. The Zunis were still suffering under the burden of the famine when the kachina clouds arrived, turning the entire sky black. Loud thunderclaps boomed, crackling in rapid succession. Lightning bolts crashed, so many that they seemed like standing shafts of light in midair. An enormous thunderstorm poured down on them, and then it began to hail huge stones, striking the Zunis with great force. When the kachina clouds saw a person, they aimed these missiles directly at them, and soon Zunis were dying left and right. So terrible was the onslaught of rain and hail that several of their houses collapsed, burying their occupants. In this fashion the kachinas wrought their vengeance. Finally, Hahay'iwuuti commanded, "Enough! We've killed a lot of them. That will do. Let's go back to Kiisiw."

So the kachina clouds departed and by evening reached their homes. Hahay'iwuuti said when they arrived, "That's the way I wanted it. We really got even with those murderers!" Turning to the kachina girls once more, she said, "All right, girls, start grinding again. This time use blue corn, please. And grind it to a fine powder."

Right away, the girls went to their grinding bins and ground the blue corn, pulverizing it to a fine powder. When they had finished, the kachinas headed to Zuni once again, as clouds. This time they dropped the blue corn powder in the form of a slow, gentle rain, and let it fall for a long time, soaking the ground well. They had also brought the seeds of various crops, which they planted by mixing them with the falling rain.

Finally, Hahay'iwuuti announced, "All right, that'll do. Everyone down there who is not dead and who paid attention to all this will be able to live again, thanks to us." The kachinas finished up the last of the planting and returned to Kiisiw.

Those Zunis who had survived the attack resumed their lives again, but there were not many of them left. When summer rolled around and the earth warmed up again, all the crops that had been sown by the kachinas sprouted—watermelon, muskmelon, and fresh corn. The Zunis who survived took good care of the plants that came up and grew a lot that year. There was plenty of food for all the people, and because of the rain, plenty of grass for both the domestic and game animals.

In this way the Zunis recovered from the famine and were able to sustain themselves once more. They began holding their ceremonies once again, and once in a while, they also included the kachinas in their dances.

And because of what happened when they first came to help the Zunis, the Hehey'a kachina is always crying when he comes, and tears are rolling down his cheeks. That's what the streaks on his cheeks stand for. And his mouth is crooked and distorted because of all the tears he shed for his dead companions.

And here the story ends.

28

Yaapontsa, the Wind God

Aliksa'i. People were living near Nuvatukya'ovi, the San Francisco
Peaks, and also here on Hopi land, where the villages of Walpi, Oraibi, Shipaulovi, and Shungopavi had been established. The people
who had settled in these places tried to plant corn during the early
planting season, but each time they did so, a fierce wind started
blowing. At times they managed to get some seed corn into the
ground, but they soon found that it would not sprout, and that the
topsoil in their fields was slowly being eroded away. Finally, the top-

soil was all swept away by the strong wind, and they only had a few kernels of seed corn left. As a result, they had to abandon their planting altogether. Frustrated and unhappy, they were at a loss what to do.

When the wind continued to rage, the village chief of Shungopavi and his partners met to discuss the situation. As they all pondered what to do, the chief made a suggestion. "Let's send some of our strongmen to the other villages and invite their leaders here to discuss this. I'd like for all of us to assemble here in four days."

The strongmen ran to the other villages and invited their leaders to meet in Shungopavi. At that time, Shungopavi was still located at the foot of the mesa, not up on top.

Four days later, the Shungopavi village chief waited for the other leaders to arrive as planned. Soon they began arriving from the various villages, asking, "All right, what is the reason for this meeting?"

"Well, as you know we're all suffering from this ferocious wind," answered the Shungopavi chief. "We're all trying to plant, but we're not having much success because of this relentless wind. So I thought we should put our heads together and discuss the situation. Maybe we can find someone who knows why the wind is blowing so hard. Perhaps if we make some pahos for him, he will have pity on us and help put an end to the wind, allowing us to plant what seed corn we have left."

One of the other chiefs suggested, "Why don't we try those lousy rascals, the Pöqangw brothers? Granted, they are badly behaved and mischievous, but there's a chance they know where the wind god lives."

All the leaders agreed with this plan, so the Shungopavi chief said, "All right, let's send someone to call upon the Pöqangw brothers." Turning to his nephew he said, "I want you to go to the place southeast of here where those no-good brothers live with their grandmother. Ask them to come see me, and tell them that I have made some pahos for them. Go and fetch them right away."

The chief's nephew immediately left for the brothers' abode. When he arrived there, Old Spider Woman greeted him in a friendly manner. "Have a seat," she said. "Nobody has ever sought us out here before. You must have an important reason for coming."

"Yes, indeed I do. My uncle sent me here. He's asking for your two nephews to go see him in Shungopavi. He has made some pahos for them, and they may pick them up there."

"Oh, thank you!" the old woman exclaimed. "We are in dire need of those prayer items. Nobody seems to make any for us nowadays. Let me call the boys over." The two brothers, as usual, were fighting with each other in a corner of the house. "You boys!" she called.

"What?" they replied, continuing their wrestling.

"We have a visitor who wants to ask you something."

But Pöqangwhoya and Palöngawhoya kept up their fighting with one another. When the old woman called them again and was once more ignored, she grew angry. Shuffling over to the fire pit, she snatched up the poker and smacked the boys on their behinds with it. "Ouch! Ouch!" they yelled. "Why are you doing that to us?"

"Well, if you'd listen to me, I wouldn't have to do it. There's a visitor here who wants to ask you something," said Old Spider Woman.

Finally, the two of them obeyed the old woman and came over to her. They looked like two dirty gray balls, with snot running from their noses. "So, what is it you want?" they asked the chief's nephew.

"My uncle, the village chief of Shungopavi, needs your help. He wants you to come see him," answered the boy.

"All right, lead the way. We'll follow you," agreed the two brothers.

The chief's nephew turned and hurried off with the Pöqangw brothers trotting along behind him. When the nephew arrived back in the village with the two, his uncle was delighted. "You've come?" he said to the two snotty-nosed dirt balls. Since the two of them had constantly runny noses and they had the habit of wiping the snot with the backs of their hands, their hands were shiny with mucous. "All right, sit down," he said to the brothers.

They replied, "Yes, your nephew told us you wanted to see us. We're wondering why."

"I'll explain, but first, thanks for coming," said the chief. "You see, we have a big problem with the wind. It just won't quit blowing. It's so strong we can hardly plant our seed corn. It's been blowing so long that just about all the topsoil has been blown away. As a result, our seeds get exposed to the wind and dry up. We were thinking that maybe you have an idea where the wind god lives, and that maybe you could go there and stop the wind from blowing."

"That should be no problem," the two brothers assured the chief. "We know him well and we know where he lives. His home is near Nuvatukya'ovi, northeast of an ice cave. There is a big crack in the ground there, and that's where his home is. His name is Yaapontsa. He owns the wind and controls what it does. Since you want our help with this matter, you must make pahos for us to take along. We'll come to pick them up in four days. Then we'll go visit him."

"Thanks," the chief replied. "We'll certainly do that." He was very happy about the brothers' response and immediately shared the news with the chiefs from other villages.

When Old Spider Woman learned what her two grandsons had so readily agreed to do, she scolded them. "You worthless brats, why did you agree to that? Do you have any idea what you've gotten yourselves into? That Yaapontsa is a very powerful being. I guess you can at least give it a try; if you're lucky you may succeed. I just have a feeling, though, that you're going to get into a fight with him."

Meanwhile, the village chiefs had gathered together and were busily fashioning pahos. On the fourth day they finished with this task and waited for the Pöqangw brothers to come pick them up. The brothers in turn, had been busy preparing for the trip by asking their grandmother to provide them with some pulverized dry sweet corn kernels. They had a use in mind for this finely ground powder when they arrived at the wind god's home.

Old Spider Woman knew what they had in mind and gave them some tips on how to use it. "There'll probably be some water near the ice cave," she said. "Stir this corn powder into just enough water, until you have a good qömi paste. Yaapontsa will emerge from his crack four times, spinning around as is his custom. When he goes back into his crack for the fourth time, throw your pahos in after him and seal the crack up tightly with the paste. Then he won't be able to escape."

After these instructions, Pöqangwhoya and Palöngawhoya headed for Shungopavi to pick up the pahos the assembled chiefs had made. The chiefs were very glad to see the brothers and thanked them profusely for being willing to undertake this task. The eyes of the little rascals really lit up when they saw what else the chiefs had made for them—some beautiful bows and arrows. The bows were finely made and the arrows were beautifully fletched with bluebird feathers.

Taking these things, the brothers set out. Of course, they had their shinny sticks and ball along with them also, and they played along their way, heading straight to Yaapontsa's home. Soon after they arrived there, Yaapontsa made his first appearance and vanished back into the great crack. They counted his appearances and when he returned to the crack for the fourth time, they cast their prayer offerings into its depths. They also fired all of their beautiful arrows into it. Then they quickly began sealing up the crack with the cornmeal paste, continuing until they were satisfied that the seal was good and tight. "There, that'll fix you!" they said. "Why did you have to blow all the time while the Hopis were trying to plant?" They really bawled him out, and when they were done they returned back to Shungopavi, where they informed the gathered chiefs that they had imprisoned the wind god. "We're sure he won't be able to escape now," they informed them.

Unfortunately, from that day on the wind did not blow at all. As a result, the weather turned really hot all across Hopiland. There was not even a breeze. It was so hot that soon the people could not stand to be inside their houses any longer and moved out onto their rooftops where it was slightly cooler. They tried again to plant their fields, but when the sprouts pierced the surface of the earth they quickly wilted. When the village chief of Shungopavi learned of this, he was distressed and once again called a meeting of all the village leaders. "We can't possibly continue to live in this sweltering heat," he said. "Now that the Pöqangw brothers have locked up Yaapontsa, there isn't even the slightest breeze blowing and the people are almost suffocating. Also, our plants are dying as soon as they come up. This is not what we had in mind when we asked them to help us the first time. I think we need to call them again. Life here is intolerable under these conditions."

The chief sent for the brothers and they came once more and listened to the chiefs' complaints. "All right," they agreed, "but you need to make a lot more pahos. Maybe when Yaapontsa sees them, he will consent to change his ways."

So the chiefs worked on a new bunch of prayer offerings for four days, whereupon Pöqangwhoya and Palöngawhoya came and picked them up and journeyed to the wind god's home once more. There they broke the seal of cornmeal paste, and opened up the crack. Instantly, the wind god came rushing out, blowing wildly. "Wait!" the brothers shouted, "don't do that. We brought you these offerings from the village chiefs. If you agree to accept them, then we won't seal you up completely. The people would like to see you blow some wind so they can breathe a little easier. Then everyone can live a little more comfortably."

Yaapontsa was glad to receive the pahos and stored them away underground. The Pöqangw brothers began sealing up the crack again, and the wind god complained that the opening was getting too small. "Make it a little larger," he urged the brothers, "I can hardly squeeze through the way it is now."

So the brothers granted him his wish and enlarged the opening a bit. Everyone was now able to breathe easier and Yaapontsa was also content. "This opening suits me just fine," he said. "I can still get easily in and out of my house. Before, when I came out I immediately turned into a strong wind. With this smaller hole, just enough of me can escape that we can all live more comfortably."

The Pöqangw brothers were happy to hear him say that and returned home. When they arrived there they noticed that the people were breathing easily again and that the heat was not so stifling because of the gentle breeze in the air. The chiefs thanked the brothers profusely for their efforts on their behalf. The corn plants were also clearly recovering in the cooler air and began to grow again. All the other plants across the land were turning green and the animals were relieved too, for the amount of wind blowing now was just right. The hole through which Yaapontsa went in and out was just the right size. No longer were there the fierce and continual windstorms the Hopis had been experiencing. Now, the Hopis fashion pahos every spring for Yaapontsa to ensure that he doesn't blow too hard.

Incidentally, as a person, Yaapontsa is quite ugly. That's why he never shows himself during the day. He only walks about at night. Probably, Hopis once met him and became so frightened that he decided never to go about during daylight.

And here the story ends.

29

So'yoko and the Shungopavis

Aliksa'i. People were living at Shungopavi, at a time when the village was still located below the mesa. The village chief had a daughter who was extremely vain and conceited, and none of the boys who courted her were good enough for her.

One day a man called on the village chief and proposed to sponsor a communal wood-gathering party. The chief had no objections, but he suggested to the man that he first go and fetch the chief's main partner, the village crier, so the three of them could plan the outing

together. The man took the suggestion and soon returned with the crier.

The sponsor of the outing now explained, "The wood-gathering party I want to sponsor is to be a social one, with both male and female participants. I would like it to take place four days from now. Therefore," he said to the village crier, "I would like you to announce the event publicly tomorrow morning. All the girls should prepare food ahead of time and then join the party. Everyone should go with a happy heart."

"All right," the chief agreed. "You have my permission to organize it. Let's get busy making the necessary pahos."

With that, the three of them began fashioning the proper prayer offerings for such an event. When they were done, they ritually smoked over them, wished each other good luck and success in this undertaking, and retired for the night.

At sunrise the next morning, the village crier made the public announcement of the communal wood-gathering party that would take place in four days. The participants were to trek to the pinyon and juniper forest in the northwest, where there was plenty of wood to cut and bring back for fuel. Girls were invited and should prepare food prior to departure, then come on the appointed day and join the boys for the trip.

And so the entire village worked toward the set date. Girls were busy grinding corn for the journey food and boys were making tumplines or renewing shoulder straps to carry the wood. During such a social wood-gathering, a boy who had a fancy for a particular girl usually collected wood for her. When he had collected enough for the girl, he tied it into a bundle for her and then collected a large amount for himself. After they finished gathering wood, they sat down to eat and then went home together.

As planned, on the morning of the big social event people could be seen heading out toward the forest. The village chief's daughter, however, was in no hurry to get ready. The chief asked his wife to urge her to hurry and dress so she could catch up with the others. His wife did so, but the daughter continued to drag her feet about it. Eventually, though, she did finish getting ready and set off toward the forest. When she arrived there, she picked up wood in various places but, since she wasn't interested in any of the boys, she didn't talk to anyone and pretty much kept to herself.

Some time passed but the girl was so self-absorbed that she

didn't realize that most of the others had already headed back to Shungopavi. When she finally became aware that she was all alone, she also decided to quit gathering wood and return home. She was just about to return to where her wood bundle was when, out of the corner of her eye, she saw an enormous man just this side of Tsuku-s'ovi.

He was huge, and as he stood there he yelled, "So'yokooo" in a long, drawn-out voice. This, and the fact that he was a repulsive-looking creature, frightened the wits out of the girl. He then started coming toward her, and she could see that he had huge bug-eyes and a large snout. In his right hand he brandished a long knife, and in his left he carried a bow and arrows. As he came, he took gigantic strides and chanted:

> Paayaaniisee'ey'ey, paayaaniisee'ey'ey
> Paayaaniisee'ey'ey, paayaaniisee'ey'ey
> Nii'ii'ii'iiy, paayaaniisee
> Paayaaniisee'ey'ey, paayaaniisee'ey'ey
> So'yookoo.

Terrified, the girl dashed for her bundle, but was too scared to load it on her back. So, she just discarded it and ran off toward Shungopavi.

Long ago girls wore heavy woolen dresses and capes and moccasins with fat leather leg wrappings. The village chief's daughter was wearing such clothes and the cape became a hindrance as she ran, so she threw it off. This helped a little, but she soon realized she was being hampered by the heavy moccasins and leg wrappings, as they made her run with her legs wide apart.

Eventually the So'yoko came across the cape where she had discarded it, and picked it up with the point of his knife. "I wonder what this is," he said to himself, as he scrutinized the garment. Then he smelled it and said to himself, "This has the smell of a girl on it. There must be one around here somewhere." Throwing it aside, he was stomping around in search of footprints when he came across the discarded wood bundle. "Aha!" he exclaimed, "that girl was here to gather firewood. She must still be around."

He found the girl's footprints and began to follow them. Some distance ahead, the girl began to tire of running in her heavy moccasins and leg wrappings, so she took them off and left them behind. She had hoped this would speed things up, but since the ground was very rough, and she was now barefooted, it actually slowed her down. So'yoko, meanwhile, was gaining on her. Fearing for her life, the girl now stopped, slipped out of her heavy dress, and discarded it. She dashed off, for she knew the monster was not too far behind. Stopping once again, she loosened the large whorls of her butterfly hairdo so that her hair fell over her shoulders. By the time she did this, she found herself in a large stand of ponderosa pines. One of the pines was very old and covered with wrinkled bark. With branches sticking out at shoulder height, it looked a little like a human being. Pressing herself along the backside of the tree's trunk, she stood there with her arms outstretched, just like the tree's branches. "If I do this," she thought, "maybe I'll resemble a tree so much that the monster will run right by me."

By now the So'yoko was getting near, his eyes closely following her tracks. "She must be here somewhere," he muttered. "What a feast she'll be when I catch her!" Once more he halted his pursuit of her and sang:

Paayaaniisee'ey'ey, paayaaniisee'ey'ey
Paayaaniisee'ey'ey, paayaaniisee'ey'ey
Nii'ii'ii'iiy, paayaaniisee
Paayaaniisee'ey'ey, paayaaniisee'ey'ey
So'yookoo.

Trying to blend in with the tree, the poor girl stood there, her entire body trembling. She was frightened nearly to death. Striding along, So'yoko finally reached the tree where she hid. Staring at it in amazement, he said, "This seems to be alive." The girl was petrified, shutting her eyes tightly as he inspected her with his large bugged-out eyes. "You're alive and you're human too," he said, running his hand over her skin. By this time, the poor girl was so scared that she began to urinate uncontrollably. The So'yoko, monster that he was, thought it was a spring and made a note of it in case he should ever come this way again and be thirsty. The So'yoko, still puzzled by the human-like tree, continued to poke and prod the girl. He stuck his finger into one of her eyes, and she yelled "Ouch!" but did not blink. The So'yoko stomped around, looking for her footprints, but they had disappeared and the girl stood there stock still, almost rooted to the ground, for fear the monster would discover her. Finally, the So'yoko grew tired of searching and strode off, muttering to himself, "I'll go home for now. I can always come back tomorrow. Those people are bound to come out looking for wood again."

Meanwhile, the girl's parents began to worry when she failed to return home from the outing. Her father, the village chief, asked the village crier to announce a search party for her, and a large group of men and boys was soon on their way. Finally, when they had climbed to a higher elevation, they found her in the ponderosa forest, crying and almost delirious. Since she was completely naked, one of the men wrapped his wearing blanket around her and led her toward home. Along the way, she eventually calmed down somewhat and related everything to them.

When the village chief learned of the So'yoko, he became outraged and immediately scheduled another wood-gathering party to depart in four days. In the past, people had failed to return from wood-gathering parties, and now he knew why. The So'yoko was obviously eating them. By ordering this new wood-gathering party, the village chief was showing that he had decided to kill the cannibal.

When the party got underway again four days later, the chief had his daughter come along again. Since the So'yoko had picked up her scent before, he would certainly be looking for her this time. He instructed her to stay near the other wood gatherers so they could keep an eye on her. When the monster came looking for her, the boys could stand and fight, and perhaps kill him.

Now, not far from the village lived Kotsoylaptiyo, Firewood Stoking Boy. When he heard of the Shungopavi's plan to go after the So'yoko, he immediately said to his grandmother, "I want to go too!"

"Oh dear!" the old woman cried. "That's really up to you. But as you know, the villagers despise us, so why would they want you along? Besides, you don't even have a weapon." The boy, who mostly spent his time stoking the fire in the fire pit, owned nothing but a poker.

Knowing that, his grandmother said, "At least take your poker with you, if you insist on going. Be careful though. Those Shungopavi boys are strong, so just wait until they catch the monster; then you can help."

Meanwhile, the party had reached the wood-gathering area near Tsukus'ovi and had begun collecting sticks and branches. Suddenly, one of the boys looked up and found himself confronted by a gigantic man. Immediately he shouted to the girls, "Run, quickly! It's him!"

Advancing toward the party, the So'yoko again began to sing his song:

Paayaaniisee'ey'ey, paayaaniisee'ey'ey
Paayaaniisee'ey'ey, Paayaaniisee'ey'ey
Nii'ii'ii'iiy, paayaaniisee
Paayaaniisee'ey'ey, paayaaniisee'ey'ey
So'yookoo.

Frightened, the girls took to their heels. The boys, meanwhile, placed themselves in strategic positions, ready to jump the monster when he came near. Way behind the boys stood Kotsoylaptiyo with his poker stick. The So'yoko came toward them, tracking the girl's footprints as before. The boys made ready to pounce on him, but as soon as the So'yoko was close enough to be clearly seen, they froze in their tracks at the sight of the repulsive creature, unable to do anything. Kotsoylaptiyo, waiting in the rear, now summoned up all his courage and strength and dashed toward the So'yoko. The giant took one leap forward and grabbed Kotsoylaptiyo around the waist. A fierce struggle ensued, with So'yoko swinging the boy around and trying to stab him with his knife. Finally, Kotsoylaptiyo slipped out of the giant's hands and scurried away with the monster in hot pursuit. The boy was just a tiny fellow, however, and quickly hid himself in the pine forest. After a lengthy search for the boy, the So'yoko gave up and went home.

As soon as he was out of sight, Kotsoylaptiyo emerged from his hiding place. Furious with the other boys, he ran back to where they were cowering and bawled them out. "You spineless cowards! Why didn't you help me? I already had ahold of him!"

The other boys were staggering around, slowly coming to their senses. Still frightened, though, they ran off when Kotsoylaptiyo started berating them and didn't stop until they were back in the village. There they told the others what a dreadful monster they had encountered and that they had not been able to catch him.

Kotsoylaptiyo was still stewing when he arrived back home and told his grandmother what had happened. "Why don't you eat a little and then go tell the village chief what really happened? He may have something to say about it."

Kotsoylaptiyo did visit the chief and explained how none of the others had come to his side when he grabbed hold of the monster. When he heard of the other boys' cowardice, the chief got angry and resolved to call for another wood-gathering party in four days. He also promised to personally talk to the village boys before they went out.

Back home, Kotsoylaptiyo told his grandmother about the chief's reaction and she said, "Well, maybe next time they'll come to your aid when you call!"

When the appointed day for the next wood-gathering party arrived, the village chief called all the men and boys of the village together and gave them a talk. "I understand that this boy here, Ko-tsoylaptiyo, got hold of the So'yoko last time, but you cowards were afraid to help him. Do you want that cannibal to devour us all? He is never going to stop kidnapping and eating us until we've killed him. Go out there and get him!" Chagrined, the men and boys of the village took off for the wood-gathering place.

The chief then turned to his daughter and instructed her as follows: "When you head back home this time, hang back a little behind the others. That is sure to draw the monster out, when he sees you alone. When he comes after you, run for the group of men and boys ahead of you, and run right into their midst. When the monster follows you, they will then have him surrounded and can attack him. Wait to be sure they can overpower him, then run straight home. Be brave now and give it your best try!"

The girl did as her father told her and lagged behind the men and boys, picking up wood here and there. Sure enough, the So'yoko showed up again and started singing his song. When he had finished, he sniffed the air and said, "Hey, that smells like the same girl that I smelled before!" Then he spotted her, all alone, and started toward her, taking gigantic strides. His legs were so long that he was rapidly getting nearer.

At this moment, the girl fled, leading the So'yoko right into the midst of the men and boys. Once again, however, they lost their courage and fled. Angered by this new show of cowardice, Kotsoylaptiyo lunged straight at the monster, grabbing him by the leg and yelling loudly. Their grunting and screaming could be heard all over as they wrestled.

Fortunately, the menfolk recovered from their initial fright this time and now came to help Kotsoylaptiyo. In spite of his small size, he was clinging fiercely to the So'yoko and aiming at the monster's eyes with his poker. When the poker stabbed him in the eye, the So'yoko cried out in pain and yelled, "I'm blind! I'm blind!" Rubbing his eyes, he stumbled around and lashed out at the ground with his knife.

The other men and boys swarmed around the So'yoko and began shooting him full of arrows, killing him on the spot. Kotsoylaptiyo leapt away as the So'yoko came crashing to the ground. It was an awful sight to see the monster lying there, stretched out to his full length, with his big teeth sticking out from his giant snout and his body bristling with arrow shafts.

Kotsoylaptiyo took the knife from the monster's giant, stiff hand, and they bound up his huge body to make him easier to carry. They then lifted him up on all sides and carried the giant corpse toward Shungopavi. He was so heavy that when one group of bearers became exhausted, another group relieved them. With some effort, they finally reached the house of the village chief, with the chief's daughter trailing along behind.

The chief was very glad to see his daughter back safe and sound and to see that the men and boys had finally killed the monster. Kotsoylaptiyo was leading the party, for he was the one who had shown the most initiative in capturing the So'yoko. "All right, here he is!" he said to the chief.

"Very well," commanded the chief, "bring him inside."

So the men and boys hauled the So'yoko inside the chief's house and dumped him on the floor. What a colossal creature he was! He stretched almost the entire length of the room. Soon, all the villagers came running to look at the monster. They all agreed that he lived up to what people had been saying about him. He was truly an ugly, repulsive-looking creature!

Kotsoylaptiyo now presented So'yoko's knife to the chief. It was quite long and very sharp. The chief looked at it, handed it back to Kotsoylaptiyo, and said, "All right, slice him open so we can rip out his heart. He was so mean and aggressive, who knows what kind of heart he has."

Kotsoylaptiyo did as the chief directed and sliced open the giant's chest, cracking those giant ribs to reach the inside. He reached in to remove the monster's heart, but it was extremely heavy and large. Finally he was able to extract it, and when they were able to examine it closely, they discovered that it was made of metal! That had to explain his nasty, aggressive disposition. Kotsoylaptiyo handed the heart over to the chief, who took it and spoke to the people gathered there: "All right, this is what we'll do. We'll cut off his head and store it away. We'll then fashion a mask in its image. Then, each time our children get mean or unruly, we will pray to it. And, in the future, if our children don't respect us, one of us will dress up as a So'yoko in the kiva, head out to a place in the northwest, and come to cleanse the children's hearts of their meanspiritedness. Whenever there is an ill-behaved child, we will warn him like this, "Obey, or the So'yoko will come and eat you!" This is how we will admonish our children from now on."

With that, the village chief made some prayer feathers for the So'yoko and stashed his heart and head away. Then he and some other men made a mask in the image of the monster.

In this manner, the monster was destroyed, and from that day on, no more Shungopavis disappeared. There was no question that the So'yoko had been feeding on them. Also, this is how there came to be a So'yoko among the various kachinas.

At some point, the So'yoko's heart disappeared from its place. Probably a witch or some other person with an evil mind stole it, since it was truly made of metal. No one knew where it went or what happened to it; it simply disappeared. At any rate, the So'yoko was killed, and he could no longer murder and eat the people of Shungopavi. As a result, the village grew into one with a large population.

And here the story ends.

30

The Witch Owl

Aliksa'i. People were living in Walpi, at a time when white men were already living on Hopi land. Also, there were trading posts, and Hopis were able to acquire guns.

Among the people living in Walpi was a girl who was in love with a certain boy. She wanted to marry him, but another girl also wanted this boy, so they were competing with each other. As it turned out, the first girl won his love and they were married.

The girl's rival was not at all happy about this. Since she was very jealous by nature, she became insanely envious and plotted to do the couple harm. Apparently she was a witch, endowed with extraordinary powers, and she pledged to herself, "That woman took my boyfriend. I'll get even with her!" The young couple had their first child by then, and soon after its birth, it became very sick.

Every night during the time that the baby was sick, an owl perched outside the couple's home and hooted constantly. Finally, the married girl's elder brother had enough of the hooting and declared, "Tonight, when the owl comes back, I'm going to shoot it! It just won't let us alone!"

So, that evening the brother was waiting for the owl when it returned. By then, it was late at night, and the world was lit by bright moonlight. No sooner had the owl started hooting, than the man grabbed his rifle and headed out the door. Guided by the sound of the bird's hooting, he headed straight toward it, taking care to stay hidden in the shadow cast by the bright moon. Then he saw it, an enormous great horned owl, perched right on top of a pole. Taking careful aim, he shot at the owl, and a moment later, it fell from the pole. The instant it hit the ground, however, it was transformed into a cat, which ran off to the southeast side of the village.

He followed the path of the cat as best he could by the light of the moon. It appeared to be headed straight for the mesa edge, and then it disappeared. When the man reached the edge, he peered down into the shadows but could see nothing. He walked a little way along the rim and suddenly he heard a noise. Freezing in his tracks, he listened intently. Someone was crying, in the dark right below him.

Climbing down to the lower terrace to investigate, he finally saw a woman crying and cowering in a corner. Stepping up near her, he looked at her and said, "I know you," but there was no reply.

Not knowing what else to do, the man turned around and went home, without uttering another word. A few days later, the young couple's baby died.

It so happened that exactly at the time of the baby's death, the jealous girl was grinding corn at her groom's house, as part of her wedding ceremony, for apparently she too was now going to be married. She was still at this task some time later when she fell very ill from an unknown cause, and it did not look as if she would survive. She refused the assistance of any kind of healer and steadily got worse. When her wedding garments had been finished and it was time for her to go home with the groom, she was so sick she could no longer walk. Her in-laws had to carry her back home. Shortly thereafter, she died.

After her death, when people were getting her ready, they discovered that she had suffered a gunshot wound. Apparently she had been so angry at not winning the first boy that she had killed his wife's child.

The wife's elder brother, who had shot the owl, commemorated this tragic event by carving, on a rock somewhere near Pigeon Spring, the image of a man pointing a gun at an owl. The image can probably still be seen there.

And here the story ends.

31

The Gambling Boy Who Married a Bear Girl

Aliksa'i. People were living at Wupatki. In addition, there were settlements all across the land. Long ago the Hopis used to migrate around quite a bit, building their houses among the buttes and cliffs, which accounts for all the ruins found there now. One such ruin exists at Wupatki. Many people once called this place their home. In spite of its small size, the place had enough inhabitants to permit gambling with each other. Gambling has been part of Hopi life since way back in time. Totolospi and sosotukwpi were the two games with which people gladdened their lives. Whenever they engaged in this form of entertainment, they usually did so at night. The stakes involved no valuables, as a rule only a straw from a hairbrush or broom. The players would tie a bundle of broom straws together and give these to each other. It was always the losers who had to hand over a straw to the winning side. When one group had lost all of their broom straws, they were beaten. The following day, then, when it got light, the losers had to cook breakfast, which the winners came to eat. Customarily, they were served boiled beans with somiviki. In this fashion people used to gamble.

Slowly but surely the fervor displayed in this kind of entertainment got out of hand, though, when the players began gambling for real possessions. Eventually, they became so addicted that they did not even quit to go to bed. Among these gambling addicts was a young man who kept losing all sorts of things that belonged to his parents. In this way, he gambled away his mother's woolen dress and shawl and his father's ceremonial kilt and embroidered sash. All these precious items he lost. When his parents noticed that these things were missing, they kept asking each other who on earth could have taken their belongings. Assuming that it was their son—after all he had participated in the gambling—they put the blame on him. When they confronted him and asked whether he had gambled their things away, he had to admit that he was at fault. There was no denying the fact that he was part of the gambling crowd. When his parents heard him confess they grew angry, for those were the clothes they really treasured. Whatever people own in the way of clothing, they like to hand down to their children. Also, whenever a child desires to participate in a dance ceremony, they must have the proper costume. And because clothing of this kind is hard to come by, the parents were understandably upset. They felt that he should never have done this, and they were anxious to learn from their son what had caused him to do it. Both husband and wife were of one mind about the seriousness of the transgression, and in return they threw their son out of the house. "You can't live here with us anymore. Go somewhere else where you can live as it suits you," they said.

So the poor fellow had no choice but to leave. It so happened that he had a younger sister who was not at all happy about this turn of events. However, she didn't know what to say to her parents and therefore didn't stand up for her brother when he left. Upon taking his leave the boy descended to the southeast side of the mesa across a slope. Somewhere there was a kiva, and crossing the area southwest of it he headed up the terrain in a southeasterly direction. He really had no idea where to go. Nor was he familiar with any other village. He had no real friends, so he was at a loss where to turn. As a result, he wandered around aimlessly. Out of frustration he finally set forth in a northwesterly direction. This route eventually led him to the large mountain range of Nuvatukya'ovi, the San Francisco Peaks.

After skirting it on its northeastern side he con-tinued on toward its northwest side. At long last he arrived in the midst of a forest. There were huge pine trees growing there and he pondered whether he should enter the place. Knowing that he couldn't return to his parents, he decided to head straight through the forest.

The boy traveled northwest until he felt like resting. He had grown tired and it was getting to be evening. He had just settled down comfortably when suddenly he clearly heard the sounds of something moving along. As he looked up and scanned the area, a bear appeared before him. Rearing up on its hind legs, it was quite tall. The boy got frightened and jumped to his feet. Intending to run back from where he had come, he was about to make a dash for it when the bear addressed him. "Don't run away. I won't harm you," the bear said. "There's no need for you to flee."

The boy remained rooted to the ground and stared at the enormous beast. The bear stood with its claws spread out like a fan, and the young man stood there with his eyes fixed on the bear for a long time. Finally, it was the bear who spoke again. "Don't run away. I won't harm you. I came just for you."

The boy continued to stand there without moving a limb. So the bear said, "You shouldn't be walking around here. Why are you?"

At long last the boy found his voice and replied, "I don't know where I'm going. I had no real destination in mind and was just wandering through here when I got tired. That's why I wound up here." The boy had no journey food with him, so he told the bear that he had nothing to eat. He explained that he was at a loss for what to do and that this was his reason for being there.

"Well, I suggest you come with me then," the bear said. "We live right here on the northwest side of the mountains, at a place slightly to the southwest. Let me take you there."

The boy now ventured near the bear, who fell back on all fours again and said, "All right, climb on top of me. Then grab hold of my fur."

The young man complied and mounted the beast. As soon as he was seated on top of the animal he grabbed its fur, and the bear lumbered downhill slightly to the northwest side and then headed in a southwesterly direction, bypassing Nuvatukya'ovi on its northwestern flank. After a while the bear veered somewhat to the southwest and then arrived at the base of a cliff. Much to the boy's surprise there was a kiva there, which the two ascended. After getting up on the roof the bear had the boy dismount. "All right, this is my home," the bear said. "Follow me inside." With that, the bear disappeared into the kiva.

The young man entered behind the bear through the hatch. Sure enough, here was a place that looked inhabited, although nobody else was at home. After getting the boy inside the bear took him to the northeastern base of the abode and said, "Stay here for the time being."

As the young man glanced about he noticed some sort of altar that was set up just outside the niche that is commonly centered at the far end of the kiva at the base of the inside wall. Evidently, whoever lived here owned an altar. The boy had no notion who they might be, for with the exception of the bear no one was home.

The bear now disappeared into the back room in the northwest side of the kiva, where there was an opening. Upon entering, the animal transformed itself by removing its skin. Much to the boy's amazement, a young woman emerged from the back room. The girl, who was extremely beautiful, turned to him and said, "I'll fix you something to eat. You must be starved."

The boy stared in shock at the girl. It had evidently been she who had brought him here. Once more she entered the back room and when she reappeared she held a tray of piki in her hands. This she set out in front of the boy, together with water and kwiptosi, fine-ground corn. "Now, eat," she urged him.

The boy began to eat and was still helping himself when there was a loud thump on top of the roof. He had expected something like this all along. When people live in a kiva and someone comes, the visitors always call out or stomp their feet on top to announce their arrival. Someone had just stomped his foot, and the light quickly darkened in the entranceway. This typically happens as a person enters, grabbing hold of the ladder in order to descend. As he climbs down then it gets dark, for on his way down he appears to block off the entire entranceway. This is what happened in this case as somebody entered from above. As it turned out, it was another bear. The boy stopped eating and stared at the beast. The girl, however, remarked, "Don't worry, he won't harm you. We live here."

Upon stepping off the ladder the bear stood there facing the boy, looking through its paws the way these animals always do when they have a mind to attack a person. Whenever Bear kachinas enter a kiva during a night dance, they behave in the same fashion. This bear did the same as it moved toward the boy. But it left him in peace and passed him by to disappear into the back room. Upon coming back out it too had changed into a human being. The boy was amazed. Once again, it was no longer a beast that reemerged but an ordinary human. "I guess they live here," the boy thought, as he resumed eating his food.

It was getting evening, and the animals had probably been hunting to have returned this late. Before long, a third beast entered. This time it was a mountain lion. It did what this animal typically does, namely jumping down from on high. It still had not come all the way down the ladder when it jumped down to the floor. In a big leap it swung around the ladder pole, landing right next to the boy. The poor boy was frightened out of his wits. But the mountain lion simply strolled about and then it too disappeared into the back room. When it reentered, it too had been transformed into a human shape.

This process continued, and each time somebody came out of the back room he said to the boy by way of greeting, "So you also stay around here?" The boy answered as was proper. The last two animals to arrive were a badger and a gopher. Apparently, they also were sharing the living quarters there.

By now all the residents had returned from their outings. When the boy was finally full, he moved away from the food and settled down on one of the stone benches. There he sat now, listening to the others as they chatted in the comfort of their home. One of them asked the girl who the visitor was that was staying there with them and where she had picked him up.

She replied, "I came upon him not far from here on the northeast side. That's why I brought him here. He said he was wandering around in self-imposed exile and so was not on the way to a specific destination. For this reason I brought him here and told him he could remain with us for the time being."

The others indicated that if indeed he had no desire to go anywhere else, it would be all right for him to stay there with them. They all agreed on this point.

Meanwhile, night had fallen as the whole group sat there whiling away the time. Finally, the bear, who seemed to be the leader of the group, suggested they entertain their guest with dancing. As a result, they all exited the kiva, probably in order to go and put on their costumes. After a while the boy could hear the approach of some beings. Then there was the sound of someone shaking a rattle. Immediately, the person tending the fire shouted up to them, "Come on down!"

Kachinas filed into the kiva. They entertained the boy by staging a dance. When they were finished, they departed, whereupon a new group came down the ladder. Different kinds of kachinas, one group after another, kept entering just like during a night dance. It was well into the night when the dancing came to an end. The leader exclaimed, "This will do. Let's go to bed now. It's late."

So they all spread out their bedrolls there. The girl who had brought the boy now turned to him and said, "Come over to me. We'll go into the back room where we can sleep."

From all appearances the girl intended to sleep with the boy. It seemed that he was going to have her as his girlfriend. There was no question, she wanted to sleep with the boy and for this reason had made her bed in the back room. The boy did as bidden, entered the room, and spent the night with the girl.

The next day, after it got light, all the animal people stayed home and did nothing.

And, as typically happens in stories, a year usually passes in no time. This was also true in this case. Meanwhile, the boy's parents and his younger sister were greatly troubled that he had not yet returned home. Sure enough, they had been very angry with him, and when he disappeared they had not really been waiting for him to come back. Nor did they have any idea where he had gone. But now, a year later, they were getting lonesome for him. The boy's parents were so distraught that they no longer even combed their hair. After all, he had been their only son. The animal people who kept the boy were certainly checking on his parents. And, as usually happens in a story, there is always someone who knows how a person's relatives are faring. So the animal people also were familiar with the state of mind of the boy's parents. They too were worried that the young man might get homesick and would show a desire to return home one day. He had never really become accustomed to their place and remembered his parents and relatives far away. One day he said to his wife—she was his wife now because he had been sleeping with her—"I wonder if I should not go back home."

His wife replied, "I think you should, for surely you must be lonesome for your parents and younger sister. Let me talk to my people here. Maybe they can advise us what is best to be done."

That same night the bear woman told her uncles that the man living there with them was toying with the idea of returning home and wondered if this would be all right.

One of her relatives replied, "Yes, it will be all right. After all, he did not grow up with us and will never get accustomed to living here in the forest. So let him return to his real home."

With that, the animal people went to bed. The following morning, as soon as it was day, they instructed the man at length in what they wanted from him after he left. As soon as they were done with breakfast they said to him, "Well, having lived here with us, you have certainly seen the condition of our altar. We always pray at this altar. Now, a game animal usually has a paho tied around its wrist. One of them may even have a taqvaho, or male paho, attached to a crook staff. A bear has the taqvaho tied to his leg. For this reason we desire from you prayer feathers and taqvahos for ourselves. When you get home, make us some pahos once in while. No one is making any for us here these days. Just do that for us from time to time because it is these prayer items that help sustain our lives. If you do that we'll be grateful to you forever.

"And make every prayer stick just like a taqvaho," they continued. "Attach a little food bag to it and place in it a mixture of cornmeal and ground-up abalone shell. Be sure this little food bag is not missing," they impressed on the man. "Carry these offerings to where you have your field and deposit them along its southwestern edge. We are then bound to notice them." This is how they talked to the man.

He replied, "Very well, I promise always to do this."

When the woman was ready to take her husband back, she changed into a bear again. Then they all dressed the man in beautiful clothes, for he had arrived rather shabbily dressed. Among other things, they had fashioned a buckskin shirt for him. The pants were also made of deerskin. In addition, he now wore leggings and red buckskin moccasins with rawhide soles, the traditional Hopi footwear. Thus, all his clothes were of leather. Dressed up like this, the bear woman loaded her husband on her back and carried him back along the same route as she had first brought him to her abode. Circling around the mountain range of Nuvatukya'ovi she turned all the way to the northeast and there set him down. From this point it was not far to his home at Wupatki.

Since the man's parents missed him so much, their daughter kept telling them that he would surely return one day. Her reassurances helped them to keep some of their strength, for they were sick from all the longing. So she was constantly saying that he would be back. That day the girl said it to them again, but her parents did not believe her anymore. "He won't be coming back as you keep telling us. He's taking forever. You're just telling us lies. He won't come as you keep insisting." That's how her parents responded to her. They simply would not take her word any longer.

Meanwhile, the man was heading home on foot from the place where his bear wife had dropped him off. Some time that evening he reached the house of his parents. Immediately, his younger sister announced his arrival to them. "Come on, get up. Your son is here!"

But the parents refused to believe her, and it was not until he actually entered that they were convinced of the truth. They had still just been lying there, for due to their grief, they no longer cared to even get out of bed. However now that he had finally returned they came to their senses again and rose at once with their hair still messy and unkempt. Since they had failed to get up they had neither washed it nor combed it. Now, however, the parents had no choice but to rise. They were overjoyed to have their son back and quickly recovered from their ordeal. By evening the whole family was living at peace again.

The next day all the villagers learned of the boy's return, for they all knew of his disappearance. Everywhere people were talking about his return. His friends came to visit him and were happy to have him back. They still remembered him well.

Unfortunately the man had only been back a few days before he resumed his old gambling habit with all the other people. Once he started he became so absorbed in it that he completely forgot his wife in the forest. Neither were any of the instructions he had received from her uncles fulfilled by him. And since he had forgotten her, he also forgot to fashion the pahos for them. He would be busy at the place where he had his field, but never did he deposit any offerings there for them. Always at daybreak his bear wife and her uncles would head out to the field for the prayer items they had asked him to make for them, but never did they find anything. There was simply nothing there. The animal people, poor things, became quite unhappy about this. On many occasions they had checked the place at the field, but always in vain. The man had never left any prayer feathers for them. This made his wife furious, for she had given birth in the meantime. Maybe the man did not know this yet, or maybe he did know. The fact was that right after his return to his parents he never thought of his wife and her relatives anymore and totally forgot his ceremonial obligations. All of this went through his wife's mind. She began to seethe with anger.

One day, after having spent a long time gambling here and there, the man once again started thinking about doing some planting. He headed out to his field and hoed weeds. It was then that he suddenly remembered his wife. He must have had some knowledge of her pregnancy for, quite by intuition, he planted corn in three places. Evidently, he assumed that his wife had twins. For this reason he planted one lot for his wife and two for the children. After preparing these three lots he also planted corn in two additional locations for his parents.

When his bear wife noticed that her husband regularly went to check on his plants, she approached her uncles and said, "I want you to go to his field, pick half of all the fresh corn, and bring it here."

The uncles obeyed and headed out to the field. It was dark night by the time they arrived there. As requested, they picked half of all the fresh corn and brought it home. Then they all feasted on it.

The following morning, as the man went to check on his plants, he noticed right away that some animals had eaten from them. He walked about trying to figure out the tracks, but he could not determine who the culprits had been. On the way back the animals had broken off parts of the corn plants and erased all traces of their tracks. They were therefore unrecognizable. The man was at a loss as to who it had been. He knew it hadn't been rabbits, so he kept wondering, "What on earth were those creatures that did this?" He was completely distraught, poor thing. Finally, he said to himself, "From now on I'll go there to spend the night. I swear, if I catch them in the act, I'll kill them." Upon his return home he therefore made arrows for himself. When he had fashioned a large pile, he said to his parents, "Tonight, after supper, I'll go out to my plants. Some animals ate from them and caused me great misery. They devoured almost all of them. If I go to guard the plants until they ripen, we can at least gather some corn at harvest time."

"All right," his parents replied. "But didn't you look for tracks to find out what animals were there?"

"Sure, I did. I walked all over, but couldn't tell what kind they were. They dragged leaves from the plants all over and erased all their tracks. Nothing is visible anymore. I have no idea who could have done the damage."

"All right, then," his parents replied, "go and sleep there. Maybe you can catch the ones responsible. They may come again during the night."

The bear woman and her relatives quickly became aware that the man slept at the field that night. So she advised her uncles, "Don't go to the field for the time being. My husband is sleeping there. I'll decide tomorrow what to do about this." The twins, her children, were quite grown by now.

When the man returned home the morning after his first night at the field he said, "Nothing happened. Maybe those animals intended to do it only once to cause me this terrible misery."

The following night he went out once more to sleep at the field. "They might come tonight if I'm not there," he thought. With that, he headed out to the field, and when he arrived he collected wood along its edge and lit a fire. The purpose of the fire was to prevent any animals from coming too close. Then he moved to the middle of the field, covered himself in a blanket, and lay down. Soon he fell into a pleasant sleep guarding his plants.

When the bear woman's uncles went out to eat some of the corn again, they spotted the fire. Because of this, they dared not approach and returned home.

The following morning when it got daylight again, the man walked about but found no trace of any animal that had come during the night. Once more he had failed to catch the culprits. In spite of this, however, he continued going to the field and sleeping there to guard his plants.

Only the portion that the man had planted for his parents was still left intact. So one night all the animals headed out to this lot and feasted on the corn once more. When an evil person intends to harm someone, he always aims at midnight. So all the animals set out in the middle of the night, the man's wife, her two children, and all their uncles. It was as if they were making a raid on the plants. Not only did they eat up all the corn, they also uprooted the stalks, just for spite. While some of them were engaged in this task, the gopher and badger were busy digging burrows and tunnels all over the place, for that is what these two are really good at. They made holes in the entire field. Finally, when they were satisfied with their destruction, they all headed home, with the exception of the bear woman and her twins. She had told them that they would stay a little longer. She now instructed her children to go to the place where their father was sleeping and chew on his bowstring. And so, when all their uncles had departed, the two approached their father while their mother waited for them at the edge of the field. He lay right next to them, pleasantly asleep, while they gnawed on his bowstring. This accomplished, the three bears went home too.

Some time later, when their father awoke, he went to inspect the plants. He had not heard a single sound of the terrible devastation, so when he saw that all his plants had been devoured and the ground churned up, he became extremely angry. This time, as he searched for tracks, he discovered some, and when he realized that they were the spoor of bears, he grew beside himself with rage. Full of anger, he returned home to inform his father that they would have to hunt down some bears who were the culprits. He explained that they had not only eaten up all of the crops but had also pulled out all the stalks and left the field in shambles.

Next the man sought out the village crier who was to broadcast the news of the bear hunt from the rooftop. The village crier did as bidden. The men who were going in pursuit of the bears, however, were somewhat reluctant because they felt inadequate for the task. A bear is an awesome creature, and they, being only humans, did not think they would be able to overpower these beasts. At least some of them who were going to accompany the man voiced opinions along these lines.

The next day the group set out in pursuit of the bears. The man who was the sponsor of the hunt had eaten his breakfast quite early and had already gone ahead of the main party. Upon reaching his field he pressed on without waiting for the others. In the area where the animals had come through he followed their tracks and eventually caught up with them. This happened soon after he had entered a forest. He was still searching for the beasts when one of them emerged from the thicket. The man aimed his arrow to shoot it. When he pulled back, however, at that instant the bowstring broke where the two bear cubs had chewed on it. Since the string was partially unraveled, it was bound to snap in two. Having failed to kill the bear the man in turn was now attacked by the beast. Bears typically kill by ripping a person's chest apart, and in this fashion the bear killed the man. Then it took off. The bear had been the man's wife. Her husband had probably recognized her in her bear's shape. She had been so filled with anger against him that she killed him. Having accomplished her mission she lumbered on home.

Meanwhile, the other hunters were following the man, traversing the same area as he. Eventually they caught up with him; when they did they saw that he was dead. Now they really lost their nerve, for they knew full well that they had no chance against those beasts. So they picked up the man's corpse and carried it back to his home.

When his bear wife arrived back at her abode she told her uncles what she had done. They became very angry upon learning of her deed. "You should not have done that to him," they scolded her. She explained that she had committed this act out of anger. Her uncles, however, insisted that regardless of whether the man neglected to make pahos for them, she should never have killed him. All of them were quite unhappy about this turn of events.

Meanwhile, the hunters had delivered the dead body of the man. After preparing him ceremonially for his afterlife, they buried him. Now that he had died, his parents and younger sister were sad and despondent.

That same evening the bear woman, the dead man's wife, all of a sudden announced to her uncles that her husband had not really died after all. She claimed that he could be brought back to life. So then the uncles ordered the two nephews to go and retrieve their father's body. The latter did as bidden. They headed out to the grave, dug the body up, and carried it back to their home. The uncles were now going to try to bring him back to life. For this purpose they had already spread out a wedding robe next to their altar, before the nephews' arrival with the corpse. After bringing it inside, they laid it on top of the robe and then covered it up with something. Next, all of them sat down by the body on all sides and started chanting. They probably used a sacred ritual prayer song. This they sang until it got daylight. Early that morning they all went outside from their abode to pray.

Upon reentering, they saw that he had evidently come back to life, for he was sitting up. The animal people were elated and expressed their thanks that he had regained his senses again. Both the badger and the mountain lion are of course medicine men. They are the ones who remove objects with malignant powers that are implanted in their patients. They were also the ones who had planned the man's revival. So now they planned to instruct him in the art of curing.

For four full days they kept the man sequestered. On the first day they taught him the sacred ritual prayer song. It took him until nighttime to learn it. The next day they showed him all the various medicines that are used to heal a sick person. On the third day they took him around to all the locations where the different medicinal plants grow. Some of them grow far away, but they went to all of them. Of course, they did not travel on foot. Since the man now had these beasts as his fathers, he did everything like them, in the form of a bear. By taking him around through all these areas, they not only taught him about these locations but also dug up the various medicines for him. Then they explained to him what a disease is. When they had initiated him like this into all the aspects of the art of healing, they reassembled back in their abode.

On the fourth day the man was supposed to return home again. His bear wife herself was going to take him back, so on the morning of the fourth day they washed his hair and ushered him outside to speak the morning prayer to the rising sun. When this ritual too was over, they dressed him in the same buckskin clothes that he had worn on his return home. As they dressed him, they also carefully bundled up all the different kinds of medicines that would be useful to him in his role as a healer. Prepared like this, his bear wife then set out to take him back. At some place she let him dismount, and from there he continued homeward on foot.

When the man arrived back home, his family could not believe their eyes. But he related to his parents how he had received a new life. People say of course that when someone becomes a medicine man, he has all of them as his children. He was now going to take care of them in that village there. He had been initiated into the art of healing, so in the role of the medicine man he would now help them.

And so, from that day on, the man took care of all the people there at Wupatki. As the word of his healing craft spread, everybody came seeking medical treatment from him, for he was extremely powerful and cured every person right away. In this fashion he worked for the people there. Soon the people from nearby villages also learned of him and came only to him for help. Once in a while Indians from far away came to fetch him, and he had to travel long distances and under great hardships. But he worked hard for everybody, no matter who it was. Since people kept coming from far away, he could not afford to be lazy. Also, he thought of it this way: He had died and had been brought back to life. He had been initiated into the art of healing and had returned to his village with this knowledge. It was as if through the art of healing he had become a member of his community again. For this reason he could not afford to be lazy.

Rather, he kept urging himself on to treat his patients. It was as if he was living for this purpose only.

From that time on the man also fulfilled his ceremonial obligations toward the animal people. He regularly prepared pahos and prayer feathers for them and went to deposit them at the edge of his field. Each time he placed them there, the beasts noticed it and came to pick them up. In this fashion the man took care of them. In a way, he was paying them back. In this matter too he now never became negligent.

He also remembered his children and his wife far away. Once, his parents asked him if he would consider bringing them to the village. Then they could all live together in one place while he continued taking care of his patients. So he sought out his beast relatives, for he knew where they lived. He asked them if they would come with him, and his wife and two children said yes.

And so they accompanied him back to his village. They built their own house somewhere and then lived there. The father continued to treat people, and once in a while when a patient wanted to express his gratitude, he gave him a gift. Occasionally, a patient would even offer him one of his belongings. However, he never accepted any material things, except food.

In this manner the man and his family lived there, and now that he had his wife there with him he was really happy. Evidently, she was a very beautiful woman. And so all four of them lived there from that time on, and I guess they still live there somewhere.

And here the story ends.

Glossary

Aala'ytaqa—Al or Two Horn society person; member of one of the four tribal initiation orders (Al, Kwan, Taw, and Wuwtsim), initiation into which bestows adult status on a Hopi male.

aliksa'i—traditional story opener with which a Third Mesa storyteller signals to his audience that he is about to begin his narrative.

Apoonivi—sandstone crest at the southwesternmost tip of Third Mesa, also known as Mt. Beautiful.

atö'ö—traditional cape, woven of white cotton, with wide black and red borders, used principally by women in formal rituals.

Awat'ovi—Howell Mesa between Hotevilla and Moencopi, in this collection; also the name of the famous historic Hopi village on Antelope Mesa that was destroyed and abandoned in 1700.

Hahay'iwuuti—female kachina believed to be the mother of all kachinas.

Hehey'a—male kachina.

Hisatsongoopavi—Old Shungopavi, a ruin below Shungopavi at the foot of the mesa.

Hootatsomi—place midway between Oraibi and Moencopi.

Hooyapi—Little Giant's Chair, a butte south of Second Mesa.

hopi—*adj*: well-behaved, mannered, civilized (not "peaceful"); *n*: human being, Hopi person.

Hotvela—literally, "juniper slope"; eponymous spring that the Third Mesa village of Hotevilla (correctly, Hotvela) was named after.

Höövatuyqa—place name.

Huk'ovi—prehistoric ruin southwest of Oraibi.

hurusuki—blue corn flour mush, a dish usually eaten by pinching pieces between three fingers.

Ismo'wala—literally, "coyote-mouth-gap"; place southwest of Oraibi, location for many Coyote tales.

Kaatoya—mythic serpent of non-Hopi origin, apparently borrowed from Keresan mythology in the Rio Grande area; foreign origin is evidenced by sound sequence *ka(a)-*, which only occurs in Hopi words borrowed from other languages.

kachina—Anglicized form of Hopi *katsina*, a term referring to a pantheon of supernatural beings or deities responsible for the welfare of the Hopi, including the production of life-sustaining moisture in the form of rain; note that the sound sequence *ka-* betrays foreign origin of the word, probably from the Keresan language at Acoma, New Mexico.

Kaktsintuyqa—Kachina Cliffs, the red cliffs south of Third Mesa.

Kiisiw—Shadow Springs, the kachina home representing the northeast cardinal direction, a shrine located in the opposite direction from the San Francisco Peaks.

kikmongwi—village leader, village chief.

kiva—underground chamber used primarily for ritual and ceremonial activities; in stories frequently the term for a subterranean dwelling reminiscent of an archaeological pit house.

Kookop clan—Fire clan, so named because of the association of fire with the clan totem Maasaw. The term *Kookop* is not translatable.

Kotsoylaptiyo—Fire Stoking Boy, a story character with greater-than-human powers.

koyaanisqatsi—life of moral corruption and social chaos.

Kuwanhehey'a—Colorful Hehey'a kachina, one of several Hehey'a kachinas, distinguished by a more colorful ceremonial costume than that worn by the plain Hehey'a.

Kwaani'ytaqa—Kwan or One Horn society person, Kwan priest; in the Hopi underworld, a god who directs the souls of the dead onto their respective paths.

Kwaatoko—mythic bird of gigantic size.

Kwan—referring to the Kwan society, one of the four tribal initiation orders (Al, Kwan, Taw, and Wuwtsim), initiation into which bestows adult status on a Hopi male.

kwiptosi—fine-ground corn flour dish prepared from white corn kernels.

Kwitanono'qa—place name.

Kyar'ovi—name of kiva at Shungopavi.

Leenangwva—Flute Spring, located on the south face of the base of Oraibi.

Maasaw—most important Hopi deity, lord of the underworld, god of fire and death; today often equated with the Great Spirit or the Supreme Being.

Masawkatsina—male kachina personifying a death spirit.

Maski—literally, "corpse-home"; the underworld, home of the dead.

Mastanga—place near Third Mesa.

Masvoksö—formation west of Oraibi overlooking Pöqangwwawarpi, the race course of the Pöqangw brothers.

Matsonpi—prehistoric ruin at the foot of Hotevilla Mesa on the northwest side.

Mishongnovi—village on Second Mesa (correctly, Musangnuvi).

Moencopi—westernmost Hopi village near Tuba City (correctly, Munqapi).

mongko—literally, "leader-wood"; emblem and badge of office in the traditional priesthood; made of wood shaped flat and oblong with notches at each end and marked to distinguish the particular priesthood order; carried by hand.

Munaqvi—Sand Springs, west of Padilla Mesa.

Na'uykuytaqa—male kachina.

Naasiwam—rock formation south of Shungopavi.

Nangöysohut—literally, "two stars chasing each other"; Hopi constellation consisting of the morning star and the evening star, both of which are the planet Venus.

Ngayayataqa—male kachina.

Nuvaktsina—male kachina.

Nuvatukya'ovi—San Francisco Peaks, the kachina home representing the southwest cardinal direction.

O'waqölt—members of the Owaqöl society, a woman's society.

Old Spider Woman—known as Kookyangwso'wuuti, an earth goddess greatly revered by the Hopi because she often comes to the aid of people in trouble.

Oraibi—village of Third Mesa, named after prominent point at the drop-off on the southwest side of the village.

Owakw'ovi—place name.

Pa'utsvi—ridge above Burro Springs, west of Shungopavi.

Paalölöqangw—Water Serpent; deity believed to control springs and other bodies of water.

Paamuya—a Hopi month corresponding approximately to January.

Paaqapa—place name.

paho—Anglicized form of *paaho*, prayer stick, or prayer feather; all three terms are used interchangeably here.

Palangw—believed to be the home of witches and sorcerers, somewhere near Canyon de Chelly.

Palöngawhoya—the younger of Old Spider Woman's grandsons.

Pangwuvi—No Trail Mesa, approximately nine miles southwest of Oraibi.

Patangvostuyqa—Pumpkin Seed Point, the cliff behind Kykotsmovi on Third Mesa.

pik'ami—a sweet pudding made from wheat and corn flour.

piki—Anglicized form of *piiki*, a wafer bread usually made from blue corn flour.

Pisisvayu—the Colorado River.

Pivanhonkyapi—prehistoric ruin site a mile northeast of Apoonivi.

Pongoktsina—male kachina.

Pongopsö—place name.

Pöqangw brothers—Pöqangwhoya and Palöngawhoya, the two grandsons of Kookyangwso'wuuti, Old Spider Woman.

Pöqangwhoya—the older of Old Spider Woman's grandsons.

Pöqangwwawarpi—a place just west of Oraibi, believed to be the running place of the Pöqangw brothers.

Qa'ötukwi—Corn Rock, near Mishongnovi.

Qöma'wa—a point of the escarpment on the road approximately halfway between Oraibi and Hotevilla.

qömi—sweet cake made with water and *toosi*, a finely ground flour made from roasted, dried sweet corn.

Qötstuyqa—White Mesa.

Qöya'oytuyqa—a point south of Hotevilla.

sakwavaho—turquoise-blue paho with a double shaft painted blue to represent the prayer for green crops.

shinny—a stickball game similar to field hockey.

Shipaulovi—village on Second Mesa (correctly, Supawlavi).

Shungopavi—literally, "place of the sand-grass spring"; village on Second Mesa (correctly, Songoopavi).

Sipaapuni—travertine dome where Hopis believe they emerged from the underworld into the present world, located in the canyon of the Little Colorado River, approximately four miles upstream from its confluence with the Colorado River.

So'yoko—cannibalistic giant deified as a male kachina.

Somaykoli—supernatural personage associated with the Yaya' ceremony.

somiviki—a tamale-like food made from blue corn flour and boiling water; it is wrapped in corn husks, tied in two places with strips of narrow-leafed yucca, and then boiled.

sosotukwpi—a guessing game played with cylindrical cups of cottonwood.

Söynapi—Grand Falls, on the Little Colorado River.

supakoyma—in the sosotukwpi guessing game, term used when the gaming stone is revealed on the first try.

taqvaho—prayer stick representing the male gender.

tiiponi—emblem of ceremonial office; a priestly object held in the arms by the head of a ceremony in certain religious rites that symbolizes the authority of the bearer.

Tiposqötö—place name.

Toko'navi—Navajo Mountain, the prehistoric home of the Snake and Sand clans.

toosi—roasted sweet corn that is dried and ground to a fine texture.

Tsa'kwayna—male kachina.

tsotsokpi—prayer stick with a symbolic perch from which the deceased's spirit begins its journey.

Tsukus'ovi—place name near Second Mesa.

tsukuviki—a dish made from blue corn flour batter that is wrapped into a crescent shape in dried corn plant leaves, then boiled and served.

Walpi—literally, "place of the gap"; village on First Mesa.

Wupakits'ovi—place name.

Wupatki—literally, "long cut or valley"; prehistoric ruin northeast of Flagstaff and the name of a national monument.

Wuwtsim society—one of the four tribal initiation orders (Al, Kwan, Taw, and Wuwtsim), initiation into which bestows adult status on a Hopi male.

Yaapontsa—the wind god, believed to reside in the vicinity of Wupatki.

Yantukya'ovi—a mesa crest approximately two miles west of Hotevilla Mesa.

Yaya'—a member of a religious society; plural, Yaya't.